THE CITY THAT KILLED THE PRESIDENT

The City That Killed the President

A Cultural History of Dallas and the Assassination

Volume 1

TIM CLOWARD

La Reunion

DALLAS, TEXAS

La Reunion Publishing, an imprint of Deep Vellum
3000 Commerce St., Dallas, Texas 75226

Deep Vellum is a 501c3 nonprofit literary arts organization founded in 2013 with the mission to bring the world into conversation through literature.

First edition 2023

Support for this publication has been provided in part by grants from the National Endowment for the Arts, the Texas Commission on the Arts, the City of Dallas Office of Arts and Culture, the George and Fay Young Foundation, the Summerfield G. Roberts Foundation, and the Communities Foundation of Texas.

ISBNS: 978-1-64605-212-7 (hardcover) | 978-1-64605-238-7 (ebook)

LIBRARY OF CONGRESS CATALOGING-IN-PUBLICATION DATA

Names: Cloward, Tim, author.
Title: The city that killed the president : a cultural history of Dallas and the assassination / Tim Cloward.
Description: First edition | Dallas, Texas : La Reunion, 2023. | Includes bibliographical references and index.
Identifiers: LCCN 2023011446 | ISBN 9781646052127 (hardcover ; v. 1) | ISBN 9781646052387 (ebook)
Subjects: LCSH: Kennedy, John F. (John Fitzgerald), 1917-1963--Assassination. | Dallas (Tex.)--Civilization--20th century. | Dallas (Tex.)--Civilization--21st century. | Dallas (Tex.)--Social life and customs.
Classification: LCC F394.D215 C56 2023 | DDC 976.4/2812--dc23/eng/20230322
LC record available at https://lccn.loc.gov/2023011446

Cover design by Steve Kinder
Interior layout and typesetting by KGT

PRINTED IN THE UNITED STATES OF AMERICA

To Robert Trammell,

who cared enough about the city to stay here and curse it, keeping track

of all the other writers it had driven away

"Your memory is a monster; you forget—it doesn't. It simply files things away. It keeps things for you, or hides things from you—and summons them to your recall with a will of its own. You think you have a memory; but it has you!"

John Irving, *A Prayer for Owen Meany*

Contents

Although schools were let out in Houston and San Antonio when the President's motorcade passed through, in Dallas we could be excused only in the custody of a parent. So like most of my classmates I was in school when it happened. It was right after lunch. I was in Algebra. Mr. Irvin Hill was describing a parabola on the blackboard when the three tones came over the public-address system and the principal started to speak. We knew something was wrong before he said a word. There was a choked pause. We could hear a radio playing in the background.

"The President has been shot."

Lawrence Wright, *In the New World*[1]

I went out before noon, to do some Christmas shopping in the Dallas stores and let others in my office go later so they could see him. No one could walk through the streets without feeling an uneasiness in the air. I saw a traffic patrolman taking off his yellow raingear; the sun was breaking through the clouds. Later, back in my office, I heard the carillon in the Mercantile Bank playing: "Hail to the Chief." And shortly thereafter it turned suddenly to "What a Friend We Have in Jesus." "What in the world are they playing that for?" I asked a secretary. Abruptly, an engineer came to my door.

"Can you stand a shock?" he asked. Sure. "The President has been shot!"

William Barney, *Words from a Wide Land*[2]

1. Lawrence Wright, *In the New World: Growing Up with America from the Sixties to the Eighties* (New York: Vintage, 1989), 63.

2. William Barney, *Words from a Wide Land* (Denton: University of North Texas Press, 1993), 175.

I went into the bedroom and sat on a wobbly three-legged stool and watched the President's arrival in Dallas. My daughter was on the bed playing with cut-out dolls. When the President and his lady got in the car to leave Love Field I got up and went into the living room and flopped on the couch and began to read a column in the *New Yorker* about television called "The Air." I was wondering what he would say to this Dallas audience, here in this essentially Republican city which was in danger of losing its commercial airport and which had lost the hoped-for Federal Center. I heard my wife call something, a question. My daughter, on the bed, paying closer attention to the TV, told her: "They've shot somebody."

My wife called out again. "Something has happened," she said.

I got up, stood stupidly. Then ran, stumbled into the bedroom.

"Kennedy's been shot," said my little girl.

Marshall Terry, *Dallas Stories*[3]

---

3. Marshall Terry, *Dallas Stories* (University Park, TX: Southern Methodist University Press, 1987), 146.

PROLOGUE

"Saving the Day"

> He has abandoned his life to understanding that moment in Dallas, the seven seconds that broke the back of the American century.
>
> Don DeLillo, *Libra*[4]

EVERYBODY HAS THEIR OWN "where-were-you-when-you-heard" story. Mine goes like this: I could not watch *Mighty Mouse*. That's the part I remember most vividly. I was just barely five years old, and I was crushed. It was Saturday morning, November 23, 1963. I had been primed for the usual ritual, stretching out on the living room carpet in front of the TV cabinet to watch *Mighty Mouse Playhouse*. The day would start with the clarion call of the *Mighty Mouse* theme song—"Here I Come to Save the Day!" I distinctly remember sitting there stewing, grubbing around on the dirt pile behind the garage in our newly developed suburban tract in Huntington Beach, California. I was banished from the TV.

While I would eventually come to understand that, at that exact moment, a monumental new era in near-instantaneous electronic communication was being initiated, I sat there alone with my brooding thoughts. As elsewhere TVs were filled with the endless stream of news of the assassination of our young and glamorous president, I believe I was experiencing my first actual

4. Don DeLillo, *Libra* (New York: Viking, 1988), 181.

moment of mature consideration. A dark revelation was coming to me: there were things that my parents, that the adults, were not telling me!

It would be decades, however, before I came back to dwell on that moment. My parents, it turned out, were pretty successful in their efforts to cocoon me from fear and discomfort. For me, someone was always there to save the day. Looking back, my Southern California childhood seems a sort of mythological paradise. When I finally got my driver's license, I could drive down palm-lined Beach Boulevard, and, with one slight jog downtown, end up riding directly to the fabled Huntington Beach Pier. I could revel in the understanding that I lived in the actual "Surf City." Orange County then was lush with citrus groves and strawberry fields, which in turn sprouted shining new indoor shopping malls and spiraling new highways. Our dads were laboring to build the New World, some of them in booming aerospace plants doing the work necessary to send our astronauts to the moon.

•

I was seventeen years old when I landed in Dallas. My father dragged all of us there in 1976 when the trucking company he was helping manage transferred him to its headquarters in Texas. I was forced to move before my senior year of high school, and, of course, I was crushed. But, if this new landscape was not Golden Age California, I soon found that it had its own sense of swagger. As a well-off white kid in the affluent northern Dallas suburb of Richardson, I could see before me once again the open fields blossoming into indoor malls and highways.

While my sisters snickered among themselves at the funny way people talked, their classmates' big hair, and the fact that the Baptists wouldn't let you buy batteries on Sundays, I quickly became more amenable to my new surroundings. There was real barbecue and Tex-Mex cooking, the rednecks had just joined up with the hippies to produce a bad-ass new outlaw music, and there was a sense of openness as expansive as the Texas horizon.

If this new place lacked the cool hipness of Southern California, it had its own consolations. Boomtown Dallas, with it microchips and State Fair of Texas cattle shows, had its own local version of Texas Mythology. It was just comically cornpone enough that you could make outrageous boasts and halfway believe you might make them come true. This was not a bad place for a kid to experience his mid-1970s coming of age—to figure out his own story in America. As a California émigré in Texas, there were a lot of things I had to figure out. The assassination of John F. Kennedy in Dallas was one of them.

As I began to understand Dallas, and myself as a Dallasite, I found trips downtown especially instructive. This was a city proud of its skyscraper-laden business center, and it was ready to show itself off. The best way to experience it, as I would on those rare occasions when I approached the city center from the west, was to enter downtown through the ceremonial portal called Dealey Plaza.

I remember the first time vividly. As I exited the highway and passed under the railway bridge, suddenly there I was. The plaza opened before me, instantly recognizable. I felt I had been here a hundred times. It took just a moment to drive through, so I scanned the plaza, made note of the familiar porticoes, the grassy knoll. There were no signs or markers, no noticeable monuments, but I knew this was a place of profound historical significance. I could not help but look up at the red brick mass of the former Texas School Book Depository and let my eyes rise to that fateful sixth-floor window.

Then I was out of the plaza, surprised by how small it was, how quick the experience. I continued on my way; I did what I had to do. But there were things I needed to process from that short moment in Dealey Plaza. I was left with a queasiness in the pit of my stomach and nothing to do with it. As I went about my day, I felt a sort of emotional void.

I realized only later, that was part of being from Dallas.

•

In that decade and a half after the JFK assassination, I had no reason to think much about Mighty Mouse. But my fixation on my first cartoon hero blindsided me one evening in 1978. This was spurred by a random skit on a rebroadcast episode of *Saturday Night Live*. The skit was from the premiere episode of *SNL* in 1975, and featured prankster comedian Andy Kaufman.

That *SNL* moment would become near legendary, emblematic of the painful-to-watch performance shtick that Kaufman would master.

This skit begins with Kaufman taking the stage and standing beside an old portable record player. Already visibly uncomfortable, he stands a long, awkward moment before placing the needle down on a spinning forty-five-rpm record. As it plays, he continues to stand, painfully and ineptly, still. But there is the song! "Mister Trouble never hangs around/When he hears this mighty sound!" It is the *Mighty Mouse* theme song! When it reaches its stirring chorus—*"Here I come to save the day!"*—Kaufman suddenly strikes a heroic pose, lip-synching along with his right arm upstretched. He then immediately falls back into his passive, angst-filled discomfort, waiting for the chorus to roll around once again so he can again strike his momentary heroic pose. It was hilarious, but painfully so. The skit amounted to, more than anything, two minutes of epic discomfort and embarrassment.

It was this one brief moment, watching TV with high school friends in Dallas, this one skit, that brought on my first real epiphany concerning my own relationship to that long-blacked-out weekend in Huntington Beach in November 1963. It connected the memory dots, linked that moment on the dirt pile directly to the death of JFK. I realized that I had my own JFK assassination "where-were-you-when" story.

There was also, in the back of my mind, a sense that there might be some eerie equivalence between this skit and my Dealey Plaza experiences. Here perhaps was a parallel expression of the embarrassment and discomfort I had felt as I drove through the plaza, something analogous to that sense of nagging inarticulateness I experienced afterward.

•

It did not take long for me to figure out that no one in Dallas was really very interested in discussing the assassination. Both the locals and the fresh-faced newcomers seemed to agree with the traditional Dallas approach to history—there is so much to do in the present, there is no use wasting time looking back. Also, by the late 1970s, the topic of the assassination had become so fouled in the tarpit of conspiracy blather that people of good sense tended to stay clear rather than risk being pulled down into the muck. This all seemed natural, but slowly I came to understand that there was more to it. The citizens of the city seemed to harbor an aversion to the subject of John Kennedy that bordered on phobia.

As I filled in the glaring gaps in my historical knowledge, I began to realize the full extent of how America had demonized Dallas because of the assassination. I began to understand the effects on the citizenry of being unjustly shamed and unfairly labeled "the city that killed the president." This was clearly an unjust slur. My understanding was that just one man, Lee Harvey Oswald, had committed the crime. It was not difficult to comprehend why we, the proud residents of this city, might be reluctant to revisit all of this, how we might even harbor some resentment.

It took me some more time, however, to understand there was a deeper, and murkier, story. We had been working on our reputation as the "City of Hate" well before Lee Harvey Oswald trained the entire world's focus on us. To comprehend that story, it is necessary to understand that cast of characters whom we would eventually come to call our Absolutists.

The Dallas Absolutists were a number of loosely related groups of far-right agitators who shared a particularly virulent version of post-McCarthyist Red Scare paranoia. Generally allied with the ideology of groups such as the John Birch Society, these activists could be seen as mid-century versions of today's most radical culture warriors. The threats they set themselves to confront were so multifarious, they formed a sort of thrashing, hydra-headed beast of Anti-Americanism. Those threats included the likes of our local museum board with its corrupting modern art, subversive Democratic Texas representatives like Lyndon Johnson, local activists who pushed dangerous demands for civil rights action, and even our own national government and Supreme Court. All of these entities, the Absolutists assured us, were working with a corrupted East Coast elite to sell us out to miscegenation, atheism, Fidel Castro, Nikita Khrushchev, and International Communism. Dallas become a sort of safe harbor for these activists, a supportive place to stage the apocalyptic struggle that would save us from the forces intent on destroying

God's America. One prominent local observer ironically labeled Dallas at the time the "Camelot of the Right."[5]

Our Absolutists became a dominant minority here, and their core attribute was their unquestioning righteousness. They shared an uncompromising certitude and were completely comfortable with closing down rational discussion. They were fearsome in defense of their ideas, and, as one local commentator noted, "They feel that their worst enemies are other Americans who disagree with them."[6]

It would be difficult today to gauge the exact number of these activists or how deeply their ideas were imprinted into our civic DNA. What is clear, however, is that these Dallas Absolutists came to dominate the national perception of our city. They became blunderingly adept at drawing national headlines, and to many in America they became synonymous with Dallas.

•

Local citizens grew accustomed to seeing Dallas in the newspapers and on TV. There we were, launching efforts to have the work of Pablo Picasso and Ben Shahn removed from our museum walls, attacking some of the most important artists of the time as Communist sympathizers and artistic modernism itself as an assault on our traditional values. There was our Communism in Arts Committee of the Dallas County Patriotic Council right in the middle of a major mid-1950s controversy that gained national arts-world attention for our fair city.

We could read that our friendly business climate had lured "the world's richest man," H. L. Hunt, to Dallas. Then we would come to understand how our political climate, so conducive to his unique Communist-obsessed conservatism, also nourished his forays into publishing, radio, and TV. It was Hunt's sponsorship of Dan Smoot's media operation that allowed it to

---

5. Wright, *In the New World*, 16.

6. Warren Leslie, *Dallas: Public and Private* (University Park, TX: Southern Methodist University Press, 1998), 90.

grow into a critical precursor of the contemporary conspiracy-driven right-wing media we have today.

We could read in the national press about the sway of our religious life and the city's most influential religious figure, the Reverend W. A. Criswell of the First Baptist Church. Criswell brought us national attention not just for his adamant stance against the civil rights movement but also, with the support of H. L Hunt, for his questioning of John F. Kennedy's ability to be both a loyal American and a Catholic.

With the rest of the nation, we read how retired General Edwin Walker, fresh from his controversial stoking of the anti-integration riots surrounding the enrollment of James Meredith at Ole Miss, chose Dallas as the launching pad for his subsequent political career. Dallas, we read, would provide him a supportive base where he could organize his conspiracy-driven Conservative Crusade. (Later, a few of us might also secretly take some glee in the suggestions that Dallas expatriate writer Terry Southern used Walker as the inspiration for General Jack D. Ripper, the earnest initiator of nuclear apocalypse in the film *Dr. Strangelove*.)

In the center of all this was Congressman Bruce Alger, the handsome and charismatic forerunner of the Republican revival in Texas. There was always news of Alger. He once introduced a bill to privatize the federal government, and, famously, was the only congressman to oppose a bill to provide free surplus milk to needy elementary children. Alger was the trailblazer for those contemporary politicians whose careers are predicated on stoking distrust of the government.

•

A distinguishing feature of the Absolutists, their unifying focus, was their sense that America was facing an existential threat from an insidious and dangerous enemy within. They were obsessed with the idea of this internal threat, and much of their activity consisted of an avid pursuit of those they considered traitors and turncoats. The apogee of this thinking would, of course, be that our own president would be in league with the enemy.

If you read the *Dallas Morning News* in the years before the president's visit, you saw this thinking delivered in daily doses. But its most blatant demonstration appeared in the "Wanted For Treason" flyers that mysteriously appeared all over town in the days before Kennedy's 1963 visit. It is all right there in the wanted poster image: the president's face, from front and side, composed in classic mug shot form, and underneath it seven charges that spelled out how President Kennedy was in league with the Communists to subvert Christianity and the Constitution.

On the day of the president's visit, the *Dallas Morning News* supplied its own broadside. It was not quite so visually arresting, but it was more effective via the number of people it reached. It consisted of a full-page advert beginning with the banner title "Welcome Mr. Kennedy." In a tone considerably less hospitable, the text made clear that the people of Dallas were not, in fact, thrilled with his visit. The advert reminded the president that this was a city "that rejected your philosophy and policies in 1960 and will do so again in 1964—even more emphatically than before." Again, there was the enumeration of charges, presented in the manner of an interrogation, all boiling down to the idea that the president had been working to advance Communism, pushing the "Spirit of Moscow." Both of these widely distributed indictments made clear: in the city of Dallas, President Kennedy was considered a traitor to his country. He was a true enemy of the people.

The hard truth of it was that when John Kennedy visited Dallas in 1963, we expected trouble.

The warnings that Kennedy received from his allies have been abundantly documented—it would be unwise to visit Dallas. According to Warren Leslie, the well-connected PR Director of the eminent retailer Neiman Marcus, "thinking people half-expected something to happen." Dallas "*was* a logical place for something unpleasant and embarrassing to happen." Dallas Police Chief Jesse Curry issued radio announcements in the week before Kennedy's visit, warning against violence, and took the unprecedented step of deputizing citizens to take action against any act that might endanger the president.

Lawrence Wright, in his memoir of growing up in Dallas, notes that as the city prepared to host the president, "We expected to be disgraced." When he heard the first announcement that someone had shot Kennedy,

"I never paused to think who *they* were. It was Dallas, of course—faceless assassins but essentially Dallas pulling the many triggers." Before anyone heard the name Lee Harvey Oswald, we knew it was the city itself that would have its reckoning. "*It happened,*" Wright writes, "—the something we had been waiting for. *It happened!*"[7]

If you lived in Dallas and had been paying attention, it was shocking, but not that surprising. Certainly, we did not all kill John Kennedy, but, as Warren Leslie would write, speaking for many others here who would not dare voice such opinions, Dallas "was not innocent."[8]

•

As a teenage transplant to Dallas, I was blissfully unaware of all this. My lone surviving memory of the assassination was of the aftermath, sitting and sulking in the dirt pile behind my suburban Huntington Beach home. I was one of the very few conscious Americans to be ignorant of what happened in Dallas that weekend.

Of course, I would eventually find out. Thinking back now about how that actually occurred, however, is a study in the vagaries of memory. I remember my first serious attempt at recalling the exact moment I found out about the assassination did not occur until well into my twenties. My first attempt at recollection took me back to one vivid moment: I am watching TV. Walter Cronkite stops mid-sentence to read a paper he has just been handed. "From Dallas, Texas, the flash, apparently official—President Kennedy died at one o'clock p.m. Central Standard Time," Cronkite removes his glasses and checks the clock on the wall. "Two o'clock Eastern Standard time, some thirty-eight minutes ago." He pauses, swallows hard for a painfully extended moment, replaces his glasses, and continues to deliver the news.

I can acutely recall experiencing that same shock, that same sinking in my stomach that Cronkite must have felt. It took me but a moment of reflection, however, to realize that I had experienced that moment years later, via a

---

7. Wright, *In the New World*, 62–4.
8. Leslie, *Dallas: Public and Private*, 8–9.

videotape recording. I had to think harder, dig deeper in the mines of my memory. Eventually, I remembered looking at those old copies of *Life* and *Look* magazine in my middle-school art class, reliving the assassination through the state-of-the-art photojournalism of that period. Certainly, there must have been, before that, TV documentaries, network news remembrances, and who knows what else. Where my memory was unreliable and things had gone missing, I realized there was this endless, ongoing media loop that could fill in the gaps. I had been reading that researchers were finding, more and more, that memory is actually a communal construct, and here was more evidence. I wondered then: how much can we actually trust our memory of our own experience?

All of this coincided with another encounter with Mighty Mouse. Andy Kaufman was dead, but, in 1999, Miloš Forman released his Kaufman biopic *Man on the Moon*. There it was again, the mythic *Saturday Night Live* rendition of the *Mighty Mouse* theme song, restaged here with Jim Carrey as Kaufman. Carrey's performance was riveting, a worthy tribute to the manic prankster who had been his inspiration. It was another beautiful example of making history a living thing, of literally saving the day through loving reenactment. I thought, *This was how we remain connected to our Golden Age*. Carrey took me back to Kaufman, Kaufman to *Mighty Mouse*, and I was again back on that dirt pile in Huntington Beach, California. It reminded me how much the tools of memory are wielded by our desires.

Woven through all this was my memory of John F. Kennedy and the gift that he had for expressing exactly this sense of participative history. His greatest legacy had been all that inspiring rhetoric that invited us to join him in his heroic version of the national narrative. That initial challenge of his—"Ask not what your country can do for you—ask what you can do for your country"—was the beginning of that sense of communal promise that he would leave with many of us. He had promised us the moon, and because he had promised, we achieved it. I have no more vivid childhood memory than that evening in July 1969 when my ten-year-old self and my family watched Neil Armstrong and Buzz Aldrin walk on the moon. I remember how we felt like this was *our* accomplishment. The fathers of my friends had worked on this; Vice President Johnson had toured one of our Huntington Beach aerospace facilities just the week before the assassination.

This was *my* Golden Age America, and John F. Kennedy was an integral part of it. It is not news that we gain strength from seeing ourselves as part of a bigger story, but as I grew older, I realized just how pervasive these desires for bigger connections actually are. I have also learned how those circuitous routes, conscious and unconscious, that we devise to create these bonds can be a very creative weave, marked as much by chance and delusion as our own agency.

•

After 1976, I rarely returned to Huntington Beach. When my recent memory work led me back there, I had to confess that I found it a somewhat different place than my nostalgic remembrance. My mid-century Orange County utopia, the bastion of sunny California chill, had become something else. In fact, one recent article in the *Los Angeles Times* has dubbed contemporary Huntington Beach "Angrytown."[9] My idyllic Pacific Coast highway pier with its color-drenched sunsets is known now as a hotspot for protest against masks and COVID restrictions, anti–Black Lives Matter events, and actions denouncing dictatorial socialist government. The scenery still looks familiar, but this is not exactly the laid-back, progressive wonderland of my memory. Huntington Beach bears, I am ashamed to admit, an uncanny resemblance to Dallas in the early 1960s.

But when I looked closer at the history of the place, delved a bit deeper into all that information that bored me so much as a youngster, I experienced a dawning realization that my childhood California was not so profoundly different from Texas. Its story was not quite as pristine as I remembered. Like Texas, this part of Southern California has an obscured history of displacing its native population and an analogous history of disenfranchising its Latino population. Huntington Beach has its own cattle ranching history; I discovered my old drag Beach Boulevard was originally a cattle route for the area ranchos. Huntington Beach also had its own oil boom—I had allowed myself

9. Gustavo Arellano, "Letters to the Editor: Right-wing media have turned Huntington Beach into Angrytown," *Los Angeles Times*, November 29, 2020.

to forget the oil derricks that lined my favorite beaches and the acrid smell that always came with them. There had even been from the beginning a significant presence of Christian Fundamentalism. One part of the original settlement had been labeled the Gospel Swamp after the revival meetings held in the marshland where the community college is today, just a few short blocks from where I lived.

More disturbingly, I found that, in the early 1960s, Orange County experienced a parallel history to Dallas. Like Dallas, the county had been a Mecca of the New Right, a bastion of growing paranoia that nurtured its own indigenous forms of Absolutism. Orange County had also been a hotbed for the John Birch Society and its conspiracy-driven ultrapatriotism. There were controversies involving supposed attempts by area schools to indoctrinate their students into Communism. The most high-profile response had been the 1961 Orange County School of Anti-Communism session, where more than seven thousand youth participants learned of the Communist Party's "treasonous" networks in the United States.[10] I would have been just a little too young to attend, but I did often frequent the popular amusement park Knott's Berry Farm. I came to learn that when I did, I was helping Walter Knott finance his California Free Enterprise Association, an operation quite similar to Dan Smoot's in Dallas, which distributed pamphlets, books, films, and tapes with the express aim "to sell Americanism back to Americans.'"

Just as in Dallas, these California activists tended to be middle-class. They were often professional, and many were recent arrivals who tended to enjoy entrepreneurial success in their thriving new home. They shared the same fundamental moorings of American success: "traditional social and normative conservative beliefs, strict moral values, unabashed individualism and faith in free enterprise." And, just as in Dallas, they shared the overheated rhetoric of apocalyptic conflict with the enemy within.

Pamphlets from Walter Knott's California Free Enterprise Association illuminate the stakes involved. Those who would speak for government actions on the minimum wage, good housing, or medical care were "choosing

10. Lisa McGirr, *Suburban Warriors: The Origin of the New American Right* (Princeton, NJ: Princeton University Press, 2001), 54.

slavery rather than freedom"; this was "the security of the penitentiary." The welfare state should best be called the "MASTER STATE where we socialists are the masters and the rest of the people are the servants." This battle demanded extreme action; victory was, after all, the "difference between a free nation and a slave nation."[11]

My Golden Age story was proving, if not false, at least somewhat delusionary. There seemed to be trouble even in paradise, and I was beginning to suspect that perhaps there is always trouble in paradise. I was reminded once again that history, done honestly, can often offer fairly humbling lessons.

•

Looking back half a century later, that period after November 1963 was indisputably this city's Dark Ages. There were great individual accomplishments and occasional good times, but collectively it was a time stained with tragedy. A pall of disgrace hung over the city. We were international pariahs; we had murdered the president.

The good news is that any story that begins at such a low point must inevitably get better, and this project will indeed be a tale of our civic recovery. It will, however, be a long and complex history—it will span three volumes before it is done. It will encompass the varied cultural reactions this city produced in its response to the murder of John F. Kennedy. Looking at the poetry and literature we have produced, the visual art, theater, music we have staged, the monuments we have constructed, and the rituals and public discourse we have produced, it will be a thorough examination of what occurred in the long aftermath of the assassination. While some might say Dallas today stands at a point of cultural renaissance, I can say we are at least experiencing an impressive recuperation.

This is a study, in a basic sense, of a city's public expression, and the story begins with the very obvious challenge presented by our Absolutists. In their tactics and ideals, the Absolutists were a clear and present danger to free

---

11. McGirr, *Suburban Warriors: The Origin of the New American Right,* 54, 88, 100.

expression. While they only occasionally focused on aesthetic matters, their presence here had its consequences. There has been little discussion of the effects of this movement on the status of our arts, but there can be little doubt it had an adverse effect on our cultural life. All this, of course, was followed by the chill that descended upon our public discourse after the assassination, and that too fell particularly hard upon the arts. As we will see, Dallas has produced a considerable amount of fascinating creative work in the last half-century, and this project will survey a considerable amount of it. This project will also, however, engage with that more difficult and speculative history, asking, "What work could have been created here but was not?"

In the pressure-cooker environment of post-assassination public discourse, there were some brave citizens of significance who did speak out against the oppressive climate that existed before the assassination. Most prominent was A. C. Greene, whose work for the *Dallas Times Herald* editorial page, in critical moments, demanded from his readers both introspection and accountability. Especially important was Stanley Marcus, whose position as chief executive at Neiman Marcus and dresser of Dallas's elite made him a cherished local figure. Marcus's most notable public effort was writing and publishing his 1964 New Year's Day full-page ad entitled "What's Right with Dallas," in the *Dallas Morning News.* In his gentle, paternal manner, Marcus begged local citizens for "the rejection of this spirit of 'absolutism,'" which produced "the man who thinks that he alone possesses wisdom, patriotism and virtue."

Marcus's close associate Warren Leslie, a Neiman Marcus PR man, went much further. In his book *Dallas: Public and Private,* published immediately after the assassination, Leslie spent a good deal of time explaining the Dallas Absolutists to the rest of the world and excoriating them for the damage they did the city. While he was somewhat gentler with the rest of us, he made it clear that Dallas had some issues to remedy.

Sarah Hughes, the federal district judge most known today as the official who swore in LBJ as president on Air Force One, was also not shy about addressing the atmosphere here in 1963. Among her most notable statements on the issue was this from an April 1964 interview: "There was a climate of hate in Dallas that was not evident in any other place." She famously asserted: "I definitely think that the feelings in Dallas contributed to the fact that Oswald would do his deed here rather than in some other city."

But there was a cost in going public. Because of his elevated social position, Stanley Marcus suffered only marginally for his honesty; he endured a tolerable stream of nasty letters and canceled Neiman Marcus credit cards. Warren Leslie, whose sins were much greater, understood he had burned away all his social capital, and he had the good sense to leave town immediately. Sarah Hughes, who was not shy about making herself a target, stayed put and persisted through a long career in jurisprudence. She did, however, accumulate an extensive file of hate mail and the reputation, as one local historian put it, for being a "pariah in the minds of many conservative citizens."[12]

These were powerful and influential members of Dallas society, and they all paid a price for making public statements concerning the atmosphere in Dallas before the assassination. For those who had less influence and less social credit, the stakes were oftentimes much higher. As many citizens pushed for solidarity in order to protect ourselves from the onslaught of outside criticism, a sort of social circling of the wagons, it became increasingly perilous to express negative views toward the city. If social ostracism was not enough to discourage loose talk, those opposed to any criticism of Dallas would—and often did—make sure people lost their jobs or received death threats. Within a year, all of this tumult hardened into a general understanding that any talk of the assassination whatsoever should simply be avoided.

•

In the Dallas of 1963, our recent history had been marked more than anything by a take-charge business community, one that had effectively taken control of civic governance. Initially, paralyzed by the shock of the assassination, this "can-do" leadership seemed stuck in the mud. There was immense pressure to do something, but no consensus on what we *could* do. For Dallas, reputation was everything, and the city had suffered considerable damage.

---

12. Darwin Payne, *Indominable Sarah: The Life of Judge Sarah T. Hughes* (University Park, TX: Southern Methodist University Press, 2004), 275–277.

Fortunately, Absolutist activity had melted away under the glare of all the scrutiny. H. L. Hunt, for instance, had fled Dallas, and while General Walker continued to stage rallies, none of them were anywhere close to Dallas. Still, there was agreement among city leaders that the right-wing agitation had compromised the city's business climate, and there was pressure to take some sort of decisive action against those who had brought about this public relations nightmare.

The real power in Dallas at this time existed in something called the Dallas Citizens Council, a tightly knit organization of Dallas business oligarchs who presided over our local political life. It was our developing tradition that we would delegate these business-oriented leaders as our public proxies and have them, meeting behind closed doors away from any ugly public spectacle, rationally chart out the best course for the rest of us. It worked so well that it came to be called "the Dallas Way." One of the things the Dallas Citizens Council did most efficiently was engineer local elections, and so our first move against the Absolutists was to remove the most politically influential of the right-wing agitators, Republican Congressman Bruce Alger. The plan was to run a reliable and electable Dallas Citizens Council (DCC) man against him, and the Dallas mayor at that time, Earle Cabell, fit the bill perfectly. He, in turn, would be replaced by J. Erik Jonsson.

The choice of Jonsson as the next mayor proved especially prescient. A solid DCC member, he was the current head of the dynamically expanding Texas Instruments. Moreover, as a native Northeasterner, he brought a fresh aura to the mayorship at a time when we badly needed a makeover. Jonsson would serve an additional three terms as mayor and initiate a program of political reform labeled "Goals for Dallas." By opening the city's government up to voices formerly shut out, Jonsson addressed some of the harshest criticism of our traditionally closed business bureaucracy. Erik Jonnson's achievements were impressive, and the city was a better place for his stewardship. His efforts produced an international airport, a state-of-the-art city hall, community colleges, and more. They were efficient and productive, but, in essence, it was the city going about the regular business of a city.

Jonsson's plan, in the main, was to reinvent the city in response to the Kennedy assassination without mentioning the Kennedy assassination, and he largely succeeded. The standard story we would tell ourselves later about how we recovered from the dark days after the assassination is that we were led through it by the steady leadership of the Dallas Citizens Council and our trusty business oligarchs. It is an attractive idea. Our entrepreneurs have always been our heroes; according to our origin myth, they are the reason we are here. The story of solid and reliable civic management leading us through those fraught and anxious times is a good story, and in some ways it is true. It is not, though, the entire story.

Ultimately, our business leaders could not heal our psychic pain with their economic prowess. It was their own blind spots, after all, that enabled the reign of the Absolutists. We could be justifiably proud of much of their physical and political achievement, but it was always a type of success through sublimation. To say that our civic leaders pulled us through the pain of the assassination is like declaring victory in a game you would not admit you were playing. What is missing here is any sign of private introspection and the type of public ritual that could nourish it. As far as our civic efforts, this is the story of a city successfully holding itself together rather than holding itself to account.

•

To be from Dallas after the Kennedy assassination was to wear the scarlet letter *A*. There was no exoneration for any of us; to be a Dallasite was to be held accountable by the outside world for the assassination of the president. A short two days after the assassination, it was already apparent. Despite the gloom that engulfed the nation, the Dallas Cowboys traveled to Cleveland for their Sunday matchup with the Browns. Sports journalist Gary Cartwright accompanied the team. "We were the first group to travel outside Dallas that was publicly identified with the city. It was terrible. People were spitting on us, calling us murderers." To the crowd in Cleveland, the Dallas Cowboys had been transformed into the "Dallas Assassins."[13] This was a legacy that would follow us for years.

13. Steven Davis, *Texas Literary Outlaws: Six Writers in the Sixties and Beyond* (Fort Worth: Texas Christian University Press, 2004), 141.

Volumes could be filled with anecdotal accounts of abuse Dallasites encountered when they traveled outside the city; it would be hard to exaggerate the extent of the abuse to which we were exposed. Almost every Dallas old-timer can share with you some story that shows the burden we shouldered. If we felt oppressed after the assassination of John Kennedy, it would be hard to say it wasn't justified. We had undergone a sort of modern-day tarring and feathering, and we became obsessively repulsed by the idea of "collective guilt."

If anyone was interested in hearing us out, our defense was simple and direct. There was only one person who pulled that trigger! It was Lee Harvey Oswald, and he was not one of us! It was difficult for us to fathom that a man could be both a card-carrying Communist and a citizen of early-1960s Dallas. The very idea of a Marxist who had left the US military to live in Russia, returning with his Russian bride to live in Dallas, seemed astoundingly preposterous. Lee Harvey Oswald was the very antithesis of what Dallas was all about. He was a loner from elsewhere, here by chance. At the heart of our defense has always been the sheer randomness of what happened. It could have happened anywhere! Oswald had no connection to the "real" Dallas. Why would we have to be responsible for the action of this one crazed outcast?

Of course, we never really had a chance to voice our defense. Beginning with those initial hours when the world media first descended upon us, we experienced stories *about* us, not by us. And as the hours marched on, what the world saw of us seemed to spiral further and further out of our control. Within forty-eight hours, in front of a national television audience, the president's suspected killer himself was murdered. When Jack Ruby stepped out of the crowd in the basement of the Dallas police headquarters and shot Oswald as he stood handcuffed to one of our Dallas Police Department deputies, we knew there would be no escape. Ruby, a local strip club operator with suspected mob ties, was definitely one of ours.

From the beginning, we understood this would be a story about Dallas, and the world would be judging us. As the disorienting events continued to unfurl, it would be impossible to express the sheer helplessness we felt. We understood the world came here with a basic narrative already in place. The president had come to Dallas knowing that it might be dangerous. He left in a coffin in the back of Air Force One.

If you lived here, you were acutely aware that the world remembered this one thing about Dallas. Ironically, ignominiously, we'd finally achieved our long-sought status as an internationally recognized city. In the course of this worldwide scrutiny, Dallas, and to a lesser extent the state of Texas, suffered through uncountable underhanded attacks and unfounded misrepresentations. For a decade, this was blatant and in your face; afterward, it was more subtle. If you wished to proclaim your innocence, there was no court in which to present your case. This was not something you could argue. It was simply the price of being from Dallas.

The result of all this constant chastening was a sort of collective paralysis. Communally, we developed any number of strategies for evasion and avoidance, a raft of ways to deflect any mention of the topic of the assassination. One conspicuous example of this civic lethargy was our perpetual inability to properly commemorate the fallen president. You can see it not only in our failure to mount any official public ceremony but also in the difficulty we experienced constructing any physical remembrance of the fallen president. First there was the halting history of the creation of our John Fitzgerald Kennedy Memorial, which took almost seven years to finally complete, and then the parallel difficulties involved in the establishment of our Sixth Floor Museum, which did not open until 1989.

From the outside, this all might seem simply more evidence of our enduring animosity toward John F. Kennedy, but it was more complex than that. We were busy protecting our own shell-shocked psyches. Celebrating a figure we stood accused of murdering was understandably problematic. If we were consumed with the desire to forget, how could we generate much enthusiasm for commemoration?

What endured was a stewing resentment. Underneath our reticence was the wounded pride of a proud city. We were bound together by the common experience of suffering the unjust judgment of the world, with any opportunity to respond stifled. No one would have said it aloud, but what united us more than anything was our victimhood. We choose to remember the murder of JFK in Dallas as "our tragedy." We kept quiet, but our sense of grievance was always there.

•

Today, it's increasingly difficult to tell what exactly we mean when we say "Dallas." The city's population has more or less doubled since 1963, and the sprawling growth of our suburbs has linked us to our sister city, Fort Worth, to form the fourth-largest metropolitan area in the United States. As in all mammoth urban centers, this has created a vibrant mess alternately glorious and horrible. A city this size, all buildings and thoroughfares, becomes something like the air you breathe—so circumferent you might not be able to explain to yourself what it is.

This is where our communal memory and its attendant rituals come into play. An event such as our civic ceremony celebrating the railroad's arrival in 1872 or, a hundred years later, the Dallas Cowboys' first Super Bowl victory can help round all this into something more graspable. As far as our civic identity goes, these events are the psychic equivalent of our downtown skyline. For better or worse, the 1963 Kennedy assassination stands atop this list of events that shape our self-identity. It is therefore a fairly astounding thing to realize that it was not until fifty years after the fact that the city officially attempted to tell its own story about what happened on November 22, 1963.

The Fiftieth, as it was called, would be the first official civic recognition of the murder of the president in Dealey Plaza. Orchestrated by then-Mayor Mike Rawlings with the assistance of long-time civic activist and philanthropist Ruth Altshuler, it would be an important breakthrough, the recognition of a long-standing void. It had taken half a century, but we had finally given ourselves permission to start the reckoning.

The Fiftieth was unique in that it was a ceremony for us, the people of Dallas. There were no towering national figures flown in to play the starring roles, not a single Kennedy to share the stage with. In its execution, the Fiftieth was a quintessentially Dallas event. It paid proper obeisance to the fallen president, but its ultimate goal was not so much to relive a painful memory as to prove that we were released from it. We were, for the first time, taking control of the story, and the ceremony was a not-so-subtle pronouncement to the world that we had recovered from the stain of the Kennedy assassination.

Mayor Rawlings proved to be the perfect man for the time. He understood the unavoidable pressure of the upcoming fiftieth anniversary of the assassination and the importance of hosting a public ceremony. Rawlings also fit the traditional profile for a Dallas mayor perfectly. He was a business man, a former CEO of Pizza Hut, and he was also an advertising man. As the head spokesperson for the city, he understood that this was an opportunity, in true Dallas fashion, to show the world the best of ourselves—for more good news.

Self-promotion is, of course, our second nature, perhaps the very essence of the city. In Dallas, history is always preface to our current Golden Age. We had survived the JFK assassination, and we were not just a drastically different city than we were in 1963. We were a better city. We could show the world we were not only bigger, with a skyline that literally dwarfed that of 1963, but also more diverse. We were a less parochial city, less culturally stifled. We were, we felt we could assuredly state, more sophisticated. We had made material progress, but we had also taken massive leaps forward culturally.

Of course, there was much more than civic self-promotion happening at the Fiftieth. More than anything, the celebration was about recognizing that we were finally released from the control of the oppressive judgment of outsiders. This ceremony was our ceremony, and we could acknowledge to ourselves this newly acquired freedom. We had been beaten down, and now all those tightly wound emotions that we had forever tamped down—and these were very real things—could be released.

As a few very prescient observers had noted, much of our considerable civic progress could be ascribed exactly to our self-effacement. It was this that had allowed us some deeper civic understanding, made us less myopic. A significant side effect of the whole assassination experience had been the fact we had been delivered a healthy dose of humility. We had our swagger back and we were less haunted now, but we had also tasted the humble pie.

There had been a painful cost to all this, and for Dallas the most significant aspect of the Fiftieth ceremony was its therapeutic value. It would be hard to overestimate the substantial good the event provided for that generation of Dallasites who had been so traumatized by the assassination and its aftermath. While the percentage of people in the area who were here in 1963 continues to dwindle, these are the most dedicated guardians of our communal memory. After fifty years, the survivors of this generation were noting the passing of many of the principal figures of the period and counting their own days. This was the chance to mark, in a very public and communal manner, what they had lived through. For so many of them, the Fiftieth provided a profound sense of closure. Finally, here was some acknowledgment of how we had suffered.

The Fiftieth gave us all official sanction to talk aloud about the assassination, and there was a great outpouring of activity. The personal stories were unloosed; people opened up. I personally witnessed, innumerable times at various events, people sharing stories that they had kept private for years. It was clear that they felt immense relief that their trauma was finally recognized, their pain acknowledged. It was truly a cathartic period, on both the individual and the civic scale.

In a larger historical sense, however, we did not open up so very much. There were thousands of relieved citizens who experienced their individual moments of release, and there was a burst of fascinating cultural introspection, but there was still something elemental missing. You could see it from the beginning, when we chose the moniker—the Fiftieth. It was fashionably concise, but it also conveniently excised any reference to many of the unsavory little details of the assassination.

Over the decades, we had accumulated certain habits, and our collective guardedness would be difficult to overcome. We had long perfected the art of telling the personal anecdote about our individual assassination experiences and dodging any of those troubling larger questions. This was, after all, a ceremony to move us past all the previous unpleasantness, so it was understandable that when it came to historical introspection, the discussion was often circumspect. After half a century, there was no real incentive to open a Pandora's box and a thousand reasons to let it be. Moreover, after half a century, it was difficult to distinguish what we had whitewashed from our memory and what had naturally faded out in the graying of our recollection.

Underneath this desire for closure, however, was a darker recognition. The reason that the Fiftieth was justifiably hailed as such a significant event was that it filled such a glaring void. The event itself was a tacit acknowledgment that there had been a breakdown—we had communally failed to adequately address the assassination of John F. Kennedy and everything that led up to it. It was an admission of a great failure of our public life.

For Dallas, the events surrounding the Fiftieth ceremony were indeed cathartic and healing. It was a landmark in our relationship with the death of John F. Kennedy, but for those interested in some historical perspective, it was just a start.

•

The story of the murder of John F. Kennedy in Dallas is today a story that belongs to the world. More than an iconic moment in the twentieth century, it exists in a way that few events in human history exist. For a great many people of a certain age, the moment they heard the president had been shot in Dallas became a place marker in their personal lives. The way we recount that story has tremendous consequences for how we situate ourselves within the world. "I think what each of us believes about the assassination says something about the kind of person we are, what we are willing to believe about our country and ourselves," writes Lawrence Wright. "It is a way of explaining everything, of giving meaning to events."[14]

Because the assassination was such momentous event, there are remarkable variations in how it is recounted, and each will have its consequential denotations. I cannot help but ponder the character of my own story, recalling that brooding November morning in 1963 when I found myself fulminating upon my dirt pile, having been banned from Saturday morning TV. At my story's core is my insatiable craving for the candy-coated cartoon narratives of *Mighty Mouse*. Surrounding it is the larger story of my five-year-old self in Huntington Beach, California, all that I knew then, and all that I did not. Imposed upon this embryonic memory is the fateful event of the assassination of President Kennedy in Dallas, Texas. In the excavation of these layered accounts, there is the introspective joy of exploring one's personal memory, but there is bigger work as well. How exactly do our personal experiences intertwine with historical moments such as these? How is it, as Lawrence

14. Wright, *In the New World*, 69.

Wright asserts, that the Kennedy assassination can be the one story big enough that an individual telling could be "a way of explaining everything?

Looking back at how a 1963 Saturday morning broadcast of *Mighty Mouse Playhouse* might look in the mind of a five-year-old mid-century American boy inevitably revives ideas of a Golden Age America. That Golden Age was not just in my head. It was built into the cartoon as well. In the *Mighty Mouse* formula, each episode begins in some version of a grand ole America. Each scenario is evocative of some classic American trope, whether drawn from folktales or showbiz clichés, and always played out through some rollicking American vernacular music. The most common *Mighty Mouse* scenario is pastoral, and the themes of family and community are presented in the anthropomorphized guise of mice or sheep, joyfully frolicking about their blameless business. Always there is the nostalgic patina of an older, Edenic America.

This formula, however, demands some drama, and there is always that fateful moment when evil enters this bucolic harmony. Inevitably, the ravenous wolves, intent on destroying and devouring, descend upon the unheeding community and wreak havoc. Suddenly, there is panic, and the American way of life is threatened! We all know the final element of the formula. Thankfully, Mighty Mouse will appear, with his stirring theme song, and the five-minute epic will end happily. Order will be restored and good will triumph over evil!

Thinking back to those super-heated Cold War days, I remember I was already doing duck and cover drills, already aware of the absurdity of hiding under my desk from an atom bomb. I had already experienced "bomb shelter envy," wondering why *my* parents couldn't have a really cool shelter like my dad's work friend. In 1963, I might not have been thinking of *Mighty Mouse* as an allegory for victory over the Communists in the great apocalyptic confrontation of the Cold War, but I knew I was missing something profoundly important on that one gloomy Saturday morning. When *Mighty Mouse* was stolen from me, I felt the loss of a great consolatory story. If I felt then my first great paranoiac, conspiratorial epiphany that "they" were not telling me "something," it was because of the efficacy of those little stories that I was being denied. Without them, I was left unprotected.

It should come as no surprise that there where those around me then, in Huntington Beach and in Dallas—and dozens of other places across America—who were making themselves compelling little stories to satisfy these same concerns. Where there is fear, there is the need for stories. Wasn't it right there in every episode of *Mighty Mouse Playhouse,* setting the drama in motion? In the boiled-down parable of this children's cartoon, it was clear that the wolves could be anywhere at hand. With each episode of *Mighty Mouse,* at least, there was always the satisfaction of an easy answer. These were stories that you could safely be put to bed with, to securely dream the dream of the sheltered.

In Conspiracy America, a similar dynamic is evident, but with one major deficiency. In the conspiracy narratives that we have collectively made over the last century, the enemy is presented to us front and center, and the threat to America is always made imminently clear. Like a *Mighty Mouse* episode, these conspiracist stories are often childlike in their imaginative leaps and cartoonish in the amount of information and context they will leave out. But it might be exactly this simplicity that makes them so very effective. The most efficient of these tightly packed little parables draws our focus right to the very core of the world where we live. This is where the enemy is—how can we look away? Unlike *Mighty Mouse,* however, where there is always a quick and cathartic resolution, the conspiracy tale leaves us with a nagging anxiety. The enemy is called out, but there is nobody to save the day.

We are made larger by our stories and myths, and our best common narratives prime us for positive action. Even in an episode of *Mighty Mouse,* you might see a potent model for our civic selves. In this great American democracy, couldn't we, the tiny citizens we are, also be made larger by association with a greater cause? Couldn't we too "Save the Day"? Surely, we become warriors first through our heroic stories.

Our Dallas Absolutists, those countless average citizens who had felt so small and unheard, were like the rest of us: they longed to be heroes. The stories they told themselves made them feel larger, and when they were able to join others, they became more emboldened. They became so enthralled with their stories that their righteousness muscled aside their logic. The weave of paranoiac narratives they created produced such a ferment of perceived enemies they knew they had to *do something!* The spasmodic confrontations that bedeviled the city of Dallas for the half decade before the Kennedy visit were the result. The translation of our fictive plots into our own real-life stories is tricky business. As Andy Kaufman so awkwardly demonstrated in his 1970s *Mighty Mouse* skit, the hollow mimicry of heroism can have painfully embarrassing results.

When, in that long, last weekend of November 1963, something happened that brought everything to a head, it proved to be a disaster for this city. When it was all over, nothing about the Absolutists' portentous conspiracy stories worked, and the citizens of this city were left with a hopeless sense of chaos. Even today, in the muddiness that has followed, there is no final story that we can agree on to encompass what happened. There are those who would argue otherwise, but I would suggest that we in Dallas, as in America as a whole, are all still trying to properly finish the story of JFK's assassination. While my five-year-old self was convinced "they" were not telling me the real story, today there are so many contradictory versions I can hear only noise.

From the beginning, on that black weekend in late November 1963, I was left to my own devices. My parents, in their confusion, uncertainty, and shame, could give me no easy answers. With JFK, as with sex, I never got *the talk*. In both areas, I've been left with the great mystery and have been bumbling forth in the dark ever since. I have given up the idea that I can come to know the whole story, and I no longer feel I have the luxury to ask what it is they are failing to tell me. Today I realize the real question is: "What do we fail to ask ourselves?"

History is a humbling business, but because I am a child of America, and particularly because I'm from Dallas, I like to think I've inherited a certain amount of optimism. I've been raised to think that just maybe the future *is* ours; I'm always waiting for the next episode. Sometimes, to this very day, I will rise out of bed in the morning and (as my long-suffering wife will confirm) sing out that stirring refrain from the *Mighty Mouse* theme song: "Here I come to save the day!" While I've lost a bit of my original innocence, I can summon up just enough mock heroism to keep hope, to believe that I can achieve that mouse-sized accomplishment of adequately preserving what happened in Dallas back then. If I'm not exactly saving the world, I can maybe "save the day" in the sense that I might preserve a better sense of those times and their fallout. I can compile this document, this object for better remembering, and lay it open here in hopes it will help us conduct our recollections with appropriate integrity.

•

Of course, the assassination of John F. Kennedy is not strictly a local matter. Our thirty-fifth president remains a figure of international significance, and he is still a profoundly pertinent historical subject. One vitally important example of this current relevance is his centrality in our understanding of America's burgeoning conspiracy culture.

Today, JFK's assassination functions as a sort of ur-event in the conspiracy world. For many Americans, the scenario of one lonely, no-account gunman killing the most powerful man in the world was deeply unsatisfying. It left a void that begged to be filled. After the press coverage, the Warren Report, and the real-life stories of Lee Harvey Oswald and his unlikely partner in crime, Jack Ruby, provided few satisfying answers, many sought more compelling narratives. The result was the proliferation of newly concocted conspiracy theories, and these supplied a sort of original template for the ever more outlandish and elaborate stories of fantasy and paranoia that followed. From those original JFK conspiracy stories, the tendrils have spiraled in a thousand directions. You can see the connections today, if you dare to look, in the expanding influence of QAnon as it goes mainstream.

As we struggle today to fathom the vast, disembodied virtual world of contemporary conspiracy theory, to put some actual flesh and bones to it, we would do well to look at Dallas, Texas, in 1963. You might find here, in this physical landscape among these real people, the place where old-style Cold War paranoia—that original "Paranoid Style in American Politics" that Richard Hofstadter chronicled—took its first mutating leap into that web-driven, hyperspeed, post-truth conspiracy landscape we inhabit today. I would propose that Dallas in 1963 is a central node in the understanding of conspiracy theory, with links that move not just forward but also backward.

The fact that pre-assassination Dallas would be a hotbed for Red Scare conspiracy theory did not make it particularly unique in mid-century America.

There were any number of communities roiled by conspiracy-tinged activism at the time; my early stomping grounds in Orange County, California, are a case in point. What set Dallas apart was its reputation for actual physical intimidation. It was here that the demonization involved in conspiracy thinking crossed that line from uncivil behavior to something more threatening.

On several occasions, liberal dignitaries visiting Dallas were harassed and attacked. These high-profile incidents brought the attention of the rest of the world and created the expectation that Kennedy might encounter the same fate. This was a city, as described by one citizen at the time, "where anxiety is high, where the opposition is cowed, where there is only one public voice and it is filled with certainty and hate." In Dallas, civil discourse had become tinged with fear.[15] It was not uncommon for Dallasites to have to make careful day-by-day calculations about what they could say, and so, of course, there was much that went unsaid.

One remarkable side effect of this conspiracy phenomenon in Dallas was how our paranoia became embedded in our, so to speak, polite society. It was our "Mink Coat Mob," the well-heeled and well-dressed supporters of Representative Bruce Alger, who brought us some of our first national notoriety by accosting and spitting on Lady Bird Johnson in the august confines of the Adolphus Hotel during that notorious 1960 campaign stop in support of JFK. (This was an especially stark demonstration of the extent of conspiracy demonization—Lady Bird was one of our own. She had attended college here and still shopped at the same downtown Neiman Marcus store as many in the mob did.) Likewise, when Adlai Stevenson's Memorial Auditorium "UN Day" event was sabotaged by a right-wing mob, the woman who accosted Stevenson outside, slamming her sign down upon his head, was a member of that same downtown social set. In a city that prides itself on offering its guests elegant hospitality and loves to define itself by its refined social display (most emblematized by the Neiman Marcus department store), it was astonishing that the most-high profile demonstrations of our bile seemed to emanate from the very core of our civic social world. The irony is heightened further by the fact that Stanley Marcus, the man most responsible for our effective display of elegance,

15. Wright, *In the New World*, 16.

accompanied Stevenson that day. In fact, both he and Stevenson were in the car that was just able to speed off before it was tipped over by the angry crowd.

Today, the importance of understanding the social dynamics unloosed by conspiracy thinking is an increasingly vital topic. For anybody willing to take up the task, pre-assassination Dallas provides a fascinating case study—a model environment in which to gauge how a subset of fervent political activists propelled by a shared conspiracist mindset could come, in some important ways, to dominate political life.

While our outside critics were generally content to paint the whole city with broad-stroke accusations, we defended ourselves with one standard mantra: "All of this was only a small but very vocal minority of our population." "They" were not to be confused with "us." Always, we had to contend with this specter of communal guilt. In truth, it was clear our radical activist groups *did* have an outsize influence on our political life. Driven by the simplified narratives of conspiracy thinking, flush with falsehood and fueled with exaggeration, they found the righteous fervor necessary to make themselves seen and heard. We could legitimately ask: "Why must the entire city be asked to answer for this few?"

We were fortunate that, under the burning scrutiny of the post-assassination spotlight, our conspiracy mongers seemed to quickly melt away. As the culprits who had created the mess mercifully disappeared, there was no willingness to ask more troubling and difficult questions. We were content then to take no more initiative as far as a specific accounting. Today, however, it might be germane to understand the answers to some of those questions. What percentage of our population *was* actually involved? How deeply did this way of thinking actually permeate local culture? And, trickiest of all: How was it *here* that this movement was able to achieve the critical mass necessary to become so prominent? Was there some social "climate" that *we* created that made this possible?

It was understandable that no one here wished to publicly ask such questions, but there has been a cost. While we resented that many outsiders would lump us all together as rabid conspiracy-mongers, we never really did the reckoning ourselves to distinguish the "them" from "us." We have had to live with that fuzziness ever since.

Today, it is worth remembering that *Time* magazine, a central arbiter of mid-century American reality, declared Dallas "A City Disgraced" less than a month *before* Kennedy's scheduled visit. Any legitimate historical review of what was going on in the city of Dallas at that time will verify that we *expected* trouble when Kennedy came in November 1963. Lee Harvey Oswald pulled the trigger and killed the president, but it is important to remember that it was our radical right-wing activists who drove that sense that something was going to happen. Oswald provided the climax, but they provided all the buildup, and they set up a narrative that would become a worldwide story.

It is worth remembering that all of those myriad conspiracy tales that flowed out of the events that occurred in Dallas that November weekend in 1963 were directly prefaced by the actions of a group of Dallas "Ultra-Patriots" who were themselves driven by a witch's brew of outlandish conspiracy stories. They created for themselves a phantom history, and we have been haunted by it ever since.

•

Again, on January 6, 2021, something happened. Just as in Dallas in 1963, it was not a surprise—the expectation was that something was bound to happen. We didn't know quite what to expect, but it was clear that momentum had been building. Again, a conspiracy-driven narrative of outlandish exaggerations and mistruths had provoked a group of self-appointed "Ultra-Patriots" to action. Again, these crazy stories had been marched out in the open and legitimized by their presence in the public square.

On January 6, 2021, the nation's capitol was attacked by a mob just as the electoral votes confirming our new president were presented. As we awaited the ceremonial certification of the election results, again we were all tuned to our televisions, sharing another ugly national spectacle. As we watched, many must have felt that same exasperation and hopelessness that we felt in Dallas in 1963. Many probably asked the same questions: "Is that us on TV?" For Dallas old-timers all of this might have evoked a ghostly familiarity. Were these our Absolutists returned and writ large?

As the fifty-year retrospective of the assassination in Dallas drew to its culmination, there were whispers among some of those doing serious reflection on our local history about disquieting echoes of 1963 Dallas in our current politics. The Tea Party movement had recently gained ascendance in the Republican Party, sparking disruptions of town hall meetings across the nation and increasing the demonization of political opponents. With their drum, fife, and flag reenactment of American history, these self-branded "Real Americans" audaciously set out to reclaim the Golden Age of our founding fathers. While this cosplay had its comic aspects, it barely disguised the combination of radical certainty and bad manners that resulted in the short-circuiting of civil discourse.

Still, with the exception of those few whispers, no one locally was talking about any national echoes of 1963 Dallas. Even at the time of the fiftieth ceremony, discussions of our conspiracy-minded Absolutists were muted. The entire point of the remembrance, after all, had been to remind us that we had left all this deep in the past. Some recent scholarship, however, has broached the subject. Undoubtedly the most vivid of these is Steven L. Davis and Bill Minutaglio's *Dallas 1963*. The most important book concerning Dallas to come out of the deluge of publishing that accompanied the Fiftieth, it is a compelling reexamination of this city's political culture in the three years before JFK's ill-fated trip to Dallas. It offers a deep dive into the distinctly American paranoia that was Dallas before November 1963, and it's a roller-coaster read, following all the major Dallas right-wing players (as well as a plethora of minor participants) as they paved the way for that moment when President Kennedy arrived in 1963 Dallas as a "wanted" man.

Dallas 1963 is a damning picture of mid-century Dallas, and a nagging reminder that we had, in some ways, earned the moniker "City of Hate." Nonetheless, *Dallas 1963* was fairly well received and well reviewed here. In the general spirit of putting things behind us, there were few who publicly complained of the treatment it gave the city. No one in Dallas, of course, could very well dispute the facts. Steven L. Davis and Bill Minutaglio were established researchers and authors. And both were certifiably Texan, with longtime Dallas connections. In print and in public, both authors were careful about making claims outside the boundaries of their book, but the parallels between 1963 Dallas and contemporary American politics were too much to ignore.

Introducing the book at the Texas Book Festival in Austin, the authors professed that many of the damnable things they had chronicled in Dallas at the time were not safely contained in the past, but were now apparent on the national stage. Bill Minutaglio noted the "really acute parallels" between today's right-wing fanatics and those in Dallas in 1963. "Our contention is that really the birth of that polarization, the real public manifestation, the outer edge of it, was born in Dallas, Texas." Steven Davis chimed in: "That virus has gone national today."[16] His concerns have only been amplified in the time since. "The most compelling aspect of Dallas and the JFK era," he said recently, "is that lunatic fringe spawned in that city has metastasized and swallowed up an entire political party and is now a mainstream movement."[17]

Coming from a man who has immersed himself in the city's pre-assassination culture and written the definitive take on the era, this begs the question: What really did happen to our Absolutists? In Dallas, the story that they were vanquished immediately upon the tragedy of the assassination has won the day and long gone unchallenged. It offers up a considerable dose of comfortable closure. But *did* all of that paranoiac animus simply disappear?

The historian Edward H. Miller has recently done important work on just this question. His 2015 book, *Nut Country: Right-Wing Dallas and the Birth of the Southern Strategy,* takes a deep look at the influence of early 1960s Dallas right-wingers on the development of contemporary conservatism and finds some things worth remembering today. Beyond chronicling our influence in pioneering the tactics that gave birth to the "Southern Strategy"—the successful use of racial animosity that helped transform the South into a bastion of Republicanism—Miller asserts that our Dallas "ultraconservative Republicans were more essential to the rise of the Right than recent historians have appreciated." After the assassination of John F. Kennedy, Miller claims, "the ultraconservatives in Dallas who did not completely jettison their predictions for

16. Bill Minutaglio and Steven Davis, "Dallas 1963," panel discussion moderated by Jessica Grogan, C-Span, October 26, 2013, https://www.c-span.org/video/?315829-4/dallas-1963.

17. Steven Davis, email message to Will Evans, December 1, 2020.

apocalyptic fantasies, overheated rhetoric, conspiracy theories and assertions of white supremacy," nevertheless retained their cultural sway. They became, he argues "even more important than the moderate conservatives."

In the decade or so since the Fiftieth, with the burgeoning influence of an alternative right-wing media and the explosion of disinformation on social media, we've entered a period ripe for the postmodern updating of our "Paranoid Style in American Politics." Donald Trump, of course, was the perfect man for this moment, and his presidency exacerbated and accelerated the predominant trends. In Dallas, while the city itself turned increasingly Democrat blue, many of its expanding suburbs went deep, deep red, becoming particularly fertile ground for the peddling of these nakedly partisan conspiracy theories.

Today, Dallas can crow about the national scope of its influence, and it is not a hollow boast. It has been clear since we hosted the 1984 Republican National Convention, and today we can proudly invite visitors to our new George W. Bush Presidential Library. We have benefited from a power shift in American politics, rightward and toward the west, and we have been in the right place at the right time. It may be, however, that we actually underestimate our national influence.

When John F. Kennedy quipped, as he approached Love Field in Air Force One in 1963, that he was descending into "nut country," we had already established a notable reputation for ourselves. Today, unfortunately, the "nuts" have established a much broader sway, one that encompasses all of America. As Steven L. Davis recently noted, a real historical examination of this city in 1963 might reveal "Dallas as the Typhoid Mary of America's political dysfunction today."[18]

•

There are very few physical markers of our Absolutists in Dallas today, no monuments that we can point to and say, "There is that thing." In some important ways, the Absolutists came to define Dallas for the rest of the

18. Davis, email to Will Evans.

world, but they left precious little here to account for the movement itself. You could point perhaps to H. L. Hunt's "Mount Vernon" home, a beautiful colonial-style estate designed as a larger version of George Washington's iconic home. It sits today still nestled on the bucolic shore of White Rock Lake. You could look perhaps to the former downtown headquarters of the *Dallas Morning News,* where Ted Dealey officed. If you looked hard enough, you might find in these physical locations the ghosts of the most prominent of our Absolutists—of Hunt, the great financier of conspiracy theory, and Dealey, the newspaperman who spread those ideas throughout the community on a daily basis.

In these physical locales, however, there are also broader stories, reminders of a deeper and richer history than a simple story of conspiracy-mongering. H. L. Hunt, whose children continue to have immense influence on this city, was an inveterate gambler who sired two separate families, became the master oil-field wildcatter, and went on to live the myth of the richest man in the world. Also packed within the building that housed the *Dallas Morning News* is much of the history of a newspaper established here in 1885, with its own long, rich history that parallels that of the city it covers. It contains stories such as that of the elder George Bannerman Dealey and his fight to suppress the considerable influence of the Ku Klux Klan in 1920s Dallas. These physical artifacts display a history as complex as the city itself—even, sometimes, illustrative of the very best of ourselves.

There is no location where the history of Dallas is more physically present than Dealey Plaza. It is the site of founder John Neely Bryan's original cabin, and the center of the settlement that would eventually radiate out from his original survey. The Depression-era WPA construction of the plaza itself is a telling glimpse into Dallas history. There is plenty of raw material here for compelling historical storytelling.

While the statue of George Bannerman Dealey, the plaza's namesake, still lords over the plaza today, none of that earlier history seems particularly present. It is obscured by another, phantom history, the more insistent narrative of the assassination of John F. Kennedy. If you were seriously digging, you might find here some traces of the Absolutists, but it is Lee Harvey Oswald at his sixth-floor window who dominates the scene. Woven through all of this physical reality is this one psychic reality, and it veils and blurs anything before or after November 1963.

Dealey Plaza literally manifests our history—if you were to dig here, you would find it in the dirt. While this rolling little amphitheater cradles almost two centuries of stories of our civic life, it is easy to forget that it is the birthplace of the city. Many Dallasites do, and they can't really be blamed. The few historical markers here are tiny and difficult to access; there are no celebrations or remembrances. Most prominent among the people you would meet here who are interested in talking history are the conspiracy buffs selling their wares.

It is important to remember that Dealey Plaza was literally designed as a portal to our impressive downtown, our proudest icon and what we most want the world to notice about us. Unfortunately, Dealey Plaza is, even today, the place where people from around the world tend to stop. It is the stage where they come for a constant replaying of November 22, 1963. Out-of-town visitors here are more likely to lower their head to ponder the X on the pavement where the president took the fatal bullet than look up at our majestic skyline. Even today, Dealey Plaza is the place where our history gets stuck. While Dallasites have always lived to tell Texas-sized stories of our city's heroic dynamism, here we stand mute.

It should come as no surprise that there is such a dearth of local historical remembrance in Dealey Plaza; there is very, very little of that in the rest of the city. We sponsor no major history-themed annual celebrations and, compared to most cities, our calendar is barren when it comes to those rituals in which we bind ourselves together through celebration of a shared past. We are a future-oriented city, famous for tearing down historical buildings to put up something new. If people wander around Dealey Plaza obsessed with the murdered president, what other alternatives have we provided them?

While we absent-mindlessly allow our past to be obscured, there is a phantom history that wafts through the plaza. It is a fickle wind in which the facts roil around within a swirling mix of myth and misinformation. What we fail to nail down as truth is overwhelmed by the force of conspiratorial elaboration. In Dallas, we stand here mute and are buffeted by this wind. We curse our fate, and then we are relieved when our out-of-town guests leave Dealey Plaza and make their pilgrimage to our preferred historical destinations. They can better learn about Dallas by reliving the rip-roaring chronicle of J. R. Ewing and his family at Southfork Ranch.

A half century later, I could sit here in Dealey Plaza, this little dirt pile on the Trinity River, and ponder again. "What is it they are not telling me?"

I suspect again I am being robbed of the stories I need.

•

Even today, when I go to Dealey Plaza, I anguish over what I should expect to experience. I feel an uncomfortable burden to express something to myself and am still unable to find thoughts that feel appropriate. I feel all tongue-tied and stumbly, like I'm standing around and don't know what do with my hands. In short, I feel like Andy Kaufman waiting for the chorus of the *Mighty Mouse* theme song to roll around so I can lip-synch along.

It's not just me. Dealey Plaza is a strange place for everybody. I have seen some bizarre behavior here. It's disconcerting to stand at a man's assassination site, where he publicly had his brains blown out, and try to craft a proper response. For me, and I suppose many older Dallasites, all that is still hanging in the air. I wonder if everyone else can still feel that twinge of shame and embarrassment?

All of this still troubles me, and I feel a little inadequate. We have, after all, performed the purge; we have officially exorcised all the ghosts. Right here, on November 22, 2013, we staged our stately ceremony—the Fiftieth. Our mayor, Mike Rawlings, stepped on stage right here in Dealey Plaza. He put the needle down on that scratchy record of history, and he made a heroic gesture. On that day, Mayor Rawlings sang the hero's song, and together we all praised President John F. Kennedy. Finally, we honored our connection to him and proclaimed that we had taken up his legacy. There was even some lip-synching. The noted historian David McCullough read selected excerpts from Kennedy's speeches, and Mayor Rawlings closed his address by reading from Kennedy's final, undelivered speech.

By all accounts, it was a monumental day for the city of Dallas. Just as with Kaufman's skit, the crowd cheered when the performance was over, and everyone felt immense relief. We had conquered a half century of stage fright and all that excruciating, pent-up silence.

I've gone back and looked at Kaufman's *SNL Mighty Mouse* homage. It always reaffirms my original appreciation of the sweet nostalgia of Kaufman's tribute. There is always the thrill I have as a fellow traveler attempting to reconnect with that golden moment of my youth. I can't help but think that, yes, maybe I too share some of that same earnest buffoonery. However, watching Kaufman walk the teetering, shaky bridge he has built to the past, I am reminded of the real danger of hurt and embarrassment. In our efforts to reclaim a cherished moment—for me my *Mighty Mouse* Saturday mornings, for Dallas those cheering crowds that greeted John F. Kennedy on the streets of Dallas—there are risks. It is difficult to reclaim paradise once you have lost your innocence.

Kaufman's genius is to always undergird his goofy playacting with elements of stark and painful reality. At his best, you see displayed before you the painful gap between what we are and what we would aspire to be. In the *Mighty Mouse* sketch, it's there in the dichotomy between the dramatic lip-synching gesture and the awkward waiting that leads up to it. There is our heroic self, and there is our real, pedestrian self.

The dynamics of the sketch are such that it is the first "Here I come to save the day!" that gets the biggest laugh, finally relieving the built-up tension. Then, instantly, Kaufman reverts back to his tedious, inept, inarticulate self. He stands there, still tongue-tied and uncertain what to do with his hands. But there is the tease; when the chorus rolls around again, *it* might just happen again . . .

When I visit Dealey Plaza today, that's the moment I am stuck in. In Dallas, we have made progress, but I'm very, very anxious for the second act.

•

Most here would be happy to proclaim that history is done with Dallas and the assassination of John F. Kennedy. We are a profoundly different city than we were in 1963, light-years beyond the anguish of that period. The Fiftieth, however, was not the close of this city's story with the death of JFK. We cannot simply declare victory over our history and march forward without paying a price. All history, if you look deeply enough, is always about the present, and this book is about who we are today. There is still a lot to unpack in the JFK assassination. The book on 1963 Dallas is not closed.

Again, something has happened. Again, we had an ominous expectation that it would, and it did—another horrific and violent attack that seems to threaten the fundamental tenets of our democracy. There is a new cast of characters, led by a reality TV actor intent on his own self-aggrandizement, falsely claiming that a presidential election had been stolen. Underneath the differences between now and 1963, however, are clear parallels. Here again are the swarms of true believers, fed the red meat of conspiracy theory and paranoic demonization of their political opponents.

The entire nation now is faced with the same gnawing questions we never adequately addressed in Dallas after the Kennedy assassination. Was there some social "climate" we created that made this possible? Could we be somehow implicated in this? As citizens, what obligations do we have now to respond?

Almost six decades after November 1963, there are benefits in asking how we can better understand what happened here. It is still worth asking: How do we hold *ourselves* to account?

CHAPTER 1

The Haunted Plaza

> The presidential motorcade is revving up on Main Street. The crowd outside the Texas School Book Depository gets ready for another round of cheering until the gunshots ring out. John F. Kennedy is about to be killed in Dealey Plaza again, and again, and again.
>
> George Lardner Jr., *The Washington Post,* May 19, 1991[19]

THE ASSASSINATION OF John F. Kennedy was a singular event, one that an entire nation felt it experienced together. Strangely, though, today the assassination seems to exist in an endless number of variations. While it is arguably the most extensively documented event in all of human history, each time we rewind the projector, a new version of the assassination seems to flicker before us.

Each version offers up those iconic elements, the inescapable clues that you are back inside that fateful day. In one recent music video, for instance, the first of these clues is the fuzzy buzz of the local news radio: "The president's car is now turning onto Elm Street and it will be only a matter of minutes before he arrives at the Trade Mart." As you watch a woman park her stately white 1964 Lincoln Continental along the curb, feed the parking

---

19. George Lardner Jr., "On the Set Dallas in Wonderland," *The Washington Post,* May 19, 1991, cited in Oliver Stone and Zachary Sklar, *JFK: The Book of the Film* (New York: Applause Books, 1992), 191.

meter, and walk back up the sidewalk, you can see that this is indeed downtown Dallas. As she walks north up Houston Street, you recognize immediately the distinctive 1930s reflecting pools and white colonnades—you are at the entrance to Dealey Plaza.

The woman's identity is obscured. She wears a black trench coat, a demure purple headcover, and big dark sunglasses. There is something regal about her, but also perhaps a little agitated. As she walks, she removes her glasses. A few steps farther, she sheds her coat, dropping it onto the pavement. She tosses aside one shoe, then the other. By the time she gets to the corner of Houston and Elm, in the shadow of the Texas School Book Depository Building, she has lost her headcover, her purple pullover, and the sheer white blouse underneath. As she turns down Elm Street toward the Triple Underpass, it's apparent where this is going. As she heads for ground zero, she is slowly disrobing.

Now, she weaves through the thickening crowd, wearing only her black underwear and bra. Thirty feet from the spot, she removes her bra. Still walking, she pulls off her underwear, and she is completely nude by the time she approaches the X. She pauses there for just a moment and—BANG! A gunshot. Her head snaps back. She falls prone to the pavement.

It all comes rushing back to you. It is November 22, 1963, all over again.

•

The provocateur in this video is Erykah Badu, Dallas's own neo-soul diva, whose previous work has earned her a national reputation for being both a very talented singer—she's occasionally spoken of as a hip-hop version of Billie Holiday—and a unique artist. A well-known advocate for Black pride, female empowerment, and bohemian do-it-your-self community-making, Badu is a graduate of Booker T. Washington, Dallas's downtown arts magnet high school. She's a local girl who, despite her Grammy awards, has stayed local.

The video of Badu's bare-all performance at Dealey Plaza occurred on March 17, 2010, and was created to promote "Window Seat," a single from her album *New Amerykah Part Two (Return of the Ankh)*. It was inspired by a similar performance by Matt & Kim, the quirky pop-punk duo whose "Lessons Learned" video was a recent internet smash. In that video, Matt &

Kim enthusiastically strip nude while walking through the throngs in New York's Times Square, pausing to enjoy the splendor of the naked city at the corner of Forty-Seventh and Broadway. Badu borrowed the idea and the minimal, damn-the-law aesthetics for her "Window Seat" video. As she wrote on her Twitter feed the day the video first aired, it "was shot guerrilla style, no crew, 1 take, no closed set, no warning, 2 min., downtown dallas, then ran like hell."[20]

"Times Square is the most monumental place in New York," Badu told an interviewer a few weeks later, "and when I was thinking of monumental places, the grassy knoll was the most monumental place in Dallas I could think of."[21] Like Times Square, Dealey Plaza is a focal point for the energy of the big city that surrounds it, but they are very different places. Times Square stands for big dreams and a good time; it is most recognized for a celebration that ushers in the new: the dropping of the illuminated ball on New Year's Eve. Dealey Plaza evokes a national nightmare. You go to Dealey Plaza to mourn a lost past, to stand where an assassin ended the life of a nation's beloved leader. While Matt & Kim's naked jaunt qualified as just another day in the Big City, Erykah Badu's sparked big outrage in Dallas.

Immediately upon its release, the "Window Seat" video went viral. Within a couple of weeks, it had provoked a national controversy. While sources as diverse as CNN International, *The Washington Post*, *Entertainment Weekly*, and *New York Magazine* joined in and amplified the discussion, the real outrage was most evident in Dallas. Badu's Dealey Plaza stunt got prominent play on local TV, and the indignation was reiterated over and over again—in man-on-the-street interviews, in letters to the editor, by bloggers and talk-show callers. It seemed, if you listened to the media echo machine, that an outraged community agreed: Erykah Badu had crossed the line!

There was a hefty amount of public posturing concerning the proper punishment for Badu. The city leaders explored various possible charges, including failure to obtain the required permit for public filming, but ultimately the

20. "Erykah Badu Strips On Downtown Dallas Street For Music Video," KWTX, March 30, 2010.

21. Hunter Hauk, "Badu speaks out about 'Window Seat' video," *Dallas Morning News*, March 29, 2010.

best they could do was a measly charge of disorderly conduct. Three and a half months later, there was noticeable disappointment and hand-wringing among her critics when the affair reached closure, and Badu unceremoniously paid her five-hundred-dollar ticket. (By comparison, Matt & Kim, even after grappling with the New York police, were charged with no crime.)

Badu's shameless and self-serving public nudity had been enough—but the desecration of a site as holy as Dealey Plaza was beyond the pale. The *Dallas Morning News,* today as in the early 1960s the self-appointed arbiter of civic morality in Dallas, trumpeted this outrage in news articles and editorials. Rod Dreher, a former *Morning News* editorial columnist, blogged: "Utterly, completely, nauseatingly tasteless. What will she do for her second single off the new album? Go to the balcony where MLK was shot and do the hoochie-koochie in her underwear?"[22] *Morning News* columnist James Ragland's March 31 piece covered similar ground, opining: "Badu, you see, is like many artists—quick to tell the rest of us that we just don't get it when we take offense to something that's rude, crude, vulgar or otherwise socially unacceptable." Ragland dismissed Badu's actions as mere cash-craving PR, and he let his readers know that he was in line with the official stance. First, he quoted Dallas Deputy Mayor Pro Tem Dwaine Caraway, a self-confessed Badu fan and the architect of the city's "Pull 'em Up" campaign to pressure young Black men to pull up their pants in public. "I want to be clear," Caraway said of Badu's actions, "We are not going to tolerate these types of things." Ragland's final source was Lindalyn Adams, the founder of the Dallas County Historical Commission and the chief mover in the establishment of the Sixth Floor Museum commemorating John F. Kennedy's legacy and death in Dallas. "I don't understand," she said, "how someone who lives here, who is a resident of this city, could do such a thing."[23]

Badu defended herself to the more sympathetic *Morning News* music writer Hunter Hauk: "'Window Seat' is about liberating yourself from layers

22. Rod Dreher, "Tactless Erykah Badu gets naked at JFK death site," *beliefnet,* March 31, 2010, https://www.beliefnet.com/columnists/roddreher/2010/03/tactless-erykah-badu-gets-naked-at-jfk-death-site.html.

23. James Ragland, "Naked Truth: Badu's latest video is more PR than art," *Dallas Morning News,* March 31, 2010.

and layers of skin or demons that are a hindrance to your growth or freedom, or evolution. I wanted to do something that said just that, so I started thinking about shedding, nudity, taking things off in a very artful way."[24] Later, more pointedly, she addressed the charges of desecrating the shrine that is Dealey Plaza on a TV talk show. "JFK is one of my heroes, one of the nation's heroes," Badu told Wanda Sykes. "John F. Kennedy was a revolutionary; he was not afraid to butt heads with America, and I was not afraid to show America my butt-naked truth."[25]

For many in Dallas, this was not a truth they wanted to confront. Indeed, it wasn't Badu's disregard for the legacy of John F. Kennedy that had ruffled so many feathers. It was her intentional evocation of that legacy. The "Window Seat" video pushed the buttons: the radio broadcast setup, the white Lincoln a negative-image echo of the black presidential touring car, the handheld video with its jumpy, washed-out quality mimicking the original Zapruder footage. It was a fairly sophisticated reworking of some of the most recognizable elements of the JFK assassination iconography. It opened old wounds.

•

Since 1963, Dealey Plaza has been the most visited tourist attraction in North Texas, drawing roughly a million visitors per year. In Texas, it has been second only to the Alamo in the number of people it draws. Dallas is the ninth-largest city in the United States, and, physically and symbolically, Dealey Plaza stands at its very center.

The plaza creates an amphitheater-shaped bowl of green space where downtown's three main thoroughfares—Elm, Main, and Commerce—converge together to pass west under the Triple Underpass toward the Trinity River. Since its distinctive white art deco–style pergolas and colonnades were

24. David Flick and Hunter Hauk, "Naked Erykah Badu video at Kennedy site stirs controversy," *Dallas Morning News*, March 30, 2010.

25. Joel Hanek, "Erykah Badu Defends 'Window Seat' On 'Wanda Sykes Show," *MTV News*, April 5, 2010, https://www.mtv.com/news/d9wvp0/erykah-badu-defends-window-seat-on-wanda-sykes-show.

built in the 1930s as a New Deal WPA project, the park has created a dramatic gateway into the city. Today, entering Dealey Plaza after exiting the Medusa-headed maze of freeways that encircles downtown, you experience a rare open space. In a flash of grass and blue sky, the western face of downtown opens itself up to you. Since Dallas is, as much as any city, a city of the car, Dealey Plaza offers up the quintessential Dallas experience—a moment of flashing brilliance that you can appreciate without slowing down on the way downtown to make money.

Dealey Plaza is also the origin point of Dallas, its birthplace. You can find the founding myths of the city inscribed in the plaza's stonework, its statues and plaques. What is often, unapologetically, called the Dallas Myth is laid out right there for any visitor to see. Nestled in this tiny green oasis, overshadowed by one of America's grandest skylines, you can begin to read that narrative of nearly uninterrupted development and entrepreneurial success that makes Dallas the "Can-Do City," a city of ambitious go-getters who made it all up out of nothing.

The most prominent single feature of Dealey Plaza is the statue of George Bannerman Dealey. On its massive marble pedestal, his larger-than-life figure dominates the Main Street entrance of the plaza in the same manner that the man himself dominated Dallas life for much of his career. George Dealey came to Dallas from Galveston in 1885 to help establish the *Dallas Morning News,* eventually buying the paper and establishing it as a powerful institution in the life of the city. Dealey would go on to become one of the earliest embodiments of the Dallas "Civic Man," a long line of city-building businessmen who saw business leadership and civic leadership as one and the same. Dealey was constantly involved in city planning, helping adopt the early Kessler Plan for civic improvement in 1910 and functioning as the driving force behind the redevelopment that led to the creation of Dealey Plaza itself.

In addition to being an influential publisher, Dealey helped shaped Dallas cultural life in other ways. He was a major force in the establishment of WFAA, the first network-affiliated radio station in Texas, and the founding of Southern Methodist University, the city's first major university. He was also instrumental in luring the Federal Reserve Bank to Dallas in 1914. But

Dealey is most famous for leading a crusade that helped quash the immense influence the Ku Klux Klan wielded in 1920s Dallas.[26]

•

Before George Bannerman Dealey, there had been John Neely Bryan, the original city father. Just off Elm Street, near Dealey Plaza's northern pergola, stands an ornate bronze historical marker that honors Bryan as the man who founded Dallas. In 1841, Bryan lay claim to this spot of land, a prominent crossing on the Trinity River that was surrounded with good timber and freshwater springs.

The former Tennessee lawyer was certain that someday the Trinity would be cleared of barriers, connecting his fledgling village to the Gulf of Mexico and transforming it into a thriving trading port. He worked tirelessly to bring his vision to fruition. He set up a trading post, persuaded a few folks to settle around him, and began running a ferry service across the Trinity. His cabin served as his office as the Republic of Texas's local postmaster, and Bryan's efforts were instrumental both in organizing Dallas County in 1846 and in ensuring that the city of Dallas became the county seat in 1850.

For twelve years, Bryan was the model city-builder, and it was his passionate vision that brought people to the tiny burg. Already, however, the city was incubating its future reputation for excessive economic ambition. When gold was discovered in California in 1848, "it was said that every man in town, save the lawyer, John C. McCoy, set out for the West." Bryan himself was among them.[27] Failing to strike it rich, Bryan returned to Dallas, but he had lost favor in the community and his influence was waning. He became gloomy and drank heavily. In 1852, at age fifty-two, Bryan sold his entire interest in Dallas to Alexander and Sarah Cockrell. Later that year, he shot

26. Jerry Dealey, *D in the Heart of Texas* (Garland, TX: JEDI Management Group, 2002); Joan J. Perez, "Dealey, George Bannerman," in *Handbook of Texas Online*, Texas State Historical Association, updated December 1, 1994, accessed December 30, 2011, http://www.tshaonline.org/handbook/online/articles/fde21.

27. Darwin Payne, *Dallas: An Illustrated History* (Woodland Hills, CA: Windsor Publications, 1982), 30.

a man for cursing at his wife and fled to the Creek Nation in Oklahoma. He returned to Dallas six years later but never fully regained his status as a civic leader, and he ended his life as a ward of the State Lunatic Asylum in Austin.[28]

While Bryan's death in 1877 was barely noted in Dallas, today he is universally recognized as the first resident and founder of the city. On the southern side of Dealey Plaza, affixed to the white art deco pergola, is a second plaque that honors Bryan, noting that this was the site where he established and ran the city's first ferry service across the Trinity River. Dealey Plaza itself is at the center of John Neely Bryan's original land claim and the site of his homestead cabin. From this spot, Bryan oversaw his 1844 survey that established the grid that undergirds today's downtown Dallas. The modern city of Dallas literally radiates out from John Neely Bryan's original homesite.

•

While Dealey Plaza is the origin point of Old Dallas, it is also where Old Dallas ended.

Currently, close to a million people visit Dealey Plaza each year, and they do not come to reminisce about the founding of Dallas. They come to commemorate the event that traumatized and, eventually, transformed the city—the assassination of John F. Kennedy. Before late November 1963, few people got out of their cars and walked the open space of Dealey Plaza. Today, crowds of pedestrians risk life and limb to cross the converging downtown thoroughfares that intersect the plaza, spreading out along the route that the presidential limousine traveled a half century ago. The pilgrims know where to go. They know what to look for; they do not need directions.

And, in Dealey Plaza, they will indeed find very little to direct them. Despite the obvious significance of the site, there is very little physical evidence that a major historical event occurred here. The casual visitor to Dealey Plaza

28. Payne, *Dallas: An Illustrated History*, 85; Cecil Harper Jr., "Bryan, John Neely," in *Handbook of Texas Online*, Texas State Historical Association, updated November 1, 1994, accessed August 20, 2011, https://www.tshaonline.org/handbook/entries/bryan-john-neely.

might miss the few small markers which commemorate the assassination; they are dwarfed by the monument that honors George Bannerman Dealey.

The most noticeable of these discreet commemorations of the assassination is the pole-mounted National Monument tablet on Elm Street, just west of the corner of the former Texas Book Depository Building. It was not installed until 1993—thirty years after the assassination—when Dealey Plaza was finally designated a National Historic Landmark. Despite its obvious significance, the plaque draws little attention. If you watch the visitors in the plaza, most will not stop and read the tablet—it is mostly ignored. They have done their own research; they are not going to learn anything from it that they don't already know.

Inevitably, the pilgrims' attention is focused just down the hill, where Elm Street coasts slightly downward toward the Triple Underpass. What they have come to see lies just a couple of feet from the white line dividing the center lane from the right lane. You can see the pilgrims gauging themselves by their proximity to it, like surveyors gauging the position of everything else against it; like haji orienting themselves to Mecca. The way that the devotees gravitate toward it, you might think it was the Holy of Holies, right here under the open Texas sun. What they are looking at is the exact spot where President John Fitzgerald Kennedy's skull was blasted open by a sniper's bullet. It is marked out in the middle of Elm Street with a simple X in white paint.

Here in Dallas, among the locals, this might as well be the scarlet letter, the yellow badge, the mark of the beast. It's a bad omen. You don't need any training in the mystical arts to know that it should be avoided. The X represents a huge blot in our collective psyche, and it is odd that something so momentous, that carries so much psychic weight, could be so small and ill defined. It's like one of those small scars or scabs on your skin that's almost unnoticeable except for the memory of its cause. The X looks more like a snatch of graffiti than a religious icon, but the passions it evokes are mammoth.

•

As Norman Mailer wrote in 1992, the assassination of John F. Kennedy became "our national obsession," and Dealey Plaza has taken on the status of that obsession's direct physical embodiment. Mailer writes that we have no answers to Kennedy's death, but, really, we have obsessively developed too many. We veer between two extremes, suspended in an "intolerable spiritual state." Was Kennedy, as Mailer asks, killed by "the concentrated forces of malign power" or was it one lone madman, leaving us in a world in which "one demented assassin could swing the ship of state wholly off its course?" We are bound between these two existential poles.

You can watch the visitors at Dealey Plaza seek their moment of solitude, attempt to find their answers, but this is not a place of peace. This is the center of a major city, and the clatter and the contestation of the busy streets never really abate. The man-made amphitheater of Dealey Plaza drains the oblations of thousands of visitors every year. They pour out their psychic libations and yet we seem no closer to any common resolution. "For what is an obsession," Mailer writes, "but a black hole in our psychic space, a zone of ambiguity into which our energies flow and do not return."[29] As one Dallas newspaper columnist remarked, Dealey Plaza has become "America's Emotional Grand Canyon."[30]

•

Dealey Plaza was finally designated a National Historic Landmark in 1993. Despite the millions of visitors and the obvious profundity of the event that occurred here, it took almost thirty years for local authorities to complete the process of officially recognizing Dealey Plaza's historic significance.

The avoidance was understandable. Like the inhabitants of Memphis after MLK, Dallasites bear a particular burden. History cannot be undone, and, as in any locale that has to live with its massacres, scandals, or slave trade, history demands its due. The Kennedy assassination is a painful legacy to carry. It is there, a whisper in the whoosh of each car that passes through

29. Norman Mailer, "Footfalls in the Crypt," *Vanity Fair*, February 1992, cited in Stone and Sklar, *JFK: The Book of the Film*, 438.

30. Max Holland, "Dealing with Dealey Plaza." *Washington Decoded*, November/December 1996, http://www.washingtondecoded.com/site/1999/12/dealing-with-de.html.

Dealey Plaza, a twinge in each glance up at that sixth-floor window. There is a well-practiced repression that comes with living in such a place. And there are a thousand ways to avoid the questions: How did we become the place of such shame? How did we become the city that killed Kennedy?

•

Today, Dealey Plaza is virtually preserved in its 1963 state. Very little has been physically altered since that fateful November day. A few street signs have been moved or altered, some lampposts have been relocated and more lighting added, but otherwise Dealey Plaza remains essentially unchanged. The Dallas Parks Department keeps the site in good shape and spruces it up a bit each year before the assassination anniversary.

The conservation of the plaza has sometimes been described as "passive preservation" since it results more from the impulse to avoid discussion of the assassination than to commemorate it. To suggest any alterations to the site would bring certain historical issues to the fore. Because "denial is the antithesis of activity," Dealey Plaza remains essentially unchanged.[31]

•

Always looming over Dealey Plaza is the former Texas School Book Depository. Perhaps the most notorious structure in American history, it will be forever linked directly to the assassination of John F. Kennedy. Even today, it is almost impossible to pass by the building without being struck with the impulse to look up at the south facade and find that far right window on the sixth floor.

Like Dealey Plaza, the building at 411 Elm Street has a history that runs deeper than just its place in JFK assassination lore. It stretches back to the early days of Dallas. The land the building was constructed on was one of the very first lots sold by John Neely Bryan back in 1849, and a recent

31. Conover Hunt, *JFK for a New Generation* (University Park, TX: Southern Methodist University Press, 1996), 123.

archeological survey of the lot discovered part of a cornfield planted by Bryan himself.[32] In 1894, the Rock Island Plow Company bought the site and, a few years later, built a five-story structure. It burned down, but was quickly replaced with the current, taller structure begun in 1901. With the exception of the Old Red Courthouse, it is arguably the oldest building on Dealey Plaza.

By 1900, the city that John Neely Bryan established in 1841 had a population of over forty thousand and was straining to catch Houston as the second-largest city in Texas. Ambitions were high. Cotton was king, and the Dallas area, with its rich black soil, had established itself as an agricultural center. The Rock Island Plow Company's building was just one structure forming the southern edge of a maze of warehouses and railroad lines called the Cotton District.

By the 1930s, Dallas's population had exploded, climbing above 260,000. Business was expanding and diversifying and, with oil gushing up on all sides, the city managed to avoid the worst effects of the Great Depression. Now, agriculture was being pushed out of downtown by other forms of commerce. The Rock Island Plow Company moved in 1937. The building at 411 Elm Street was then purchased by Colonel D. Harold Byrd and leased to the Texas School Book Depository Company, a private brokerage firm that supplied books to Texas schools.

•

Colonel D. Harold Byrd was, in many ways, the perfect embodiment of Dallas's mid-twentieth-century nouveau riche. He was a geologist who made it big in the wild and woolly world of Texas oil, and he earned his nickname, "Dry Hole," from the fact that, after he brought in his first big gusher, his next fifty-six wells produced nothing. Using his oil millions and the connections he developed at the Dallas Petroleum Club, Byrd diversified and continued to expand his fortunes. (In fact, Byrd's connections to the likes of H. L. Hunt

32. Conover Hunt, *A Visitor's Guide to Dealey Plaza National Historic Landmark* (Dallas: Sixth Floor Museum, 1995), 70.

and Lyndon Baines Johnson would ensure that his name would later occasionally pop up in rumors of a plot by right-wing Texas oilmen to murder JFK.)

Byrd translated his wealth into the type of larger-than-life reputation possible only with the playful cultivation of Texas frontier mythology. That he helped finance the Arctic expeditions of his cousin, Admiral Richard Byrd, and had the snow-laden Harold Byrd Mountains named in his honor did not hurt. Nor did his considerable philanthropic work, most notably his gift of "Big Bertha"—the world largest bass drum—to the marching band of his alma mater, the University of Texas. Byrd's reputation as a Texas eccentric with the means to satisfy his every whim earned him great notoriety. He landed a number of mentions in *New Yorker* writer John Bainbridge's bestselling 1961 inquiry into the lifestyles of the new Big Texas Rich, *The Super Americans*. *Life* magazine, in its 1948 "Southwest Has a New Crop of Super Rich" article, featured a photo of Byrd "in a top hat, cutaway coat, and false mustache and goatee, stepping down the street with his arms around two pretty girls" while on a self-financed jaunt to Mexico with thirty of his friends whom he had flown down in two of his own airplanes.[33]

For all of his notable eccentricities, Byrd fully understood his responsibilities as a Dallas civic mover and shaker. As part of the self-appointed power structure, with its obligation to protect the reputation of their city, he understood the particular and painful dilemma he faced in late 1963. The dilemma is visible even today on the street-level historical marker attached to the base of his building at 411 Elm Street. The plaque dutifully spells out the building's unique connection to Dallas's earliest history, from Bryan's original plot through the Rock Island Plow Company days to its incarnation as the Texas School Book Depository. This is all mere preface, though. "On Nov. 22, 1963," the plaque closes, "the building gained national notoriety when Lee Harvey Oswald allegedly shot and killed John F. Kennedy from a sixth-floor window as the presidential motorcade passed the site." The plaque has been repeatedly defaced—the word "allegedly" has been underlined with repeated gouging.

33. John Bainbridge, *The Super Americans* (New York: Doubleday, 1961), 375.

Colonel D. Harold Byrd's happy-go-lucky days of high-profile living would be tempered now with a new reality. He had a major public relations problem on his hands. His property at 411 Elm Street had become a lightning rod—the one physical structure that would attract all the clamor and electricity generated by the assassination of John F. Kennedy.

•

After November 1963, many people in Dallas suggested that the Texas School Book Depository Building be demolished and replaced. Unlike Dealey Plaza, the building could easily be made to disappear. When the Texas School Book Company moved to another location and vacated the building in 1970, demolition seemed to many a palatable option. For Colonel D. Harold Byrd, its owner, it was a no-win situation. He could bulldoze the building or continue to lease it; there would be controversy either way. After considering the options, Byrd eventually chose to auction off the warehouse.

The eventual buyer was Aubrey Mayhew, a Nashville music producer, who obtained the building for $650,000. Mayhew's record label had produced no major hits, but the artists he had worked with included Dallas rockabilly rabble-rouser "Groovey" Joe Poovey, and two singers who would later produce hits that helped define modern country music: Jeannie C. Riley with her "Harper Valley PTA," and Johnny Paycheck with his "Take This Job and Shove It." As Mayhew recounts it, he had been in Houston in November 1963, trying to purchase some George Jones tapes from maverick record man Pappy Daily. When the first assassination reports came over the TV, he recorded everything he could during the first twelve hours of those broadcasts. He then hurried back to New York with the material and put out the first album collection of Kennedy speeches. Mayhew claims that Pickwick Records, his employer at the time, sold three million of these albums in the next four months.[34]

Mayhew became a passionate collector of artifacts associated with John F. Kennedy; he would eventually open up a small JFK Museum on Nashville's

34. Tony Russell, "Obituary: Aubrey Mayhew," *Guardian*, May 25, 2009.

Music Row. His obsession drove him to assemble what was arguably the largest collection of Kennedy-related items in the world, including the largest, and presumably the only, complete collection of JFK medallic art. He transformed himself into a numismatic authority and literally wrote the book on the subject. His *The World's Tribute to John F. Kennedy in Medallic Art* contains vital information about every coin, token, key chain—anything metal—bearing JFK's image.[35]

Mayhew's plan was to turn the Texas School Book Depository into a commercial museum commemorating Kennedy's life, but his venture never got off the ground. The city permits necessary to start the renovations for the museum were repeatedly turned down, and the state ignored his requests to recognize the building as historically significant. In the early 1970s, local nerves were still raw. A group called Dallas Onward formed to protest efforts to turn the building into a national Kennedy landmark. The city leaders recoiled at the idea that an outsider would have such control of the city's reputation. Mayhew's plan seemed to celebrate the moment of the city's greatest shame, and they found the idea that the museum would be run for profit especially distasteful. Just before the purchase of the Texas School Book Depository, Mayhew had already caused a furor with the purchase of some letters written by Jacqueline Kennedy.[36]

There had been one other serious attempt to operate an assassination-themed museum adjacent to Dealey Plaza. A cheesy little storefront John F. Kennedy Museum had opened in 1970 across the street from the Texas School Book Depository in the Dal-Tex Building. For a mere $1.50 admission fee, this privately run operation offered a papier-mâché model of the city mimicking the presidential parade route, with electric lights blinking out the points of action while a narrator described the tragedy. As one visitor wrote: "All forms of Kennedyana [were] offered, from ashtrays to velvet

35. Andrew Mayhew, *The World's Tribute to John F. Kennedy in Medallic Art* (New York: William Morrow and Co., 1996).

36. A. C. Greene, "A. C. Greene on the Texas School Book Depository." *Washington Decoded,* January/February 1997, http://www.washingtondecoded.com/site/files/a.C.%20Greene%20on%20 the%20Texas%20School%20Book%20Depository.pdf.

art."[37] The John F. Kennedy Museum was tolerated, and it stayed open until 1982, because it was a small-scale affair. It kept a relatively low profile, and it was not located in the Texas School Book Depository Building.

Mayhew, in contrast, never had a chance. He was continually harassed by the powers that be. By April 1972, he was reduced to using the lobby of the Texas School Book Depository as a visitor's center. He financed the venture by selling one-dollar "deeds" for a square inch of the ground where the building stood.[38] By July of that year, after a couple of years of frustrated efforts to get the museum off the ground, one of Mayhew's warehouse employees was arrested for attempting to torch the building. Mayhew proclaimed his own innocence in the matter, but he was, he claims, warned by Dallas authorities to leave town as quickly as possible. Soon after, Mayhew officially defaulted on his loan, the bank foreclosed, and Colonel D. Harold Byrd repurchased the building.[39]

Colonel Byrd immediately put the property back up for sale, this time asking $1.2 million, hoping whoever purchased the site "would use the building in a way that would not be a slam on Dallas . . . that would not blame Dallas for having the right environment for causing Kennedy's death."[40] While the policy of benign neglect had been sufficient for Dealey Plaza, the Texas School Book Depository had always posed a more pressing problem for the city's leaders. By 1973, they could no longer avoid the issues surrounding 411 Elm. After Mayhew's ownership, according to a *Dallas Morning News* report:

> There has been a change in attitude by the city's business leadership on the disposition of the Depository. Previously, city leaders tried to ignore the assassination . . . and have not wanted any tangible reminders. They would have been happy if . . . the highest bidder [when Byrd

---

37. Jerry Organ, "Murder Perch to Museum," McAdams's Kennedy Assassination Home Page Index, accessed May 17, 2011, http://mcadams.posc.mu.edu/organ4.htm; Dealey, *D in the Heart of Texas,* 121.

38. Organ, "Murder Perch to Museum."

39. Anne Zimmerman, "Stained glass," *Dallas Observer,* November 27, 1997, https://www.dallasobserver.com/news/stained-glass-6402278.

40. Zimmerman, "Stained glass."

> sold it] had been a real estate developer who wanted to tear the building down . . . Fearing it would become a "tourist trap" over which they had no control, the city's business and civic leadership finally sat up and took notice. [41]

Now the fate of the building had become a public issue. In the glare of the spotlight, Colonel Byrd considered a number of offers, even one that proposed to tear down the structure and sell it off at five dollars a brick. Personally, Byrd preferred to save the building, but this was no longer purely a personal matter. Feeling the pressure, Byrd resolved to allow the city council to settle the issue.

The passions that the assassination aroused, even a full decade after the fact, were clearly evident in the council's debate. Councilman Fred Zeder quickly organized a pro-demolition group. He sought to prevent any federal, state, or local tax monies from being spent to preserve "this terrible blight on the city," and he raised $100,000 for the cause. His ally Councilman Russell Smith echoed the feeling of many Dallasites when he said: "This building will never be a memorial to John F. Kennedy, only to Lee Harvey Oswald. It should be torn down and a park or something positive built there." Zeder echoed this, writing in a newspaper editorial that the Texas School Book Depository could never properly memorialize the president; it could only create a memorial "to the fanatic fool deed of a sick little man."[42]

Mayor Wes Wise blocked Zeder's demolition bid, and he and his political allies passed an ordinance preventing the building from being torn down. Mayor Wise had his own connection to the assassination. On November 22, 1963, he had been a reporter for KRLD-AM, the local CBS affiliate, and had covered the presidential motorcade as it passed Lemmon Avenue on its way downtown. He had then gone on to the Trade Mart, where he was to be a guest for the president's scheduled speech. As a journalist who had worked the assassination, Wise understood the importance of preserving its

41. Greene, "A. C. Greene on the Texas School Book Depository."

42. Beverly Lowry, "Thanks For The Memories," *Texas Monthly*, March 1973; Hunt, *JFK for a New Generation*, 123.

physical relics, and he worked adamantly to preserve the old Texas School Book Depository. He not only led the initiative to block demolition, but he also went on to help lead the movement that would eventually land the building at 411 Elm on the National Register of Historic Places.

By 1977, the tide had turned. City of Dallas voters approved the use of bond money to purchase the building from Byrd in order to protect it from commercial exploitation.[43] The Dallas powers that be were settling into a middle path between "let's-tear-it-down" denial and "let's-make-a-buck" entrepreneurship, and there was budding momentum to preserve the structure as a space to celebrate Kennedy's life as well as commemorate his death. As one writer noted, the endless throng of Dealey Plaza visitors had "exerted a pressure on the city akin to Chinese water torture."[44]

As *Morning News* reporter Laura Miller, who would herself later become Dallas mayor, wrote, plans were taking shape that would give Dealey Plaza's visitors "something to do besides stand in the middle of Elm Street"[45]

•

By 1977, it was clear that the building at 411 Elm would be preserved, but the shape that preservation would take was not at all clear. The building was renamed the Dallas County Administration Building (the "Texas School Book Depository" title was still being used by the previous tenant), and the first five floors were refurbished and turned into offices. When the building was officially dedicated on March 29, 1981, the top two floors, including the infamous sixth floor, remained empty.

There continued to be opposition to any sort of assassination commemoration at 411 Elm. Dallas Cowboys coach Tom Landry and local cosmetics entrepreneur Mary Kay Ash made a nationally televised joint appearance in

43. Bob Huffaker et al., *When the News Went Live: Dallas 1963* (Lanham, MD: Taylor Trade Publishing, 2004), 129–130; Lowry, "Thanks For The Memories"; Greene, "A. C. Greene on the Texas School Book Depository."

44. Holland, "Dealing with Dealey Plaza."

45. Laura Miller, "Panel Unveils Plan for JFK Museum," *Dallas Morning News,* April 20, 1983; Hunt, *JFK for a New Generation*, 125.

1984 to propose that the School Book Depository Building be demolished and all memory of the Kennedy assassination scrubbed from Dealey Plaza, but the wheels continued slowly turning.[46]

Several city leaders, including influential real estate developer Raymond Nasher, were increasingly drawn to the idea of creating a private, nonprofit museum commemorating Kennedy and the assassination on the site. There were ongoing discussions, and, despite some continuing opposition, there was soon some real progress. The Dallas County Historical Commission spearheaded these efforts. Led by Lindalyn Adams, who had headed a number of recent local historical projects, the organization conducted ambitious fundraising campaigns and garnered support for the establishment of an interpretive center in the former Texas School Book Depository Building.

Finally, in 1989, twenty-six years after the assassination, the new Sixth Floor Museum opened. The entire sixth floor of the former Texas School Book Depository Building was given over to an interpretive center dedicated to the assassination of John F. Kennedy and his legacy as president. Its establishment had been a tricky business, but overcoming the long-held desire to repress the subject was only half the task. The next great challenge was figuring out exactly what to say. Given the controversy that still swirled around the assassination, any attempt at interpretation was like walking a minefield. A step in any direction could bring trouble.

The Sixth Floor Museum board determined, ultimately, that the Warren Commission Report would provide the museum's guiding principles. The Sixth Floor Museum would acknowledge the existence of the myriad conspiracy theories, but "controversy about these findings would be presented within the framework of the government's original conclusion." The museum would seek neither to turn JFK into a saint nor to reduce him to a corpse in a detective story. Finally, there would be no *mea culpa* for the host city, "no attempt to apologize for Dallas."[47]

---

46. "Assassination's shame lingers," UPI Archives, November 22, 1986, accessed July 18, 2022, https://www.upi.com/Archives/1986/11/22/Assassinations-shame-lingers/9155533019600/.

47. Hunt, *JFK for a New Generation*, 125.

•

The person who ultimately became the voice—and guiding light—of the Sixth Floor Museum was Conover Hunt. A native of Virginia, Hunt came to Dallas in 1978. She was hired as a consultant early in the development of the museum and helped raise the first funds to develop the institution. Still only in her early thirties, Hunt was a promising prospect whose previous project had been an immense success. Working with historian Linda Grant DePauw, Hunt had curated the groundbreaking museum show *Remember the Ladies: Women in America (1750–1815)*. Exhibited just four years after the Equal Rights Amendment had passed Congress and designed to coincide with the US Bicentennial, the show brought together sponsors from across the political spectrum, such as the fervently patriotic Mount Vernon Ladies' Association and the overtly feminist National Organization for Women. (As Hunt later quipped, "Fortunately they never saw each other in the same room.") The *Remember the Ladies* show established Hunt as a curator who could get the job done while juggling the demands made by diverse and often contentious clientele—attractive attributes for anyone about to wade into the JFK Assassination Wars.[48]

The lushly illustrated book that accompanied the *Remember the Ladies* exhibition was also, coincidentally, the first book that Jacqueline Kennedy sent to press as she began her publishing career with Viking Press in the mid-1970s. Hunt recalled one New York editorial meeting they had together. "I thought she would be as big as Mount Everest," she wrote, "Instead, this tiny little woman in black slacks and white silk blouse comes in. Very quiet. Said nothing. Great presence in her quiet way."[49]

Conover Hunt, in her own way, would come to establish that same kind of great presence around Dallas. It was Hunt, more than anyone, who would set the tone and define the message at the Sixth Floor Museum. She would become its first director and chief curator, serving there until 1989. She was

---

48. William Kuhn, *Reading Jackie: Her Autobiography in Books* (New York: Doubleday, 2010), 121.

49. Kuhn, *Reading Jackie*, 121.

not only at the center of the delicate deliberations that determined the exact mission of the Sixth Floor Museum, but she would also go on to work as a consultant with almost all the area's major museums and historical organizations before her time in Dallas was done.

Hunt's most significant insight was her recognition that the legacy of the JFK assassination is not settled history. It is a contested landscape, and there are still certain aspects that might just be too hot to handle. The Sixth Floor Museum takes great care to get the facts right and put things into proper context, but it does not attempt to answer all the questions swirling around the assassination. Rather than strive to settle all the disputes, the museum allows, more than anything, for the visitor to experience Dealey Plaza, enter the former Texas School Book Depository, and stand next to the sniper's nest. It invites the visitor to relive and reimagine the event themselves.

•

In many ways, Conover Hunt's book *JFK For A New Generation* is the culmination of her work at the Sixth Floor Museum. Produced by the museum in conjunction with SMU Press and published in 1996, seven years after Hunt left the museum, the book embodies her open approach to the topic. "This is a book *about* history," she writes, "but it is not *the* history of JFK's legacy."[50]

From the book's first chapter, "Being There: November 22, 1963," Hunt's focus on active, "experiential" engagement is evident. By the second paragraph, the narrative has shifted to the direct second person: you, the reader, are a resident of Dallas experiencing the day of the assassination firsthand. "When you wake up around 7:30 AM (CST) it is raining. Will they cancel the parade for President Kennedy? You hope not . . . You hope nothing will disturb the president's trip." Hunt leads you through your morning routine: reading the the *Dallas Morning News,* seeing the notorious "Welcome Mr. Kennedy" ad—the locally produced, full-page broadside that accused Kennedy of being a Communist fellow traveler. "The ad makes you feel ill at ease; it does not seem appropriate."

50. Hunt, *JFK for a New Generation*, xi.

You decide to go witness the motorcade anyway, and you are listening to the radio reports of the president's arrival at Love Field as you park your car in a lot just south of Dealey Plaza. Hunt's time-tunnel approach surrounds you with all the appropriate historical background, and, by the time you take your place in Dealey Plaza, just as the president's motorcade arrives, you are a fully informed and involved participant. You experience the crowd around you, flush with anticipation.

> "Hey Mr. President, look over here! We want to take your picture," shouts the woman in the bright red raincoat.
>
> You see photographers moving in and notice that a man carrying a little boy has moved near the location of the kerchiefed lady; other people in the crowd run along the curb of the south side of Elm Street, trying to keep up with the motorcade. One little girl skips along the grass.
>
> Crack!
>
> Abruptly, she stops.
>
> What's that? A backfire? A firecracker? Perhaps someone's playing a sick joke; it's not funny.

But we all know what's happening. In Hunt's narration there is the terror and confusion of what it might have been like to be standing there in Dealey Plaza at 12:29 PM on November 22, 1963. There is no unifying narrative; the event collapses into fragments and quick impressions, the clamorous disorientation of the moment.

> Gunshots! Someone is shooting at the president!
>
> A Secret Service man is sprinting toward the Lincoln from the follow-up car.
>
> They're directly in front of you.
>
> Don't slow down.
>
> Another shot! President Kennedy's head explodes, throwing his entire body backwards and to the left.
>
> Oh my God! . . .

"Keep in mind the confusion, the shock, and the tremendous fear that these people experienced," Hunt writes. "Close your eyes and count to six or eight. All the shots rang out in that short space of time. History changed in a matter of seconds."[51] Hunt's narration takes you there—and you experience it all as a Dallasite.

Hunt goes on to lead you through the shock and numbness of that entire day. You turn on the TV when you get home and hear the announcement—the president is dead. You read the evening news and follow the chaotic search for the killer. You are reminded that all residents of Dallas, whether they witnessed the assassination or not, whether they wish it or not, are participants. During the afternoon coverage, Hunt notes, Jay Watson, program director for Dallas ABC affiliate WFAA-TV, halts the coverage and extends an apology for the tragedy on behalf of the city of Dallas.[52]

•

In her *JFK for a New Generation,* Hunt reminds us that, even if we were not there (of course, only a very few actually were), we all shared the long weekend of the assassination. We all felt the shockwaves emanating from those seven seconds. While the residents of Dallas experienced the assassination in a particularly intense manner, it is understood today that *all* Americans old enough to be aware of the world in 1963 share in a profound collective memory that remains vivid after fifty years.

Occurring just at the start of the TV age, at a time when big photo magazines like *Life* and *Look* ruled the newsstands, the assassination occurred in a unique time period ripe for the creation of a new brand of instantaneous communal experience. This combination of new media, fascinating personalities (a young, charismatic world leader and his glamorous wife), and stunning action (a presidential assassination in the most public manner possible, followed, two days later, by a live TV broadcast of the murder of the accused assassin), created an Event, a moment that made clear there was a new way to experience the world.

51. Hunt, *JFK for a New Generation,* 1–15.
52. Hunt, *JFK for a New Generation,* 15.

If we all share the common experience of the JFK assassination, we each underwent that experience in our own way. In the second chapter of *JFK for a New Generation,* "The Weekend," Hunt chronicles the days following the assassination in a manner that reminds us how our memories interweave personal history with a larger dialogue. Early in the chapter, she interrogates her own experience, examining her own "where-were-you-when" story:

> On Friday, November 22, I had just finished a "Great Books" class at Hampton High School in Virginia and was heading down the hallway on the second floor towards the parking lot where our car pool had parked. Suddenly, I spied my classmate Prentis Gandy, who was clutching a transistor radio to his ear. "The president's been shot!" he shouted. The time was about 1:35 (EST).

Hunt relates her subsequent conversations with old school friends who shared that morning with her, comparing their memories, noting how tenuous and spotty those original memories were. In fact, her friends' stories of the same events were often contradictory. But because they were attached to an event of profound significance, these memories remained fluid and active. Hunt examines how she, and those around her, learned more from TV, from newspapers, from each other, and how a communal, "collective" memory developed. "As time goes by," she notes," the importance of firsthand experience lessens, and communicated information becomes dominant."[53]

In "The Weekend," Hunt lays out not just what happened in days following the assassination, but how people found out what happened—how it was reported and when. She weaves in a considerable amount of poll information concerning what people thought at the time. Even as she meticulously reports these verifiable, quantifiable facts, however, Hunt remains always cognizant of how truth is mediated. She understands that cold, hard history does not always jibe exactly with the stories we end up telling—and that those stories may change over time.

In the organizational scheme of *JFK for a New Generation,* you can see

53. Hunt, *JFK for a New Generation,* 17.

how Conover Hunt addresses this interplay between history and experience. Her third chapter is "JFK: the Man and Myth." The fourth, "The Endless Trail of Lee Harvey Oswald," followed by "The Media as Messenger," and—finally—a chapter entitled "JFK as Commemoration." It is clear throughout her text that the essential meaning of the Kennedy assassination is still in process, unstable, and negotiable. Nowhere, as Hunt is well aware, is that flux more evident than in Dallas.

•

If you pick up the most recent *A Visitor's Guide Book to Dealey Plaza National Historic Landmark*, you will see that it is also authored by Conover Hunt. Published in 1995, after Dealey Plaza was finally designated a National Historical Landmark, it is the official guidebook of the Sixth Floor Museum. Moreover, it is organized to mimic, almost exactly, the physical layout of the Sixth Floor Museum as developed by Hunt and her compatriots.

When you exit the elevator from the ground floor and step out onto the former Texas School Book Depository building's sixth floor, you are introduced to "The Early '60s" just as in the guidebook. Displays set forth the period's popular books and Broadway plays as well as its political world: the Cold War, Castro and Cuba, the Space Race, MLK, the March on Washington—and John F. Kennedy's place in the middle of it all. Just as in the guidebook, as you turn right and proceed down the museum's next corridor, there are the displays depicting "The Trip to Texas." You are presented with the details of Kennedy's late November 1963 campaign stops in Houston and San Antonio, the early morning November 22 speech in Fort Worth, and, finally, the landing of Air Force One at Love Field. The tumultuous reception erupts, Jackie receives her roses, and the presidential limousine pulls out to begin the motorcade through downtown Dallas. It's all fast and lively: blow-up photos, documents such as the notorious *Dallas Morning News* "Welcome Mr. Kennedy" ad, audio recordings of the local newscast. You could almost forget that you are being pulled down the hallway toward "The Assassination" and the sniper's nest.

Your first clue is the glass-paneled enclosure in the far corner ahead of you, filled with its stacks of generic brown storage boxes. It would be fairly nondescript if you didn't already know what happened there; the sight of it raises the hair on the back of your neck. You are finally approaching the real thing, here in the southeast corner of the sixth floor of the former Texas School Book Depository—the physical actuality of the assassination. You know it is only a re-creation of the shooter's perch as Oswald had arranged it. Still, when you stand at the window next to the enclosure, look down and follow the sightlines from the sixth floor across Dealey Plaza and down Elm Street, then focus your eyes on the X in the center of Elm Street—*you are there.*

If you are a conspiracist, your mind will race with the alternate tellings, with what really happened and what is wrong here; with what is misrepresented, missing, and covered up. If you believe the Warren Commission, you might imagine, focusing your sight below on the X on Elm Street, the dead-eyed calculation of the assassin. What might it have been like to pull the trigger and kill the American Century?

•

It is a disorienting experience—standing there at the sixth-floor sniper's nest. It takes you back to when the trigger was pulled, the bullets unloosed, and the chaos begun. The confusion of the moment is evident in the initial United Press teletype that went out just after the assassination. Displayed on the wall next to the sniper's nest, the text on the fading brown roll is gibberish. The language is scrambled, as if the author could not gather his thoughts, his fingers and head disconnected. The museum's next display, in its hulking glass case, is "The Original Sniper's Nest Window." It turns out the window you have been looking at is not the actual 1963 window; it was removed for protection by Colonel Byrd and only returned to the museum in 1994. But you know, if you are an assassination buff, that there is yet a third window in the possession of Aubrey Mayhew that may be the actual 1963 window. You know this is not an easy story to tell; it can be framed a number of ways, all conflicting, all contested.[54]

54. Zimmerman, "Stained glass."

As you turn away from the sniper's nest, the Sixth Floor Museum opens up into "The Crisis Hours" and the museum's clear linear path bifurcates and splits into a number of different possible directions—the bedlam of November 22, 1963, is replicated in the floor plan. The chronology of events becomes scrambled; everything seems to happen at once. No longer is this an intimate and local story (the citizen calling out to the president to turn this way for a photo), but an event with worldwide implications and consequences. "The Crisis Hours" bleeds into the next section—"National and World Response"—and, moving between them, you experience the pandemonium of everything happening at once. Simultaneously, there is the chaos at Dealey Plaza, the confusion at the Trade Mart, where a crowd waits for the president to deliver his speech, at Parkland Hospital, where the press desperately clamors to discover the president's fate, at Love Field, where Air Force One awaits the president, and on the streets of Dallas as the mad search for the assassin commences. The layout of the Sixth Floor Museum makes you subconsciously aware that the age of the new media is beginning before your eyes: the medium is becoming the message. As the news breaks, it is scrambled with the reaction of the rest of the nation and the world, the common man and heads of state mixing with newscasters, ramifications rippling in all directions. The museum replicates this barrage of information, delivering it with the buzz and flash of the electronic age.

•

Some of the most compelling images that whizzed across the airwaves in those early hours were recorded by Dallasites who had come downtown to welcome the president. There is a display in "The Crisis Hours" which features replicas of the still and movie cameras those witnesses used to record those moments just before, during, and after the assassination. The very physicality of these old cameras in their Plexiglas enclosure reminds you that those images America was witnessing were, for all their power, just pale slivers of actual experience.

One reason people come to Dealey Plaza is to be in the physical presence of history, to transcend mediated experience, and *A Visitor's Guide to Dealey*

Plaza National Historic Landmark assumes that visitors, after touring The Sixth Floor Museum, will take the elevator downstairs and walk the plaza. As the guidebook recommends: "The best way to tour the assassination site is to review accounts provided by the people who actually witnessed the tragedy." So it provides a schematic map of Dealey Plaza marked with twenty-three specific spots. These are the locations of some of the critical witnesses, all of whom provided their stories to the Warren Commission. The guidebook suggests that visitors seek out these twenty-three spots, stand there, and relive each specific perspective of the assassination.

Visitors expecting clarity might be sorely disappointed as they stand in each spot and read the experience of each of these witnesses as recounted in the guidebook. Looking through these twenty-three sets of eyes returns you again to the confusion of the "Crisis Hours," but in a more direct and intimate way. William Eugene, a twenty-two-year-old former military man who stood just a few feet from the motorcade, heard shots from the grassy knoll in front of Kennedy's limousine as he and his wife fell to the ground, protecting their young son. Malcolm Couch, a twenty-five-year-old theology student and television photographer standing at the corner of Elm and Houston, heard shots and looked up just in time to see a rifle barrel being drawn back into a sixth-floor window of the Texas School Book Depository. S.M. Holland, a fifty-seven-year-old signal supervisor for the Union Terminal Railroad, saw a puff of smoke come from the trees above the grassy knoll. Howard Brennan, a forty-four-year-old steamfitter standing a few feet away from Malcolm Couch, thought he heard two shots. Twenty-seven-year-old car salesman James Tague heard three shots; Holland, watching from the top of the Triple Overpass, reported four.

"Notice," the guidebook says, "how their recollection varies about the sequence, timing and number of shots." There seem to be as many variations as witnesses. (The Warren Commission used interviews from 190 eyewitnesses but, of course, the exact number of eyewitnesses will always be in dispute.) On the Dealey Plaza witness tour, it seems the more you see, the less you know.[55]

•

55. Hunt, *Dealey Plaza National Historical Landmark*, 73–79.

After the chaos of the "Crisis Hours" and "National and World Response" sections, the Sixth Floor Museum starts to pull the strands back together. They reconverge in "The Investigations" section, at one of the centerpiece exhibits of the museum: the FBI model of Dealey Plaza. Encased in glass, this commanding twelve-by-twelve-foot dioramic mock-up of the plaza dominates the post-assassination section of the museum.

After exiting the whirlpool of images and information in the assassination sections, the Sixth Floor Museum's model of Dealey Plaza presents a welcome reprieve. Like the downtown park itself, the openness of the model plaza spreads out before you as a relief from the claustrophobic scenes you have just left. Just past the replicas of the Dal-Tex, Criminal Courts, and Records Buildings, you scan the simulated green of the park, past the Texas School Book Depository Building, sloping south to the center of Main Street and west to the grassy knoll, ending just as Elm disappears under the Triple Underpass. The diorama, streamlined of all unnecessary detail, is a perfect simulacrum—it's completely unmarred by the imperfections of daily life. Silent and motionless, the scale-model Dealey Plaza presents itself with the incipient calm of the laboratory, where, with detached objectivity and the appropriate formulas, the proper experiment will inevitably produce a final resolution.

This replica Dealey Plaza was built by the FBI, based on information gathered by the agency immediately after the assassination. It was installed in the office of the Warren Commission on January 20, 1964. It played an important role in the commission's investigation, but the *Warren Report* did not, ultimately, resolve all the issues surrounding the assassination. As the guidebook reports: "Accepted at first, the *Report*'s inconsistencies later launched a controversy that has led to more than three decades of inquiry and spirited public debate." Subsequent government investigations, like the late-1960s Clark Panels and the mid-1970s Rockefeller Commission and Church Committee, served only to muddy the waters. The Dealey Plaza diorama was pulled out of mothballs to be used again by the late 1970s House Select Committee on Assassinations.[56]

"The Investigation" section of the Sixth Floor Museum presents both

56. Hunt, *Dealey Plaza National Historical Landmark*, 44–49.

these government inquiries and the various points of contention raised against them—how investigation after investigation, and publication after publication, exposed inconsistencies, disputed evidence, alleged various cover-ups, and attacked the original *Warren Report* in every conceivable way. The neat and clean resolution promised in the FBI scale model of Dealey Plaza never materialized. In fact, as the museum guidebook notes, there were inconsistencies even between the *Warren Report* and the original setup of its own Dealey Plaza model. "The model was designed to be a working exhibition, with movable cars and pedestrian figures. Strings were attached at the presumed location of the presidential limousine at the time the shots were fired, then drawn back to the sixth floor corner window in order to determine trajectories." But the Warren Commission got the original placement of the tiny model limousine and the trajectory string wrong. Consequently, the guidebook tells us, the museum "has placed the limousine, following cars and many bystanders in their correct positions for the fatal shot."[57] Using their own research, the museum staff have also placed the tiny Dealey Plaza pedestrians in their proper places.

On one 2013 Sixth Floor visit, I noticed one of the trajectory markers had worked itself loose, leaving the tiny model pedestrians staring at an unattached string lying coiled in the middle of Elm Street.

•

Despite all of its unique historical attributes, the Sixth Floor Museum's FBI model of Dealey Plaza is like all dioramas. It needs its viewers to imagine movement and motivation; to string sequences of actions together. There is a spectral hollowness here—the dots have not been connected.

Of course, you have seen the sniper's nest and photographs of Lee Harvey Oswald posing in his Oak Cliff backyard with the very same 6.5 Carcano-type 91/38 rifle that police found in this building, just a few feet from the sniper's nest. But is that the whole story? Polls have consistently

57. Hunt, *Dealey Plaza National Historical Landmark,* 49–50.

shown that the majority of Americans do not believe so.[58] The tour of the Sixth Floor Museum, and its guidebook, eventually steers you to a section entitled "Who Did It?" Even here, you are left with open questions rather than closure; there is no final word.

Looking at the Sixth Floor Museum's FBI model of Dealey Plaza, it is hard not to imagine conspiratorial shadows lurking behind the blank windows: Cuban operatives or anti-Castro activists in their tiny rooms, CIA or KGB agents behind brick walls, right-wing Dallas oilmen looking down from their high-rise offices, mob assassins and their mistresses, John Birchers and manipulative politicians just out of sight. Our current imaginative landscape of Dealey Plaza could contain a dozen alternate universes, at least.

It is an eerie feeling, staring out the arched windows of the former Texas School Book Depository Building, over the top of a scale model of the very building in which you stand. You can look across the sloping, simulated grass of the diorama Dealey Plaza, out the window, and onto the actual trees and grass of the real Dealey Plaza. Beneath the buzz and rush of the city scene, it is hard not to see the milling people and the passing automobiles as spectral gameboard pieces. You might recall a phrase, reiterated over and over by Don DeLillo in his classic JFK assassination novel *Libra*: "There is a world inside the world."[59]

•

It is not surprising that in America today, we most commonly play out that world within a world in film. Through movies, we enact our mythology and transform the ghosts of our history into celluloid phantoms. The JFK assassination has undoubtedly become one of the most contested of our national legends. It was inevitable that the topic would become prime fodder for Hollywood.

Like Monument Valley, Dealey Plaza has taken its place as one of our

58. Hunt, *Dealey Plaza National Historical Landmark*, 56.
59. DeLillo, *Libra*, 13.

mythic stage sets. Just like the red sandstone buttes and spires of Monument Valley, Dealey Plaza's distinctive white pergolas, the Book Depository's arched windows, and the grassy knoll are all instantly recognizable, bringing with them a bundle of immediate associations. Even for Dallasites who drive through the plaza daily on the way to work, it is impossible to forget that this is an active landscape where one glimpse of these iconic landmarks can take you back fifty years into the myth-time of November 22, 1963.

David Miller's 1973 film, *Executive Action,* was the first major motion picture to take us back to that momentous moment. The film is inspired by Mark Lane's 1966 bestseller, *Rush to Judgment,* the first really influential book-length attack on the conclusions drawn by the Warren Commission. The movie presents the manipulations of a group of nefarious right-wing men of wealth as they coolly and efficiently conspire to have the president assassinated on the streets of Dallas. *Executive Action* intersperses the stock black-and-white news footage of the assassination with new color footage. You see the well-known moments on the parade routes: the Kennedys waving to the crowd, the crowd swooning in return, but then, back and forth, there are the gunmen taking their positions, assembling their weapons, taking aim. By Hollywood standards, it is all rather crudely done; the jumps between the vintage documentary and new color footage are unintentionally jarring and less than convincing. But the film did make an impact. It garnered a generous amount of controversy for itself, and it presented the idea of a conspiracy involving multiple gunmen to a Hollywood audience for the first time, helping ensure that the assassination debates would expand.

Since *Executive Action,* it has become if not commonplace then at least not surprising to find parts of Dealey Plaza closed off, the traffic diverted, and the area filled with all the lights, screens, and booms of modern film production. The plaza has become the stage set for dozens and dozens of major and minor films, ranging from the fictional to the nonfictional, from spoofs to serious documentaries. When B-movie king Roger Corman came to Dallas in 1970 to make *Gas-s-s-s,* an apocalyptic youth-culture comedy that begins with reactionaries sealing off the city to convert it into a police state, Dealey Plaza made a fifteen-second cameo appearance. As the young heroes drive out of town to escape the fascists, you see them pull past the Texas School

Book Depository Building. "Say goodbye to Dallas . . ." says the driver, "we've seen that type of law here before." Then you hear four gunshots as they disappear under the Triple Underpass. Just a glimpse of Dealey Plaza, an off-hand remark, and the gunshots become a sort of shorthand for a whole matrix of larger associations.[60]

•

If Dealey Plaza was to serve as a stage set for the conflicting narratives of the assassination, it would need, just as the Sixth Floor Museum's FBI model of the plaza did, human figures that could be easily moved around to bring the scene to life. Filmmakers, of course, call them extras, and they are vital for large-scale moviemaking. They move a scene from the closed box of the theater stage to something bigger: a complete and believable world.

You can see extras in *Executive Action*, scattering in panic before the police motorcycles as they move to seal off the entrance to the Texas School Book Depository. You can see them spread across Dealey Plaza in movies like *The Trial of Lee Harvey Oswald*, a two-part television film shown on ABC in September of 1977. There is a woman cheering and waving, reliving the thrill of standing on a downtown curb, just a few dozen feet away from the president and the glamorous Jackie. There is another woman reacting to the first blast by grabbing her young daughter and pushing her down beneath her onto the grass of Dealey Plaza. There is a man pointing from atop the Triple Underpass, attempting to direct the scrambling police officers to the source of the gunfire. There are a hundred common people here, citizens of Dallas, all trying to get it right.

They are leaving their lives for a moment to enter another life, leaving their time for another. They are throwing themselves into their roles. They strive to be convincing—to dress right, to talk right, to move right. But I'm guessing a good number of these extras did not concern themselves with the politics of the alternate world they were stepping into. Most of the supernumeraries in

60. Don Graham, *Cowboys and Cadillacs: How Hollywood Looks at Texas* (Austin: Texas Monthly Press, 1983), 76.

Executive Action probably did not perform a close reading of the script portraying Dallas businessmen as the assassins of an American president, and most of the extras in *Gas-s-s-s* probably did not lose sleep over the depiction of their home city as a fascist police state. Later, the on-screen locals in Oliver Stone's *JFK* probably spent little time pondering the film's implication that fellow Texan Lyndon Baines Johnson may have had a hand in the killing of the president under whom he served. And why should they? An important addendum to the American Dream is the idea that any American, no matter how insignificant, might somehow have the opportunity to spot themselves on the big screen. And, if the modern movie theater is the temple where we house our myths, we Americans have never been too concerned with minor issues of theology. If we play the happy pawns for Hollywood producers, the payoff is the glow of our own image in the myth machine. It might be that we share more an abiding faith in the spectacle than the sense such a spectacle might make of the world.

Many of these Dallas-area role-players did understand that, by taking part in these cinematic reenactments of the JFK assassination, they were making themselves stand-ins for a previous generation of Dallasites who had been pulled into the story involuntarily. In November of 1963, the residents of North Texas, simply by living in the area, had been sucked into the single most traumatic moment in the city's history. It would be difficult to determine the exact number of Dallasites involved in the filmed reenactments of the assassination, but it is certain that the number would dwarf the number who were present in Dealey Plaza as the actual 1963 presidential motorcade passed by. Like the players in those primal rituals in which a tribe reenacts their foundational tales, making them active and present, these Dallasites understood they were representing their local kin in the myth-time of November 22, 1963—that they were activating some powerful mojo.

•

The single biggest Hollywood spectacle ever to grace Dallas is, without a doubt, the show that Oliver Stone brought to town in 1991 to make his film *JFK*. The film brought the national debate about the JFK assassination to a fever pitch, but that was nothing compared to the stir its filming caused locally. Oliver Stone is a producer of grand ambition, and *JFK* was to be his personal opus. From the first announcements of his intentions, Stone had Dallas abuzz. The director was already a known quantity in Dallas, having helped fuel Texas's incipient Third Coast film movement by filming his *Born on the Fourth of July* here in 1988–89. The movie injected $10 million into a depressed local economy and kept a host of local film professionals employed. Stone even thanked the citizens of Dallas when he accepted his Academy Award for the film in 1990.[61]

Oliver Stone is legendary for his attention to historical detail. So, when production of *JFK* began, one of his primary tasks was to take Dallas back to 1963. Stone expended immense effort on restoring specific assassination-related sites back to their early-sixties form. Oak Cliff's Texas Theatre, where Lee Harvey Oswald was arrested, had its front doors replaced and a new ticket booth installed, and a number of adjacent businesses received make-overs and period-appropriate window displays. At the downtown Dallas police headquarters, the center of the assassination investigation, a current lieutenant's office was restored to the Homicide captain's office it once had been. Signs were replaced on the glass doors, and the names of the old bureaus were revived in fresh black paint. Old-style light fixtures were salvaged from vacant Deep Ellum warehouse buildings to replace the modern fluorescent fixtures that had been installed since the assassination. And downstairs in the basement where Oswald was shot by Jack Ruby, steel doors were torn out and replaced.[62] In his quest for historical verisimilitude, Stone even sought access to the sniper's nest in the former Texas School Book Depository Building. At first Conover Hunt and the Sixth Floor Museum staff resisted the intrusion, but Stone was relentless. He eventually arranged to pay a fee big enough to retire the museum's entire debt—Oliver Stone would have the sniper's nest!

---

61. Oliver Stone, acceptance speech for Best Director at the Sixty-Second Annual Academy Awards, March 26, 1990, Awards Acceptance Speech Database, accessed December 28, 2011, http://aaspeechesdb.oscars.org/link/059-8.

62. Todd Copilevitz, "Recreating the Past: Police Headquarters carefully made over for 'JFK' scene," *Dallas Morning News*, May 4, 1991.

After Stone arranged the required permits to film at Dealey Plaza, the rest was easy. The plaza required little work to restore it to its condition in 1963. The paralysis that had kept the city fathers from altering anything for fear of provoking any controversy had kept the plaza virtually unchanged. Crews pruned some trees and repainted some of the surrounding buildings to match their 1963 color.[63]

But if Stone was going to take Dallas back to 1963, there was more to do than just prep the physical landscape. Stone would need people—a lot of people. When Stone made the first casting call for extras (offering forty dollars and a couple of free meals per day, along with a lot of standing around), ten thousand people responded.[64] Ultimately five hundred people, who passed the rigorous inspection for historically correct 1960s garb, were chosen as street scene extras.[65]

It was clear to the participants that Oliver Stone was up to important historical business, and they had their parts to perform. Contemporary Dallas held an obligation to do old Dallas right—there were ghosts to reckon with. Jim White, veteran area broadcaster and news director of KLRX-FM (97.9 "Lite"), was given a small part as a newsman who interviews a key assassination witness. Feeling those ghosts, he watched as much of the original 1963 TV footage as he could find. Conscious of the legacy he was embodying—those Dallas newsmen who spearheaded the initial coverage—he sought out the local journalists who had covered the assassination and spoke to them about their memories.[66]

One of the five hundred extras felt an even more direct connection to the assassination. Estella Faggan was a forty-one-year-old unemployed security guard who had been thirteen when Kennedy was killed. She had, she claimed, skipped school to see the president that day, and was downtown when he was shot. She had personal ghosts to exorcise. When the time came for the

---

63. Hunt, *JFK for a New Generation*, 112.

64. Hunt, *JFK for a New Generation*, 112.

65. Jeffrey Weiss, "Scores heed call for extra extras," *Dallas Morning News*, April 18, 1991.

66. "Local radio newsman plans to make the 'JFK' cut," *Dallas Morning News*, April 23, 1991.

JFK extras to do their work in the infamous scene on the grassy knoll, Faggan spontaneously pushed her way to the front and began to sob dramatically, yelling hysterically, "Oh my God, they shot him!" and collapsing into uncontrollable weeping. "It was," she said, "the greatest experience of my life."[67]

•

As the film crew and actors meandered through the local scene—leading man Kevin Costner's whereabouts were discussed almost daily in the society section—the filming of *JFK* became topic number one in Dallas. For weeks, Stone's movie was an important news beat. Here was a slice of Hollywood excitement come to downtown Dallas. But the glamour could not seal, much less heal, the wounds the city had suffered because of the assassination. Longtime *Dallas Morning News* columnist John Anders, whose office was just down the street from Dealey Plaza, was one of the local journalists who observed the thousands of spectators who pushed in around the set to witness the filming. Anders noted the near-carnival atmosphere that prevailed on that April day in 1991 as the assassination was finally about to be reenacted—"Hit Day Wednesday," as the movie crew called it.

"The motorcade starts." Anders writes. "The mood sobered abruptly as a crew chief yelled, "'Everybody in their cars—let's go!' and moments later the motorcade was 'flagged' to a start."

As he watched the reenactment and waited for The Moment to arrive, Anders could not help but be reminded of his own experiences back in 1963:

> Seeing the 'movie' Jackie in her pink suit and pillbox hat, I was taken back to the blur of pink that sped past me at the juncture of Lemmon and Oak Lawn where several Bryan Adams High School seniors had assembled on that day to see the president (against the announced wishes of our high school principal, an archconservative).

---

67. Norma Adams Wade, "Scene Stealer: 'JFK' extra sobs her way to emotional one-line part," *Dallas Morning News*, May 1, 1991.

> I recalled walking out into the then two-lane Lemmon Avenue only a few feet from where the convertible carrying the president went past. And I remembered thinking, "Why, I could reach right out and touch the car." My gaze focused on John Kennedy—full-faced, handsome and deeply tanned. He looked more like a movie star than the actor who portrays him in the film. President Kennedy was smiling confidently and waving in what were to be the final five minutes of his life.
>
> All these memories came back as I watched the limos revving up and the extras who played Secret Service men began adjusting their hats.
>
> Moments after the entourage drove past us toward the Texas School Book Depository, it was strange and eerie to hear shots ring out.
>
> This was only a movie, after all. The woman standing next to me said, "My God—they shot him!"

While the downtown filming of Oliver Stone's *JFK* had taken on many of the trappings of a Hollywood circus, the events that it was re-creating could still expose some very sensitive nerves. "Yet as I walked away from 'hit day' filming," Anders writes, "the middle-aged man walking beside me expressed the way I was feeling when he told his friend, 'It still hurts, man . . . It still hurts.'"

•

After the "Hit Day" staging of the assassination that Anders witnessed, many of the spectators filed into the street and began to head back to work: "What happens now?" one onlooker said to another. "They bring him back and shoot him again," said the other.[68]

The truth is that, over the years, reenactments of the JFK assassination

68. John Anders, "Movie shoot triggers our '63 memories," *Dallas Morning News*, April 22, 1991.

in Dealey Plaza have become fairly common. Typical of these is a 2011 session documented by Jim Schutze in the *Dallas Observer,* the city's alternative press magazine. He recounts that the day was a fairly typical sunny April Saturday on the plaza. The usual odd mixture of tourists and locals inhabited the site: a group of elder African American Shriners, a JFK conspiracist setting up to hawk his goods, a group supporting Syrian freedom setting up for a hip-hop party, a half dozen clowns, and three out-of-town rockers who had played Poor David's Pub the previous night. On this day, however, a *National Geographic* film crew was also on hand and in the middle of filming:

> President John F. Kennedy, his wife Jackie, Governor John Connally and his wife Nellie are parked at the fatal X on Elm Street in that famous 1961 Lincoln Continental convertible limousine. At the meticulous direction of a *National Geographic* film crew working on a new conspiracy theory, the actors move their heads ever so slightly this way and that, just a tick at a time. They look like robots on the blink. An intense burr-cut man in his 20s is up on a boom lift in front of the famous Sniper's Nest in the former School Book Depository Building, clicking off silent shots with a replica of that famous 6.5 Carcano-type 91/38 rifle. About 50 tourists have gathered on the sidewalks to watch.[69]

This scene echoes another recorded in *Texas Monthly* in 1998, thirteen years before:

> A dark blue 1961 Lincoln Continental convertible limousine is sitting in the center lane of Elm Street, which has been blocked off. Stills of the Zapruder film line the sidewalk, serving as the storyboard for the day's activities: a restaging of the century's most famous murder, the assassination of John F. Kennedy, for a television documentary that will try to determine, with the help of lasers, where the shots came

69. Jim Schutze, "City Hall's Kennedy Conspiracy," *Dallas Observer,* April 28, 2011.

> from. Three men in white shirts are huddled around the convertible, bending and shifting the limbs of its foam rubber passengers. A gray dummy sits in the back seat, just as Kennedy did, while another—in John Connally's place—rests on the jump seat in front of him. "His arm has got to come over more," insists one man, pulling the president's left arm farther across his spongy torso. A film crew circles the scene, while tourists, ballistics experts, conspiracy buffs, and reporters watch the goings-on.[70]

Like these two sessions, the original reenactments of the assassination were investigative exercises. They were somber, forensic re-creations, conducted just after the assassination, aimed at understanding very specific aspects of the crime—a form of truth-seeking. Any real assassination buff will have a copy of the original Secret Service reenactments that were made immediately after the assassination. This film relic from the initial investigations shows, in grainy black-and-white footage, the simulated motorcade, an open-top sedan escorted by the same two motorcycle cops who rode alongside the president's limo on the day of the shooting. The simulated motorcade follows the route from Main Street, the jog up Houston Street, and the slow turn onto Elm Street. There is footage from within the car and then from the sixth-floor sniper's nest, made among the very boxes that Oswald had arranged for cover. You can watch the simulated motorcade from the window, first in plain view and then magnified through the same type of rifle scope that Oswald used. Visible still in these images are the bouquets and memorial wreaths piled on the Dealey Plaza lawn to honor the recently murdered president, and the dumbstruck crowd still lined up at the curb behind yellow crime scene tape, watching.[71]

Photographs from 1978 would show Dealey Plaza filled with electrical wiring and banks of stanchioned microphones, as scientists empowered by the House Select Committee on Assassinations took over the park. Gunshots

---

70. Pamela Colloff and Michael Hall, "The Conspiracy Theories," *Texas Monthly*, November 1998.

71. *JFK Assassination: The Definitive Guide*, Quality Information Publishers, 2006, DVD.

once again rang out across the plaza as technicians ran acoustic tests in an attempt to determine the exact source of the original assassin's bullets.[72] While not as cinematic as most other reenactments, these acoustic tests belong to a long and ongoing tradition. We live with the almost routine blockage of Dealey Plaza for assassination reenactments. It is an accepted, if unacknowledged, consequence of being a Dallasite. It is a silent reminder that the western entrance to our stately, glass-towered downtown is still recognized worldwide as the scene of "the crime of the century."

•

Most Dallasites would like to forget Dealey Plaza ever existed. We have a long history of trying to block out the pain, but there is also something else—a sense of embarrassment. There is an air of cheesiness that has attached itself to Dealey Plaza. We have grown accustomed to ignoring the moon-eyed Kennedy groupies, the amateur criminologists, and the conspiracy nuts who descend here annually for their conventions. The plaza is often filled with crooks and charlatans, people just out on a lark. We'd like to ignore it, but we understand—it's magnetic.

Before Jim Schutze became an iconoclastic columnist for the *Dallas Observer,* he was an award-winning investigative journalist. He has continually raised the hackles of the Dallas establishment, most notably with his 1987 book, *The Accommodation,* which probed Dallas's troubled approach to race issues in the 1950s and 1960s. In the late seventies, Schutze had just recently moved here to work for the *Dallas Times Herald*; "a Yankee carpetbagger," he called himself. Some northern friends were in town for a newspaper convention and they asked him, as a Dallasite, to take them to the site of the JFK assassination. They arrived at Dealey Plaza sometime after midnight. "I believe drink may have been involved," Schutze recalls.

> We decided to reenact it. We arranged ourselves out in the lanes of Elm Street. The streets were silent as a tomb. My friend, Ladd Neuman,

72. Hunt, *JFK for a New Generation,* 95.

> was Kennedy. Others were Jackie, the Connallys, the driver, the Secret Service agents. Someone was Oswald, hiding behind a sapling. We moved slowly in unison with our knees and waists bent so our heads were at convertible-seat level, bent-walking down Elm until we got to about where the X is now.
>
> Oswald shouted, "Bang! Bang! Bang!"
>
> Neuman threw his head back.
>
> . . .
>
> We thought we were funny. For a minute.
>
> A glistening black car, the size of Kennedy's limo, purred slowly down Elm and rolled to a stop right next to us. A tinted rear window rolled down, and an old man with white hair leaned forward. In the musically genteel accent of old upper-class Texas, he said, "Do you boys not have anything better to do with yourselves tonight?"
>
> We froze. I was ashamed of myself. Standing there like an oaf in the street, I felt naked. But it was not a good naked. That was the first time I heard even a whisper of the pain of this place for Dallas. The man in the car shrugged. The window rolled up, and the big black car rolled off into the night.[73]

If Dealey Plaza has become a joke, we laugh at it at our own risk. If the plaza oftentimes resembles a circus, it is worthwhile to remember that this circus is erected on a graveyard.

There is an inescapable tension that inhabits Dealey Plaza, an air that begs for some kind of protocol or direction. If you watch people in the plaza,

---

73. Jim Schutze, "Schutze Says We Should All Do a Badu and Get Naked at Dealey Plaza—and That Includes Him," *Dallas Observer*, April 15, 2010.

you can see it. Typical is an instance I witnessed not too long ago as I watched a young couple wander the plaza. Eventually, the young woman stepped out into Elm Street and stood a moment on the X that marks where Kennedy had been shot. "Bang!" her companion yelled. She jumped, and they laughed awkwardly as they walked off in each other's arms

The "Bang!" remained there in the air. It had no place to go.

•

There are currently no official civic ceremonies that occur in Dealey Plaza. Dallas does not observe a Founder's Day to celebrate its original heroes like John Neely Bryan. Nor are there any officially sanctioned events at Dealey Plaza to recognize John F. Kennedy or the events of November 22, 1963. Those events have been scheduled elsewhere. After 1970, Dallas County began conducting an annual ceremony marking the November 22 anniversary of the assassination at the Philip Johnson–designed John F. Kennedy Memorial, located a block east of Dealey Plaza. Those ceremonies were finally abandoned in 1983 at the request of the Kennedy family, who asked that commemorations of the former president be held upon the day of his birth rather than his death. However, these sanctioned events have never prevented large spontaneous gatherings from occurring in Dealey Plaza each November 22. Since 1964, these gatherings have come together with such regularity that the Dallas Parks Department cleans up the plaza each year in preparation, and the Dallas Police Department schedules extra plaza patrol units, although real disturbances are quite rare.[74]

According to Conover Hunt, these unplanned annual assemblies qualify as authentic "happenings."[75] Each year, hundreds of pilgrims appear from all over the United States, wandering the park, seeking some sort of cathartic experience. Eventually, the gatherings seem to have developed a set of informal, unspoken protocols. Probably the earliest of these rituals congealed around Penn Jones, the author of *Forgive My Grief*. This 1967 publication was

74. Hunt, *JFK for a New Generation*, 121.
75. Hunt, *JFK for a New Generation*, 121.

one of the first to seriously question the findings of the Warren Commission. As his conspiracist followers gathered around him on the grassy knoll just at 12:30, Jones would offer a prayer "for God to save the country from corrupting influences," then ask for a moment of silence. Although Jones himself passed away in 1998, conspiracy buffs still convene at Dealey Plaza every year and continue this tradition.[76]

From the time of her arrival in Dallas in 1978, Hunt has seen numerous impromptu ceremonies take shape. In a 1983 example, she watched from her perch near the sniper's nest on the then unrestored sixth floor of the old Texas School Book Depository Building:

> People began to move into the park during the morning and shortly after noon, they formed into loose lines on both sides of Elm Street, the original route of the 1963 motorcade. I learned later that some people came every year from out of state to participate in the event. Then, at 12:30 PM, everybody stood at the curb and waited for the limousine to miraculously reappear. Of course, it never did.[77]

Five years later, on the twenty-fifth anniversary of the assassination, Hunt witnessed much the same thing. This time, three thousand people showed up at the plaza, holding an "impromptu vigil that lasted from morning until night."

> At the appointed time, participants lining the curb joined hands. Suddenly, one person walked out into the middle of Elm Street and placed a rose near the spot where the fatal head shot had found its mark. Cars moving west on Elm managed to avoid hitting the pedestrian, but they squashed the flower. Soon, other people followed suit and created a little triangular street shrine, composed of coins, flowers, rosaries, and other mementos. Traffic stopped. Without a word

---

76. Marc Ramirez, "JFK ceremony attracts diverse group," *Dallas Morning News*, November 23, 2011.

77. Hunt, *JFK for a New Generation*, 121.

> the police quickly moved in and placed protective cones on either side of the street sculpture. Then as by signal, cars moved out of the middle lane and traffic continued towards the triple underpass."[78]

Hunt came to understand that Dealey Plaza had become hallowed ground. After the assassination, memorials were dedicated to John F. Kennedy all over the world. There was the Eternal Flame at Kennedy's gravesite in Arlington National Cemetery. Washington, DC, offered up The John F. Kennedy Center for the Performing Arts, and Boston, The John F. Kennedy Presidential Library. Dallas eventually commissioned its own John F. Kennedy Memorial, the cenotaph designed by Philip Johnson, which was dedicated in 1970. "The gravesite, the Kennedy Center and the Kennedy Library were clearly intended as memorials," writes Hunt, "but the assassination site was transformed into one by the public."[79]

Hunt saw firsthand how Dealey Plaza has been transformed—not by official fiat, but by spontaneous public activity—and she compares the plaza today to places like Gettysburg, Mount Vernon, and the Washington Monument. All these sites have become what she calls "debate parks" where people go to "ponder the meaning of life, the meaning of government, and they will talk about it."[80] Our national history is never a simple thing, and the JFK assassination is mired in as much controversy as any single event in that history. Dealey Plaza is a place, as Hunt says, where you can "feel the power of history under your feet." Dealey Plaza and these other great national memorial sites, she notes, "evoke passion and emotional responses with the public. They tie us together in this weird, loose thing called our civil religion."[81]

•

78. Hunt, *JFK for a New Generation,* 122.
79. Hunt, *JFK for a New Generation,* 115.
80. Schutze, "City Hall's Kennedy Conspiracy."
81. Jim Hodges, "10 Questions with Conover Hunt." *Newport News Daily Press,* June 18, 2007.

If there is such a thing as a civil religion, Dealey Plaza, in the heart of downtown Dallas, is one of our great temples. It is, however, a temple without a recognized priesthood, a defined liturgy, or any definite ritual. Each year, hundreds of thousands of people make the pilgrimage to the plaza. But when they get there, they don't know what to do or how to act. You can sense their confusion, the pressure they feel; they are looking to experience something profoundly significant but aren't sure how to achieve it. If each Thanksgiving we reenact that first feast of the Plymouth Puritans, if each Fourth of July our fireworks recreate the battles of the War of Independence, then what should we do here?

Dealey Plaza demands ceremony and ritual, but everything here works against it. Crammed in its urban bowl beneath towering skyscrapers and raised highways, cars, trucks, buses, taxis rushing through it in every direction, there is no time here for meditation on loss, no solitude for rumination. But people come here—many obviously on a lark, others merely curious, but many as faithful pilgrims, as if they were visiting a holy site.

Kennedy, along with Martin Luther King, is our great twentieth-century martyr. His passing marked not just the death of an individual but something much larger, something that needs its proper commemoration. Just as medieval travelers developed the traditions of the Stations of the Cross in their desire to more profoundly enter into the landscape of the Holy Land, many visitors to Dealey Plaza feel a similar urge for active commemoration. It's not hard to imagine them following the last route of the doomed president in the same manner that the pilgrims of Jerusalem still walk the path of Jesus's last day.

You would follow the route of the presidential limousine along the motorcade route—the right turn off Main Street, down to the slow left turn from Houston Street onto Elm Street—as if you were walking the *Via Sacra*. At the former Texas School Book Depository, you would ascend to the sixth floor. After paying homage there to the sacred relics, you would take the elevator down to street level, walk down the Elm Street incline to the final station on this local *Via Dolorosa*: the white X sprayed onto the center lane of Elm Street. You would imagine this as our own national Golgotha, the place where the beloved suffered his final agony.

Throughout your entire pilgrimage, you would have been gauging your position by your proximity to this final destination—the very center of it all. You could step out onto Elm Street and stand upon the very spot. Take yourself back there: 12:30 PM, November 22, 1963.

•

When Erykah Badu, in her video for "Window Seat," reaches the X in the center of Dealey Plaza, a gunshot rings out and she falls, naked.

There is a moment of slow-motion vertigo. The handheld camera twirls, beginning a slow spin that takes in the entire plaza: a flash of the surrounding crowd; a fleeting glimpse of the former Texas School Book Depository Building; the flags across Dealey Plaza; the Old Red Courthouse; behind it, the skyline of modern Dallas; and, finally, the great geodesic dome of Reunion Tower, the city's current iconic symbol. By the time the camera eye completes this circle and returns to its starting point, it is clear: you are in the center of contemporary Dallas, not the Dallas of 1963. In the camera's swirling arc, you have experienced a disorienting swoon that takes it all in—the swarming city emanating from this original hub, reaching all the way back to John Neely Bryan and its historical founding. It all spirals back to this singular point in the middle of this green plaza, this vortex at the very center of Dallas: the X.

In the "Window Seat" video, after the camera eye has made its rounds, it returns to Badu. She has risen up a new person, been reborn. More than fifty years after the event, writing about the JFK assassination and Dallas, this is a good place to begin.

CHAPTER 2

Conspiracy A-Go-Go

(When the true King's murderers
are allowed to roam free
a 1000 Magicians arise
in the land)

Jim Morrison, "An American Prayer"[82]

JOHN SLATE IS THE Dallas city archivist. Since 2000, he has gone to work among the stacks of boxes and interminable rows of files lined up in the basement of Dallas City Hall, that massive inverted concrete wedge that I. M. Pei designed for the city in 1972. The building is the final and most monumental result of Dallas Mayor Erik Jonsson's "Goals for Dallas" program, the post-assassination initiative designed to move the city beyond the shame of the events of November 1963.

In that cavernous space, crammed with years' worth of city council proceedings, zoning requests, and parks department annual reports, sit the city's police department records relating to the assassination of President John F. Kennedy. A minuscule part of the entire Dallas Municipal Archive, these records remain the most vexing materials on John Slate's watch. While

82. Jim Morrison, *The American Night: The Writings of Jim Morrison*, (New York: Vintage Books, 1991), 2:5.

requests for Kennedy assassination–related materials have slowed down drastically since most of the pertinent police records have been posted online (after the release of Oliver Stone's *JFK* in 1991, there was a nationwide push for the opening up of all related records), Slate occasionally still gets one of those calls "from out in left field."

As an archivist, Slate is the consummate professional. He does not interject his personal opinion or interpretation into the process of meticulously preserving and sharing the materials put into his care. Over the course of his career, researchers from all over the country—and of every possible ideological bent—have called upon Slate for assistance. He provided conspiracist Robert Groden with information he's since used in his efforts to prove the JFK assassination was part of a vast intrigue. Slate also assisted Vincent Bugliosi, the world's primary debunker of JFK conspiracy theories. (Slate's name appears a number of times in the notes of Bugliosi's 2007 *Reclaiming History: The Assassination of President John F. Kennedy.*) "I'm interested in the materials," Slate says, "but as far as being a junior detective, I'll leave that to the professionals."[83]

•

Most of Slate's current coworkers at the City of Dallas are unaware that he has a secret life—that, over the years, dozens and dozens of people have run into him on the street and asked, "Hey, aren't you the 'Conspiracy A-Go-Go' Guy?"

John Slate is indeed the "Conspiracy A-Go-Go" Guy, one of the most memorable characters to appear in the 1990 cult film classic *Slacker.* "Richard Linklater's sly ode," as one critic put it, "to Austin's anarchists, yahoos, and UFO obsessives,"[84] *Slacker* has been hailed for defining the zeitgeist of its age. It helped popularize the use of the term "slacker," and, as Chris Walters has suggested, it was "one of the first American movies ever to find a form so apropos to the themes of disconnectedness and cultural drift" that are at the core

83. John Slate, interview with Tim Cloward, December 22, 2010.

84. Christopher Kelly, "Grounds for Suspicion: Texas and the Conspiracy Movie," *Texas Monthly*, September 2007.

of slackerdom.[85] An eternal Austinite, Linklater defends the slacker ethos: "The dictionary defines slackers as people who evade duties and responsibilities. A more modern notion would be people who are ultimately being responsible to themselves and not wasting their time in a realm of activity that has nothing to do with who they are or what they might be ultimately striving for."[86]

Viewers of Linklater's film will understand that slackers have opted out of the game because they have figured out the game is fixed. The most obvious "fix" is, of course, the conspiracy—the sinister connivings of those secret cabals that control our lives. John Slate's Kennedy assassination "Conspiracy A-Go-Go" Guy is a potent representation of our cynical age: the embodiment of that slacker fascination with paranoia. "Paranoia plus a generation," Linklater said in a piece in *Salon,* "equals pretty much the world we're living in today."[87]

•

Conspiracy paranoia is nothing new in America. Almost three decades before Linklater made *Slacker,* the historian Richard Hofstadter delivered his soon-to-be famous lecture, "The Paranoid Style in American Politics." Speaking at Oxford University in November 1963—the same month that John F. Kennedy was gunned down in Dallas—Hofstadter reminded his audience that America had a long history with obsessive political paranoia.

At that time, Hofstadter's concern was not left-wing bohemian anarchists like the slackers in Linklater's film, but America's right-wing paranoiacs. There *was* an enemy within, but, in mid-century America, the malignant force that threatened our way of life was not UFO infiltration or CIA subversion, but Communism. Dallas was in the thrall of the Red Menace. While much of

85. Chris Walters, "Slacker," review of *Slacker,* directed by Richard Linklater, *Austin Chronicle,* July 5, 1991.

86. Andrew Kopkind, "Slacking toward Bethlehem," *Grand Street,* no. 44, 1993, 176–78.

87. Brian Raftery, "*Slacker*: 15 Year Later," *Salon,* July 5, 2006, https://www.salon.com/2006/07/05/slacker/.

America shared our concerns, we—with our John Birchers, our rabid support of Barry Goldwater, and our McCarthyite oilmen—were a bit more fanatical than most places.

Like Hofstadter, Hollywood was just then beginning to sketch out the outlines of this distinctly American paranoia. In 1962, the film *The Manchurian Candidate* was released. If *Slacker* represented the paranoid zeitgeist of 1990s America, *The Manchurian Candidate* represented that of the early 1960s. Some have called it the first film in what would eventually be dubbed the conspiracy movie genre, and the *New York Times* called it "arguably the most chilling piece of cold war paranoia ever committed to film."[88]

Directed by John Frankenheimer, *The Manchurian Candidate* was based on Richard Condon's 1959 political thriller of the same name. The novel plays on the then-prominent right-wing phobia of Communist infiltration, revealing how a company of American soldiers captured during the Korean War is brainwashed by the Soviets, becoming unwitting pawns who are manipulated to overthrow the US government. The story climaxes with an attempted assassination of a prominent politician just as he accepts the nomination to become president of the United States.

At the time, the assassination of a prominent American politician was considered a touchy subject for a mainstream film to address. When Frankenheimer approached United Artists with the idea, they would not proceed with the project. It wasn't until Frank Sinatra, who was lobbying for the part of the heroic protagonist, Bennett Marco, got assurances directly from his friend John F. Kennedy that the president had no objections to the production of the film that the project got underway. When Kennedy was assassinated, *The Manchurian Candidate* was still making the rounds of America's theater houses, finishing a very successful first run.

The creepy similarities between *The Manchurian Candidate*'s fictional plot—a planned presidential assassination by a Communist sleeper agent—and the actual events of November 22, 1963, were too profound to miss. After November 1963, the film seemed to disappear. Condon asserted that

88. Mel Gussow, "Richard Condon, Political Novelist, Dies at 81," *New York Times*, April 10, 1996.

it had been suppressed because of its eerie parallels with the JFK assassination—"frozen," he said, "because it was felt that the assassin might have seen it and been influenced by it." In a December 28, 1963, article in *The Nation*, "Manchurian Candidate in Dallas," Condon lashed out at his critics, noting that his fiction was not the cause of violence but a reflection of our society's violent tendencies. "All of us are nothing more than the result of our conditioning," he wrote, and "for some time all of us in the United States had been brainwashed to violence."

While many noted that his novels were close to prophetic, Condon admitted only that they were "sometimes about five and a half minutes ahead of their time."[89]

•

If *The Manchurian Candidate*'s first run was cut short in early 1964, the conspiracy thriller genre it helped pioneer was just coming into its own. In 1966, Michelangelo Antonioni's *Blow-Up* artfully articulated what would become the most common conspiracy film trope: the individual who stumbles upon the hidden truth and then is hunted down to be silenced. In 1974, this theme of dangerous knowledge was expanded in Alan Pakula's *The Parallax View*. Here, the murderous culprit turns out to be a multinational corporation whose primary enterprise is political assassination.

By 1979, when William Richert's film *Winter Kills* was released, things had come full circle. That film, starring Jeff Bridges and John Huston, was based on the book of the same title by one Richard Condon. Almost two decades after having drawn so much attention for the striking similarities between the JFK assassination and his *The Manchurian Candidate*, Condon produced something more than just another conspiracy thriller. He had written a black comedy, and *Winter Kills* was an intentional takeoff on the JFK assassination. The novel's plot features many parallels to the Kennedy assassination. Tim Kegan is the doomed president. With his boyish charisma and toothy grin, he has been groomed for

89. Richard Condon, "Manchurian Candidate In Dallas," *The Nation*, December 28, 1963, 449–51; Gussow, "Richard Condon, Political Novelist, Dies at 81."

the presidency by his domineering father (played in Richert's film by John Huston). Tim is survived by his brother Nick (Jeff Bridges), who strives heroically to come to grips with the family legacy. The killing occurs not in Dallas but in Philadelphia; Dealey Plaza becomes Hunt Plaza; and the *Warren Report*, the *Pickering Report*. Nevertheless, *Winter Kills*' convoluted plot is nothing if not a working out of many of the conspiracy theories that had begun to swirl around the Kennedy assassination. In its shocking conclusion, Condon's novel presents that event as "a cold-assed business proposition," the work of a cabal of businessmen who "controlled the CIA, the Secret Service and the FBI."[90]

In another ironic twist, by the time the film *Winter Kills* had finished its run at the theaters, Richard Condon had moved to Dallas. A longtime Hollywood writer, Condon had left the United States just before *The Manchurian Candidate*'s publication. His self-imposed exile lasted for almost two decades, until he returned to the country in the early 1980s to be near his daughter and granddaughter in Texas. His most well-known work from his Dallas period was the mafia-themed *Prizzi's Honor* series, but Condon—the man the *New York Times* would call "a visionary, a darkly comic conjurer, a student of American mythology and a master of conspiracy theories"—continued to churn out political thrillers here until his death in 1996.[91]

In 1984, the Republican National Convention met in our downtown convention center to re-coronate Ronald Reagan, and, once again, Dallas was at the center of an ascendant right-wing movement, Condon transformed that ruckus into *Emperor of America*. The novel was a vicious satire of America in the late 1980s, portraying Dallas as the grateful capital of a militaristic fascist state led by an Oliver North–like despot kept in power by *People* magazine–style media manipulation. (The paranoia here was provided by the hyped-up threat of an invasion by Communist Nicaragua.)

Emperor of America sold reasonably well, but what brought Condon the most attention at that late stage of his career was the 1988 rerelease of the film that had started it all—*The Manchurian Candidate*. In the years since the assassination, the film had collected a certain mystique. Not only had it been

90. Richard Condon, *Winter Kills* (New York: Dell, 1974), 305, 329.
91. Gussow, "Richard Condon, Political Novelist, Dies at 81."

increasingly mentioned as a founding document of the burgeoning conspiracy film genre, but there had also been growing rumors that the film had been pulled from circulation and hidden away because of the ghostly similarities between its plot and the circumstances of the JFK assassination. Those rumors weren't true; the film's disappearance had more to do with contested licensing arrangements than any conspiracy. But the conspiracy buzz made the better story.

•

In Austin in 1988, there would have been plenty of interest in checking out the rereleased *The Manchurian Candidate*. By then, film culture was thriving in the state's capital. Richard Linklater and a group of like-minded young film buffs from the flourishing film community developing around the University of Texas had founded the Austin Film Society in 1985. John Slate, who had grown up in Austin, had been drawn to UT to study film and soon found himself connecting with this cadre of young, enthusiastic filmmakers. While there was a lot of ambition floating around at the time, there was very little available funding. Linklater, looking to produce the one film that would establish his name, went to work with the materials at hand: maxed-out credit cards and the help of friends. He assembled the barest of crews and a rabble of fascinating misfit actors and began work on *Slacker*.

This was a scheme thoroughly befitting of Austin, which has always been the anarchistic antithesis of its northern neighbor, serious, hard-driving Dallas. In late 1980s Austin, Hofstadter's "Paranoid Style" had transformed itself into a thoroughgoing yet laid-back skepticism. In *Slacker*, the superheated Cold War conspiracy action of *The Manchurian Candidate* gives way to meandering, rambling monologues delivered by characters like Tommy Pallotta's "Looking for a Missing Friend" guy. He warns his listener about the UFO cover-up during the NASA moon landing, the government's secret occupation of Mars, and the memory-destroying programs initiated by the "secret group" that actually runs the government. Everything is relatively harmless, though, because, in the slacker world, the participants have already dropped out of the conspiratorial rat race.

Richard Linklater was drawn to cast John Slate in *Slacker* after learning of his JFK assassination obsession. Linklater and Slate worked together to create the movie role (which Slate estimates eventually earned him fifty dollars or so), developing a simple script that Slate could hold on three-by-five-inch index cards. Slate's big scene was filmed at the old Austin Half-Price Books at West Thirty-First and Guadalupe Street. Referred to locally as "The Drag," Guadalupe Street was then legendary for the eclectic mix of bohemian dropouts and college kids who frequented its establishments. Slate's scene opens, as do all the scenes in *Slacker*, with a character wandering off from one encounter, then entering another location and initiating another seemingly random encounter. In this case, a young woman enters the bookstore and begins haphazardly browsing. Slate, in his blue jeans and assassination-themed T-shirt, passes behind her, recognizes her from a class they had together at UT, and approaches her. You can see the handwritten Half-Price Books section labels hanging from the shelves—both characters are a standing a few feet from the "True Crime" section, among the literature classified as "Conspiracy."

"Hey," he introduces himself, "I see you're reading *Rush to Judgment*." (Written by attorney Mark Lane and published in 1966, this was the first major publication to propose an assassination conspiracy and cover-up.) The two exchange pleasantries, and she asks what he's been doing. "You know me," he says, "I've been keeping up with my JFK assassination theories." And then he is off and running, recommending to her *Best Evidence* because "that's the one, you know, with all the head-snap stuff in it," then *Six Seconds in Dallas* "'cause, you know, it's got all the trajectory and triangulation of the bullets and stuff." His "real favorite," though, is *Forgive My Grief* because it reveals the "Breakfast of Infamy" where Oswald and Officer Tippit share eggs at Oak Cliff's Steak'n Egg Kitchen.

Slate's character goes on nonstop for five and a half minutes, even as he leaves the bookstore and runs into a friend on the street working on his car. He has discovered things about Jack Ruby and his relationship to his dogs. Ruby's dachshund, Sheba, was "like a wife" to him. And we learn that he is, of course, working on his own JFK book. He hasn't written it yet, but he's in discussions with his "small press" editor, and they've decided it should be called *Conspiracy A-Go-Go*.

•

A used bookstore is a pretty good place to gauge the current obsession with conspiracy theories. (In the course of my research, I myself have bumbled inadvertently into a number of conversations with rabid conspiracists while browsing shelves.) Reliable sources estimate that between one and two thousand books about the JFK assassination have been published. According to Vincent Bugliosi, 95 percent of those books are "pro-conspiracy and anti–Warren Commission."[92] Used bookstores are filled with them. The first image you encounter in the Sixth Floor Museum guidebook (it is also the last photo panel you pass as you leave the museum) offers an eloquent visual depiction of this mass of literature. It is a black-and-white photograph of a series of bookcases, part of Mary Ferrell's famous collection of JFK assassination material. This label reads: "A small selection of the many books written about the Kennedy assassination." In the photo, the books literally pour over each other. They are crammed into every available space and still overflow: *A Higher Form of Killing*; *Jack Ruby's Girls*; *J.F.K Must Die!*; *Best Evidence*; *Oswald: The Truth*; *Marina and Lee*; *Accessories after the Fact*; *And We Are All Moral*; *The President Is Dead*. The books mount up at the base of the shelves and obscure each other. This is what the "Conspiracy A-Go-Go" guy has been reading.

By the time *Slacker* was released in 1990, it wasn't just right-wing paranoia that bedeviled America, it was more widespread. The paranoia was in the fabric of our society. And it all started on November 22, 1963. The Kennedy assassination was when it all came apart, the story goes, and *they* took control. Americans continue to believe, at an astounding level, that the killing of JFK was the result of a conspiracy. Polls taken within the last two decades reflect that 75 percent of Americans do not believe that Lee Harvey Oswald acted alone; 70 percent suspect that there was a broader plot behind the assassination; 66 percent think there was a conspiracy; and 74 percent think there was

92. Vincent Bugliosi, *Reclaiming History: The Assassination of President John F. Kennedy* (New York: W. W. Norton and Co., 2007), 974; Peter Knight, *The Kennedy Assassination* (Edinburgh: Edinburgh University Press, 2007), 75.

a cover-up.[93] James F. Broderick and Darren W. Miller, in *Web of Conspiracy: A Guide to Conspiracy Theory Sites on the Internet,* have labeled the JFK assassination "the greatest and grandest of all conspiracy theories," and Peter Knight in *Conspiracy Theories in American History: An Encyclopedia,* calls the JFK assassination "the mother of all conspiracies."[94] The fact that there are numerous guides and encyclopedias tracking conspiracy theories is itself an important indicator that America has become a conspiracy-crazed nation.

If the Camelot myth dominated the early years of the post–JFK assassination era, simplifying our history into a tale of a Golden Age and a fallen present, then the Conspiracy myth, which dominates today, has built onto that narrative. It proposes that our present, fallen condition is the result of a series of interlocking, all-encompassing schemes conducted by secret, malignant powers. The Kennedy assassination in Dallas, "the mother of all conspiracies," has become the foundation of this current craze, the starter kit for the conspiracist mindset.

It is a mindset that allows the crafting of an all-encompassing narrative that can contain virtually any historical material, forming a hydra-headed monster that seems to sprout two new heads for each offshoot that is severed by fact or logic. (The old Dallas Conspiracy Museum had a large wall mural depicting a "Conspiracy Tree," showing the various plots branching off from the central trunk.[95]) The root—where this modern paranoia has sprouted and grown so monstrous—is Dealey Plaza. The plaza, as Dallas columnist

93. Lydia Saad, "Americans: Kennedy Assassination a Conspiracy," Gallup News Service, November 21, 2003, http://www.gallup.com/poll/9751/Americans-Kennedy-Assassination-Conspiracy.aspx; "ABC NEWS POLL: WHO KILLED JFK?," *ABC News,* November 9, 2003, http://abcnews.go.com/images/pdf/937a-1JFKAssassination.pdf; "Poll: Most Believe 'Cover-Up' of JFK Assassination Facts," *Fox News,* June 18, 2004, http://www.foxnews.com/story/0,2933,102511,00.html.

94. James F. Broderick, "The JFK Assassination," in *Web of Conspiracy: A Guide to Conspiracy Theory Sites on the Internet* (Medford, NJ: CyberAge Books, 2008), 203; Peter Knight, ed., *Conspiracy Theories in American History: An Encyclopedia* (Santa Barbara: ABC-CLIO Inc., 2003), 383.

95. Wade Goodwyn, "It's No Mystery: Rent Hike Kills Conspiracy Museum." *NPR,* December 9, 2006, http://www.npr.org/templates/story/story.php?storyId=6600771.

Jim Schutze asserts, has become "a black hole of conspiracy drawing every possible plot to its breast with such a powerful suck that finally nothing, not even light itself, can escape."[96]

•

After almost fifty years, Dallas is considerably less obsessed with defending itself against accusations that we are the "City of Hate." Time has passed, and we are no longer consumed with anguish about suspicions that we established the conditions that resulted in the death of the president. We are happy to think that today most people understand that we did not kill Kennedy. Unfortunately, the question of our civic guilt has been subsumed by a larger and more existential one. If we didn't kill Kennedy, who did?

Even if we have been absolved of the murder of the president, the inescapable fact is that Dallas is still the crime scene. For a city as concerned with its image as Dallas is, that our primary tourist attraction is the location of a presidential assassination makes for an extremely uncomfortable situation. While the Dallas Convention & Visitors Bureau trumpets our tradition of local hospitality and advertises our obvious ability to entertain in style, its officials must feel a deep sense of ambivalence about the fact that we are ground zero for the contemporary conspiracy movement.

Every year around November 22, they come, bringing steady and reliable business to Dallas. By the hundreds, they pay their airfare, cab fare, hotel bills, pay for meals, drinks, and gifts for those left at home. They fill the beds and the meeting rooms at the Hyatt Regency, the Adolphus, and the Hotel Lawrence. And, each year, the conspiracy conventions mark the anniversary of the JFK assassination in the blocks surrounding Dealey Plaza. Typical of these conventions was the event staged by ASK (Assassination Symposium on John F. Kennedy) in 1993, on the thirtieth anniversary of the assassination.

Joe Nick Patoski, a longtime Texas journalist, helped satisfy his lifelong fascination with the assassination by helping organize the event. That year's ASK conference featured many of the big names—important conspiracy

96. Schutze, "City Hall's Kennedy Conspiracy."

buffs like Robert Groden and archivist/researcher Mary Ferrell, all joining together to bash Gerald Posner, whose just-published *Case Closed* purported to prove definitively that there was no conspiracy. The biggest buzz that year surrounded Norman Mailer. Mailer's 1991 CIA conspiracy novel *Harlot's Ghost* was still hot property, and he was just starting to immerse himself in the newly declassified information from the former Soviet Union that would form the core of his book *Oswald's Tale*.[97]

For the six hundred attendees of the ASK conference, "a loose community of conspiracy celebrities, self-appointed archivists, and independent researchers," each of whose members had paid $175 to participate in five days of activities, there was plenty to do. The trade show offered over two hundred assassination-themed books and other related merchandise, but the real bonus of the symposium, as related by Patoski later in *Texas Monthly*, was the chance to meet our local assassination celebrities—people who *were there!* You could mingle with witnesses like Jean Hill, the "famous lady in red" who was one of the individuals standing closest to the presidential limo when the shooting started, or Tom Alyea, the WFAA-TV cameraman who was the first to film the sixth-floor sniper's nest. You could even meet Marina Oswald Porter, the "alleged" assassin's Russian-born wife.[98]

Two decades later, the conspiracy business was even better. In the 2010s, Dallas hosted two major assassination/conspiracy conferences. JFK Lancer, a historical research company dedicated to the revealing of truth surrounding the assassination of President John F. Kennedy, has been hosting its annual conference at the Adolphus Hotel since 1996. The COPA folks—COPA being the acronym for the Coalition on Political Assassinations—have been meeting in Dallas since 1993. In 2011, they stayed at the Hotel Lawrence a few blocks south of Dealey Plaza. While the JFK Lancer conference tends to focus specifically on the JFK assassination, the COPA conference is more expansive, assuming conspiratorial links between various well-known political assassinations. They presented not only speakers like Ed Haslam—whose most recent book is *Dr. Mary's Monkey: How the Unsolved Murder of a*

97. Joe Nick Patoski, "ASKed Out," *Texas Monthly*, January 1994.
98. Patoski, "ASKed Out."

Doctor, a Secret Laboratory in New Orleans and Cancer-Causing Monkey Viruses are Linked to Lee Harvey Oswald, the JFK Assassination and Emerging Global Epidemics—but also discussions of whether the FBI was, as part of its war on Black leaders, behind the shooting of Tupac Shakur. Of special note was the appearance by celebrity forensic pathologist Dr. Cyril Wecht, a figure familiar to TV audiences for his theories on the actual cause of death of not just President John F. Kennedy, but Senator Robert F. Kennedy, Elvis Presley, Nicole Simpson, and JonBenet Ramsey as well.[99]

•

The contemporary conspiracists making their annual trek to Dallas view themselves as researchers, as part of a larger movement intent on discovering the code that will unlock the secret nature of things. They understand that they are contributing to a larger body of work, a critical mass of evidence that has been collected by their forebears. At the conventions, they take pains to honor the pantheon of earlier searchers, the giants upon whose shoulders they stand.

The first of those great questioners was Mark Lane. A Jewish American lawyer-activist from New York, Lane was an early Kennedy supporter. Less than a month after the assassination, he published his influential "Oswald Innocent? A Lawyer's Brief" in the a special edition of the *National Guardian.* With that piece, Lane became the first national voice to challenge Oswald's presumed guilt. After Marguerite Oswald read the piece, she asked Lane to represent her son before the Warren Commission. (He eventually visited her in her Fort Worth home in March of 1964.) Lane went on to make even more of a name for himself during the Warren Commission proceedings. He demanded that he be allowed to cross-examine witnesses and generally made himself a thorn in the side of committee members.

After the *Warren Report* was published later in 1964, Lane came back

99. "JFK Lancer's November in Dallas Conference," *JFK Lancer*, July 12, 2012, http://jfklancer.com/Dallas.html; "COPA Dallas Conference November 22–25, 2012," *COPA/Coalition on Political Assassinations*, June 11, 2012, http://politicalassassinations.com/conferences/dallas/.

to Dallas. For two weeks in March and April 1966, he interviewed a couple of dozen assassination witnesses who he felt had been ignored or misrepresented by the Warren Commission. The fruits of those investigations would become *Rush to Judgment,* Lane's scathing attack on the conclusions of the Warren Commission. Subtitled *A Critique of the Warren Commission's Inquiry into the Murders of President John F. Kennedy, Officer J. D. Tippit and Lee Harvey Oswald,* the book spent seventeen weeks on the *New York Times* bestseller list. It became the first significant book to challenge the Warren Commission, and was quickly adapted by Emile de Antonio into a documentary film. *Rush to Judgment*'s popular success is generally credited with transforming discussion of a possible JFK assassination conspiracy from random chatter into the beginnings of a movement.

In 1973, Lane helped take the message to Hollywood. He cowrote the screenplay for the feature film *Executive Action,* starring big-name actors Burt Lancaster and Robert Ryan. The film, which was released two weeks before the tenth anniversary of the assassination, presented a plot by a covey of right-wing business leaders to assassinate the president—"The way it *could* have happened," proclaimed the film's advertising. A decade after the event, the idea that the assassination of John F. Kennedy was the result of a conspiracy was becoming mainstream.

•

That same year, another JFK assassination film, one that would have an even more profound impact, had its major public premiere. In November 1973, Robert J. Groden presented the Zapruder film to a spellbound national symposium of Kennedy assassination researchers at Georgetown University. The 26.6-second silent color footage was taken by Dallas women's clothing manufacturer Abraham Zapruder on his Model 414 PD Bell & Howell Zoomatic Director Series camera just as the bullets started to fly in Dealey Plaza. The film was already legendary, but it had been rarely seen. *Life* magazine, which owned its rights, guarded it religiously. They had published still frames, but *Life* had only allowed the film to be screened in its entirety twice before: for the Warren Commission and at Jim Garrison's New Orleans conspiracy trials.

Groden had previously presented a couple of low-profile screenings on local news programs, and a few bootleg copies had begun to make the rounds, but they were of notoriously poor quality.

What the audience at Georgetown University saw was complete and of much higher quality. In 1969, Groden had been hired on as a technician at a New York City motion picture processing lab. A test copy of the original Zapruder film was stored in its vault, courtesy of previous work the lab had done for *Life*. "And let's just say," Groden told *Dallas Observer* columnist Jim Schutze, "an extra copy was made." Groden transferred this test copy from eight-millimeter home movie film to thirty-five-millimeter, minimizing the camera's shakiness in the process. He hoarded his treasure for four years—until the Georgetown premiere. After that, things started happening for Groden. Less than two years after the Georgetown screening, on March 6, 1975, he and comedian and political activist Dick Gregory showed this same copy of the Zapruder film to a national television audience on ABC's *Goodnight America*. It was hosted by Geraldo Rivera, and it was footage that could not be ignored. The debate on the Kennedy assassination was recharged, and Robert Groden was thrust into the conspiracy limelight.

As it turns out, Groden, a native of the Queens borough of New York, was celebrating his eighteenth birthday on November 22, 1963, when he heard what had happened in Dallas. From that point forward he felt a deep connection with the assassinated president. In 1967, he chanced to visit Washington, DC, just as the eternal flame at the JFK gravesite in Arlington National Cemetery was consecrated. Groden, then twenty-one and just back from military duty overseas, stood in line for hours to have his moment before the sepulchre. "I made a promise to President Kennedy at his gravesite that day that I would do everything in my power to try to find the truth, no matter how long it took and no matter what it cost me," he later recounted. "And I have kept my word."[100]

•

100. Schutze, "City Hall's Kennedy Conspiracy."

Groden's resolve has made him a hero among conspiracy buffs. In 1975, he published his first book, *JFK: The Case For Conspiracy*, and, in the late 1970s, he served as a staff photographic consultant for the House Select Committee on Assassinations. By the 1980s, his technical expertise had made him the go-to consultant for the myriad documentary films being made about the JFK assassination. He worked with Oliver Stone on *JFK*, even appearing in a cameo as the projectionist showing the Zapruder film during the climactic courtroom scene. As Groden gained notoriety and influence, he began to feel increasingly pulled toward leadership of the conspiracy movement. In 1995, feeling that he could make a difference, Robert Groden left his wife back in their Philadelphia home and moved permanently to Dallas to be on the front lines of the battle.

Today, you can find Robert Groden in Dealey Plaza on most any weekend day. On a foldout sales table set up near the northern pergola, not too far from the point where Abraham Zapruder shot his famous film, you'll see his wares: his video magazine, *The Killing of a President*; the Dealey Plaza Memorial DVD edition of his *JFK: The Case for Conspiracy*; his 1992 *New York Times* nonfiction bestseller *High Treason*. The table will also hold a host of magazines, books, videos, and DVDs, all of which Groden will sign on request. Groden will engage anyone who is interested in conspiracy talk; it is his mission. Although he ekes out only a modest living this way, he has no regrets. "The other side was winning by default," he said recently. "They had the Sixth Floor Museum that was lying to everybody who walked in the door, and still does. My wife and I felt there needed to be a voice of reason here."

In fact, Groden is convinced that the Sixth Floor Museum and the City of Dallas are intent on driving him out of Dealey Plaza. The city, he says, has a vested interest in promoting the *Warren Report* and quashing any talk of conspiracy. To Groden and many of the conspiracists who see him as their standard-bearer, the city and the museum are allied with larger forces that will stop at nothing to muzzle the truth-seekers. There is ample evidence of a program of suppression, Groden asserts, in the fact that the City of Dallas has engaged in a cyclical campaign of legal harassment against him. Groden claims he was ticketed eighty-one times between 1995 and 2016. He's been arrested twice, most recently on June 13, 2010. His legal battles with the city, sympathetically documented by the *Dallas Observer*'s Jim Schutze, garnered plenty of publicity for the cause, and Groden sued the city for denying him his free speech rights. The case remained in litigation until 2017, when it was finally resolved and Groden received a modest settlement.[101]

•

It is difficult, given the opacity of its operations, to determine exactly what the City of Dallas's specific motives are in its harassment of Groden. It is clear, however, that since November 22, 1963, the City of Dallas has never known quite what to do with Dealey Plaza. The primary impulse has always been to sanitize the park, cleanse it of anything that would evoke memories of the assassination. As millions of visitors continued to show up, making their pilgrimages, it became more and more clear that ignoring the historical significance of Dealey Plaza was not a viable option.

The Sixth Floor Museum is the answer to that dilemma. Since its 1989 opening, the museum has offered those millions of visitors a conduit to an informative and dignified commemoration of the president's death. Also, despite the attacks by Groden and his conspiracist allies, the Sixth Floor Museum does not deny the fact that there are many people who dispute the conclusions of the Warren Commission. While the museum generally accepts its conclusions, it does devote a considerable amount of space to criticism of the Warren Commission. The museum's "The Investigation" section even includes a "Who Did It?" display which reviews the various possible conspiracy scenarios: the Soviets and the KGB, the Cuban government, anti-Castro elements, the New Orleans scenario, Jack Ruby, organized crime, US investigative agencies (FBI, CIA), the far right, even the Vietnam angle. The museum acknowledges these competing views, and it takes pains to present a fair and reasoned discussion of the various investigations. All told, the Sixth

101. Schutze, "City Hall's Kennedy Conspiracy"; Michael Scott, "Warren Commission Critic Arrested in Dealey Plaza," *JFKMurder.com: The Official Robert Groden Website*, June 13, 2010, http://www.jfkmurder.com/plazanews1.html; Jim Schutze, "Robert Groden, JFK Expert, Settles with Dallas After 82 Bad Arrests," *Dallas Observer*, March 10, 2017.

Floor Museum does an admirable job of straddling that fine line between contemporary controversy and the settled pronouncements of history.

While the Sixth Floor Museum is not the demonic suppressor of truth it is sometimes accused of being by the conspiracy theorists, it is guilty of a certain institutional conservatism that is part of the bargain of its origins. It has never been blatantly stated, but it is clearly present in the subtext: if the city is going to sanction an official organization that will confront the legacy of the JFK assassination, that organization's subsidiary mission will be to serve as a bulwark to protect the image of the city in all matters concerning the assassination.

•

The city of Dallas is deservedly famous for being image-conscious. In the 1980s, during the early discussions that would lead to the creation of the Sixth Floor Museum, that was especially obvious. By then, the city had grown considerably, becoming one of the glittering jewels of the New South. When we were chosen to host the 1984 Republican National Convention, it was perceived as a sterling opportunity for Dallas to show the world that it had remade itself after the dark days of the assassination. In anticipation of all the national attention, Texas Monthly Press issued a guidebook to the city. Simply titled *Dallas USA*, it is a fascinating artifact of its time.

Dallas USA was written by A. C. Greene. Greene, of course, had been the *Dallas Times Herald* editorial writer most noted for exhorting the city to undertake some necessary soul-searching after the 1963 assassination. Twenty years later, Greene was for the city of Dallas what Frank Dobie had recently been for the state of Texas: our folksy cultural spokesman. He was the local raconteur who could speak assuredly for all of us. In his guidebook, Greene affects the tone of a swaggering Texas tour guide, blustering his way through the expected Dallas civic background, the sites to visit, the people, and the weather.

When Greene gets to the unavoidable topic of the assassination, however, the playful braggadocio turns defensive. By the mid-1980s, Greene was a noted author and a PBS commentator, a public figure who could talk frankly and authoritatively about, and for, the city of Dallas. Offering up a vigorous vindication of the city, Greene aggressively confronts the early post-assassination attacks on Dallas: "a shocking number of visitors disregard facts and rules of fairness in their zeal to ascribe guilt and heap scorn on Dallas," and the "national critics who seemingly were willing to be duped if charges against Dallas were severe enough." Calling the *Warren Report* "the work nearest to accuracy," Greene is especially dismissive of the conspiracy theorists, claiming there is "nothing to intelligently discredit evidence that Oswald was the lone gunman, and nothing to link Jack Ruby to any other person than the man he killed." His message to visiting out-of-towners is clear. We will no longer be willing to have outsiders dictate to us their narrative of the assassination. In *Dallas USA,* Greene announces in no uncertain terms that Dallas "now feels it is the guardian, the protector, if you will, of the history of the event."

One assumption that Greene, and many Dallasites, made was that Dallas's image problems were imported: the result of renegade outsiders. "It is also interesting to note," Greene wrote in *Dallas USA,* "that Dallas has not been home base for any of the thousands of assassination cultists and theorists." However, in his assertion that the area has produced no conspiracy theorists of note, A. C. Greene was dead wrong.[102]

•

Before almost anyone else, there was Penn Jones Jr. In the early 1980s, when a young John Slate visited a nearly deserted Dealey Plaza, he recognized a lone figure standing near the grassy knoll, not too far from the X on Elm Street that marks the location of the second shot. It was Penn Jones. As a young conspiracy buff, Slate could not pass up the opportunity to meet one of the original pioneers. As they spoke, Slate relates, Penn "pointed out to the X and said: 'Young man, that's the spot where democracy died.'"[103]

---

102. A. C. Greene, *Dallas USA* (Austin: Texas Monthly Press, 1984), 116, 114, 119.

103. John Slate, interview with Tim Cloward, December 22, 2010.

It was not unusual to see Penn Jones at Dealey Plaza. The apocryphal story goes that Penn Jones had been at Dealey Plaza every November 22 from 1964 until 1997 (he passed away in January 1998). It was Penn Jones, the same story goes, who initiated the tradition of commemorating the death of John F. Kennedy with a moment of silence exactly at 12:30 each year on the anniversary of his murder—a tradition that continues to this day.

But Jones is probably most remembered for publishing *Forgive My Grief*, a series of four books distributed between 1966 and 1976, which became early compass points for the JFK conspiracy movement. The title, taken from Tennyson's *In Memoriam*—"Forgive my grief for one removed/Thy creature whom I found so fair./I trust he lives in thee, and there/I find him worthier to be loved."—reflects the romantic dedication that Jones, and his followers, felt for their cause. Today, the books are collectors' items, sacred artifacts of the early years.

Before the JFK assassination, Penn Jones was already recognized as a crusader for truth. He was born the son of a sharecropper in tiny Annona, Texas (in the extreme northeast corner of the state), and had been a hobo during the Great Depression. He ultimately worked his way through, and graduated from, the University of Texas. After his Army service during World War II, he moved to the small former cotton town of Midlothian. Intent on becoming a newspaper man, Jones bought and edited the *Midlothian Mirror*, "a weekly, six-page journal," one source commented, "which successfully defied all the laws of typography." Jones's paper, with its circulation of eight hundred or so, was printed on "a strange, coarse newsprint which had the look of a recycling experiment that had failed," and it covered "the boredom of Midlothian like its dust."[104]

In was a small stage, but Jones made a name for himself as a prairie populist unafraid to pick a fight. After criticizing town officials for their shabby job of paving the negro section of town, Jones picked up fifty pounds of the hard-packed gravel, which contained jagged clumps of discarded nails, and displayed it in the window of the *Mirror* office. Soon after his editorial attack

104. Robert Bonazzi, "One Man's Grief," *Texas Observer*, September 29, 1967, 12.

on the local John Birch Society, the *Mirror* office was firebombed. Jones was recognized nationally with the 1963 Elijah Parish Lovejoy Award for courage in journalism, and, locally, the *Southwest Review* published a Jones piece, "Philosophy from a Weekly Editor," which chronicled his personal endeavors in "the history of the fight for the freedom of the press."[105]

•

Penn Jones vividly remembered his reaction to the Kennedy assassination. "I went home and cried for two days," he told Robert Bonazzi of *The Texas Observer.* "Then I started knocking on doors and asking questions."[106] Unsatisfied with the original press coverage of the assassination, Jones started looking closer, investigating the loose ends and apparent contradictions in the official accounts. This inquiry quickly became his big cause. Using his pulpit as editor of the *Midlothian Mirror,* Jones started to spread the word that something was fishy.

Jones's first significant breakthrough came when he began tracking the deaths of assassination-related figures. After Lee Bowers, a Dealey Plaza witness who had testified about a "flash of light" from the grassy knoll in his 1964 Warren Commission testimony, was killed in a mysterious one-car accident in Midlothian two years later, Jones started to pursue what he perceived as a trend. Less than two years after the assassination, Jones had chronicled in his work the deaths of 188 people who had some association with the assassination. They knew, Jones speculated, too much about the assassination to be permitted to live.

This speculation went national when the Leftist magazine *Ramparts* published excerpts of *Forgive My Grief* in 1966. That issue of *Ramparts* sold out, went back to press, and Penn Jones found himself catapulted to the status of instant folk hero. There was an article in *Time,* and coverage on NBC's *The Huntley–Brinkley Report.* Walter Cronkite even dispatched a film crew to

105. Penn Jones, "The Philosophy from a Weekly Editor," *Southwest Review* 49, no.1, Winter 1964, 36–43; Barry Schlachter, "Penn Jones, JFK theorist, editor," *Fort Worth Star-Telegram,* January 28, 1998.

106. Bonazzi, "One Man's Grief," 12.

Midlothian and devoted long segments of three consecutive CBS newscasts to Penn Jones. By September 1967, Jones's small-time operation had made a huge impact—he had sold 6,400 copies of *Forgive My Grief* by mail or over the counter at his Midlothian office.[107]

As editor of the *Midlothian Mirror*, Jones continued to mercilessly pursue every possible lead. When he finally retired the *Forgive My Grief* series, it was only to start his monthly assassination newsletter, *Continuing Inquiry*. He was instrumental in helping New Orleans District Attorney Jim Garrison develop his well-publicized charges against Clay Shaw, and he consulted with Oliver Stone when Stone came to Dallas to film *JFK*. By the time Jones, who retired to Waxahachie, thirty miles south of Dallas, passed away in 1998, he had become one of the true legends of the conspiracy movement.[108] He died convinced that Kennedy had been killed by a conspiracy, probably involving military intelligence, and that America could not be redeemed until the murderers were found.

•

Like Penn Jones, Mary Ferrell would also become a major inspiration for those who found something suspicious about the Warren Commission's explanation of the Kennedy assassination. At the time of the assassination, she was a forty-one-year-old legal secretary and mother of four who had moved to Dallas just six years earlier. The morning of November 22, she lunched at the Chaparral Club in the downtown Southland Center, about ten blocks from Dealey Plaza. A lifelong Republican, she had not been interested enough to go down to Elm Street to watch the motorcade.[109] But, like all Dallasites who followed the

107. Bonazzi, "One Man's Grief," 13; Warren Hinckle, *If You Have a Lemon, Make Lemonade* (New York: G. P. Putnam's Sons, 1974), excerpted in Spartacus Educational, accessed July 13, 2012, https://spartacus-educational.com/JFKjonesP.htm.

108. Schlachter, "Penn Jones, JFK theorist, editor."

109. John Kelin, *Praise from a Future Generation: The Assassination of John F. Kennedy and the First Generation Critics of the Warren Report* (San Antonio: Wings Press, 2007), 6, 108.

newscasts that afternoon, she was shocked when she heard about the shooting. She was also astounded that the crime was solved so quickly. Hungry to chronicle the event, she called her husband, Buck, and instructed him to grab their teenage sons and "place one boy at the loading dock of both papers in Dallas to get a copy of each edition that weekend."[110]

Those newspapers would form the foundation for a legendary collection of books, newspapers, magazines, reports, and declassified documents that would earn Ferrell the title "the great archivist." In the following years, she "labored diligently to collect and index everything ever written about the assassination, every document, every clipping, every scrap of potential evidence." Her husband built a room in their backyard to hold the ever-expanding files, and they bought two German shepherds to protect their storehouse. The most famous part of that project was "her ultra-authoritative, supercomplete name index to the JFK assassination." Those original typed and hand-annotated notes fill forty thousand three-by-five-inch index cards and contain an estimated 8,200 names. They are now accessible via the Mary Ferrell Foundation website, "the largest searchable electronic collection of materials related to the JFK assassination" in the world.[111]

A photograph of Mary Ferrell appears on the header of each page of the foundation's website. There, against a black background crossed with the simple and dignified text, "Mary Ferrell Foundation: preserving the legacy," she looks every bit the ordinary, middle-aged Dallas legal secretary and mother described in the foundation's biography. The organization's website, however, is a sophisticated electronic clearinghouse of information, one whose focus is not confined to the JFK assassination. It also features documents relating to other prominent political assassinations and alleged government cover-ups that have occurred since then. It has become one of the most important resources used by the current generation of conspiracy theorists.

Like Penn Jones, Mary Ferrell, who passed away in 2004, will remain an icon among conspiracy theorists. Along with Jones, her initial skepticism about

110. "About Mary Ferrell," *Mary Farrell Foundation,* accessed July 13, 2012, http://www.maryferrell.org/wiki/index.php/About_Mary_Ferrell.

111. Ron Rosenbaum, "Still on the Case," *Texas Monthly,* November 1983.

the assassination investigation produced a body of work that would lay the foundation for a movement that sought to reclaim America from the murderers of the president. As she remarked in Dallas before a 1992 symposium of admiring Kennedy assassination researchers, "a conspiracy and government-sponsored cover-up blotted out the rights of our citizens and sanctity of the rule of law." Like Jones, she challenged the next generation: "If we are truly living in the land of the free and the home of the brave, we'd better damn well prove it now."[112]

•

By the mid-1970s, it was becoming increasingly clear that new technology would be the engine that would drive conspiracy research. Locally, Gary Mack was the "industrious young Turk" who would usher in "the new generation of high-tech audiovisual aids buffs who have supplanted the old-style document-indexing types." In 1975, Mack, a Fort Worth native, was working as program director for that city's KFJZ-FM radio station when he caught Robert Groden's enhanced Zapruder film broadcast on ABC. He was entranced.[113]

In December 1976, just a year later, Gary Mack was meeting with Penn Jones. (He would soon contribute to *The Continuing Inquiry,* eventually start his own journal, *Coverups!,* and become one of the talking heads most sought-after by the plethora of documentary filmmakers who continued to revisit the JFK assassination.) This conversation with Jones focused on the police motorcycle in the presidential motorcade that had activated its radio microphone thirty seconds before the first shot and stayed open for the next five and a half minutes, blocking all police traffic on Channel 1. Mack proposed to Penn that the motorcycle audio tape, if collated with the visual record provided by the Zapruder film, could reveal the pattern and location of the shots in Dealey Plaza. They both agreed this was something to explore, and Gary Mack embarked on a research project that would have profound consequences for the conspiracy movement.

---

112. "About Mary Ferrell."

113. Rosenbaum, "Still on the Case."

When Mack discovered that the available recordings of the original motorcycle tape were of very low quality and would be of no help, it was Mary Ferrell who came to the rescue. Reviewing some of her forty thousand three-by-five-inch index cards, she found that the original tape—the Dictabelt of the transmissions from the motorcycle cop's open mike to police headquarters on November 22—was in a box in a retired police intelligence officer's closet.[114]

The interest generated by Mack's inquiry, along with the hubbub surrounding Groden's repeated screenings of his Zapruder film, helped prompt the formation of the House Select Committee on Assassinations in 1976 and the opening of new investigations into the assassinations of John F. Kennedy and Martin Luther King Jr., and the attempted assassination of Alabama Governor George Wallace. The committee was interested enough in Mack's theory to send an investigative team to Dallas. On August 20 of that year, Dealey Plaza was shut down while four committee staff members, seven acoustic experts, a photographic consultant, thirty-seven Dallas police officers, and two hundred spectators observed the firing of fifty-seven test shots over five hours.

Once the smoke had cleared and the committee issued its final report, it lent support to the idea that there were two gunmen who had fired upon the president. The Dealey Plaza acoustic tests indicated there was a "95 percent probability that a shot came from the grassy knoll." The committee also surmised "that President John F. Kennedy was probably assassinated as the result of a conspiracy."

Conspiracy theorists cheered the final report of the House Select Committee on Assassinations. In many ways, the report was the high-water mark of the conspiracy movement, and Penn Jones, Mary Ferrell, and Gary Mack had all made vital contributions to helping it claim vindication.

•

114. Dale K. Myers, "Acoustics," Secrets of a Homicide: JFK Assassination, accessed August 18, 2012, http://www.jfkfiles.com/jfk/html/acoustics_2.htm; Rosenbaum, "Still on the Case."

In the late 1970s, there was a rising sense of euphoria among local conspiracy theorists, a sense that they were near the truth and that the big cover-up was close to unraveling. Unfortunately, that enthusiasm allowed them to get pulled into the controversy surrounding the "KGB imposter" theory advocated by British writer Michael Eddowes in his book *The Oswald File.* Eddowes claimed that the Oswald who returned from his trip to the Soviet Union in 1962 was not the same man who left—he was a *Manchurian Candidate*–style plant. Mary Ferrell enlisted in the campaign for the exhumation of Oswald's body, "drawing a flotilla of Dallas buffs behind her," even pulling in the assassin's widow. In 1981, Marina Oswald's lawsuit finally led to a very public opening of the tomb at Fort Worth's Rose Hill Cemetery.[115]

When the medical examiner determined that the exhumed body was the same Lee Harvey Oswald who had served in the Marines before he defected to the USSR, it strained the unity of area conspiracy theorists. To exacerbate matters further, Gary Mack, who had become one of the most recognizable faces in the conspiracist movement, would eventually join the "dark side." He signed on as curator at the Sixth Floor Museum, dealing a major blow to the conspiracy researchers who see the museum as a bastion of monolithic Warren Commission orthodoxy.

To make matters worse, the conclusions of the House Select Committee on Assassinations, rather than leading to more breakthroughs, came increasingly under attack. The acoustic evidence suggesting a second shooter was questioned in 1988 after testing by the FBI, then discarded as faulty in 1992 by the National Academy of Science and the Justice Department. As journalist Ron Rosenbaum suggested, that evidence, "like almost every other piece of 'definitive' evidence in the case—is now lost in that limbo of ambiguity, that endless swamp of dispute that swallows up any certainty in the Kennedy case."[116]

•

115. Rosenbaum, "Still on the Case."
116. Rosenbaum, "Still on the Case."

Because of the very public nature of the assassination of John F. Kennedy—it occurred on a major thoroughfare in a major city in a ceremonial motorcade covered by all the major American news media—the American public requires a narrative worthy of the event. Something this visible and momentous needs a story that can make some sense of it. Although we're still struggling with our inability to settle on the exact nature of that narrative, its necessity was clear from the very beginning.

William Manchester, in *The Death of a President*, recounts a moment, maybe ten hours after the shooting, when Jackie Kennedy is beckoned aside by Robert Kennedy. They are in a waiting room at Bethesda Naval Base, waiting as the autopsy is done. He tells her: "They think they've found the man who did it. He says he's a Communist."

> She stared. *Oh, my God*, she thought, *but that's absurd*. Later, she would think about hatred and the highly charged atmosphere of Dallas; at the moment, however, she just felt sickened. It was like existentialism, entirely purposeless, and she thought, *It even robs his death of any meaning.* She returned to her mother. "He didn't even have the satisfaction of being killed for civil rights," she said. "It's—it had to be some silly little Communist."[117]

Even in those traumatic early hours, Jackie Kennedy understood the necessity of forming a meaning-making narrative around the assassination of her husband. Oswald—that "silly little Communist"—would not do. Within a week, Jackie had self-consciously tailored the Camelot allegory, summoning Theodore H. White to the White House and making sure that the editors of *Life* magazine got it down right.[118]

Twenty years later, that romanticized myth of the Kennedy administration had become codified into our modern American version of the Fall—our expulsion from the Garden. The time of the assassin had robbed us of our

---

117. William Manchester, *The Death of a President* (New York: Harper & Row, 1967), 407.

118. Theodore H. White, *In Search of History* (New York: Warner Books, 1978), 665–81.

Golden Age. "Jacqueline Kennedy's farewell to Camelot," wrote Theodore H. White, "was farewell to an America never to be recaptured."[119] As White quoted her in that fateful December 6 article: "*Don't let it be forgot, that once there was a spot, for one brief shining moment that was known as Camelot*—and it will never be that way again."[120]

The Camelot myth fulfilled its original function admirably, enabling the proper heroic memorializing of the young president. But it left us without much to grasp onto. There is a general consensus that the JFK assassination was a historical watershed that changed everything, but it has been a trickier business to determine what type of new world it has left us with.

Norman Mailer diagnosed this condition, this unique cognitive dissonance, in his *Oswald's Tale: An American Mystery* in 1995: "If a figure as large as Kennedy is cheated abruptly of his life, we feel better, inexplicably better, if his killer is also not without size."[121] Oswald, as Jackie recognized immediately, was too absurdly small, too ephemeral—Jack Ruby's rubout job had left nothing for us to flesh out. When polled on the subject, the majority of the American population has repeatedly indicated that they find the "Lee Harvey Oswald as single gunman" story unsatisfying.

The "official" narrative of the assassination, the report of the Warren Commission, has progressively proven less and less convincing to most Americans. From its inception, the committee's task was, more or less, to rubber stamp the original police and press accounts of the assassination. The commission's report did present ample evidence to authenticate the original conclusion that Oswald was the man who killed the president, but something got lost in the translation.

The Warren Commission's report opens with a "Narrative of Events," but presents that narrative in a scant eighteen pages. In the short, single-volume edition of the Warren Commission report published by the *New York Times* in 1964, that narrative gets lost in its 726 pages. Once that volume is

---

119. White, *In Search of History*, 683.

120. Theodore H. White, "For President Kennedy: An Epilogue," *Life*, December 6, 1963, 159.

121. Norman Mailer, *Oswald's Tale: An American Mystery* (New York: Random House, 1995), 607.

supplemented with its twenty-six volumes of supporting documents, the narrative is completely subsumed. There would be no murder trial for Lee Harvey Oswald, no dramatic courtroom revelations. Instead, there would be this library shelf-sized mass of bureaucratic gobbledygook, with all its obligatory supplements, statements of methodology, disclaimers, recommendations, and appendices.

The report of the Warren Commission failed in its mission to provide historical closure. It strove to provide a clear, fully documented narrative supporting the Oswald-as-solo-gunman scenario. But, in twenty-seven volumes, it presented the case with all the messiness, clutter, and ambiguity of real life. As the commission attempted to include everything in order to avoid accusations of participating in a cover-up, the final product turned murkier and murkier. The more encyclopedic the report became, the more loose ends, omissions, and contradictions it contained. "The great volume of information gathered," writes conservative scholar James Piereson, "was never pieced together in the form of a narrative that was understandable to the American people." Rather than convincing the American public of the veracity of its conclusion, the Warren Commission's report ultimately proved to be the greatest source of ammunition for those interested in attacking the "official" version of events. As Piereson also points out, the majority of the Kennedy assassination conspiracy theories "are based on some claimed weakness or inconsistency in the *Warren Report*."[122]

By the mid-1970s, it was the conspiracy theorists, using these attacks on the Warren Commission report, who were producing the most compelling narratives.

•

In Dallas, the original conspiracy was, of course, International Communism. This was the narrative that our city leaders, our police force, and a good number of our citizens clung to in the first days after the assassination. Dallas had

122. James Pierson, *Camelot and the Cultural Revolution* (New York: Encounter Books, 2007), 129.

not killed President Kennedy—it was a Communist! Within hours of the killing, the Dallas Police Department had arrested the killer, and all the evidence showed that he was indeed a self-confessed Marxist and vocal supporter of Fidel Castro. On the day of Oswald's arrest, Assistant District Attorney Bill Alexander had drawn up charges that Oswald had murdered the president "as part of an International Communist conspiracy."[123] Outside political forces, desirous of avoiding a Cold War confrontation with Russia, quickly forced Alexander to drop his international conspiracy approach, but there were also other motivations at play that would discourage casting John F. Kennedy as a victim of the struggle against Communism.

"The thought that Kennedy was a martyr to the Cold War was never seriously considered," notes James Piereson, "though it fit the known facts better than any alternative interpretation." As Piereson—and many other right-wingers today—are eager to point out, Oswald was obviously a Communist and, thus, evidence that the Republican fear of the internal threat of Communism at that time was not an irrational obsession but a legitimate concern.[124] Locally, the framing of Communism as the culprit for the president's death was central in the city's self-defense, and there were many voices nationally who defended Dallas in those same terms. Right-wingers then, however, found themselves stuck in an awkward position. With the shocked nation in mourning, their anti-Communist arguments were preempted by the imperatives of national unity. It was a time of crisis, a time to gather around the fallen leader, not foment political tension.

Inevitably, the memorialization of the dead president was dominated by his supporters. The Kennedy team, recognized masters at working the East Coast establishment media, would control the story. Jacqueline Kennedy, the president's grieving widow, would herself take firm control of the commemorative process and assume the greatest voice in shaping her husband's legacy. As indicated by her first reaction to Oswald's reported Communist affiliations, she was not interested in making her husband a martyr to the Cold War. A Communist assassin in Dallas did not fit a narrative she could accept.

---

123. Manchester, *The Death of a President*, 287.
124. Pierson, *Camelot and the Cultural Revolution*, 59.

Moreover, Oswald himself did not prove to be a particularly fearsome example of the Communist menace. The Communist Party would not claim him, and Oswald had denounced the Soviet Union as a failed society when he returned to the US from Russia in 1962. He had even failed in his efforts to establish any contact with Cuba. He was clearly more of a hopeless loser than a lone-wolf agent of chaos. As Cold War paranoia decreased and the country moved toward détente, Oswald's Communist affiliation became less and less a part of the public debate.

Dallasites who clung to the assertion that the president was a victim of the war against Communism were perceived, more and more, to be, themselves, victims of an outmoded Cold War paranoia.

•

If Communist conspiracy didn't kill the president, then who or what did? From the beginning, there was a mad scramble to establish a purpose for JFK's death, to give it meaning as a sacrifice for *something*. As Jacqueline Kennedy understood almost immediately, the demise of a man of his stature must provide some sort of edification for the nation he led. While the exact nature of his martyrdom had to be worked out, there was, within hours of the president's death, already a working script. Chief Justice of the Supreme Court Earl Warren observed in a written statement on the afternoon of the assassination: "A great and good President has suffered martyrdom as a result of the hatred and bitterness that has been interjected into the life of our nation by Bigots."[125]

The president had died, the story would go, not because of an external campaign he was waging against Communism, but because of the internal fight he led on behalf of various progressive causes, especially civil rights. He had been killed by the irrational Right, the hate-filled opponents of his liberal policies. For the locals, unfortunately, this narrative would require that Dallas be a punching bag, the stand-in for all of the president's right-wing political opposition.

This story had already begun to write itself before John F. Kennedy got

125. Pierson, *Camelot and the Cultural Revolution*, 92.

off Air Force One at Love Field. There was already the expectation that trouble was waiting for the president in Dallas. No matter how many enthusiastic citizens met the Kennedy motorcade on the streets of Dallas on November 22, 1963, what most Americans would remember about the city was LBJ and Lady Bird being spat upon in the Adolphus Hotel lobby, or Adlai Stevenson being knocked on the head by a sign-waving superpatriot outside the Dallas Memorial Auditorium Theater. The popular predilection would be to remember the "Wanted for Treason" flyers that peppered the city before the president's visit. People, even Dallasites, would remember that when the first shots rang out, their initial suspicions were that Dallas right-wingers were responsible. They'd remember how the list of possible suspects had scrolled through their heads: right-wing oilmen? John Birchers? Maybe the supporters of Edwin Walker, the former US Army general whom Robert Kennedy recently had institutionalized after his participation in the anti-integration riots at the University of Mississippi?

Dallas had already earned itself the title the "City of Hate," and, as a high-profile hot spot of conservative fervor, would make the perfect civic foil for the manufacturing of John F. Kennedy as a civil rights martyr. It was already enemy territory before he arrived. The president himself, when presented the notorious "Welcome Mr. Kennedy" ad in the *Dallas Morning News* on the morning of his arrival in Dallas, had called the area "nut country."[126]

Of course, a Dallas right-wing zealot did not kill John F. Kennedy; Lee Harvey Oswald did. Locals were quick to point out—and the *Warren Report* confirmed it—Oswald *was* a Communist sympathizer. He emerged from the far left, not the right. The political atmosphere in Dallas, they insisted, *did not* contribute to the killing of the president. But we could not exonerate ourselves; we could pose no argument that could effectively quiet our accusers. We would be the "City of Hate." We had sown the seeds and now we had to reap our just reward. There was no way to retell the story—that train had left the station.

Within a week of the assassination, the newly sworn-in president, Lyndon Johnson, addressed Congress. "No memorial oration or eulogy

126. Manchester, *The Death of a President*, 121.

could more eloquently honor President Kennedy's memory," he said "than the earliest possible passage of the civil rights bill for which he fought so long."[127] Using the same script as Jackie, LBJ's message was that Kennedy had died for civil rights; his life was about confronting racism and bigotry. LBJ would purposely use the emotions aroused by Kennedy's death to push through the landmark Civil Rights Act of 1964, along with much of the liberal legislation that would define his Great Society. In retrospect, JFK's death undeniably provided a huge impetus for civil rights legislation and a more progressive America.

Like all martyrs, Kennedy would become something else after his death. Dallas, however, would be stuck with the history it had made for itself prior to his assassination—it would remain the "City of Hate."

•

What would eventually save Dallas and allow us to escape the pall of national reproach for our role as in the killing of a president was the expansion of the conspiracy narrative. While our defensive talk refuting our reputation as the "City of Hate" seemed only to draw more attention to our failings, we could take some solace in the fact that attention was being increasingly diverted away from Dallas toward other culprits. As the alleged assassination plots grew larger and more elaborate, it seemed clear that the murder of John F. Kennedy was beyond the capabilities of a single tight-knit group in one locale. The stories made it obvious: this thing was bigger than just Dallas.

By the late 1960s, a more complex world was replacing the black-and-white "Communism vs. Capitalism" paradigm, and Kennedy's original Cold War adversaries, the Russians and Castro, were being replaced by a growing list of internal assassination suspects. Kennedy's right-wing foes—Texas millionaires concerned about their oil depletion allowance and violent opponents of civil rights—were joined by a raft of new suspects. There were rogue CIA agents intent on revenge for the president's failures at the Bay of Pigs, out-of-control imperialists angry about his rumored plans to abandon Vietnam,

127. Pierson, *Camelot and the Cultural Revolution*, 93.

Pentagon militarists fearful of losing war profits, police-state extremists like J. Edgar Hoover eager to protect their turf, and mobsters angered by Attorney General Robert Kennedy's constant attacks. There were a thousand possible variations, a million schemes and plots with all sorts of unseemly amalgamations of culprits. The bottom line in all of these scenarios was that somehow John F. Kennedy had challenged these forces, and, to protect their malevolent activities, these forces had killed him.

But it wasn't all just about Kennedy. Another game was afoot. "A conspiracy theory," James Piereson writes in his 2007 *Camelot and the Cultural Revolution*, "is a moral explanation of things gone wrong, at once an account of how things happened and also an assignment of blame against those responsible." By the late 1970s, the big conspiracy story, as "an understandable attempt to impose order and meaning on a confused and perplexing situation," had to explain an entire country that had, since the JFK assassination, come to perceive itself as in decline. When Jimmy Carter delivered his "Crisis of Confidence" speech in 1979, the conflicts of the sixties and the continuing civil rights struggle had become more complex and problematic. We had suffered through defeat in Vietnam and the fiasco of Watergate. Consequently, JFK conspiracy theories expanded to include these larger concerns, growing until they "dovetailed with the emerging radical critique of American society as violent, racist, and corrupt." [128]

Then the expanding conspiracy narrative began to gain official sanction from the federal government itself. America's late-1970s obsession with self-scrutiny manifested itself in a series of post Watergate congressional investigations: the 1975 Rockefeller Commission, the Church Committee in 1975–76, and the House Select Committee on Assassinations in 1978. These inquiries repeatedly reopened questions about the Kennedy assassination. Senator Richard Schweiker, for instance, commenting on national TV on his experience on the Church Committee, charged that CIA and FBI officials had engaged in various JFK assassination–related cover-ups, and that the recent inquiries had caused the *Warren Report* to collapse "like

128. Pierson, *Camelot and the Cultural Revolution*, 108, 112, 126.

a house of cards."[129] Just as significantly, these congressional investigations brought to public view a plethora of additional governmental misdeeds that pointed to a larger pattern of official malfeasance. The American people were informed that the FBI had initiated a plot to blackmail Martin Luther King Jr. over details of his sex life, and that the CIA conspired with the mob to have Fidel Castro killed. They learned there was a systematic pattern of illegal surveillance within America involving the unethical use of governmental agencies and even the opening of personal mail. They learned that, overseas, our intelligence services had initiated numerous assassination plots and attempts to subvert foreign governments.

These congressional investigations brought to light a secret, cloak-and-dagger world—a world that operates just below the surface of our own, where the rules are different. Underneath the orderly workings of our democracy, it seems, was a secret government. It was, in short, the world the conspiracy theorists had been warning us about. As a result, the Kennedy assassination came to serve, more and more, as a central hub around which all these other interlinking conspiracy tales could orbit.

As the nefarious forces confronting American democracy multiplied into a huge, nebulous, far-flung conspiratorial network, the image of Kennedy himself expanded. While recent historical appraisals of his short presidency tend to depict him, despite his rhetorical ambition, as a cautious, pragmatic liberal, his cultural representation trends in the opposite direction. "Kennedy came to be viewed," Piereson writes, "as a liberal visionary and path-breaker, more as a revolutionary cultural figure."[130] This John F. Kennedy, the story goes, shook up the existing order to such an extent that the powers that be could no longer tolerate his existence. The fact that his brother Robert Kennedy was assassinated during his 1968 presidential campaign amplified John F. Kennedy's personal martyrdom into a family martyrdom. Chronicled by an American media entranced by its charismatic and glamorous characters, the political saga of the Kennedy

---

129. Richard Schweiker, interview on *Face the Nation*, June 27, 1976, transcript, CBS.

130. Pierson, *Camelot and the Cultural Revolution*, 29.

family has been propelled into a realm of mythic depiction unique in modern American political history.

In late-twentieth-century America, the various representations of the Kennedy Camelot myth have made compelling drama and been staples of our increasingly celebrity-crazed media culture. The flipside of that Camelot mythology has become, more and more, the Big Conspiracy. If Camelot was our Golden Age, then the story of its fall requires a compelling narrative; the glorified and martyred ruler needs a properly substantial antagonist. A Big Conspiracy, with its shadowy tentacles rooted in the mire of American political corruption, was just the thing.

In both T. H. White's book *The Once and Future King* and the Broadway adaptation that Jackie Kennedy drew from, King Arthur moved to establish a government based on reason and civility, opposing the forces of darkness and disorder. Likewise, John F. Kennedy (and, later, his brother Robert) fought against reactionary forces in order to move America forward. In the Camelot myth, the kingdom falls apart from within. The noble ambitions of the ruler—in the New Frontier just as at the Round Table—come to a tragic end because the internal forces that the rulers sought to eradicate conspire to destroy them. Just as England falls from its Golden Age because of the betrayals of Arthur's half-sister Morgause, his bastard son Mordred, and his most trusted knight, Lancelot, so our own American Camelot is undone by the internal rot of the Big Conspiracy.

It's all there—the conflation of the Camelot and conspiracy myths—in the "Preface" of prominent local conspiracy author Jim Marrs's *Crossfire: The Plot That Killed Kennedy*. Marrs is, like many of his fellow conspiracy investigators, looking not just for criminals—the murderers of one man—but something much bigger, almost mythical. "Not only do I seek the killers of President Kennedy," he tells us. "I seek the persons who killed Camelot—who killed the confidence and faith of the American people in their government and institutions."[131]

131. Jim Marrs, "Preface," in *Crossfire: The Plot That Killed Kennedy* (New York: Carroll & Graf, 1989).

•

By the mid-1970s, a new type of modern freedom fighter was taking shape—the conspiracy theorist. These individuals spoke a language of desperate American patriotism, proclaiming that they had appeared out of the countryside, common citizens like the original Minutemen, to do nothing less than to save America. On August 22, 1976, just a month and a half after the celebration of the country's two-hundredth anniversary, Penn Jones Jr. mailed out the first edition of *The Continuing Inquiry,* his monthly newsletter and follow-up to *Forgive My Grief.* On the opening page, Jones proclaimed that "[o]ur democracy is in mortal danger." A president had been murdered, and "[i]t is now established beyond a doubt that killings are being accomplished in order to maintain the cover-up." Jones warned that all the monstrous powers of the social order—the legal profession, law enforcement, the government, the media—were now working together to perpetuate that cover-up. Like Paul Revere, Jones and his fellow conspiracists were "shouting the danger signal."[132] They were linked together by what, according to Norman Mailer, had become our "national obsession": finding out who was behind the assassination of John F. Kennedy.[133]

By 1976, the conspiracy tale was already becoming the story of the age. *The Parallax View* by Loren Singer, published in 1970, was just one of a growing tide of post-Kennedy assassination conspiracy novels. By the time noted director Alan Pakula turned it into a major Hollywood film in 1974, the JFK conspiracy film *Executive Action* had already been in the theaters for a year. If Penn Jones had gone to the theater to catch a screening of *The Parallax View,* he might very well have seen something of himself in the film's lead character. Joe Frady, played by Warren Beatty, is, like Jones, a newspaper man who finds himself confronted with evidence of the cover-up of the assassination of an important political figure. As Frady digs deeper and gets closer to uncovering the truth behind the killing, the bodies begin to pile up: his former girlfriend

132. Penn Jones Jr., "Our Aim," *The Continuing Inquiry* I, no. 1, August 22, 1976.

133. Mailer, "Footfalls In The Crypt," cited in Stone and Sklar, *JFK: The Book of the Film,* 444.

dies of an apparent drug overdose; a small-town sheriff drowns; a bomb explodes aboard a yacht, then an airplane; finally, his editor is poisoned.

Jones would certainly have noted the unmistakable congruency between *The Parallax View* and his own reporting. It was Penn Jones who had, in his *Forgive My Grief* series and the 1966 article in *The Ramparts,* pointed out to the world the remarkable number of deaths that occurred among assassination-related figures between November 1963 and November 1965. Jones had documented 188 deaths during that short period, many of them occurring, he claimed, under very suspicious circumstances. The thrill Jones might have experienced in seeing his investigative work dramatically replicated on the big screen might have been tempered, however, by the film's conclusion: Frady, framed for murder, is gunned down by an assassin. Shortly after his death, his guilt is confirmed by a Warren Commission–like official tribunal.

While Penn Jones himself had never been chased by mysterious cars, shot at by snipers, or threatened with poisoning, he might have experienced a deeply held sympathy for Joe Frady. Jones understood the dilemma of those few who had been called to the ominous task of "shouting the danger signal" as well as anyone. He also understood that, in the real world, the serious conspiracy theorists did not have to be killed because very few people took them that seriously. Like Frady in *Parallax View,* Jones and his fellow conspiracy theorists were realizing that it was not enough to discover the truth. You had to convince a cynical and apathetic public. What had emerged as a common trope of the conspiracy movie—the hero, proclaiming the truth, being shunned and pronounced crazy by the very public he would save—became a constant concern for the real-life conspiracy theorist.

The great irony was that people *were* listening; the masses were, theoretically, with them. All the polls consistently showed that the great majority of those people asked did not believe Oswald acted alone. The evidence indicated that most people assumed President Kennedy's murder had been the result of some sort of conspiracy, and that the *Warren Report* should not be trusted as the final word. These same people had been flocking in droves to buy pulp novels based on conspiracy themes and had been making conspiracy-based films big box-office hits. Penn Jones himself had become a media figure, attracting a significant amount of national press coverage to the cause.

For the true believers, however, a huge gulf separated them from the apathetic general public. They felt a real frustration with the vagueness of the public's apprehension of the issue. What to the conspiracy theorists was an existential crisis often seemed, to the general public, a suitable source for entertainment. The masses had not worked out the consequences: if the president had been killed in a conspiracy, it meant our democracy had been hijacked, and we were actually ruled by a secret government, one completely beyond our control. Yet, despite what the American people told the pollsters, there was no huge movement to get to the bottom of things. Like Joe Frady, Penn Jones and his followers often felt the isolation of being the lone voice crying in the wilderness.

If the conspiracy theorists often felt like outcasts, they at least had each other. There were a lot of them, and they were academics, lawyers, teachers, private investigators, journalists, and experts in any number of arcane forms of knowledge. They were, by and large, competent and professional; they were not insane. Nor were they going away. They had kept the JFK assassination debate alive, kept the case open and under investigation, and, if they had not experienced the big breakthrough yet, they would continue the work until they did.

Increasingly, they referred to themselves as "researchers," and saw information itself as their primary weapon. Like Penn Jones, they established networks to stay in contact with each other and published newsletters like *The Continuing Inquiry*. Already they were finding ways to get their work distributed by publishers, large and small, and soon they would update to new technology—email LISTSERVs, online chat groups, then assassination-related blogs. As they forged links, sharing all manner of conspiracy-related information, they also began to develop a type of conspiracy theorist professionalism. They established informal standards and rules of conduct, critiqued each other's methodology, and weeded out the obvious kooks who would do damage to the cause. While it was often hard and thankless work, somebody had to save America.

•

Finally, the one voice that would get people to listen, that could not be ignored, was Oliver Stone. After the filmmaker blew through Dallas in the early 1990s, the conspiracy movement would enter the mainstream in a way it never had before. Stone's *JFK* would act as a lightning rod for conspiracy theorists, crystallizing the conspiracy vision into a compelling new cinematic narrative. After the film, conspiracists would no longer be lone voices crying in the wilderness—they would take command of their story.

Stone had something important to say, and he was as ambitious as a filmmaker could be. Working with Warner Brothers, his Camelot Productions poured $40 million into the production of *JFK* and produced a three-hour epic. It was nominated for eight Academy Awards, including Best Picture, and ultimately won the Best Cinematography and Best Film Editing awards. It grossed more than $205 million worldwide. Most importantly, it ignited a broil of controversy, returning the JFK assassination, almost thirty years after the event, to the center of the national consciousness.

Stone dove into that debate, taking on all comers. In his *JFK: The Book of the Film*, Stone published the work of his many prominent critics and then appended his own acerbic responses. In both the film and his myriad public pronouncements, the director was vehement: a huge injustice had been perpetrated and the nation was being held hostage by a conspiracy cover-up. "The achievement of the film is not that it answers the mystery of the Kennedy assassination," wrote Roger Ebert in his review of *JFK*. "Its achievement is that it tries to marshal the anger which ever since 1963 has been gnawing away on some dark shelf of the national psyche."[134]

JFK was the conspiracy movie of all conspiracy movies, a no-holds-barred act of cinematic propaganda aimed at revivifying the conspiracy myth. There was intense debate about its historical veracity, but Stone was adamant that those debates were a red herring—those same issues existed with the *Warren Report*. He knew his film could offer something that those twenty-seven volumes of loose ends and incomplete investigations could not: a clear and compelling narrative. With a little poetic license and the dream

---

134. Roger Ebert, "JFK," review of *JFK*, directed by Oliver Stone, *Chicago Sun-Times*, December 20, 1991.

machinery of American film, *JFK* tied up all those loose ends and gave us a story with a coherence that the official version lacked. Armed with that coherence (one that crystallizes much of their previous research), the conspiracy theorists took command of their story—they would no longer be lone voices crying in the wilderness.

Stone himself described the film *JFK* as a "counter-myth" to the "fictional myth" of the Warren Commission. But Norman Mailer best summed up Stone's approach. "Several generations have already grown up with the mind-stultifying myth of the lone assassin," he wrote in the 1992 *JFK: The Book of the Film*. "Let cinematic hyperbole war then with the Establishment's skewed reality. At times, bullshit can only be countered with superior bullshit."[135]

•

By the time Dallas caught wind of rumors that Oliver Stone was coming to town to film a JFK movie, he had not only begun scouting locations. He had also established serious connections with the local conspiracy research community. In fact, before Stone had even opened negotiations with city officials about the necessary permits and permissions, he had made the rounds in the area's conspiracy underground. He consulted with conspiracy pioneer Penn Jones Jr., looked into the current research Gary Mack was doing on "Badgeman"—the grassy knoll shooter Mack proposed was evident in a blown-up and enhanced witness photograph of Dealey Plaza—and brought on Robert Groden, who would move to Dallas three years later, as a primary technical advisor.

Stone's arrival was a true godsend for the struggling JFK Assassination Information Center. Located on the third floor of West End Marketplace, an old warehouse-turned-shopping-mall located three blocks north of Dealey Plaza, the center's stated mission was to educate the public and act as a clearinghouse of assassination information. As you entered its three-thousand-square-foot

135. Mailer, "Footfalls in the Crypt," cited in Stone and Sklar, *JFK: The Book of the Film*, 447.

exhibition and office space, you'd see, on one side, continuously running video highlights of the assassination and, on the other, looming life-sized photographs of Ruby and Oswald. Above Oswald was printed the quotation: "No, sir, I didn't kill anybody. I'm just a patsy." Near that was another quotation, this one from mobster Carlos Marcello, often rumored to be involved in the JFK conspiracy: "Three can keep a secret, if two of them are dead."

Stone flew Larry Howard, who helped run the JFK Assassination Information Center, to Hollywood to hear his pitch, and he liked what he heard. When Stone returned to Dallas, he arranged a deal that would pay the struggling center $80,000 for its most important asset—access to twenty-one key local witnesses, including Marina Oswald, former District Attorney Henry Wade, and James Leavelle, the lawman handcuffed to Oswald when he was shot.[136]

While Stone has been roundly criticized for "fictionalizing" the assassination, he did go to extraordinary lengths to document his conspiracy assertions (his *JFK: The Book of The Film* contains the fully annotated screenplay). A legendary stickler for detail, Stone also put great effort into getting the look of 1963 Dallas right. Larry Howard was on the set every day with Stone and saw the director at work. "During the filmmaking, Oliver asked me things like the exact license plate number on every car in the motorcade," he said. "He wanted the inspection stickers exactly like they were in 1963. He wanted the trees cut back to the size they were in 1963. He wanted the fence just right. The clock had to be just right at the Texas Theatre, exactly on the minute. He wanted this to be as historically correct as it could be." Historical truth, however, had its limitations—this was movie mythmaking. "There are things we don't know," admitted Howard. "And it's not a documentary. It's a motion picture."[137]

•

136. Gary Cartwright, "I Was Mandarin," *Texas Monthly*, December 1990, cited in Gary Cartwright, *Turn Out the Lights: Chronicles of Texas During the 80s and 90s* (Austin: University of Texas Press, 2000), 187–88.

137. Grover B. Proctor Jr., "Larry Howard: A Man Under Fire," *The Saginaw News*, December 21, 1991.

Oliver Stone built his *JFK* upon two foundational texts. The first was *On the Trail of the Assassins* by former New Orleans District Attorney Jim Garrison. That book was Stone's original inspiration for the film, and Garrison's story forms the core of *JFK*'s plot. The second text was *Crossfire: The Plot That Killed Kennedy* by former Dallas journalist Jim Marrs.

Marrs's *Crossfire* gave Stone a wealth of ideas to work with. At six hundred pages, this 1989 publication is a grand compendium of every major JFK conspiracy theory then in circulation. Marrs, an expert compiler and synthesizer, cast a wide net, poking holes in the official lone gunman version of the assassination with a comprehensive listing of every known challenge to its veracity.

Nevertheless, Marrs admits that because of the nature of the cover-up, there is still difficulty in determining exactly what happened on November 22, 1963. "Since so much information concerning the plot to kill Kennedy has been destroyed, altered, or masked by false leads, it remains impossible to state with authority details of the plan." However, Marrs does offer what he calls "A Likely Scenario." "The Kennedy assassination was a true coup d'état—a sudden and violent shift in power to the right in this country."

In Jim Marrs, Stone found the perfect fellow traveler. *Crossfire* gave Stone a model for connecting all the dots into one nefarious, all-encompassing plot. Stone's film, like Marrs's book, assembled its grab bag of theories in just such a way as to demonstrate, as Marrs puts it, that, "Camelot was killed from within, by men whose fear and ambition overpowered their faith and loyalty to the United States Constitution and the people it was designed to protect."[138]

•

Jim Marrs hadn't always been so concerned with the legacy of John F. Kennedy. He was born in 1943 and grew up on the south side of Fort Worth. Like the earlier noted Dallas writers Bud Shrake and Dan Jenkins, he attended Paschal High School and fell into journalism while working on the school paper. He enrolled at the nearby University of North Texas (then North

138. Marrs, *Crossfire*, 580, 590.

Texas State University) in the early sixties to continue his journalism studies. He was asleep in his Denton dorm room on November 22, 1963, when his roommate woke him to tell him the news. All Marrs could say then was one word: "Good." Marrs admits to being a "typical Texas redneck" at the time. Like many in North Texas, he assumed that Kennedy was determined to hand the country over to liberals and Blacks, and that his assassination was the work of "Commies."

As an ambitious student of journalism, Marrs was already wondering how he might get involved in the biggest news story to ever come out of North Texas. He eventually ended up back in Fort Worth at the *Star-Telegram*, and occasionally found himself in Dallas covering stories. Marrs took those opportunities to investigate what really happened in 1963. As he talked to Oswald's friends, like George de Mohrenschildt, and Oswald's mother, Marguerite, he became more and more suspicious. Occasionally, he wrote a story on the assassination for the *Star-Telegram*, but his focus became much more concentrated in 1976 when he was asked to teach a course on the assassination for the University of Texas at Arlington (a growing mid-city outpost of the state university system). In 1980, Marrs quit the Fort Worth paper, took occasional freelance work in Dallas, and started the serious research that would eventually become *Crossfire*.

Marrs devoted himself obsessively to his conspiracy work. Within months of the 1981 shooting of President Ronald Reagan, his name popped up in *D Magazine*. There, he proposed that the Reagan shooting might not have involved, as the mainstream press suggested, only John Hinckley Jr. There might have been a second gunman, possibly the pawn of a top-secret government program that could induce a person, against his will, to commit a *Manchurian Candidate*–style assassination.[139] Marrs's JFK assassination course became an ever more popular fixture at UTA, and, with his impressive book sales after the 1989 release of *Crossfire*, Marrs could not escape the attention of the newest flag-bearer of the conspiracy brigade: Oliver Stone.[140]

139. "Twenty Questions: Who Shot Reagan?" *D Magazine*, December 1, 1981.

140. Robert Wilonsky, "The truth is way out there," *Dallas Observer*, July 6, 2000.

•

Jim Marrs, who passed away in 2017, was not the hero type. Affable and bearded, he was typical of the researchers who are the shock troopers of the conspiracy battles. They generally work in the arcane worlds of libraries and archives, scrutinizing film in photo studios or reviewing evidence in laboratories—these are their battlefields. Marrs must have been ecstatic then, during the filming of *JFK,* to hear the text of *Crossfire* transformed and dramatically delivered by A-list Hollywood star Kevin Costner.

Stone had brought on Costner to play the starring role of Jim Garrison, the New Orleans district attorney who had, with the 1969 trial of Clay Shaw, presented the only JFK assassination–related charges ever brought to court. Like Stone himself, Garrison was passionate, tireless, and single-minded. Using all the resources he could muster as the district attorney of New Orleans, Garrison had single-handedly taken on the powers that be to bring the JFK conspiracy into the public eye. In Stone's hands, this galvanizing figure in the conspiracy debates would become the ultimate conspiracy hero.

The most important element the Garrison story provided Oliver Stone was the courtroom scenario. In American theater, there is no better stage on which to work out the themes of justice and truth than the courtroom. When Jack Ruby shot Lee Harvey Oswald, he denied the American public an important ritual: a trial. Stone's restaging of *State of Louisiana v. Clay L. Shaw* would remedy that. The crime of the century would have its day in court.

Stone's compacted reenactment of the Garrison trial, running from February 15 to March 1, 1969, would be the grand finale of *JFK.* Kevin Costner as Jim Garrison, the brave and passionate crusader for truth, would seek to prove that New Orleans businessman Clay Shaw had sought to conspire with David W. Ferrie, Lee Harvey Oswald, and other shady New Orleans figures to murder John F. Kennedy.

From Garrison's original closing arguments, Stone fashioned an extended monologue, interwoven with numerous flashbacks, which climaxed in the film's dramatic final summation. The scene displays Stone's great technical brilliance, but also the ambition of his storytelling. In this final courtroom scene, Stone transcends his influences. He's both more passionate than Marrs and more articulate than Garrison, and he adds historical and literary flourishes not to be found in either *Crossfire* or *On the Trail of the Assassins*. (Stone, along with cowriter Zachary Sklar, was nominated for an Academy Award for Best Adapted Screenplay.) "The President was murdered by a conspiracy planned in advance at the highest levels of the United States government and carried out by fanatical and disciplined Cold Warriors in the Pentagon and CIA's covert operations apparatus," Costner's Jim Garrison tells the jury. "It was a public execution and it was covered up by like-minded individuals in the Dallas Police Department, the Secret Service, the FBI, and the White House—all the way up to and including J. Edgar Hoover and Lyndon Johnson."[141]

In the hands of Oliver Stone, *State of Louisiana v. Clay L. Shaw* became an epic confrontation, the stakes of which were nothing less than the fate of America. The conspiracy theorists had finally found that oracle who could fully elucidate the import of their cause. The closing segment in *JFK* has Garrison, sitting alongside his Deep Throat–like source on a park bench in Washington, DC, musing about the consequences of the assassination and its cover-up: "Just think . . . just think. What happened to our country . . . to the world . . . because of the murder . . . Vietnam, racial conflict, breakdown of law, drugs, thought control, guilt, assassination, secret government, fear of the frontier . . . "

In the climactic moment of his courtroom summary, Costner's Garrison intones: "We have all become Hamlets in our country—children of a slain father-leader whose killers still possess the throne. The ghost of John F. Kennedy confronts us with the secret murder at the heart of the American dream."[142] By his audacity, Oliver Stone had come to Dallas and galvanized the debate on the death of John F. Kennedy. Conspiracy researchers nationwide, seeing their research dramatized so potently on the big screen by a spokesman as fearless and influential as Oliver Stone, were reinvigorated. Jim Marrs, and the rest of the local conspiracy community that Stone had so carefully cultivated, were now happily assured of a much higher profile for their work.

141. Marrs, *Crossfire*, 177–78.

142. Stone and Sklar, *JFK: The Book of the Film*, 176–78, 183.

•

These triumphant notes aside, Garrison lost his case. Stone's *JFK* ends just after the jury returns to the courtroom and declares Clay Shaw innocent of all charges. Jim Garrison's big gamble has failed. As he leaves the court, accosted by the jackals of the press, he is unrepentant. He will not quit: "If it takes me thirty years to nail every one of the assassins, then I will continue this investigation for thirty years. I owe that not only to Jack Kennedy, but to my country."[143]

Stone's message is that the story is not over. When Garrison lost his 1969 case, he was disgraced—ostracized, even—by many in the conspiracy community for going too far. There was general agreement that his overreaching had done great damage to the conspiracy-hunting cause. Two decades later, however, here was a big-screen reincarnation of Jim Garrison, reviving interest in the cause to an unprecedented level. The case would continue to be retried in the imaginations of every viewer who witnessed Oliver Stone's JFK.

Across America, Stone's film caused immense controversy, much of it focusing on his use—or abuse—of history. By the early 1990s, the historical record was a quagmire where it seemed every fact was in dispute. Journalists, law officers, politicians, and researchers had engaged in such incessant wrangling that there was no agreed-upon bottom line on which to build consensus. There had been so much written about the case that it was nearly impossible for the layman to distinguish between good and bad, truth and untruth. One could despair completely of ever finding firm footing in the body of work called, paradoxically, nonfiction. Most reputable historians, loath to step into the muck, wisely chose to wait it out until things had settled down.

Ironically, the most important work dealing with the JFK assassination published over the last thirty years has not been investigative journalism or history. Rather, the enlightening work resides in the realm of social mythology. Hadn't Stone himself described *JFK* as a "counter-myth" to the "fictional myth" of the Warren Commission? From the beginning, hadn't the narrative of the JFK assassination been fraught with popular mythology? First, there

143. Marrs, *Crossfire*, 181.

was Camelot; then, increasingly, there was the conspiracy myth, "an understandable attempt to impose order and meaning on a confused and perplexing situation." The assassination had become the parable for the age. So, with the world of fact stuck in a stasis of dispute, it was perhaps inevitable that most of the significant recent work dealing with the JFK assassination would be fictional.

•

Don DeLillo's novel *Libra* was published in 1988, just as Oliver Stone was beginning to formulate his ideas for *JFK*. It was one of the landmark books of the decade, and a telling emanation of our increasing national obsession with conspiracy and the JFK assassination. Unlike the assassination thrillers that had preceded it in such numbers that they came to form their own genre, DeLillo's *Libra* was concerned with the process of the making of the story as much as with the story itself. With *Libra*, DeLillo achieved that rare feat of producing a novel that was both a bestseller and a postmodern examination of the construction of reality.

DeLillo's authorial alter-ego in *Libra* is Nicholas Branch, a retired senior CIA analyst assigned to write the secret history of the assassination of President Kennedy. To Branch, the twenty-seven volumes of the *Warren Report* are "the megaton novel James Joyce would have written if he'd moved to Iowa City and lived to be a hundred," the unfinished "Book of America" in which "nothing is left out." Branch, throughout *Libra*, sits in his one-room apartment as every possible piece of assassination information is provided to him. Everything ever published or produced in any form is at his disposal—a huge, impossible sprawl of information.[144] Woven around Branch and his attempt to create a single, coherent history of the JFK assassination are the narratives of the active participants in the assassination conspiracy: a host of CIA plotters, various subterranean schemers, and Oswald himself. As these characters, already moving in an underworld hidden beneath our apparent reality, create their various aliases and conspire in their creation of alternate

144. DeLillo, *Libra*, 181–82.

narratives, it becomes clear that the conspiracy cover-up is the ultimate constructed story. Like a Russian matryoshka doll, it features stories nested within stories, smaller plots within larger ones, and, if the conspiracy is successful, the real story is, ultimately, unknowable. As DeLillo propels his quasi-historical figures toward the fated event, a refrain surfaces, to be repeated again and again: "There is a world inside the world."

At the conclusion of *Libra*, Nicholas Branch is still trapped in his room, attempting to write the final, definitive history of the event, and "he knows he can't get out. The case will haunt him to the end." Like all of us, he knows the president is dead, but he can't quite bring the story into exact focus. Ultimately, he is stuck in his own "world inside the world," his "room of growing old, the room of history and dreams."[145]

•

Like DeLillo's *Libra*, James Ellroy's Underworld USA trilogy is a major rewriting of the JFK assassination conspiracy narrative. It comprises three novels published between 1995 and 2009: *American Tabloid*, *The Cold Six Thousand*, and *Blood's a Rover*. Even more ambitious than *Libra*, Ellroy's trilogy, which he describes as his "secret history" of the mid to late twentieth century, takes on that large arc of American history that stretches from just before the JFK assassination through the assassinations of both MLK and Robert Kennedy to the years just before Watergate.[146] Also like DeLillo's novel, Ellroy's series chronicles a group of rogue American law enforcement officers who, entangled in a web of interconnecting associations between the FBI, CIA, and Mafia, eventually become important players in the big conspiracies that transform American history. While Oliver Stone's *JFK* self-consciously reshaped the assassination conspiracy narrative to promote the Camelot myth and exhort us to find its destroyers, Ellroy's game is to "demythologize" the era. He is intent on bringing down the castle of Camelot: "America was never

145. DeLillo, *Libra*, 445.

146. Keith Phipps, "James Ellroy," interview, *AV Club*, December 1, 2004, https://www.avclub.com/james-ellroy-1798221577.

innocent," he asserts. "Jack got whacked at the optimum moment to assure his sainthood." Kennedy was, according to Ellroy, simply "the mythological front man for a particularly juicy slice of our history."[147]

While DeLillo uses the cool, detached prose of postmodernism in *Libra,* Ellroy's novels are wonders of the hyper-noir style, mixing the staccato cadences of gangster films with percolating hipster jargon. Taking his reader on a roller-coaster ride that links John and Robert Kennedy, Martin Luther King, drug running in Southeast Asia, mob action in Cuba, Howard Hughes, Jimmy Hoffa, and J. Edger Hoover, Ellroy, like DeLillo, creates a comprehensive "world inside the world," using the great explanatory power of the conspiracy tale to connect the dots.

Both DeLillo and Ellroy work within history, but traditional historical truth is not their specific concern. Ellroy concedes he is content with "a reckless verisimilitude," and DeLillo has called *Libra* "a work of imagination" that "makes no claim to literal truth" but might serve as "a way of thinking about the assassination."[148] Their novels are ambitious works, in some ways attempts to sum up an entire historical epoch. The irony—or paradox—of fiction is that it creates small stories that tell the bigger tale. In this regard, the JFK conspiracy saga has proven to be a particularly potent mode for telling the tale of our troubled age.

As Lawrence Wright writes in his memoir of growing up in Dallas, *In the New World*: "The assassination sent a shaft through our society, throwing unexpected light on creatures used to the dark—spies, mobsters, informers, mistresses, all of them surprised in strange alliances. It would forever change our understanding of how our country worked." Observing the volume and variety of stories we have told ourselves about the assassination, Wright further notes: "It is odd that a single moment of reality—Oswald's assassination of Kennedy—can be folded and refolded into infinite origami constructions." The consequences of the creation of these stories, Wright realizes, are profoundly important; they are "a way of explaining everything, of giving meaning to events."

147. James Ellroy, *American Blood* (New York:Vintage, 1995), 3.
148. Ellroy, *American Blood,* 3; DeLillo, "Author's Note," in *Libra.*

As he closes this meditative passage, Wright offers a final question: "Reality is twisted into art. Is there such a thing finally as truth?"[149]

•

By 1980, the general populace was much more concerned with who shot J. R. than who shot JFK. First airing in the spring of 1978, the prime-time soap opera *Dallas* had become a runaway hit for CBS. The show's third-season finale, a cliffhanger ending with the cutthroat, backstabbing businessman J. R. Ewing gunned down by an unknown assailant, aired in March of 1980. Again, Parkland Hospital (posing as the fictional Dallas Memorial Hospital) became the scene of maniacal speculation. Who was responsible for this terrible crime? J. R., it seemed, had just as many enemies as John F. Kennedy.[150]

Dallas's stories of the dysfunctional Ewing family, with its incredible wealth accumulated through ranching and oil, had elicited a strange local pride. While the show seemed to confirm the worst stereotypes about the crassness of the Texan nouveau riche, it was immensely successful—and Dallas loves success. So the Ewings—especially J. R.—were happily adopted here as our cultural emissaries to the world.

Indeed, many locals argued that the attention the TV show *Dallas* brought the city was a great boon, a blessed distraction from our inevitable association with the JFK assassination. Dallas boosters were especially happy when they could announce in 1982 that Southfork, the suburban Rowlett ranch house that served as the fictional home of the Ewing clan, had surpassed Dealey Plaza as the area's number one tourist attraction.[151]

There was little public demand for introspection concerning the assassination, and we were content to spend our time watching the manipulations of J. R. Ewing rather than reading literature on the death of JFK. Not that Dallas has produced any great literary conspiracy epics to match the works

149. Wright, *In the New World*, 68–69.

150. Barbara Curran, *25 Years of* Dallas*: The Complete Story of the World's Favorite Prime-Time Soap* (College Station, TX: VBW Publishing, 2004).

151. Greene, *Dallas USA*, 92.

of DeLillo or Ellroy. While we've had more than our share of conspiracy researchers, very few of our local fiction writers have shown any interest in treating that topic. (Richard Condon published his *Winter Kills* in 1974, six years before he moved to Dallas.) Mostly, it's been poets from outlying areas in North Texas who have been the rare literary voices to have explored the theme of JFK conspiracy theory.

•

Dave Oliphant is a longtime Fort Worth poet who has carved out a literary career surveying the regional landscape. His long poetic journey *Memories of Texas Towns & Cities,* first published in 2000 but two decades in the making, is representative of that work. Modeled after William Carlos Williams's *Paterson,* it chronicles Oliphant's engagement with a geography that's both autobiographical and historical. At one point within this sprawling poetic sequence, Oliphant recollects the trauma he experienced while pondering the possibility of a JFK assassination conspiracy as a young school teacher in the South Texas town of Hebbronville.

> in Zapruder's movie through all the smoke
> made out shots in the front from a raised manhole
> saw others fired nearby on the grass knoll
> felt ill then cheated feared Penn Jones' theory
> even viewed LBJ in on that vast conspiracy
>
> a cover-up so all pervasive none untouched
> anti-Reds caught up in suspicion's spider web
> thinking poisoned by all Jack might have been
> his face & cresting hair so refreshingly vigorous
> quoting in crisis Milton's "only stand & wait"

A stanza later, Oliphant strains for the language to express the disillusionment that followed.

now his Peace Corps goes hardly anywhere
its plumbing lessons aren't found suspect
another capitalist trick to sell the fixtures
the in-fighting continuing after all the tears
over speeches had moved them to volunteer[152]

For anyone of Oliphant's generation, the assassination was inescapably woven into the experiences that marked the passage into adulthood. Those experiences also stuck with Paul Foreman. Foreman grew up on the Brazos River in rural Granbury, sixty miles southwest of Dallas. A proud Texas poet, much of his work is set in the natural setting of the area in which he grew up. He did much of his important work, as a poet and an influential small-press editor, in Berkeley, California, but even there he established TAWTE—Texas Artists, Writers, and Thinkers in Exile. While he eventually returned to Austin, he remains tied to North Texas through his passionate concern with the events of November 1963. His "Cursed by Eidetic Imagery," composed in 2003 and included in the collection *Feather River,* displays the sustained fervor of a true conspiracy theorist. It begins:

How can you ever forget
The year Jack Kennedy died?
All the doctors at Parkland Hospital
Declared the throat wound an entrance wound.
Why then the tracheotomy
When he was through the mortal door?

Such things do not admit of poetry.
The poet must wait a hundred years
Or more before bespeaking this kind of evil.[153]

152. Dave Oliphant, *Memories of Texas Towns & Cities* (Austin: Host Publications, 2000), 283–84.

153. Paul Foreman, *Feather River* (Berkeley, CA: Thorp Springs, 2003), 40.

For Foreman, the conspiracy was still an obsession more than five decades after the assassination. At the time of his death in 2012, has was still working on a historical memoir on the deaths of JFK and RFK called *Dare to Ask Why*.[154]

•

The assassination of John F. Kennedy, the assassinations that followed, and the political chaos of the sixties and early seventies have produced a more cynical America. While growing cynicism has increased the prevalence of conspiratorial thinking, it is a double-edged sword for conspiracy theorists—that inbred skepticism is often directed at the conspiracy buffs themselves. In Dallas, an optimistic city that tends more than most to accept standard doctrine, the conspiracy researcher gets an extra dose of special scrutiny.

The conspiracy theorists also have another local problem. For decades, the city has been trying to move beyond that dark splotch the JFK killing has left on its history. Increasingly, it is the conspiracy buffs who will not let the subject rest. While the percentage of local citizens who distrust the official version of the JFK assassination is, more or less, in line with that of the national population, Dallasites are much less likely to invite discussion on the matter. If official city policy, when it comes to all matters relating to the assassination, leans toward denial and neglect, it is because those policies mirror the general desires of the local populace. There is, here in Dallas, a general assassination fatigue.

In 2000, Gary Cartwright, who experienced the original assassination frenzy in Dallas firsthand and has spent a career covering the fallout, wrote about this fatigue from the perspective of a jaded journalist.

> Since that seminal autumn in the summer of my youth I've spent hundreds of hours reviewing the assassination, only to return again to the beginning, older but never the wiser. I've read most of the

154. Paul Foreman, email message to Tim Cloward, August 19, 2010.

> twelve-volume Warren Commission Report and all the other official documents I could find, interviewed countless people who claimed to have inside information, re-thought, wrote and rewrote the events of November 1963. Every time I believe I've put it behind me, another report or source surfaces to stir up the old memories and muddy the picture.[155]

The JFK assassination was the story that would not go away. By 2000, Cartwright had done major pieces for *Texas Monthly* on Jack Ruby, whom he knew personally, and the Mandarin case. ("Mandarin" was the supposed code name of Roscoe White, a Dallas police officer who had served in the same military unit as Lee Harvey Oswald and married a woman who had worked for a short time for Jack Ruby. It was claimed that White had left a journal, now missing, in which he confessed to shooting Kennedy from the grassy knoll.) In the course of his journalistic work, Cartwright has heard a lot; he's interviewed two different sources, for instance, who claim they had witnessed a pre-assassination meeting between Lee Harvey Oswald and Jack Ruby at the Carousel Club. Speaking of his immersion in the arcane world of conspiracy investigation, Cartwright can only write: "The crazier it gets, the more reasonable it sounds."[156]

Cartwright remains deeply unsettled about the possibility of a conspiracy. His assassination reporting and experiences living amid the craziness of 1963 Dallas weave their way through his other writing, popping up in all sorts of unexpected places. "Over the years I heard hundreds of stories, bits and pieces of information that suggested a wide but highly confusing conspiracy, but they tended to bump together. Gradually, I compartmentalized them, afraid that my brain might otherwise explode."[157]

•

155. Gary Cartwright, "My Most Unforgettable Year," in *Turn Out The Lights: Chronicles of Texas During the 80s and 90s* (Austin: University of Texas Press, 2000), 3.

156. Cartwright, "My Most Unforgettable Year," 8.

157. Cartwright, "I Was Mandarin."

In the major works of fiction produced by area writers which deal with the JFK assassination, the conspiracy angle is conspicuously absent. In both Bryan Woolley's *November 22* and Marshall Terry's *Dallas Stories*, there is no hint of larger conspiratorial forces, just the vague pall of local guilt. Only in Bud Shrake's *Strange Peaches* do the conspiracy researchers make an appearance. And, in this novel, they descend on Dallas immediately after the assassination:

> By Monday morning the amateur assassination-investigators had begun to arrive in town. Several who were friends of friends called me up and asked questions and confided that the President had been killed by a Batista Cuban conspiracy, by a fanatical Fascist faction of the CIA, by an international opium syndicate afraid Kennedy intended to interfere with their sources in Indochina, by a German intelligence organization with ties to the Nazis, by the Mafia, by a secret right-wing group with headquarters in Dallas and Alabama and by a combination of these."[158]

The skeptical narrator who is being canvassed by these assassination-investigators is John Lee Wallace, the alter-ego of Bud Shrake himself. Using his own fictional variation on Gonzo Journalism, Shrake collapses the history of JFK conspiracism into the first few days after the assassination. In addition to weaving his own personal experiences into the narrative, Shrake also weaves in the figure of his 1963 Dallas roommate—none other than his lifelong friend Gary Cartwright, here rechristened Buster.

In *Strange Peaches*, John Lee and Buster have taken a Zapruder-like film of the actual assassination, and so they are of particular interest to the assassination-investigators. A character named Harrison Jones has latched onto them and their film, and has Buster screen it for him, over and over.

> "There, do you see it," he cried. "Three Cubans with rifles!"

158. Edwin Shrake, *Strange Peaches* (Austin: Texas Monthly Press, 1987), 295.

> We backed up the film and showed it again in slow motion and stop-frame. When the President's hand reached for his throat, when Connally slumped, when the brains flew out, Jones said, "They're shooting at them!"
>
> We saw some dim figures on the trestle.
>
> "No doubt about it," said Jones. "Kennedy was hit in the front of the head by rifle fire from the trestle. See the police running up the grassy knoll? They knew where the shots came from."
>
> "I'm willing to believe it, but I don't see it," Buster said.
>
> "Run it again," said Jones."[159]

Shrake's John Lee Wallace keeps his distance, but Buster is drawn in. "The more Buster drank, the more interested he became in Jones's theory about the anti-Castro New Orleans homosexual ring." Soon he and Harrison run off to photograph a Texas School Book Depository employee who was said to resemble Oswald. After more drink, Buster has fully "accepted Jones's theories and was fitting in extra pieces of his own."

Shrake plays Buster's openness to the suggestions of the conspiracy theorists against John Lee Wallace's cynical distance. In *Strange Peaches*' final summation, you can hear Shrake's own dismissive skepticism. Already John Lee, and Shrake himself, is experiencing assassination fatigue.

> I thought it was interesting that none of the amateur-investigators believed the President had been murdered as the result of a Communist plot, or that Oswald had acted alone in the crime, or that Ruby had acted on his own, or that the FBI or the government commission would ever reveal the truth.[160]

159 Shrake, *Strange Peaches*, 298.

160. Shrake, *Strange Peaches*, 295, 298, 300, 303, 295.

•

For the last thirty years, there has been an uncomfortable stasis here in Dallas, a slow-broiling stalemate between the forces of the Warren Commission apologists and the conspiracy theorists. It has become manifestly obvious that all the official efforts to deny a conspiracy have produced no closure. While the conspiracy theorists have never been able to produce that one Holy Grail of evidence that would prove the grand conspiracy plot, they have dug in for the long haul, having produced a mountain of claims and speculations that cannot be simply swept under the rug.

With this constant wear and tear on our public psyche, Dallasites often long for some type of humorous relief. What can we do but joke about it? But it is a sensitive matter, the nature of the tragedy being what it is. By the 1980s, when it became obvious the JFK assassination wasn't going away, however, some sort of relief was necessary. With so few acceptable targets for humor available, it became clear the easiest was the conspiracy theorists. They would become the first victims of JFK assassination humor.

Thanks to the ongoing newspaper war between the *Dallas Morning News* and the *Dallas Times Herald*, the 1980s was a good time for public humor in Dallas. At the time, the *Times Herald* was actively challenging its longtime rival and had actually matched the *Morning News* in Sunday circulation.[161] In this no-holds-barred fight for readers, the *Herald* snagged nationally recognized political commentator Molly Ivins. The paper's editors set her and her iconoclastic wit loose, letting her write whatever she chose and putting up billboards proudly advertising the fact: "Molly Ivins Can't Say That, Can She?" They also allowed an up-and-coming young film critic, John Bloom, to take on the moniker Joe Bob Briggs and bill himself as "the Drive-in Movie Critic from Grapevine, Texas."

Up to that point, Dallas-born Bloom had negotiated a completely respectable career as a journalist. After graduating from Vanderbilt, he did first-rate

161. Matthew Hayes Nall, "Dallas Times Herald," in *Handbook of Texas Online*, Texas State Historical Association, updated July 2, 2016, accessed June 17, 2012, http://www.tshaonline.org/handbook/online/articles/eed13.

newspaper work, receiving accolades and awards, and earning a staff position at *Texas Monthly*. Upon returning home and joining the *Dallas Times Herald,* he made a name for himself with his intelligent reviews of foreign films and a greatly admired "Metro" column. He even coauthored a book on the suburban housewife/axe murderer Candace Montgomery, *Evidence of Love,* which became a TV movie. He was a rising star in his field.[162]

In 1983, *Times Herald* editors signed off on a new John Bloom experiment—"Joe Bob Goes to the Drive-In." The weekly Friday column featured as much rambling narrative about life in the white-trash underclass as it did film criticism, and always ended with a fast movie evaluation based on the basic drive-in movie criteria: blood, boobs, and beasts. The column became an instant hit, and Joe Bob developed a large and loyal following, quickly finding his way into syndication.

But on Friday, April 12, 1985, Joe Bob went too far. His infamous "We Are the Weird" column, an unusually tasteless takeoff on the "We Are the World" celebrity video soliciting money for humanitarian aid for Africa, created a furor. By the next Tuesday, 350 protesters, led by Black activist and county commissioner John Wiley Price, appeared at the *Times Herald* office, demanding that the column be dropped. On Thursday, *Times Herald* management bowed to the pressure and killed the column. John Bloom, however, was not ready to let Joe Bob go. He resigned from the *Times Herald* and plotted an appropriate Joe Bob response. He had already angered women and racial minorities with his political incorrectness. He resolved now to take on the city's touchiest subject—the JFK assassination.

In the June 1985 issue of *D Magazine,* alongside an article detailing the *Times Herald* blow-up, Joe Bob made his official response. Under the banner title "Joe Bob Goes to the Drive-In," the subtitle read: "Drive-In Movie Critic of Rockwall, Texas November 22, 1963–April 16, 1985. They said it couldn't happen again." The text began this way.

I guess I'll always remember where I was when they killed me on

162. Chris Tucker, "The Further Adventures of Joe Bob Briggs," *D Magazine,* October 1992.

> national TV, right after the Maybelline commercial. I guess we all will. Who could remember the look on the High Sheriff's face when he said, "Joe Bob's dead!" I know a lot of people ran through the streets of downtown Dallas, screaming hysterically:
>
> "The drive-in critic's dead!" "Oh my God Joe Bob is history."

Bloom threw around any number of the standard JFK assassination tropes, with Joe Bob himself in the role of the martyred hero. After the hyperbole and hubris of the opening, the rest of the piece plays fast and loose with the notions of America's conspiracy obsessions.

> There were immediate rumors of an international Communist conspiracy, the "three-gun Theory," the "act of God theory," the bizarre "one-gar-bonza theory" and the "What would happen if you dropped Joe Bob Briggs off a seven-story building and watched him splatter all over the pavement?" theory.

After reviewing the circumstances surrounding his "death" at the hands of "The Crimes Herald," Joe Bob closes with what he calls "a few 'Miracle' facts of world history," a variation on a lesson familiar to everyone who had taken US history in high school.

> 1. Lincoln and Kennedy were both assassinated on a Friday. Joe Bob was assassinated on a Tuesday. Makes you think.
> 2. Lincoln and Kennedy were both succeeded by a man named "Johnson." Joe Bob was killed by a High Sheriff named Tom Johnson.
> 3. Lincoln and Kennedy put their pants on one leg at a time. Joe Bob puts his on two legs at a time.
> 4. Lincoln and Kennedy never could get a laugh either.

•

Joe Bob did survive the killing of his column at the *Times Herald*. Bloom went on to expand the syndication of "Joe Bob Goes to the Drive-In," and repackage Joe Bob for television in shows like the Movie Channel's late-night "Joe Bob's Drive-In Theater." And Joe Bob lives on, very profitably, in a series of books, an early example of which is his 1988 *A Guide to Western Civilization: Or My Story*.

Here, Bloom cannot help but take up his JFK shtick again, and by the book's penultimate chapter he meanders into "How I Solved the Kennedy Assassination." Again, Bloom mines the tropes of the conspiracy movement. Here, for instance, he plays with one of the staple elements used by any worthwhile Kennedy researcher—the detailed chronological timeline.

1. Kennedy and Jackie go to Dallas.

2. Kennedy gets sick on the plane, but nobody thinks much about it.

3. On final approach, Kennedy turns to Jackie and says, "Do you realize there are seven letters in 'Kennedy' *and* seven letters in 'Lincoln,' that Lincoln was killed on a Friday by a lone gunman shooting at the back of his head, and that Lincoln was succeeded by a Vice President named 'Johnson'?"

4. Jackie replies, "Oh, honey, don't be silly. A lot of names have seven letters. Like , oh, 'Onassis.'"

Later, Bloom parodies the growing catalog of conspiracy publications (and Dallas's literary life) with a trip to Dallas Public Library. There he will "read the complete works of A. C. Greene, because A. C. Greene wrote all the books in the Dallas Public Library, beginning with *Famous Drunk Indians That Visited Dallas in the 1860s and Got Killed with Muskets,* continuing right on through *Dallas in the Eighties: Gimme Some Money*." Joe Bob will also read all the important JFK literature, books like: "*Rush to Judgment* by Mark Lane, *Highlights from Rush to Judgment* by Mark Lane, *Another Rush to Judgment*

Book He Put Out Right After That One by Mark Lane, *How the Dirty Commies Did It* by John Wayne, as told by Irving Reinfeld, and *Please Forgive My Bullet: What Really Happened Out There,* by Marina Oswald, as told to Mikhail Stepanovich Grigorin."[163]

By the time the chapter ends, Joe Bob's research has led him across the sprawling Dallas metroplex—from a gun-photo studio in Oak Cliff to the Ridiculous Belts Department of Neiman Marcus—and he's taken his reader through all the misadventures of a good private-eye tale. If Joe Bob's final unraveling of the great secret of the JFK conspiracy proves to be nothing but a shaggy dog story, John Bloom had still provided one important public service. The Kennedy assassination had been used as the fodder for public humor. It had been scandalous, and some feathers had been ruffled, but after that the laughs would come easier.

•

If we vaguely suspected that the official story of the JFK assassination was not quite right, we were too busy to give it much thought. In the late 1980s, what many of us really wanted was to see family photos of Jackie and the kids at Camelot or to learn the most salacious details of JFK's rumored affair with Marilyn Monroe. We knew the conspiracy theorists were hard at work trying to save us from ourselves, but, in the Age of Irony, their earnestness could be so off-putting. So we were content to read *People* magazine. It had been founded a decade before by Dick Stolley, the man who had first acquired the Zapruder film for *Life* magazine. By 1988, the weekly publication was a tremendous success. Twenty-five years after he obtained the film that documented the father's death, Stolley was able to help honor the son, John F. Kennedy Jr., tendering him *People Magazine*'s annual "Sexiest Man Alive" award.

John and Jackie Kennedy had had their fifteen minutes of fame as Warhol images, and now their secret lives were standard fodder for tabloids

163. Joe Bob Briggs, *A Guide to Western Civilization: Or My Story* (New York: Delacorte Press, 1988), 165–83.

like the *National Enquirer*. By 1988, the time was ripe for all the JFK assassination tropes to be used as kitsch. It was no surprise, then, that John Bloom could vault Joe Bob Briggs to fame using parodies of conspiracy theories—or that, a few years later, another area writer could gain in literary stature by producing a novella in which a still-living John F. Kennedy joins forces with Elvis Presley to destroy an Egyptian mummy rampaging through rural East Texas.

•

Joe Lansdale, the author of *Bubba Ho-Tep*, is a self-styled "champion mojo storyteller," and, like Bloom's Joe Bob Briggs, an aficionado of drive-in movie aesthetics. He published his first novel just about the time Bloom's *Times Herald* career was beginning, and he has gone on to enjoy a wildly diverse career, writing over thirty novels as well as working in comics and film.

If Bloom's Joe Bob represents a Western style of redneck, Lansdale tends to speak for an Eastern version. While Dallas likes to fashion itself as a frontier city, using the iconography associated with the western half of the state, it is actually closer, geographically and culturally, to the southeastern Piney Woods.

There is a local adage here: "Dallas is where the East ends, Fort Worth is where the West begins." Dallas founder John Neely Bryan was from Tennessee, and, likewise, the migrants who followed him through the first half century of the city's existence were primarily Southerners moving to the West. Our Southern culture is evident in the open-armed hospitality that we Dallasites so pride ourselves on. Dallas has also always been the sophisticated hub city for the farming communities of East Texas, the place where people from Marshall, Tyler, and Paris come to shop and seek entertainment. And, although those days are long gone now, Dallas bankers flocked to the area to help service the flourishing East Texas wildcatters during the big oil boom.

Lansdale, who was born in 1951 in Gladewater, a midsize hamlet a two-hour drive east of Dallas, has always lived somewhere in East Texas. His work tends to create an East Texas remote from the sophisticated glamour of its nearby hub city, a place often closer to the swampy, mossy ambience of next-door Louisiana. While his pulp genre take-offs are often reminiscent of the wild genre-mixing humor of Mark Twain, his style is more often likened to William Faulkner's Southern Gothic.

In *Bubba Ho-Tep*, first published in 1994, the past is not dead; it has come back in an extraordinarily strange new form. Lansdale uses that classic conspiracy trope—the departed hero is not actually dead but living a hidden life removed from public view—to bring us contemporary versions of two of our greatest culture heroes. Here we find the seventy-year-old Elvis Presley, bedridden and hopeless, more or less waiting for death in the Mud Creek Shady Grove Convalescence Home. He has traded away his life of stardom and exchanged places with an Elvis impersonator. Among the home's residents are a number of individuals who are, in their elderly dementia, losing their previous sense of identity: a Dillinger character, Kemosabe (who wears a mask and styles himself the partner of the Lone Ranger), and an elderly Black man who claims to be John F. Kennedy.

It takes only a small step to travel from some of the most outrageous conspiracy speculation to Lansdale's fictional JFK. "The bullet only wounded him and his brain is in a fruit jar at the White House, hooked up to some wires and a battery," we learn. "The Powers-That-Be had dyed him that color to keep him hidden." The government takes care of the former president, occasionally sending a woman who says she is his niece in Dallas, but he has to be careful because "everyone was in on trying to assassinate him. Even Elvis Presley."

The real action begins when Elvis finds Jack prone on the floor. Jack's initial suspicions—"Lyndon Johnson. Castro. They've sent someone to finish me"—prove false. The culprit, it turns out, is a soul-sucking mummy who has found itself a pair of cowboy boots and a hat. In its getup, the mummy is "[e]ven uglier," Jack says, "than Lyndon Johnson." What follows from Lansdale's wacky premise is an epic geriatric adventure.[164]

•

164. Joe R. Lansdale and Don Coscarelli, *Bubba Ho-Tep* (San Francisco: Night Shade Books, 2005).

In 2002, director Don Coscarelli released a lovingly adapted film version of *Bubba Ho-Tep*. Its expansion of the original novella features a number of wonderful touches—the miniature diorama of Dealey Plaza by Jack's bed being just one example. Most importantly, Coscarelli lured one of the elder statesman of the theater, Ossie Davis, to play JFK, thus amplifying Lansdale's core theme: the redemption of two great American icons who had never been able to achieve their full promise in their actual lives. Although Elvis had squandered all his immense talent when he died at forty-two, and JFK was assassinated at age forty-six, *Bubba Ho-Tep* gives both figures a fictional second chance.

You cannot help but root for these aged avatars of the two greatest culture heroes of the second half of the twentieth century. The film climaxes with a big face-off with the soul-sucking cowboy mummy—the eponymous Bubba Ho-Tep. Despite their bumbling and various infirmities, our heroes succeed. Bubba Ho-Tep is vanquished, and Coscarelli's low-budget film became a great success as a cult movie favorite.

The JFK in *Bubba Ho-Tep*, of course, bears only a passing resemblance to the historical JFK. The man Ossie Davis plays is JFK as a cultural icon, and such icons are like coins that we can spend as we choose. In a media-saturated world, where our common imagery is transformed as it jumps from the news to novel, to film, to tabloid, it should come as no surprise that an event as profound as the JFK assassination should continually metamorphose. Like the mummy that rises from the dead, the JFK assassination still, in any number of horribly mutated forms, walks among us.

•

One especially fascinating recent mutation of the JFK assassination mythology involves *Times Herald* staff photographer Bob Jackson's image of Jack Ruby shooting Lee Harvey Oswald. It is one of the most well-known photographs in history—Oswald, bent over and scowling, just at the moment when he takes Jack Ruby's bullet in his stomach. The photo is burned into our collective consciousness, recording the exact moment of the nationally televised murder of an alleged presidential assassin. It is a profoundly important moment in our national history. Yet today, it is not all that unusual to see that image, in a slightly altered version, on the front of a T-shirt.

This mutated image will sometimes be captioned: "The Oswald Band Last Live Performance Dallas 1963." In this version of the photograph, Jack Ruby's gun is replaced with a guitar, police escort James Leavelle is playing keyboards, and Lee Harvey Oswald is shouting into a microphone. In an ironic variation on the conspiracy trope of the altered photo—a little darkroom magic and you have a different story, a murder scene transformed into a rock show.

The altered image is the work of New Jersey Photoshop expert George Mahlberg. He had been struck by the passions evident in Jackson's photograph. "Jack Ruby was in a posture that spoke of conviction and drive, and there was something in Oswald's face, a look of passion that's hard to duplicate," he explains. "It struck me that he was certainly screamin' the blues; in fact, he looked to me like a young rock and roller beltin' out a serious tune."

On a lark, Mahlberg, a self-admitted artistic terrorist, altered Bob Jackson's Pulitzer Prize–winning photograph. After Mahlberg posted the image on an internet newsgroup for JFK assassination theorists, the image went viral. "It was particularly popular," says Mahlberg, "in the Bay Area of California, where there are a lot of Dead Kennedy heads. It's on refrigerators all over the place." It hit the mainstream when it was published in the August 1997 edition of *Wired* magazine.

When Bob Jackson discovered the altered image, he, in Mahlberg's words, "flipped out." Jackson had been understandably protective of the image, and he had never licensed the commercial use of his photograph. Mahlberg's mutation was certainly not the ideal form of the image that Jackson would have hoped to sanction, but it was wildly popular. By the time Jackson realized what had happened, he had lost control of his image. It was out there in this new form and it could not be brought back.[165]

If you look very closely underneath every "The Oswald Band Last Live Performance Dallas 1963" T-shirt image, you can read these tiny letters: "Adaptation by G. Mahlberg Photo Permission © By Bob Jackson." This

165. David Walker, "Oswald, Ruby sing the blues." *Photo District News* 17, no. 10, October 1997.

copyright notice reinforces how, for Dallasites, Mahlberg's T-shirt is an abject demonstration of one of our salient local dilemmas. How can we protect the sanctity of our historical memory in a postmodern world where the artifacts of historical memory have become playthings?

•

Another fascinating recent local mutation of the JFK assassination story, sparked by concerns about the hijacking of our historical memory, is a 2008 novel entitled *JFK Conspiracy: The Missing File.* This book is particularly interesting because it was authored by an actual participant in the JFK investigation—as the book's cover claims, "the last officer assigned to the assassination of President Kennedy."

Jim Bowles, a lifelong resident of Dallas, served thirty years with the Dallas Police Department. He was eventually elected sheriff of Dallas County, a position he held for two decades until he lost a reelection bid in 2004. At the time of the assassination in 1963, Bowles was the Dallas Police dispatch supervisor. His direct association with the investigation of the assassination began in 1976 when he was assigned to work with Jack Moriarty, the chief investigator of the House Select Committee on Assassinations. He would serve as the Dallas Police Department liaison in the examination of the motorcycle Dictabelt recordings that Gary Mack had proposed might contain audio evidence of the shooting.

Bowles is a very unlikely novelist, having spent a lifetime in law enforcement and very little time studying the literary arts. But he had been tinkering with the idea of a novel for three decades, and, finally finishing it at age eighty-one, he contracted with a self-publishing house to produce a run. There are not many of copies of *JFK Conspiracy: The Missing File* in circulation, but they are fascinating documents.

In Bowles's novel, the narrator, a lifelong police officer, receives a file from a coworker who is dying from cancer. He requests it not be opened until November 2007. Only when the narrator opens it does he realize the earth-shaking nature of its contents—the secret of the JFK assassination conspiracy from the last survivor of the group that perpetrated it!

In the first hundred pages of *JFK Conspiracy*, we learn that the confessor is David Wright, a thirty-five-year veteran of the Dallas Police Department. Because of his ultraconservative views, Wright is befriended by the Old Man, a mysterious and powerful Dallas businessman who has gathered around himself a cadre of similar-minded individuals with connections to the Secret Service, CIA, and FBI . This group meets intermittently at a secret rural lodge outside of Dallas. Intent on combating "the insidious and encroaching nature of Communism in America" and the related "tide of liberal politics and creeping socialism," they make the decision to assassinate John F. Kennedy.

Bowles spends the next two hundred pages relating how the Old Man's cadre of agents successfully puts the scheme into action—having the president shot, assigning Oswald the role of the patsy, then arranging for Ruby to rub him out. Bowles is able, despite his obvious literary shortcomings, to maintain some narrative momentum, and the book has some merit as pulp fiction.

However, the last hundred pages of *JFK Conspiracy: The Missing File* are not so kind to the reader. The action lags terribly as the members of the conspiracy regroup at the lodge to review their plot and manage the cover-up. The plotters sit in a room and talk through, in excruciating detail, all the aspects of the scheme—they cover *all* the bases. It is tedious even to the characters themselves.

While Bowles is no literary master, the primary reason *JFK Conspiracy* falls apart is that the author is writing at cross-purposes. Bowles's intention in writing *JFK Conspiracy* is not to write a convincing conspiracy tale, but to discredit the very idea of a JFK assassination conspiracy. The problems are evident from the beginning, and you can see the dilemma even in Bowles's preface:

> It is my intention, through a fictional format, to weave a conspiracy into the true account of the assassination. Hopefully, readers seeing how impossible it would be to organize, develop, control, finance and conduct such an undertaking, they will then be able to finally acknowledge: It just didn't happen![166]

166. Jim Bowles, *JFK Conspiracy: The Missing File* (Booksurge Publishing, 2008).

Bowles has tied himself into knots, writing a conspiracy thriller in order to discredit conspiracy theories.

•

For decades, Jim Bowles has been asked for his views on the JFK assassination. He's a go-to guy for the local press, and he has worked as a consultant for authors of numerous books. When asked if there is any evidence of a conspiracy, his response has been incredibly consistent. As he told one area newscaster: "Lord no! Never has been, ain't now, ain't never gonna be." He has authored "The Kennedy Assassination Tapes—A Rebuttal to the Acoustical Evidence," which seeks to disprove the "fourth shot, second shooter" theory. He has been unequivocal in his statements: "There is no acoustical evidence from Dealey Plaza except in the minds and imaginations of conspiracy buffs who must put it there because that's the only way they can create a second shooter."[167]

His immense frustration that, decades after the event, the great majority of the public still holds the belief that there was some conspiracy is evident in his book. When he has his *JFK Conspiracy* characters complain of the "meddlesome spook hunters," it is because those are his views. "It is appalling," he says, "that so many people have gone to such extreme lengths to prove something that's not there."[168]

In the final 1964 meeting of the conspirators in *JFK Conspiracy*, David Wright makes a final prediction. "Scholars and nuts will have a field day for years to come. In the year 2000 there will still be conspiracy buffs looking, people who weren't even alive in 1963." As the book closes, the narrator agrees:

> Time proved his predictions to be true. The assassination investigation didn't die a natural death. Each year seemed to generate a new crop of "experts" determined to find something all the others had

167. "Part 19, DPD's Jim Bowles," in *JFK 40: Forty People, Forty Stories*, produced by Lance Liquez, WBAP 24/7 News, 2003, accessed June 25, 2012, http://www.youtube.com/watch?v=eg6RjmV2gLk.

168. Kevin Krause, "Former Dallas Sheriff Jim Bowles pens novel about JFK assassination," *Dallas Morning News*, November 19, 2008.

> missed. Each placed his critical significance on the most trivial detail. Some twisted the truth to serve their purposes while other invented new "truths." And then there were others who mostly guessed at it.[169]

By the time Bowles decided to write *JFK Conspiracy,* it was clear that the conspiracy narrative was not going to disappear. During his tenure with the Dallas Police Department and in Dallas city government, Jim Bowles had seen that rational counterargument or contradictory evidence was not enough to rebut the conspiracy theorists; it all fell upon deaf ears. The conspiracy story had become an inescapable part of the local landscape. In the convoluted fictionalizations of *JFK Conspiracy,* Bowles is seeking a way to undo that spell.

Bowles's recent novel doesn't stand alone, however. It is emblematic of a movement against the conspiracists from within the Dallas establishment.

•

In the early 1970s, just as the unfolding revelations of Watergate were confirming the worst suspicions of anyone with conspiratorial leanings, Texas was experiencing a New Journalism renaissance. *Texas Monthly* began publishing out of Austin in 1973 and immediately made a name for itself, winning Outstanding Editorial Achievement recognition from the National Magazine Awards in 1974. As editor William Broyles Jr. sent out his staff of crack writers to canvass the state, the JFK assassination and the conspiracy theories that surrounded it were a common topic. Among the magazine's most important contributors, of course, was Dallas expatriate Gary Cartwright.

Closer to home, *D Magazine* was created in 1974 to emulate the success of *Texas Monthly* and its regionally focused New Journalism on a more local scale. Justifiably famous for the number of cosmetic surgery ads contained in each issue, *D Magazine* is glossy and slick, steadfastly upholding the tradition that the voice of Dallas is the voice of money. Nonetheless, it has given considerable space to many of the area's best writers. However, *D Magazine* has never known quite what to do with the Kennedy assassination.

---

169. Bowles, *JFK Conspiracy: The Missing File*

The original, unspoken *D Magazine* policy toward the Kennedy assassination, much like that of official Dallas, was to ignore it. In the November 1976 issue, for example, there was a cursory treatment of the subject in an article titled "Thirteen Years After: Where Are They Now?" Fourteen locals, connected one way or another with the assassination, were profiled, but only accorded a paragraph each. Until the twentieth anniversary of the assassination in 1983, the only other mention of the assassination in *D Magazine* was Chet Flippo's August 1980 review of Anthony Summers's book *Conspiracy*.[170]

If *D Magazine* was to have any credibility as the chronicler of the local scene, the JFK assassination could not be ignored—it was the proverbial elephant in the room. When the twentieth anniversary did roll around in November 1983, the cover of *D Magazine* featured a profile photo of JFK framed in red. Above it, a banner proclaimed: ASSASSINATION IN DALLAS. In her "Editor's Page" introduction, "How the Assassination Changed Dallas," Lee Cullum acknowledged the need for a little historical introspection, recognizing the negative perceptions of Dallas that had persisted so long after the assassination and, just as significantly, the "agony of self-accusation" that Dallasites had endured. By 1983, however, Cullum argued, the city had overcome. "Out of the turmoil came a new style of public life," one that was "more complex and less complacent," she asserted in the tone of civic boosterism for which *D Magazine* is famous. "The generation that came to the fore to put the pieces back together after the assassination laid the groundwork for the ascendancy that Dallas enjoys today."[171]

The centerpiece of this twentieth-anniversary issue was a first-person account of that frantic November 1963 weekend from the newsman who was, more than anyone else, on the scene: Hugh Aynesworth. Aynesworth is our undisputed journalistic expert on the subject. He had not only witnessed the assassination in Dealey Plaza; he was also present at Oswald's arrest, and when Oswald was shot by Jack Ruby. He was everywhere that weekend, and, afterward, he continued to produce groundbreaking investigative reporting

170. Chet Flippo, "Puppet Theater: Who Was Pulling Oswald's Strings," *D Magazine*, August 1980.

171. Lee Cullum, "Editor's Page: How the assassination changed Dallas," *D Magazine*, November 1983.

on the assassination. "Assassination in Dallas: A veteran journalist looks back on the day the president died," offered Aynesworth's concise summary of his on-the-scene experience. While it conveyed all the drama of the moment, the piece offered no hint of any of the pressing contemporary issues surrounding the assassination. That was left to its companion piece (not mentioned in Cullum's introduction), one written by another Dallas author, Earl Golz.

Like Aynesworth, Golz was a veteran journalist, an investigative reporter for the *Dallas Morning News* who specialized in financial stories and then established himself as a JFK assassination expert. His article, "Did Oswald Act Alone?: Twenty years later, the question remains," begins: "After twenty years of debate and dead ends, the question of who shot Kennedy is still very much alive." Golz presented a summary of the current conspiracy theories as they stood in 1983: "Russian Riddles"; "Links with Organized Crime"; "Cuban Connections"; "Questions of Evidence." In each section , Golz reminded his readers that there were more than enough open-ended questions to keep the assassination debate alive. "Critics have doubted the lone-assassin theory since the assassination," Golz wrote. "Their questions have not only remained unanswered, they have proliferated."

Although *D Magazine* had made its first serious attempt to deal with the topic of the JFK assassination, its stance ultimately remained one of ambivalence. Like the local news stations that traditionally breezed through their perfunctory obligations, making fast mention of each passing anniversary, *D Magazine* had broached the subject. The magazine had even given the conspiracy theorists their due. But there was plenty left unsaid. Earl Golz summed it up succinctly: "Many unsettling aspects of Kennedy's death still hang in the air."[172]

•

By the assassination's twenty-fifth anniversary, *D Magazine* was ready for a little civic self-examination. Its November 1988 issue featured Lawrence Wright's "Was Dallas a City of Hate?", an extended essay, part of which would

172. Earl Golz, "Did Oswald Act Alone?" *D Magazine,* November 1983.

appear in his soon-to-be-published memoir, *In the New World*. This was heady stuff for Dallas, a serious and sustained look into what the city had been like at the time of the assassination. In it, Wright asked some serious questions about himself, his family, and his city. While this level of introspection was groundbreaking locally, the piece's impact was mitigated somewhat by the fact that Wright had published a very similar piece, "Why Do They Hate Us So Much?", five years earlier in *Texas Monthly*.

For the next few years, not much on the topic of the assassination was to be found in the pages of *D Magazine*. The silence was particularly obvious in the early nineties, when Oliver Stone took over the city to film *JFK*. While the national press was experiencing paroxysms of ecstasy and spleen over the politics of the film, and the local press was going all agog over the comings and goings of Kevin Costner and the visiting Hollywood contingent, *D Magazine* remained oddly quiet. There was a short but appreciative acknowledgment of the newly opened Sixth Floor Museum in the 1991 November issue, but the most telling clue to *D Magazine*'s eventual editorial direction was a short piece that appeared in its June 1995 issue.

That article dealt with the Sixth Floor Museum's new competition. In April of that year, the new Conspiracy Museum had opened at the corner of Commerce and Market Streets, just around the corner from Dealey Plaza. "Dedicated to eradicating government lies and exposing possible, albeit improbable, truths," the new museum had been founded by Boston architect and JFK ballistics expert R. B. Cutler. "Some scholars," author Dan Michalski suggested, "believe him to be a single bullet short of having a fully loaded chamber." The museum went far beyond simply asserting that John F. Kennedy was not killed by a single shooter. The voice-over narration to one video on exhibit at the Conspiracy Museum explained: "Complete with hit squads, planted evidence, diversionary fire and fake arrests [conspirators] assassinated the president in a paramilitary ambush on Elm Street." The Conspiracy Museum further proposed that the JFK assassination was just one link in a vast web of nefarious underground activity that shapes the world we live in today.

In his article, Michalski was content to let the Conspiracy Museum folks damn themselves with their own words, giving them just enough rope to hang themselves. "There is a single conspiracy that began with the killing of JFK and went on to eliminate Martin Luther King and Robert Kennedy," museum president Tom Bowden told him. "They also killed Mary Jo Kopechne and shot down Korean Air Lines 007." [173]

D Magazine, it seemed, would no longer be as deferential to the conspiracy theorists as they had been in 1983.

•

By the thirty-fifth anniversary of the assassination, *D Magazine*, as the self-appointed guardian of Dallas's image, was ready to fight back. Six years after Oliver Stone had come to Dallas and reinvigorated the conspiracy movement, the editors geared themselves up to take a stand and protect the city from the conspiracy stain. The November 1998 issue of *D Magazine* amounted to a full-frontal assault on the idea that there was any other explanation for what happened over the weekend of November 1963 than the actions taken by Lee Harvey Oswald and Jack Ruby. There would be no more accommodation of the conspiracy theorists; it was time to cut them loose.

D Magazine's editors brought in the big guns to do the job. For example, New Yorker Gerald Posner was imported to write the opening essay, "The Conspiracy Lure." Posner was the author of *Case Closed*, the 1993 tome that, to that date, had provided the definitive defense of the Warren Commission's conclusion. In his essay, Posner was unequivocal in his denunciation of the conspiracy theories. "Not a single witness saw anyone suspicious on the grassy knoll," he asserted. "A single bullet," he declared, "did strike JFK and Gov. Connelly almost exactly as the Warren Commission set forth." He announced, "Not one key witness died mysteriously," and proclaimed that "Ruby was not a member of the mafia." All the myriad conspiracy theories? "None of it is true."

Joining Posner in *D Magazine*'s onslaught on the conspiracy theorists was local ringer Hugh Aynesworth, the reporter who had been everywhere. This

---

173. Dan Michalski, "Modern Times: Who Really Dunnit?", *D Magazine*, June 1995.

was a different Aynesworth than the man who had, in 1983, recounted his experiences in Dallas during the week of the assassination. Now, a decade and a half later, he was back to address the tainted legacy of that week. Aynesworth had not only been everywhere the week of the assassination—he had been deeply involved in follow-up investigations. He had watched close at hand as the conspiracy movement unfolded and gained momentum. He didn't like what he had seen. In his *D* feature, "JFK Special Report: How Hucksters & Crazies Built the Big Lie and Why We Still Believe It," Aynesworth focused on debunking.

In the process, he had plenty of stories to tell. Aynesworth related how, two months after the assassination, a practical joke he had played on a pesky investigator had resulted in a bogus story on the front page of the *Houston Post* identifying Lee Harvey Oswald as an FBI operative. Aynesworth also related how he had agreed, just after the assassination, to loan a file of documents—witness accounts gathered by the Dallas Police—to an earnest investigator intent on helping the Oswald family clear Lee Harvey's name. A few weeks later, Aynesworth wrote, he read of that same investigator, Mark Lane, at a European press conference waving those documents in the air, claiming, erroneously, that the papers proved that witnesses in Dallas contradicted the authorities. "*My* documents," Aynesworth wrote, "I was livid."

Aynesworth's depiction of his personal dealings with Jim Garrison—the New Orleans District Attorney later glorified in Oliver Stone's *JFK*—functioned as a microcosm of his dealings with the conspiracy theorists. Always in the middle of things, Aynesworth had been invited by Garrison to visit him and share his expertise. That visit, Aynesworth related, resulted in "one of the strangest days of my life," just the first in a series of encounters with Garrison that convinced him that Garrison would be a "likely object of interest at the state mental hospital."

The thirty-fifth anniversary *D Magazine* also included a half-page insert titled, "He Never Had a Chance." It recounted JFK assassination researcher David Perry's attempt to determine an accurate count of all the possible presidential shooters chronicled in the conspiracy canon. The final list did not include Jackie Kennedy, who one book claimed was in on the plot, but did include "Umbrella Man, who is suspected of firing a dart through a special

CIA-designed umbrella gun." The message, it was clear, was that the conspiracy theorists were not to be taken seriously.

•

In Austin, *Texas Monthly*, the magazine after which *D Magazine* had modeled itself, had always been more open and active in its treatment of the topic of the JFK assassination. For instance, the issue it published on the twentieth anniversary of the assassination in 1983 not only featured the original Lawrence Wright "Why Do They Hate Us So Much?" article, but also Ron Rosenbaum's "Still on the Case," one of the best and most incisive article-length investigations into the JFK conspiracy movement at that time.

By 1998, *Texas Monthly* already had a history of having fun at the expense of the conspiracy theorists, but its November issue that year took on a much more serious and deliberative tone. Thirty-five years after the assassination, the editors were now setting out to "make the case that one man alone did the deed and try to show how knowing that can be a kind of solace." It was time, they felt, to directly confront the prevalence of the conspiracy mindset and the debilitating cynicism it engendered.

> We think the millennium is changing in 2000, but since eras change by events and not by the calendar, the new millennium began 35 years ago, on November 22, 1963. That was when the confidence and the security of the years following World War II were abruptly destroyed and replaced by suspicion and insecurity. Immediately after that came the unthinkable—the assassination of Martin Luther King, Jr., and Robert Kennedy, a losing war, Watergate, and Iran-Contra. Belief in conspiracy and powerful forces working against us became part of the national consciousness, reaching its apotheosis in the 1991 film *JFK*.[174]

In their special 1998 "The Assassination" issue, the editors of *Texas Monthly* devoted a good deal of space to explaining the attractions and allures

174. "The Assassination at 35," *Texas Monthly*, November 1998.

of the various conspiracy theories. Ultimately, however, they asserted that there is only one truth. Gregory Curtis's lead article, "The Lone Gunman" was subtitled "Lee Harvey Oswald Killed John F. Kennedy. End of Story." It concludes: "To believe Oswald was the lone assassin is to believe the clear evidence, however mundane it might be." On the other hand, "those who insist on conspiracy are adding to the general confusion, leading innocent people astray, unjustly undermining confidence in the structure of the country, and that unwarranted confusion is the reason for our problems." For Curtis, and the editors of *Texas Monthly*, "until ghosts are proved to be real, it is far better to accept the clear and certain evidence and move on."[175]

•

While polls continued to show that the majority of Americans suspect that the death of John F. Kennedy was the result of some type of conspiracy, that didn't necessarily translate into unquestioned mainstream acceptance for the conspiracy movement. By the turn of the millennium, it had become more and more common for the established Texas press to target conspiracy theorists for ridicule. Even the *Dallas Observer*, an influential weekly alternative magazine generally more amenable to the offbeat and controversial, got in on the pile-on. In one July 2000 issue, longtime *Observer* writer Robert Wilonsky took on the most venerable of the Dallas-area conspiracy theorists: Jim Marrs.

Since his 1989 book, *Crossfire*, and his collaboration with Oliver Stone, Marrs had actively expanded his conspiracy credentials. In 2000, Marrs published his *Alien Agenda: Investigating the Extraterrestrial Presence among Us* (in which he repeats a story "suggesting that Kennedy was really killed because he was about to reveal the existence of UFOs to the American public"). The next year, Marrs followed with his *Rule by Secrecy: The Hidden History That Connects the Trilateral Commission, the Freemasons, and the Great Pyramids.* When Wilonsky profiled him, Marrs was just beginning to turn himself into a one-man conspiracy publishing empire.

175. Gregory Curtis, "The Lone Gunman," *Texas Monthly*, November 1998.

Wilonsky's article, "The Truth Is Way Out There," begins: "The Nut lives just outside a small town called Paradise." Through the next four paragraphs, Wilonsky continues to refer to Marrs as simply "the Nut." In fact, he is referenced as "the Nut" eight more times before he is introduced by his given name. This type of treatment was nothing new to Marrs, however. As he told Wilonsky: "Years ago, when I was trying to tell people there was a big conspiracy to kill Kennedy, I was the nut, the fringe guy, the conspiracy theorist, the buff, but I'm used to it." Marrs felt more than justified by the fact that the majority of Americans had also come to feel that there was something fishy about the official version of the Kennedy assassination. "So that's all pretty accepted, so now, of course, I'm on to other things, and now I'm still the nut, the conspiracy theorist, so I guess I'll just be branded with that for life."[176]

What, more than anything, encouraged Marrs in his pursuit of the truth was his continuing success as a bestselling author, and his output accelerated with that success. Among the major nonfiction books Marrs has published since Wilonsky's article are: *The Terror Conspiracy: Deception, 9/11 and the Loss of Liberty* (2006); *The Rise of the Fourth Reich: The Secret Societies That Threaten to Take Over America* and *Above Top Secret: Uncover the Mysteries of the Digital Age* (2008); *The Trillion-Dollar Conspiracy: How the New World Order, Man-Made Diseases, and Zombie Banks Are Destroying America* (2010); *Our Occulted History: Do the Global Elite Conceal Ancient Aliens?* (2013); and *The Illuminati: The Secret Society That Hijacked the World* (2017).

The titles speak for themselves. Jim Marrs was and is the modern master of conspiracy theory. Via his research and extensive bibliography, he created a sort of grand unified theory that connects almost all the major extant strains of American conspiracy theory into one unified web of nefarious intrigue. While a local journalist like Wilonsky might heap ridicule upon him, there are thousands of readers more than ready to throw their money down and take a ride with Marrs.

•

176. Wilonsky, "The truth is way out there."

For all his publishing success, however, Jim Marrs never cornered the conspiracy market. Even in hard economic times, it continues to be one of our premiere growth industries. "You might be forgiven for thinking that paranoia is as American as apple pie because in recent decades it has become such a visible and widespread part of the cultural landscape," writes Peter Knight in his 2002 book, *Conspiracy Nation*. "From the Kennedy assassination to Hilary Clinton's accusation of a 'vast right-wing conspiracy' against her husband, and from the novels of Thomas Pynchon to *The X Files*, talk of conspiracy is everywhere. We're all conspiracy theorists now."[177]

If we are all conspiracy theorists, then Jim Marrs remains the most prolific local embodiment of our species. With his voracious appetite for all things conspiratorial and his impressive talent for patching them all together, he was the master synthesizer of all those movements that feed our common fear that we are losing control of our lives—that there are secret forces out there who have taken over. From space aliens to 9/11 Truther theories, Cold War psychic warfare techniques to the clandestine machinations of the Masons and the Trilateral Commission, Marrs touched all the conspiracy bases, with one notable exception—the ever more popular Biblical Apocalypse conspiracy movement. Marrs was an extremely rationalist paranoiac. Even though the modern American millenarianist movement has deep roots in early-twentieth-century theological traditions developed out of Dallas-area fundamentalist strongholds, Marrs gave no truck to the explanatory powers of the Antichrist or Satanic influences.[178]

If Marrs kept his distance from these local theological roots, he remained foundationally rooted in one local conspiracy tradition. For Marrs, as for the modern conspiracy movement itself, it all started with the Kennedy assassination. *Crossfire: The Plot That Killed Kennedy* was his first synthesizing effort, weaving together of all the extant major JFK conspiracy theories. For Marrs, just as it was for two generations of assassination researchers, the killing of JFK was the cataclysmic event that convinced him that there was a hidden

177. Peter Knight, *Conspiracy Nation: The Politics of Paranoia in Postwar America* (New York: New York University Press, 2002), 5–6.

178. Michael Phillips, *White Metropolis: Race, Ethnicity, and Religion in Dallas, 1941–2001* (Austin: University of Texas Press, 2006), 49–50.

story that had to be unearthed in order to save the country. Look at Marrs's 2006 book, *The Terror Conspiracy,* and his description of a suspected cover-up of a government plot behind the 9/11 attacks. There is a direct and clear lineage connecting *Crossfire* and this more recent conspiracy research:

> If the game plan of the masterminds behind the 9/11 attacks was to curtail American freedom, centralize more power in the federal government and set back the social agenda of the United States in favor of an open-ended military and intelligence buildup, then they succeeded admirably. To many longtime researchers, it all has a familiar ring to it.
>
> In many ways, the aftermath of the 9/11 attacks fit the same template as the assassination of President Kennedy in 1963.[179]

Jonathan Kay, in his 2011 study of 9/11 conspiracy theorists, *Among the Truthers: A Journey through America's Growing Conspiracist Underground,* noted: "Scratch the surface of a middle-aged 9/11 Truther, and you are almost guaranteed to find a JFK conspiracist." There is an obvious parallel between the career arc of Jim Marrs and the development of the larger conspiracist movement. "It is impossible to overstate how influential the legacy of JFK's murder has been in the formation of the flourishing and variegated conspiracist subcultures of later decades," Kay writes. "In fact, the death of JFK acts as a sort of universal hinge point for conspiracy theorists everywhere."[180] Fellow scholar Timothy Melley, in his 2000 *Empire of Conspiracy: The Culture of Paranoia in Postwar America,* agrees, writing that the JFK assassination was "the postwar source of conspiracy theory par excellence."[181]

For all his wild excursions into the world of international and interstellar conspiracy, Jim Marrs never strayed far from home. He lived less than an

---

179. Jim Marrs, *The Terror Conspiracy: Deception, 9/11 and the Loss of Liberty* (New York: Disinformation, 2006), 399.

180. Jonathan Kay, *Among the Truthers: A Journey through America's Growing Conspiracist Underground* (New York: HarperCollins, 2011), 51, 45, 50.

181. Timothy Melley, *Empire of Conspiracy: The Culture of Paranoia in Postwar America* (Ithaca, NY: Cornell University Press, 2000), 134.

hour's drive northwest of his Fort Worth birthplace, in the rural splendor of a spacious ranch house just outside the little burg of Paradise, Texas. Until his death in 2017, he continued working out that original ambition that struck him as a young journalism student in November 1963: how he might get involved in the biggest news story to ever come out of North Texas. He stayed on the case. Through his work with the *Fort Worth Star-Telegram,* his classes at the University of Texas at Arlington, and all his subsequent research and writing, one center of gravity defined Jim Marrs's orbit—the assassination of John F. Kennedy in Dallas, Texas.

•

"There is a world within the world." That is the refrain Don DeLillo repeats throughout *Libra,* a book predicated on the idea that we *do* live in a nation where paranoia is as American as apple pie and where we *are* all conspiracy theorists. In *Libra,* stories are embedded within stories, and people live clandestine lives, relaying cryptic codes and secret signs. The real story is always lying just underneath the surface. In Dallas, nearly sixty years after the JFK assassination, there is also a world within the world. Beneath the hustle and bustle of one of America's biggest and most thriving metropolitan areas, there exists, for those willing to look, an underground world of clandestine drama.

Today, just a mile or so southeast of Dealey Plaza, in the basement of Dallas City Hall, there is a literal underground world of file cabinets, stacked boxes, and stored documents of every size and shape. It is the City of Dallas Archives, and like the room occupied by DeLillo's secret CIA historian, Nicholas Branch, it is a windowless expanse spread out beneath the aquarium–like glow of fluorescent light. We are back where John Slate goes about his business as the City of Dallas's chief archivist.

The history that Slate has most recently mined from the treasure trove of this concrete cavern is something called *Historic Dallas Parks.* Part of Arcadia Publishing's extensive "Images of America" series, the 2010 book is a visual history of the City of Dallas's four hundred public parks. Culled from the files of the city archives, it is a collection of black-and-white photos, design plans, artist's renderings, and mementos that relates the history of the city through its park system. Lovingly curated and captioned by Slate, *Historic Dallas Parks* notes that some parks, deemed to have "interest far beyond Dallas," receive a bit more attention than others. Dealey Plaza, for instance, receives more space—five pages—than its measly fifteen acres would seem to merit.

The location, Slate informs us, has a central significance in Dallas history. It was the site of an important Trinity River crossing, "the intersection of two major American Indian traces," and thus a logical spot for John Neely Bryan to plant his original homestead. Slate spends most of these five pages chronicling the site's 1930s transformation into one of the gems of the city—the western gateway into downtown Dallas. Excerpts from its design plans and photos of its construction document its creation, and the 1936 *Annual Report of the City of Dallas* proudly displays a completed Dealey Plaza on its cover.

The final photo of Dealey Plaza included in John Slate's *Historic Dallas Parks* was taken on November 22, 1963, the day of the assassination. It shows the plaza undergoing yet another transformation. The northern section of the plaza is filled with bouquets and wreaths, "as the park became a makeshift memorial to the slain president."[182] From that date on, Dealey Plaza would have a second, shadow life—a parallel and powerful existence well beyond its "official" life as the core of historic Dallas or its function as the gateway to downtown.

•

Like Dealey Plaza, John Slate has his own shadow life. Beneath his "official" *Historic Dallas Parks* chronicle of Dealey Plaza lurks another history of Dealey Plaza that Slate helped write. Like *Historic Dallas Parks,* this other text features black-and-white photos and diagrams of historical Dallas, but here the tone is different. The section concerning Dealey Plaza is labeled "Bushwack Park." The section on the Triple Underpass is subtitled "Vituperative Viaduct"; that

182. John Slate, *Historic Dallas Parks* (Charleston, SC: Arcadia Publishing, 2010), 63–68.

on the Texas School Book Depositary is subtitled "Crosshairs & Chicken Wings"; and the grassy knoll is the "Assassin's Ant Hill." The accompanying text and captions relate the movement of a team of coordinated shooters, including a "fake" Lee Harvey Oswald, spread around the plaza in order to lay down triangulated fire into the president's touring car. All of this commentary serves to confirm "that there was a conspiracy to murder the thirty-fifth President, John F. Kennedy."

This text was the creation of a younger John Slate, something only a handful of his closest acquaintances might know about. In 1988, Slate and a few of his Dallas rock 'n' roll buddies put together this twenty-four-page Xeroxed packet. Copyrighted by the Sixth Floor Press, the first edition of one hundred copies was stamped across the cover page "TOP SECRET." Its title? *Conspiracy A-Go-Go: A Guide to Selected Sites in Dallas Associated with the Assassination of John F. Kennedy*.

•

Today there continues to be a number of JFK assassination–related tours tooling daily around the streets of Dallas. The Dallas Historical Society once offered an "In the Steps of Oswald" tour. "Learn about the motorcade and events surrounding the assassination as well as individuals like Oswald, Ruby and Tippit by visiting the sites where it all took place." Or there is the JFK Assassination Trolley Tour, whose website recently implored potential customers to "Take the 1 hour JFK trolley tour . . . and go back in time to November 22, 1963." A visitor to Dallas can simply search the internet for "JFK Assassination Tours" and choose from a dozen options.

In 1988, a JFK assassination tour was a more novel and dangerous idea. When John Slate and his friends compiled *Conspiracy A-Go-Go: A Guide to Selected Sites in Dallas Associated with the Assassination of John F. Kennedy*, it was to be the guidebook for a very tongue-in-cheek twenty-fifth anniversary assassination tour. Slate was then himself twenty-five years old and still living in Austin at the time, but he had fallen in with a group of quasi-intellectual Dallas rock 'n' rollers who called themselves the Potatoes. He occasionally helped them out with sound and lights. Like Slate, the group was fascinated with JFK assassination conspiracy theories, and their song "Jack Ruby's Girls" was a staple in their repertoire.

"I got interested in the various sites related to the JFK assassination," Slate recently related, "so in 1988—the twenty-fifth anniversary—I figured, 'Why don't we do something silly?' So I drove up to Dallas, hung out with friends, and we rented a limo-type car and put together a driving tour. *Conspiracy A-Go-Go* was a driving tour booklet." Slate and select members of the Potatoes packed an ice chest into the rented vehicle, filled it with free beer, loaded up their passengers, and embarked, "like Gilligan's Island—a three-hour tour." [183] The tours started on Saturday and continued into Sunday evening, and, by the time they were done, "perhaps two dozen people had paid twelve dollars each for the booklet and a narrated ride around the city."

The lighthearted tour seemed to be well received. It got some PR on prime-time radio, was the subject of an article in the *Dallas Times Herald,* and received only one "hate call." The organizers, however, kept their real identities secret. As the *Times Herald* reported: "The tour leader"—in actuality, head Potato John Kays—"was a 35-year-old Dallas musician and conspiracy buff who had adopted the name 'Dr. Noel di Grassi.'" The other participants adopted such monikers as Dr. Warren Piece, Ruby Payola, and Tarr D. Pans. John Slate, described as "a 24-year-old library assistant from Austin," was Dr. Harvey O. Kliff.[184]

It was this brief foray into assassination tourism that brought Slate's obsession with Kennedy conspiracy lore to Richard Linklater's attention, eventually resulting in the birth of the "Conspiracy A-Go-Go" Guy. With *Slacker*'s runaway success, Slate's character—the annoying nut that you can't get away from—became an underground icon. People began to recognize him as he traveled around the country, often assuming he *was* the character he played.

By 2011, the film *Slacker* had taken on a life of its own. In celebration of its twentieth anniversary, the Austin Film Society commissioned *Slacker 2011*, a retrospective tribute in which twenty-six local filmmakers

183. John Slate, interview with Tim Cloward, December 22, 2010.

184. Jim Morris, "Tour with a twist visits obscure JFK sites." *Dallas Times Herald,* November 21, 1988.

reinterpreted segments of Richard Linklater's original. Director John Bryant happily grabbed the opportunity to update the "Conspiracy A-Go-Go" segment. The new version of this scene takes place not in Half-Price Books but in a video store. Actor Chris Trew, with his long black hair and full beard, bears no resemblance at all to the young John Slate, and Slate's original white T-shirt depicting Ruby shooting Oswald has been replaced with a black T-shirt emblazoned with "9/11 Was an Inside Job." Trew, however, mimics the original "Conspiracy A-Go-Go" Guy mannerisms lovingly. As the 2011 version of this archetype latches on to his female victim, Trew's nervous shuffling, his head shake, even his voice, with his rambling "you know"s and "yeah"s are near-perfect takes on the original. Trew's character is still working on his book, *Conspiracy A-Go-Go*. But, as he regales his victim, his exegesis is not focused on JFK conspiracy literature. It's all about 9/11 Truther video documentaries. The times have changed, but the conspiracy narrative lives on.

When *Slacker 2011* premiered in Dallas, it was given the royal treatment at that year's annual Dallas Video Festival. The festival, one of the most elaborate of its kind and an important Dallas cultural event, kicked off its celebration with a special screening of *Slacker 2011* at Oak Cliff's newly renovated Texas Theatre (famous, of course, as the site of Lee Harvey Oswald's arrest just hours after the assassination). That screening featured the premiere of four additional *Slacker*-tribute segments produced by Dallas-area directors. The most notable of these new shorts was created by University of Texas at Arlington film grad and longtime John Slate friend Ryan Hartsell. Hartsell's clip has Slate himself reprising his "Conspiracy A-Go-Go" Guy role, but, as in John Bryant's tribute to Linklater, the character has been updated for a new generation.

In Hartsell's video, Slate is back in a bookstore, but his victim now is a kid in the children's book section; he's reading *Phantom of the Muppet Theater* when Slate confronts him. The plot, as Slate explains it this time, involves the covert murder of Muppets puppeteer Jim Henson at the hands of the Disney Corporation. Slate, in dialogue he and Hartsell worked up together, spells out how Disney manipulated the death of the famous children's entertainer, and recommends that his young listener stop in the conspiracy section and grab the book *Surrender to the Mouse* to find out more about Disney's malevolent power grab. Or, Slate tells the kid, he can wait for his new book to come out—it's called *Death by Disney*. ("My Kennedy book," Slate's "Conspiracy A-Go-Go" Guy confesses, "didn't turn out too great").[185]

By the time Hartsell's video premiered, doubles of John Slate's project were popping up faster than fake Lee Harvey Oswalds, and the term "Conspiracy A-Go-Go" had already become a part of the popular lexicon. Today, it is the moniker of a current hip-hop/alternative band, the title of two CDs (one rock and one jazz), the name of "the world's only conspiracy theory and sticker magazine," and, increasingly, the phrase of choice when we wish to denote our contemporary mania for paranoia. *Texas Monthly*, for instance, titled its November 1998 piece on alleged JFK assassination plots "Conspiracy A-Go-Go."

•

To look today at *Conspiracy A-Go-Go: A Guide to Selected Sites in Dallas Associated with the Assassination of John F. Kennedy* is to be reminded that, in Dallas, there is always a parallel reality. Because of the JFK assassination, the city lives a double life. The *Conspiracy-A-Go-Go* guidebook exhorts us to come to grips with the history of the JFK assassination. "Some people," it reminds us, "have lived in Dallas all their lives and never seen these places." In its own campy and ironic manner, it reminds us that a second look at the local landscape might just reveal a geography of secrecy and intrigue. What the *Conspiracy A-Go-Go* guidebook (and the conspiracy movement in general) proposes is that the world we see is simply a sort of stage set for a parallel drama, a counterfeit world that fronts the one where things *really* get done.

In the *Conspiracy A-Go-Go* guidebook, this philosophy is explained courtesy of the "Nerraw Commission." "Nerraw," of course, is the "Warren" of the Warren Commission run backward. If the official *Warren Report* presents a version of Dallas where law and order reign and the Kennedy assassination case

185. Robert Wilonsky, "It's No Conspiracy as Dallas's Official Archivist, John Slate, Reprises His Slacker Role." *Dallas Observer*, September 22, 2011.

is closed, the Nerraw Commission presents the opposing, mirror image—Dallas as a vast, sprawling crime scene.

Follow the *Conspiracy A-Go-Go* guide and you will experience the city as a conspiracy investigator. In the spirit of tongue-in-cheek public service, Slate and his conspiracy crew exhort you to stop and see the city with fresh eyes: "These structures stand in mute testimony to the lurid misdeeds of the persons involved in the Crime of the Century."

•

The first stop is perhaps the most unlikely: a lower-middle-class suburban neighborhood in the mid-city of Irving. Located halfway between Dallas and Fort Worth, at 2502 West Fifth Street, is Ruth Paine's former home. This is where Oswald spent his last free night, visiting his estranged wife, Marina. This boxy little tract home (restored to its original condition in conjunction with the fiftieth anniversary of the Kennedy assassination and now open to the general public as the Paine House Museum) is also where Oswald stored his Mannlicher-Carcano rifle, removing it from its garage hiding place, disguising it as curtain rods, and carrying it to his job at the Texas School Book Depository. In our guidebook, this is the "Casa de Curtain Rods."[186]

The next stop—"Redrum Runway" in the guidebook—is Dallas's Love Field. A thriving regional airport and the corporate center and operational hub for prosperous Southwest Airlines, it is a very busy place. If you look beneath the bustle, however, you will see the ghosts of 1963. This is where, if you believe the LBJ conspiracy angle, the public face of the coup d'état was on full display. Love Field is where President Kennedy and his beautiful wife first stepped down from Air Force One into an adoring Dallas crowd. It was also where, just a few hours later, he was returned in a coffin, his wife forced to stand by as Lyndon Baines Johnson took his presidential oath.

Due east from Love Field, following Mockingbird Avenue across Central Expressway, the guidebook takes you to Campisi's Egyptian

186. Avi Selk, "It's '63 again at place that hosted Oswald," *Dallas Morning News*, December 22, 2012.

Restaurant—"Carcano Carbonara." The restaurant has expanded since Jack Ruby ate dinner there on the night before the assassination, but the figure of founding owner Joseph Campisi still holds court in the form of a nearly life-size portrait hanging on a back wall. In the darkened dining room, you can imagine that the whispers at the bar and between the booths hold the clues that might reveal the truth of Campisi's links to the mob, and, through him, Ruby's links to that mysterious underworld.

Back on the west side of town, the guidebook takes you into Highland Park, the affluent city within a city that has traditionally housed Dallas's elite. There, among its meandering avenues, you'll find 4011 Turtle Creek Boulevard—the "Pad of Tiberius of Olde Dallas" according to the guidebook. This is the home once owned by General Edwin A. Walker, the well-known right-wing zealot once institutionalized by Robert Kennedy for inciting anti-government violence during the 1962 integration battles at Old Miss. This is also the mansion where Lee Harvey Oswald supposedly attempted his first assassination, and where, some speculate, the plot to kill the president might have been hatched.

After the *Conspiracy A-Go-Go* tour clears Dealey Plaza, it veers deeper into downtown Dallas, to 1312 ½ Commerce Street, the site of "The Brotherhood's Burlesque"—Jack Ruby's Carousel Club. Today you see this address has been subsumed into the towering edifice of One AT&T Plaza, but, in 1963, this was the swinging nude dance club that, in our guidebook's words, "served as a focal point of the people and forces that conspired to eliminate the Chief Executive." A few blocks away, at 2014 Main Street, sits the Municipal Building. This is where Dallas citizens pay their traffic fines or stand trial for local misdemeanors. Most of them wouldn't necessarily realize that downstairs, in the basement parking garage, is where America experienced its first televised murder—"Oswald's Last Stand." This is the site where Jack Ruby stepped out of the crowd and shot dead the one man who could tell us the real story of John F. Kennedy's assassination.

Parkland Hospital is an obvious stop on our *Conspiracy A-Go-Go* tour. Here, our guidebook suggests, the "Magic Bullet" was placed on Governor Connally's stretcher, perhaps by Jack Ruby himself. Parkland is still Dallas County's primary public hospital, although today it is buried in the center of a sprawling medical complex and almost unrecognizable from its 1963 incarnation. Despite the immense activity that has occurred here—decades of the constant cycle of birth and death—Parkland Hospital cannot escape its infamous past. This is where President Kennedy was pronounced dead; where, two days later, Oswald was pronounced dead; where, three years after that, a cancer-ridden Jack Ruby died. According to our guidebook: "Its low-slung roof, announcing 'Emergency' in casual modern letters," spells out for those in the know, "death and conspiracy and wrath and lawlessness and horror."

The one barrier that truly breaks up the sprawl of Dallas is the Trinity River. It separates the northern regions of the city from its smaller southwestern Oak Cliff and West Dallas neighborhoods. In Dallas, however, the pall of conspiracy knows no physical boundaries. In Oak Cliff, the structures of the older white, working-class underside of Dallas now shimmer with the bright colors that have flowed in with the new Hispanic majority. Today, if you visit 1221 North Beckley Street, you will find the Vet Stop Animal Clinic. In 1963, your guidebook explains, you would have found the Dobbs House "Steak 'n Egg Kitchen," the site of the "Breakfast of Infamy." We know that Jack Ruby often ate breakfast there, and we know that here, at 10:00 AM on November 20—the Wednesday just before the assassination—Lee Harvey Oswald and Dallas Police Officer J. D. Tippit, whom Oswald would kill two days later, ate breakfast just a few feet apart from each other. Our guidebook suggests this might have been more than simply a coincidence.

Just a few blocks due south, at 1026 North Beckley, you'll find Lee Harvey Oswald's last residence. This is where he was living at the time of the assassination, and where he first fled just after the shooting in Dealey Plaza. The mystery here, the guidebook explains, revolves around the testimony of Earlene Roberts, the woman who ran the boarding house. Roberts testified that a police car pulled up in front of the house and signaled—two fast horn honks, "tit-tit"—just before Oswald slipped out of the house. Who was in that car? The guidebook suggests it was Tippit and Ruby.

Next, not too far away, is a rickety old apartment building at 214 Neely Street. This is the site of one of Oswald's earliest Dallas residences. It is most famous as the locale of the famous photo session during which Marina snapped Oswald (the guide labels him here the "Shutterbug Socialist") with his Mannlicher-Carcano rifle and his socialist pamphlets. Or did she? The guidebook suggests that a closer examination of the photo shows "unlikely-sized shadows." Could it be the photo has been doctored?

Finally, the *Conspiracy A-Go-Go* tour ends, just as it started, in a nondescript housing tract far from the bustle of downtown and Dealey Plaza. Today, at 404 Tenth Street, just down the block from where Tenth intersects with Patton Street, a freshly dedicated plaque commemorates what some might say was the first sacrifice to the JFK assassination cover-up. The inscription on the new historical marker begins: "On November 22, 1963, at this intersection, Dallas Police Officer J. D. Tippit was murdered by Lee Harvey Oswald." Our guidebook, however, cautions us that Tippit was shot "by a man that bore a likeness to Lee Oswald." It also suggests that, if the killer *was* actually Oswald, he very well might have been "on a bee line to [Jack] Ruby's Apartment."

•

By its conclusion, the three-hour *Conspiracy A-Go-Go* tour has covered a fairly large swath of Dallas. Humor aside, the *Conspiracy A-Go-Go* tour represents the core ideas of the JFK conspiracist movement with some accuracy. To take it is to replicate the detective work done by the conspiracy researchers. When it's over, you've seen the city—rather, you've seen underneath the surface of the city, and you've seen that nothing is as simple as it has been presented in the *Warren Report*. Questions remain; the case is far from closed. You understand when the *Conspiracy A-Go-Go* guidebook leaves you with its clever tagline: "The plot thickens."

The Kennedy assassination and its immediate aftermath have become an indelible part of the Dallas landscape—a stain that cannot be removed. It has its own inescapable images, icons, and mythology that cannot be washed away with public relation campaigns or rubbed out with high-profile seminars. The assassination is integral to our identity. While we have mercifully outgrown the label "City of Hate," we have not been able to seize complete control of our own story or explain what it means to have hosted the death of a president. We have officially acknowledged our part, built a museum and put up carefully contrived markers, but managing the comprehension of that watershed event has proved beyond the power of our city leaders. It has a life of its own, and it is always there underneath the surface, barely suppressed. We cannot put it to rest.

If you live in Dallas, there is always another world inside the world.

CHAPTER 3

Goodnight Mr. President

Tragedies of this dimension could be approached only as myths.
Norman Mailer, *Interview March 1, 1997*

JUST AFTER MIDNIGHT ON November 23, 1963, Jay Hogan of Dallas's KRLD radio, the local CBS affiliate, signed off for the evening. It had been an extraordinarily long and breathtakingly taxing workday. It had started with the excitement of covering the visit of the president and his wife, and it had ended with the president dead, a police officer shot, the suspected assassin arrested, a new president sworn in, and, just as Hogan was saying his good-night, the body of the fallen leader returned to Washington, DC, aboard Air Force One. Throughout the mad rush of the day's events, Hogan manned the controls at the KRLD radio desk, working behind the mic and switching between the accounts of his local reporters in the field and updates from the national network. When he wasn't on air, he was writing copy and editing wire stories; within a few hours of the shooting, he had conducted the first interviews with Dealey Plaza witnesses Mary Moorman and Jean Hill. Hogan stayed on the air all day, struggling to make sense of the chaos and maintain a sense that someone was in control.

Described by a coworker as "a scholarly old pro" who "was genteel, private, and soft-spoken," Jay Hogan kept an old leatherbound copy of Omar

Khayyam's *Rubaiyat* in his office desk drawer. As he completed his extraordinary day of live reporting, he chose to end his shift by stepping beyond the bounds of journalism. It seemed appropriate to Hogan to take up the prerogatives of poetry, to cast about for the myth that might properly memorialize the tragedy of the newly assassinated president. He ended his newscast with this verse, an original work he had managed to compose amid all this confusion.

> It has all been a long dark night since last Friday,
> And daylight hours are still needed here.
> But Mr. President, may we say one last good night,
> When there must be perpetual light
> In your faraway Valhalla, wherever,
> Reserved for souls like yours.
> And we can still see your bright smile
> And your vigorous stride
> Through some mystic Elysian fields.
> Good Night, Mr. President—good night.[187]

•

The assassination of John F. Kennedy has long been acknowledged as the beginning of a new era in mass media communication—the one event that propelled us into the world of electronic saturation that we live in today. The three TV networks broadcast continuous assassination coverage for roughly seventy-five hours. During those long hours while the news was live, broadcasters were hard-pressed to fill on-air time. To fill the pauses and lulls, they ad-libbed and improvised. While politicians were temporarily dumbfounded by the gravity of events and law enforcement officials were stifled by the pressure of the moment, the broadcast journalists were left to make it up as they went along.

---

187. *The Lost JFK Tapes: The Assassination.* National Geographic, 2000, DVD; Huffaker et al., *When The News Went Live*, 38.

Unlike our current period of cynicism toward the media, the early 1960s was a time when broadcast journalists enjoyed nearly unquestioned credibility—when Walter Cronkite was cementing his reputation as "the most trusted man in America." In those chaotic days after the assassination, our on-air news personalities didn't just bring us the news. They were our most trusted oracles, sifting through the tea leaves of fragmentary reports and jumbled intelligence to bring us the story.

But this news was so big; the victim, arguably the most important and powerful man in the world, was senselessly done in before our eyes. Here was the oldest human burden—making sense of death for the living—and this was no ordinary man. This was the governing president of the United States, the ruler in whose destiny the masses saw their own small fates writ large. And so it was that Jay Hogan, eleven hours into the new era of electronic media, turned to poetry in an attempt to deliver the appropriate eulogy for this fallen hero.

In his midnight benediction, Hogan could not help but raise his rhetoric to the level of mythology. First, he evoked the warrior tradition of the intrepid Norse, placing the departed president in Valhalla, his "perpetual light" sheltering in the great god Odin's hall of slain heroes. The president's death was too profound for a single image, however, and Hogan was compelled to offer another glimpse of the fallen hero, with his "bright smile" and his "vigorous stride," disappearing "Through some mystic Elysian fields." In his mythopoeic searching, Hogan closes by linking Kennedy to Greek mythology and its final resting place for the souls of the virtuous and righteous.

Norman Mailer, writing about the JFK assassination in 1992, explained that "Tragedies of this dimension can be approached only as myths." He also cast the JFK assassination in terms of Greek tragedy, asserting that we still lived "in the mystery, the awe, the horror, and the knowledge that a huge and hideous event did, yes, take place on that day, and the gods had warred, a god fell, and a nation could never be the same."[188]

Jay Hogan's elegy was just one local expression of a larger movement

188. Mailer, "Footfalls in the Crypt."

powerful enough to remake John F. Kennedy, the man, into a myth. As William Manchester, who himself would do much to shape that myth, wrote: "The Kennedy we knew in life vanished forever on November 22, 1963."[189]

•

That people would speak of John F. Kennedy in mythological terms so quickly after his death would not have surprised anyone who had been paying close attention to Kennedy's career as he lived. Throughout his lifetime, John F. Kennedy was constantly and consciously engaged in the business of mythmaking, with himself as the primary product. His political success, in large measure, was the result of his proficiency in writing his own story and creating his own heroic persona.

Joseph Kennedy, his father, was himself an accomplished and powerful public figure. He was the first chairman of the Securities and Exchange Commission and the American Ambassador to England at the beginning of World War II. As the dynamo who created RKO Radio Pictures, one of the Big Five studios of Hollywood's Golden Age, and the man behind the production of at least seventy-six movies, the elder Kennedy knew a little about the creation of an effective public persona.[190] After his oldest son, Joe Jr., was killed in action in the summer of 1944, John became Joseph Kennedy's primary PR project. John was groomed from an early age for success, and as Joseph became more and more aware of his second son's natural charisma, he began scripting his path to the presidency.

With his father's help, twenty-two-year-old Harvard undergrad John Kennedy transformed his graduation thesis into his first great success. Taking advantage of his ambassador father's connections in England, John produced a historical study of England's entrance into WWII. With the assistance of his father's friend, the influential publisher Henry Luce, this

189. Manchester, *The Death of a President*, 623–24.

190. David Lubin, *Shooting Kennedy: JFK and the Culture of Images* (Berkeley: University of California Press, 2005), 6.

thesis became the 1940 bestseller *Why England Slept*. Beneath this impressive early literary accomplishment, John Hellman has suggested, young John Kennedy was writing his own coming-of-age story. Ostensibly about England overcoming its post-WWI lethargy and rising to confront the Nazi menace, *Why England Slept* could also be read as an allegory of John Kennedy's own journey from carefree undergrad to serious scholar, anxious to actively apply the lessons of history.[191]

John Kennedy's transformation into a war hero was also ably abetted by Joseph Kennedy's media manipulations. In 1943, John, then commander of torpedo boat PT-109, went missing in the South Pacific after a sea battle. His subsequent rescue was a huge relief to the Kennedy clan. It also represented a great opportunity. Through Joseph's cultivation of a family friend, the up-and-coming journalist John Hersey, the incident metamorphosed into "Survival," a dramatic piece published by the *New Yorker* in 1944. While John Kennedy's actions during the Solomon Islands campaign displayed obvious heroism and leadership, Hersey's groundbreaking New Journalism turned them into something larger than life. "Joe Kennedy seized upon his son's unfortunate accident as a public relations bonanza," wrote Thomas Maier, "turning the episode into an ocean-faring myth of Melvillean proportions, a virtual Jack Kennedy and the Argonauts."[192] The story of PT-109 would play a critical part in the shaping of Kennedy's public persona.

In his public statements, Kennedy was quite self-effacing about the PT-109 episode. "It was involuntary—they sunk my boat," he famously quipped. He could, however, conveniently benefit from strategic retellings of the story. His father, for instance, had one hundred thousand condensed versions of Hersey's "Survival" reprinted for use in his son's 1946 congressional campaign. Later, when the 1963 film *PT-109* entered production, the White House was very much involved. The three conditions Kennedy demanded were that the film had to be historically accurate, that any profits from the venture should go to the survivors of the PT-109 incident and their families,

191. John Hellman, *The Kennedy Obsession: The American Myth of JFK* (New York: Columbia University Press, 1997), 21–27.

192. Thomas Maier, *The Kennedys: America's Emerald Kings* (New York: Basic Books, 2004), 170.

and that he would have his choice of the actor who would portray him. (He picked Cliff Robertson. Peter Fonda, Warren Beatty, Jeffrey Hunter, and Edd Byrnes were all left to wonder what might have been.)

In the mid-1950s, when Kennedy was a struggling backbench senator recuperating from serious back surgery, he spent his recovery time working with Ted Sorenson to produce the book *Profiles in Courage*. By writing about great political figures who had resisted the easy or popular options and taken more difficult but brave action, Kennedy projected a similar self-portrait before the eyes of the reading public. Rewarded with a 1957 Pulitzer Prize, *Profiles in Courage* was of as much importance to John F. Kennedy's political career as anything he had accomplished on the Senate floor. It did not hurt, either, that Jacqueline Bouvier, the beautiful Eastern establishment debutante he chose to marry, had some experience in the media world herself, having worked for the *Washington Times Herald* as the "Inquiring Camera Girl." She had already interviewed Vice President Nixon and covered both Eisenhower's inauguration and the coronation of Queen Elizabeth II. With her social savvy and highly developed sense of the public's perception, Jackie would make an astute partner, as well as the perfect romantic lead for the charismatic and ambitious young senator.

One has only to review Kennedy's 1961 inaugural address to perceive that he was a man who understood you could speak new realities into existence, and his great rhetorical powers remain at the heart of his legacy. As his patronage of the arts subsequently made clear, Kennedy knew the value of celebrating the great works of human creativity, and he understood the opportunities inherent in poetry for national mythmaking. His invitation of the venerable New England bard Robert Frost to read at his inauguration initiated the new tradition of incorporating poetry into one of the nation's most solemn and significant common rituals. At Kennedy's request, Frost composed "Dedication" (later titled "For John F. Kennedy His Inauguration"), repaying tribute to the new president by tracing American history from its inception until that point. He noted that, with the inauguration of the new, dynamic president, "There is a call to life a little sterner, / and braver for the earner, learner, yearner." The poem's stirring conclusion proclaimed the promise of the new administration in classically heroic terms.

> It makes the prophet in us all presage
> The glory of a next Augustan age
> Of power leading from its strength and pride,
> Of young ambition eager to be tried,
> Firm in our free beliefs without dismay,
> In any game the nations want to play.
> A golden age of poetry and power
> Of which this noonday's the beginning hour.

•

That next Augustan age, the "golden age of poetry and power" that Robert Frost trumpeted on January 20, 1961, would end abruptly on November 22, 1963. After just "A Thousand Days"—as Kennedy's hand-picked personal historian, Arthur M. Schlesinger Jr., would title his chronicle of the Kennedy administration—it was all over. There was no need for Virgilian tributes to the august ruler now; it was the time for elegies.

After November 22, 1963, the throats of America were unloosed in a common mourning wail. William Manchester wrote that, on the evening and day after the assassination, writers in Washington, DC, "went on writing. In crises literacy may eclipse every other passion. Drunks were sober, lechers were chaste, and aspirants for the Presidency . . . were free of Potomac fever, but the stream of words swelled hourly."[193]

All over the country, people were writing, seeking to work their grief out in language. As Manchester saw it:

> The amount of unpublished material [was] overwhelming. There were literally tons of it. Judging from the mail that reached 1600 Pennsylvania Avenue immediately after the funeral, at least fifty

193. Manchester, *The Death of a President*, 446.

> thousand adults and children were writing poems Sunday evening . . . They were more than just inquisitive; profoundly moved by the historical catastrophe, they wanted to participate in the country's homage, and if their doggerel was often trite and their gestures clumsy, they were expressing themselves with all the eloquence they had, and sometimes it was a lot.[194]

Poetry is, of course, the genre most available for the spontaneous outpouring of emotion, a universal conduit for the purging of powerful feelings. In Dallas, those emotions must have been particularly raw. It would seem inevitable that Dallas and its environs must have produced a huge amount of spontaneous poetry during those traumatic days after November 22, 1963. One would think that here, where the assassination occurred, there would have been thousands of poems written in response to the shock, dismay, and helplessness that people were feeling. It would seem logical to expect this reflex to generate an outpouring of short lyrics, confessional screeds, rants, reflections, a thousand stabs at therapeutic verse.

It is surprising, however, how little local poetry from that period can be found today; next to nothing remains for us to read. Certainly, a good amount of it would have been deliberately destroyed almost as soon as the ink dried. It is very possible that much of it has been, more or less, hidden away. It could be lost in attics, closets, garages, anywhere old journals, notebooks, or loose papers are stored away; a huge archive, buried away beyond recovery.

But if such poems exist in Dallas, there has never been a call for them: no editor who sought them out, no anthologist who solicited local works dealing with the assassination. In a city not entirely comfortable with the literary pursuits, these poems must have simply sunk further and further beneath the surface. Poetry, as the most personal and intimate form of writing, often tends to stay private, and, in the literary world of Dallas at that time, there was no stomach to revisit the trauma we had just lived through.

But it may be that some of this writing—assassination-related poems or self-consciously literary epistles—was sent out. "Doggerel," as Manchester

194. Manchester, *The Death of a President*, 56.

termed it, "trite" with its "gestures clumsy," most of it would never have met the test of art or reached the standard that would separate it from self-therapy. Some of it must still be out there, locked away in the tons of letters sent to the widowed Jacqueline Kennedy, or filed away in the thousands of messages received by Dallas Mayor Earle Cabell. Some of it would have been long ago purged from newspaper files, tossed out from the folders of now-defunct literary journals, buried away too deep for retrieval.

While the rest of America was writing and purging their grief through that work, in Dallas we generally kept it to ourselves. We were ashamed and embarrassed because we had killed Kennedy. And, even if that accusation wasn't the truth, we heard it coming from all directions. What right did we have to eulogize the president, to share in the grief that we knew the rest of the world perceived us to have caused?

The other option is that the words never even met the page—that the trauma was so great here the local populace could not even bring themselves to express what they were feeling. It could be that the events surrounding November 22, 1963, had left us mute.

•

John F. Kennedy would have his proper eulogies. Perhaps the finest and most moving moment of poetic invocation in memory of the slain president would come nine months later in Atlantic City. While addressing the assembled delegates at the 1964 Democratic Convention, Robert Kennedy introduced a filmed tribute to his fallen older brother by borrowing from scene 3, act 2 of Shakespeare's *Romeo and Juliet*.

> . . . When he shall die,
> Take him and cut him out in little stars,
> And he will make the face of heaven so fine
> That all the world will be in love with night,
> And pay no worship to the garish sun.

While the convention was a rally for the election of Lyndon Baines Johnson,

Robert Kennedy's brief invocation was its most powerful moment. It sparked a fifteen-minute ovation.[195]

In the days immediately after the assassination, the newspaper editorialists, television commentariat, and community and religious leaders made their shocked initial decrees. In the unfolding new era of media saturation, there was a chaos of remembrance and fast-breaking news, but there was nothing that could satisfy the American public's need for sanctified common ritual. The world waited impatiently for the president's funeral.

As orchestrated by Jacqueline Kennedy, the state funeral of John F. Kennedy was a masterpiece of stately ceremony. But it was not an occasion for especially memorable oration. At Saint Matthew's Cathedral, Cardinal Richard Cushing conducted the traditional Catholic ceremony in Latin. Apart from one sudden break into English ("May the angels, dear Jack, lead you into paradise. May the martyrs receive you at your coming"), the mass and the ceremony at the grave in Arlington National Cemetery were delivered in a language foreign to most Americans. What survived in the national memory was visual symbolism: Black Jack, the riderless horse with the symbolic empty boots in its stirrups; the black-veiled widow Jacqueline Kennedy, marching with the fallen president's brothers beside her; three-year-old John Kennedy Jr. saluting his father's coffin; fifty jet fighters, flying in a V formation with the last plane missing to symbolize the fallen leader; the lighting of the eternal flame. A huge television audience soaked it all in, and, while the hushed TV commentary has receded from our memory, the visual poetry of Kennedy's funeral still resonates with us today.

•

On November 25, 1963, the nation came together to memorialize John F. Kennedy. In Dallas, like the rest of the country, we watched the ceremony on TV. We too experienced the regal pageantry and shared in the common mourning. Many Dallas-area churches went a step further and held their own

195. William Manchester, *One Brief Shining Moment* (Boston: Little Brown, 1983), 271.

memorial services; some even set up television sets so that mourners could also watch the national services. One interdenominational service (a rarity for the area at the time) at Fort Worth's Farrington Field drew five thousand people.[196]

As we watched the great leaders of the world—France's Charles de Gaulle, Emperor Haile Selassie of Ethiopia, Chancellor Ludwig Erhard of West Germany, South Korea's Park Chung-hee—parade past the grave site, we knew that our leaders were there too. Determined that Dallas be represented at the funeral services, the Dallas Citizens Council scrambled to assemble an appropriate contingent of civic leaders. Mayor Earle Cabell led the group. He was joined by Erik Jonsson, then head of the DCC and chairman of the board of Texas Instruments; Willard Dawson Sterling, chief executive officer of Southwestern Life; and Rev. Luther Holcomb, a prominent area minister.[197] They represented the civic/business elite that we held in such unquestioned respect, but we worried: Would our fellow Dallasites be seen as pariahs in Washington, DC?

Whether we liked it or not, we were part of the story. On the same day that the state funeral of John F. Kennedy was being broadcast to the nation, we held our own funerals. Just as the roar of the Navy jet was dissipating over Arlington National Cemetery, the funeral of Dallas Police officer J. D. Tippit was commencing. Those who could not fit into the 450-seat South Dallas Beckley Hills Baptist Church had been ushered into Sunday school rooms equipped with closed-circuit television. Among these and the few thousand others who milled around outside the church were about seven hundred police officers from all over the state.

Just as in Washington, DC, there would be very little said here that could pass for memorable poetry. The Reverend C. D. Tipps Jr. delivered a sermon worthy of the burial of a noble foot soldier. "Today we are mourning the passing of a devoted public servant," he intoned. "He was doing his duty when he was taken by the lethal bullet of a poor, confused, misguided, ungodly

196. "Kennedy's Funeral Timeline: Minute by minute timeline of President John F. Kennedy's funeral." *Dallas Morning News*, November 22, 1988.

197. Darwin Payne, *Dallas Citizens Council: An Obligation of Leadership* (Dallas: Dallas Citizens Council, 2008), 58.

assassin—as was our president."[198] The organist played "The Old Rugged Cross," and the visitors filed by to pay their last respects. Then, having valiantly sacrificed himself for the greater cause, Tippit was buried, the first person laid out in a special section of Laurel Land Memorial Park dedicated to those who gave their lives in community service.

As the three local TV networks cut back and forth between the small, red brick church in the working-class Oak Cliff neighborhood and the events in Washington, DC, there was the prevalent sense that events in Dallas were shrouded in a great shadow. As *Life* magazine reported, "The choir, conscious of the TV cameras on them, sang with unwonted stiffness."[199]

The scene thirty-five miles to the west at Fort Worth's Rose Hill Cemetery was even more dismal. Because the gravediggers needed more time to complete their work, the funeral of Lee Harvey Oswald had been delayed. When it finally began at 4:00 PM (just as the new president, Lyndon Johnson, was hosting his elaborate reception for foreign dignitaries at the State Department), there were no TV cameras, just a group of anxious press reporters milling about with a large security detail of police and Secret Service men. Because no one had thought to arrange for the casket carrying Oswald to be moved from the chapel to the grave site, seven members of the press had to be recruited to assist. While there was some grumbling among them, the stoic reporters stepped up to the task. According to AP reporter Mike Cochran, Jerry Flemmons of the *Fort Worth Star-Telegram* turned to him and said, "Cochran, if we're gonna write a story about the burial of Lee Harvey Oswald, we're gonna have to bury the son of a bitch ourselves."[200]

The Revered Louis Saunders experienced a similar predicament. The executive secretary of the Fort Worth Council of Churches, Saunders recognized that, given the extensive media coverage of Oswald's burial, there was the potential for "an international incident." When the two other ministers

---

198. Kent Biffle, "Heroic Patrolman Lauded at Rites," *Dallas Morning News*, November 26, 1963.

199. Thomas Thompson, "In Texas a Policeman and an Assassin Are Laid to Rest Too," *Life*, December 6, 1963, 51–52.

200. Mike Cochran, "Ex-AP writer recalls serving as Oswald pallbearer," *AP News*, November 21, 2013.

who were called to oversee the service failed to show up, the funeral home director asked Saunders to perform the service. Despite the fact that he had not performed a burial service in eight years, Saunders consented. "No man," he said, "should be buried in Fort Worth without a minister."[201]

It was as bare a ceremony as could be imagined. Five members of the immediate family—Oswald's wife, Marina, his two infant children, his brother Robert, and his mother, Marguerite—joined Saunders on the five battered folding chairs grouped before the wooden coffin. As Saunders explained it: "I made a brief statement to the effect that we were here to lay away Lee Harvey Oswald, not judge him." He then quoted from memory the twenty-third Psalm ("The Lord is my shepherd . . .") and a passage from John 14 ("In my father's house are many mansions . . ."). Saunders closed with this statement: "Mrs. Oswald tells me that her son, Lee Harvey, was a good boy and that she loved him. And today, Lord, we commit his spirit to Your divine care." His only words for Oswald were: "May God have mercy on his soul."[202]

The service took about ten minutes. "There was a dim awareness in me," Saunders said later, "of the tremendous contrast between the beautiful and carefully worked-out service for President Kennedy and the very humble and stark service we were having." (It was estimated Oswald's funeral cost roughly five hundred dollars.

•

If the funereal oratory following the assassination of John F. Kennedy did not entirely fill the public's need for a common language in which they could voice their grief, the nation's poets were quick to charge into the breach. The public eulogies were quickly supplanted by the more private efforts of the elegists. If poets in Dallas were reticent to broach the topic, poets from every other corner of the nation were hard at work searching for the words that might make some sense of the tragedy.

---

201. Thompson, "In Texas a Policeman and Assassin Are Laid to Rest Too."

202. Robert Thomas Jr., "Rev. Louis Saunders, 88, Dies; Buried Oswald," *New York Times*, April 17, 1998.

Just as Lincoln, after his assassination, had been eulogized by Walt Whitman, James Russell Lowell, and Herman Melville, many of the best poets of John Kennedy's generation produced works to commemorate his passing. (America's poets responded to Kennedy's friendliness to the arts and his appreciation of poetry. In fact, less than a month before his assassination, the president had spoken eloquently for the "full recognition of the place of the artist" and "poetry as a means of saving power from itself" at the dedication of the Robert Frost Library.) A good number of those poets are anthologized in *Of Poetry and Power: Poems Occasioned by the Presidency and by the Death of John F. Kennedy*. Collected and edited by Erwin Glikes and Paul Schwaber in the months just after the assassination, the book takes its name from Frost's inaugural poem for Kennedy. It contains eighty-two poems by seventy-eight poets, including W. H Auden, John Berryman, Gwendolyn Brooks, Gregory Corso, Allen Ginsberg, Donald Hall, Mary Swenson, and Lois Zukofsky. There are poems in every style and form, all dedicated, in one way or another, to the memory of John F. Kennedy.

Of Poetry and Power is a very diverse collection, but it includes only one Texan—only one poet who could speak for the state where Kennedy was killed. He was Thomas Whitbread, an Easterner, born in New York, educated at Amherst and Harvard, who had voluntarily become a Texan. Hiring on at the University of Texas in 1959 at age twenty-eight, Whitbread quickly dove into the Texas literary life. He became a fixture in the UT English Department, where he taught poetry and creative writing, and his first book of poetry won the Texas Institute of Letters annual Poetry Award. He became an active member of the Poetry Society of Texas, and one of the most recognized poets in his adopted state.

Whitbread's contribution to *Of Poetry and Power*, simply titled "November 25, 1963," bore a particular burden. As the only work by a Texan in the Kennedy tribute anthology, the poem faced inevitable scrutiny for indications of the area's post-assassination state of mind. Whitbread, however, was not going to give up much.

The assassination of the President,
Among its many effects, confers upon

The slightest act a clarity of precision.
The sharpening of a pencil with a knife,
My old Scout knife, twenty years old, today
Sharply reseen as its invented self.
The cutting of my nails with the old small scissors,
Trying, as always, not to hurt the quick.
Then encountering, taking up the pencil,
Tooth marks, not mine, and breaking it in half
In the frustration of rage, despair, and grief
At life not being as it ought to be.
She bit it. Our love should be alive, as he
Much more should be, and stupidly is not.

Unlike almost all of the works collected in *Of Poetry and Power*, Whitbread's poem avoids direct engagement with the assassination. The title of the poem references the date of Kennedy's funeral, but it is not a funeral poem. It is not a celebration of the life of the hero or a memorial to his death; it is the chronicle of a failed attempt to avoid dealing with the emotions attached to the assassination.

Just as the memory of a failed love affair can be denied and displaced, so can the memory of the death of the president. But, try as he might to lose himself in the repetition of mundane actions, Whitbread's narrator cannot maintain the veneer of forgetfulness. In this regard, Whitbread's "November 25, 1963" is typical of much of the poetry produced in the state of Texas after the assassination—it exemplifies our penchant for evasion.

•

In the early 1960s, much of Texas suffered from an inferiority complex. The state had not yet come into its own in the eyes of the larger literary world. But Dallas, at least, could legitimately hold itself up as the regional Mecca of literature. Of particular local pride was the *Southwest Review*. Today, the Dallas-based literary journal is the third-oldest continuously published literary quarterly in America. Established as the *Texas Review* in 1915 at the

University of Texas, it moved to SMU in 1924, and it proclaimed its intention of representing the "new Southwest" as it made "the transition from cotton and cattle to skyscraper and city."[203] The journal was where you would find the best local and regional writers chronicling what it meant to live, think, and create in this environment. The famed folklorist and Texanist J. Frank Dobie was a frequent contributor, and Jerry Bywaters used the journal to trumpet the Texas modernism of a group of visual artists known as the Dallas Nine.

In short, the *Southwest Review* was a lively regional journal when regionalism in America was fashionable. Readers expected to see the important events of the region's intellectual life reflected in its pages. But the Winter 1964 issue of the *Southwest Review* contained very little type devoted to the JFK assassination. "The Editors Notebook" section, always a good indicator of the area's sense of itself, offered no mention of the assassination, and there was only one literary work that addressed the issue—a poem by James Hoggard.

James Hoggard would eventually enjoy a sterling literary career as an essayist, translator, and poet, working primarily at Midwestern State University in Wichita Falls, an hour-and-a-half drive northwest of Dallas. In 1981, his *Trotter Ross* would be acclaimed one of the best novels the region has ever produced. He would later be elected president of the Texas Institute of Letters and, in 2000, named poet laureate of Texas.

In the fall of 1963, however, Hoggard was an unpublished twenty-two-year-old. He had recently graduated from SMU, where both his father and mother had studied, and had just started graduate study at the University of Kansas. He was teaching in Lawrence when he heard the first reports of the president's death. Hoggard quickly penned a poetic response to the event, and when he returned to the family home in Dallas for Thanksgiving the following weekend, he stopped by SMU to submit the work to Decherd Turner. Turner, who had just taken over editorship of the *Southwest Review*, accepted the poem, telling Hoggard it was exactly what he was looking for. When the poem was published a couple months later, it amounted to the *Southwest Review*'s one and only acknowledgment of the assassination.[204]

---

203. "History," *Southwest Review*, February 11, 2012.

204. James Hoggard, telephone interview with Tim Cloward, February 15, 2012.

Hoggard's poem was entitled "November 22, 1963." Just as in Whitbread's "November 25, 1963," the narrator's first impulse is denial. It begins:

Caught up in memory's struggle to deny
The fact of absence, we forget our loss
For but a blessed moment, fleeting by,

Over the course of five stanzas, the poem goes on to bemoan the senseless violence and unsettled nature of the times: "The tension has not been resolved; the war/Of ideas rambles vainly on, so what/Use were the efforts of Conviction?"

But, also just as in Whitbread's "November 25, 1963," here there is no elegy or tribute to a fallen hero. Again, a date is all the scene-setting the author allows; there are no allusions to any of the event's particulars. Unlike much of the work collected in *Of Power and Poetry*, which explores the well-known imagery of the assassination and the funeral with excruciating variety, both "November 22, 1963" and "November 25, 1963" avoid the painful details. There is no "place" in either poem, and almost no specifics to latch on to.

With James Hoggard's "November 22, 1963," the state's premier literary journal, famous for its regional color, introduced a promising young writer who would go on to be a leading voice for the region. But the poem itself possesses no local flavor. It closes with the prevalent aura of senseless tragedy, but one that is generic.

A man's become a legend in the twist
Of nonsense in an insane plan—the thought
Seems callous but it is true, for little mist
Is left when tears have flowed, for then the mist
Is all too thin to hide what has been learned
And reaffirmed: the fatal involvement
Of man with man.

•

Dallas was a hotbed of poetic activity in the early 1920s. The city had not only lured the *Southwest Review* from Austin but had also been the foundation site of the Poetry Society of Texas. Organized in 1921, it remains today the second-oldest statewide poetry society in the country. By the early 1960s, it had already established itself as one of Texas's leading literary institutions. The society's broad influence can be seen in its *A Book of the Year,* the annually published journal chronicling its activities for that year, and, most importantly, its members' monthly prize-winning poems. While the journal has always published a certain amount of amateurish doggerel, it has also kept the state's poets in touch with each other and offered them support in the form of recognition as well as contest winnings. In the 1960s, most Texas poets of any ambition were active members—Thomas Whitbread, for instance, joined the society when he moved to the University of Texas, and published both on the national level and within the PST throughout his career.

If you were looking for a window into the state's poetic zeitgeist in the aftermath of the Kennedy assassination, the most obvious place to look would be the 1965 Poetry Society of Texas's *A Book of the Year.* There you would have assembled before you a representative survey of much of the state's best poetry written in the previous year—a grassroots review of the region's state of mind regarding recent events. Not surprisingly, the first poem you encounter in 1965's *A Book of the Year* is, in fact, an elaborate pastoral elegy honoring the assassinated president.

"Menalcas," the winner of the illustrious Lan and Willie Davis Award, is perhaps the most elaborate and accomplished poetic work published in the state of Texas in response to Kennedy's death. The title of the three-page poem references the rustic shepherd from Virgil's *Eclogues* and Theocritus's idylls, and it begins with a quote from John Milton's *Epitaphium Damonis* (his Latin companion to *Lycidas*). Like Milton's poems, "Menalcas" works out of the classical tradition of the pastoral singer praising the recently departed. It begins:

> Yet once more were we called upon, once more
> to be a nation of pallbearers.

Two hundred million pairs of arms strained to hoist
and tote a crushing load . . .
. . . .
carrying the load to Arlington,
He must not travel, we said, to his fateful rest unsung,
Once he sang too. He rang vibrant changes on a few choice tunes
and now his voice is still—ours forlorn, wrung dry.

The modern-day singer sings here along with the TV audience of two hundred million, and they honor the fallen president who himself was the master singer who "sang the world." Here our poet unites the imagery of the grand ceremony of the state funeral with the imagery and themes of the traditional pastoral elegy. He deftly joins the narrative of a nation joining together in its common mourning with the classic themes of nature and regeneration: death inevitably leading to resurrection, winter to spring. The poem ends: "bid us grow towards a fresh tomorrow and a new."[205]

"Menalcus" was a fitting gesture on behalf of the Poetry Society of Texas, a worthy way to open a volume that carried the burden of addressing a terrible tragedy that continued to haunt the state. But this poem—the poem that opens the 1965 *Book of the Year*, and the most important and accomplished work the journal contains—was not written by a PST member. It was not written by a Texan at all. Despite all the usual strictures of the journal of the Poetry Society of Texas, it was written by Leo Haber of Brooklyn, New York.

•

If the assassination cast a pall over the nation, that cloud was darkest over Texas. Just as the *Southwest Review* contained no other mention of the Kennedy assassination after Hoggard's "November 22, 1963," the 1965 Poetry Society of Texas *Book of the Year* contained absolutely nothing that specifically mentioned the Kennedy assassination other than Haber's "Menalcus."

205. Leo Haber, "Menalcus," in *A Book of the Year 1965*, Poetry Society of Texas.

In the hundred or so poems by Texas poets in that volume, there was not one other work that directly alluded to the president or his death.

There were in the shadows, however, a number of works that, if they didn't directly allude to the events surrounding the assassination, at least paralleled them. In this handful of works, you could see analogous situations where Texas poets might be elliptically commenting on an otherwise onerous and oppressive subject. The most accomplished of these poems, "The Mask," was written by Violette Newton. A native of Beaumont, Newton was fifty years old at the time of the assassination. She would go on to become an honored member of the Poetry Society of Texas and was designated the Poet Laureate of Texas ten years later. Proud of her home state, much of Newton's work celebrated its virtues, and she once opened a poem with lines that read, "Up East, they do not think much / of Texas poetry."[206]

Although there is no explicit reference to the assassination in "The Mask," the poem's depiction of a misunderstood funeral attendee seems to beg a fairly pointed question. Whose recent funeral had left a larger "legacy of gaudy blooms" than John F. Kennedy's?

Waiting to be done with words and flowers,
I stand apart, while others plead your cause
In supplications to the higher powers
And affirmations that you kept God's laws.
They glance at me, and lean in whispering groups;
They note my tearless cheek, my patient pose,
And with much drama, place the rosy hoops
About you, as a parent places toys
Before a child.
        O callow, callow love,
To leave this legacy of gaudy blooms
and pious friends. I twist my right hand glove,
I read inscriptions on the nearby tombs

206. Violette Newton, "Texas Poetry," in *Texas in Poetry 2*, Billy Bob Hill, ed. (Fort Worth: Texas Christian University Press, 1971), 75.

And wish that this were done, that I might go
To sit awhile in rooms we used to know.[207]

How might a proud, longtime Texan feel at the time of JFK's burial? In a nation full of mourners suspicious of all things Texan, largely convinced that the state was somehow complicit in the assassination, might some locals feel a little defensive ("they glance at me, and lean in whispering groups")? Could it be that "The Mask" is, itself, a masked commentary of the state funeral by a mourner who cannot properly take part in public mourning because of the national animus against the state and its people?

Carolyn Ellis's "Brief Interlude" is another funeral poem included in the 1965 PST *Book of the Year*. It explicitly commemorates a fallen president, but one from a century before—Abraham Lincoln. Ellis takes the reader on a Whitmanesque journey from the box at Ford's Theater to the presidential funeral train moving toward Springfield. In language typical of the Victorian-era doggerel, moralistic and safely ensconced in the historical past, the poem celebrates the mighty virtues of the great leader who led the nation through the Civil War: "O fallen Captain! with peaceful brow:/ Your ship in harbor, safe anchored now." What is striking here—conspicuous by its absence—is the lack of any reference to the recently deceased president. While the rest of America was knee-deep in the process of drawing analogies between the assassinations of Kennedy and Lincoln, it is striking that the Texan Ellis would omit any mention of the relationship. An astute reader might ask: Why?

Julia Hurd Strong's entry in the 1965 *Book of the Year* is entitled "Day of Crisis." Paired on the same page with Newton's "The Mask," it too could be read as a shrouded allusion to the mourning after the president's assassination. What recent crisis could be more analogous to the nameless calamity depicted in "Day of Crisis" than the Kennedy assassination? It reads:

While cities shudder at the newsboy's cry

207. Violette Newton, "The Mask," in *A Book of the Year 1965*, Poetry Society of Texas.

and workers leave their instruments to buy
details before the printer's ink is dry . . .

while stocks begin to tumble, and despair
spreads like a whispered rumor till the air
is filled with gloomy prophesy—and prayer . . .

while even little children's nerves are fraught
with this contagion which their minds have caught,
a scrawny squirrel, immune to human thought,

runs tightrope on his acrobatic paws,
clowning his lithe performance because
he holds tomorrow's acorn in his jaws.[208]

Strong's "Day of Crisis" deploys imagery strongly associated with the classical elegy—nature's cycle of new life redeeming death. Here, however, the standard acknowledgment of the painful grief surrounding death has been replaced by the ironic "clowning" squirrel; the gloomy "contagion" of crisis is minimized and trivialized.

If these poems are indeed oblique responses to the assassination, their most prevalent themes are displacement and evasion. Like much of the poetry produced by Dallasites just after the assassination, they are not attempts to find forms by which the emotions cut loose by recent events could be mediated. They are attempts to deny those emotions.

•

In the early 1960s, real modernism in verse was still just taking root in Texas, and most of the state's poets chose not to follow the avant-garde. To honor and elegize the fallen president, they utilized the abundant arsenal of traditional

---

208. Julia Hurd Strong, "Day of Crisis," in *A Book of the Year 1965*, Poetry Society of Texas.

modes already at hand. At Lincoln's death a century earlier, poets like Herman Melville ("The Martyr") and James Russell Lowell ("Ode Recited at the Harvard Commemoration") had masterfully employed formal verse to elaborate upon themes of patriotism and sacrifice. A century later, those forms, in the hands of our local poets, showed little such daring or ambition. Their formalism and worn-out tropes read today like borrowed tools inadequate to the task at hand.

It would not be the poets—and certainly not the poets of Texas—who would shape the new, post-assassination incarnation of John F. Kennedy. The mythopoeic tropes that would inform the national narrative of the JFK assassination would take shape on the East Coast, in the power centers of Washington, DC, and New York City. More than anyone, Jacqueline Kennedy, the president's widow, would control the process of memorializing her deceased husband.

With her stoic dignity and deft staging of the profoundly moving ceremonials of her husband's funeral, Jackie had made herself a national treasure. In the most trying of circumstances, she had maintained the presence of mind to consider both her husband's significance in history and the best way to communicate that significance to the public. The state funeral, however, was only the first step in the orchestration of her husband's legacy.

A week after the assassination, Jacqueline Kennedy contacted Theodore H. White and asked him to meet her at the Kennedy compound at Hyannis Port. White, one of *Life* magazine's top writers, had already established his reputation with the publication of *The Making of a President* in 1961. The book broke new ground in insider campaign coverage. And its hero, of course, was the dynamic young senator from Massachusetts who would become president. White's loyalty and the momentousness of the occasion were such that he literally left his mother as she was having a heart attack to heed Jackie's call.

The editors of *Life* had arranged, at huge expense to the magazine, to hold the printing presses while White finished his interview with Jackie. What the magazine got for these efforts was not just an exclusive look into the psyche of the grieving first lady but also a eulogy that would take on a life of its own. Entitled "For President Kennedy: An Epilogue," White's piece did not so much wrap things up as open a new door. White pushed Jackie, and he gave her the room to spell out her version of the royal Kennedy White House years.

> "Once, the more I read of history the more bitter I got. For awhile I thought that history was something that bitter old men wrote. But then I realized history made Jack what he was. You must think of him as this little boy, sick so much of the time, reading in bed, reading history, reading The Knights of the Round Table, reading Marlborough. For Jack, history was full of heroes. And if it made him this way—if it made him see the heroes—maybe other boys will see. Men are such a combination of good and bad. Jack had this hero idea of history, the idealistic view."
>
> But she came back to the idea that transfixed her: "*Don't let it be forgot, that once there was a spot, for once brief shining moment that was known as Camelot*—and it will never be that way again!"

The interview continues—Jackie talks about the eternal flame that her children could now see from miles away, her future plans for more tributes to her late husband, the Kennedy Space Center.[209] But White concludes with the one theme Jackie insisted on:

> She said it is time people paid attention to the new President and the new First Lady. But she does not want them to forget John F. Kennedy or read of him only in dusty or bitter histories:
>
> For one brief shining moment there was Camelot.[210]

•

209. White, *In Search of History*, 674–80.
210. White, "For President Kennedy."

Images of Kennedy's presidency and assassination dominated the December 6, 1963, issue of *Life* magazine, but none would be more influential in the formation of the fallen leader's legacy than White's short article. It would give us the seeds that grew into our modern Camelot myth, creating a convenient new vessel in which to collect all our disparate remembrances.

In Dallas, one local poet spoke to that same theme of post-death transformation. The poem "Epitaph," would appear later in the 1965 *Book of the Year*. Its author, John Davenport Womack, did not himself leave much of a poetic legacy, but here, assuming the voice of the dead, he reminds us that the living, after they pass, inevitably become something else.

Grieve not for me
When I am gone from here,
And place no tall, black candles
At either end of my bier;

For when I go
I shall have had enough,
Let me go quietly and in peace.
I am not made of stronger stuff

Than what you see,
Nor metal nor the flame
That has devoured me daily.
Call not my name—

I might return to you,
And be not he you know.[211]

•

211. John Davenport Womack, "Epitaph," in *A Book of the Year 1965*, Poetry Society of Texas.

While the mythopotic work of remaking the JFK legacy through the prism of Camelot was taking place on the East Coast, the Arthurian connection had already been noted in Texas a week earlier. Ralph Yarborough was the senior senator from Texas. Ending his feud with Texas Governor John Connally had been one of the goals of Kennedy's Texas visit. Yarborough had been in the motorcade, riding with Lyndon Johnson two cars behind Kennedy at the time of the shooting, and he followed the president to Parkland. Just moments after the prone president was wheeled into Trauma Room 1, Yarborough was approached by the first wave of reporters descending upon the hospital. In those first moments at the hospital, it was becoming clear to those closest to the president that he was, in fact, dead. According to William Manchester, Yarborough, who "had been bred in the fulsome tradition of Southern oratory," replied brokenly to those first journalistic questions: "Gentlemen, this has been a deed of horror." As his eyes filled with tears and as he turned aside, he whispered, "Excalibur has sunk beneath the waves . . ."[212]

Camelot was in the air then. A month after the assassination, the young King Arthur would make the rounds of America's movie theaters in Walt Disney's *The Sword in the Stone.* Opening on December 25, 1963, the animated Disney fantasy was the story a bumbling and good-hearted youth who, with the help of the magician Merlin, discovers his powers and becomes the King of England. The movie was based upon British author T. H. White's 1938 book of the same name. White's *The Sword in the Stone* was later republished in 1958 as the first book of White's tetralogy *The Once and Future King.* That book became a vast success—its generation's equivalent of our Harry Potter phenomenon. It garnered a huge readership, capturing the imagination of both child and adult, and soon began to pop up on required school reading lists.

With its knights and chivalry and mix of myth and magic, the medieval world of Arthur and his Round Table had long been a Hollywood staple. But following the success of White's *The Once and Future King,* Broadway saw the potential for a stage version of these legendary adventures. Less than two months before John F. Kennedy was inaugurated, on December 3, 1960,

212. Manchester, *The Death of a President,* 172.

Camelot opened at the Majestic Theater. At the time, it boasted the biggest budget of any show in Broadway history. The musical comedy-romance, Lerner and Loewe's follow-up to their massively successful *My Fair Lady*, had star power galore: Richard Burton as Arthur, Julie Andrews as Guinevere, Robert Goulet as Lancelot, and Roddy McDowall as Mordred. It was an immediate success, running for two years and 873 performances. Its original cast recording can be seen advertised in the December 6, 1963, *Life* magazine that featured White's "Epilogue," and it became one of the top-selling albums of that period.

It was this Broadway reworking of T. H. White's popular book that would function for Jackie as her analogy for the Kennedy White House. Lerner and Loewe portrayed King Arthur as a man intent on bringing order and civilization to his realm, establishing the rule of law that would ensure a safe, free, and democratic country. Now Jackie would recast her husband as Arthur and herself as Guinevere—the king and queen presiding over the Round Table, attracting the noblest warriors of the realm to help create a new world.

This was obviously a contraption of fiction, a show-business concoction, and, in Theodore White's "Epilogue," Jackie is apologetic: "When Jack quoted something, it was usually classical," she said, "but I'm so ashamed of myself—all I keep thinking of is this line from a musical comedy." Here was an intimate detail from the bedroom of the king and queen, and the masses were happy for the offering.

> All night, before we'd go to sleep, Jack liked to play some records; and the song he loved the most came at the very end of this record. The lines he loved to hear were: *Don't let it be forgot, that once there was a spot, for once brief shining moment that was known as Camelot.*
>
> Jackie wanted to make sure her claim was clear: "There'll be great presidents again—and the Johnsons are wonderful, they've been wonderful to me—but there'll never be another Camelot again."[213]

213. White, "For President Kennedy."

•

The conception of the Kennedy administration as a type of modern Camelot—with both the beauty of its original ambitions and the tragedy of its fall—would strike a chord that still echoes to this day. The idea would be reproduced and replicated in so many ways that it has since become a national cliché.

The first notable local literary application of the Camelot myth appeared in Gene Shuford's elegiac poem "The Death in Our Family," first published in the *Arlington Quarterly*. In 1963, Gene Shuford was already an established Texas poet with a national reputation and numerous awards to his credit. He was also very active in the Poetry Society of Texas and would be named alternate state poet laureate in 1975. "The Death in Our Family" is one of Shuford's most ambitious works, and it brought him his greatest recognition to date when it won the Poetry Society of America's William Marion Reedy Award for 1965–66.

Because of this, "The Death in Our Family" would become the most widely disseminated local poem dealing with the assassination. Like Whitbread's and Hoggard's poems, Shuford's reveals that same tendency toward denial. There it is, thirteen lines into the first section of the poem:

> Already this is legend, a myth we only half believe
> saying, surely it must not have happened; surely, it must
> have been a dream; surely, it was long ago,
> but now is already encrusted with myth and passion
> for forgetting, [. . .]

But, unlike Hoggard or Whitbread, Shuford's "passion for forgetting," is overcome by a force as "strong as the passion for remembering." In "The Death in Our Family," for the first time, we find a Texas poet ready to accept the burden of memorializing the fallen president. And he does so in the most efficacious way possible—by adopting the Camelot myth lock, stock, and barrel.

•

The first section of "The Death in Our Family," is entitled "The Visit." It begins: "One can never tell what November will be in Texas." Shuford then notes that the North Texas autumn days are warm enough to "let the lilacs bloom"—a nod to both the traditional pastoral mode and Whitman's elegy to Lincoln from a hundred years earlier. Then the poem's protagonists are introduced.

> and the big jet will slip down out of the cottony clouds
> and the prince and the princess descend and all the banners
> will wave above the spirit's shining armor.

The "big jet" is, of course, Air Force One, and the "prince and princess" are clearly John and Jackie. By the end of this first stanza, Shuford has already situated the reader within the myth-time of Camelot.

An important element in much of Shuford's poetry is his exploration of the tension between history and myth. Shuford was a lifelong journalist, a reporter who eventually rose to become chair of the Journalism Department at the University of North Texas. His poetry constantly plays with the ironic disparity between real life and the stories that we make of it. But "The Death in Our Family" is an exception is this regard. Here, there is no irony, only a tragic romance on a national scale.

The poetry produced just after the assassination was inevitably soaked in the imagery that the unprecedented media coverage of the event had provided. Before the poet could put pen to paper, there was already a common memory, a field clogged with preprocessed images and ready-made information. Like the majority of post-assassination poetry, "The Death in Our Family" is constructed upon this landscape.

Appropriately enough for a tragic romance, the poem's central recurring image is a red rose. These specific roses, however, have been taken straight from two photographs appearing in the November 29, 1963, issue of *Life*. The first is a full-page color photo of Jackie stepping off Air Force One at Love Field. As she stands next to her husband, looking radiant in her pink dress and pillbox hat, she holds the bouquet of red roses presented to her by Elizabeth Cabell, the wife of Dallas Mayor Earle Cabell. The second photograph appears on the facing page. It is in black and white and was taken a few short hours later. It is a close-up of the back seat of one of the motorcade limousines as it sits parked and abandoned outside of Parkland Hospital. Across the back seat, what appear to be those same roses are now strewn, mingling, apparently, with the blood of the murdered president.

Shuford does not explicitly reference these photographs or the moments they document, but they provide the core visual imagery which weaves its way through the poem: an elegant shorthand for a more brutal reality. Early in the poem, a bullet "bleeds the roses of their deepest red," and the poem closes at the final graveside ceremony at Arlington National Cemetery. Here, Shuford plays out the tragic romance of the modern Camelot by drawing parallels between the blood rose and the Eternal Flame.

> Sweet prince, who was no prince, but king in spirit,
> lifting us all to some high hill, to some
> tall burning, this is your legend, the myth that you
> have forged, a myth truer than true, the flame
> you lighted for us all, the flame we mourn
> as vanished, but a torch that somehow pierced
> the darkest corners of our night, that burns
> like roses in our hearts, bleeding a red
> that stains our minds with grief, as red as blood
> you bled, as red as roses that your princess dropped
> from her trembling fingers on the day you died.

•

What differentiates Shuford's poem from his fellow Texans' earlier assassination-themed poems is its rejection of evasiveness and unapologetic adoption of common imagery. "The Death in Our Family" directly adopts the inventory of powerful tropes that had already been developed in the electronic and print media. The poem structures itself around that same narrative that the nation, glued to their TV sets over that long weekend in November 1963, had already shared together. The first section, "The Visit," recounts the dark events in Dallas. The next, "The Dark Flight," depicts Air Force One on its sad journey back to Washington, DC; "The Walking Time" describes the solemn promenade of the funeral procession; and the final section, "The Flame" leaves the reader at Kennedy's graveside.

Shuford's tactic of reworking the imagery that had already been harvested by the national press was by no means remarkable. The great majority of the work in *Of Power and Poetry* does exactly the same thing. What sets Shuford's poem apart is that it combines the reworking of that shared iconography with an unapologetic, full-scale adaptation of the Camelot myth. (*Of Power and Poetry* includes only one very fleeting reference to Camelot.)

Shuford's greatest accomplishment in "The Death in Our Family" was to overcome the muteness and evasiveness that had prevailed among Texas poets on the topic of the assassination. Unlike his local predecessors, Shuford moved with the assurance that came from deferring to a developing national myth. He had the aesthetic savvy to surrender to a larger, communal narrative. If his images were not exactly original, Shuford could work with the confidence that comes with an established mythopoeic trope.

Certainly, the judges of the William Marion Reedy Award must have found themselves drawn to the idea of a North Texas poet actively joining in the eulogizing. During a time that begged for a unifying response, it could not have hurt that Shuford's was a Texas voice reminding us that we are all a family and that JFK belonged to all of us—that he was *our* leader.

So soon after the assassination, however, most Dallasites would resist such wholehearted acceptance of that myth. Although Shuford's "The Death in Our Family" is significant for being among the first attempts by a local literary artist to counter the national perception that Dallas was populated exclusively by Kennedy-haters, few of us living here in the mid-1960s were ready to assume the role of protectors of the president's legacy. A different, decidedly non-Texan, group of writers would take on that responsibility.

•

If Shuford's "The Death in Our Family" was a capitulation, it was a capitulation to an extremely powerful cultural force. John Kennedy's inner circle was an especially adept crew of mythmakers. He had consciously assembled around himself a bevy of writers who shared his monumental sense of mission. They were aware they were helping shape history and that there was a mythic dimension to their work. Jackie herself was remarkably savvy in her ability to craft symbolic meaning. It was Jackie who developed the Eternal Flame, which Shuford utilized as his final poetic image. It was Jackie who had orchestrated the funeral ceremony upon which Shuford, like so many other poets, structured his poem. And it was Jackie who had intentionally scripted the Kennedy White House version of the Camelot myth.

Even so eminent a historian as Arthur M. Schlesinger Jr., a Pulitzer Prize–winning historian (for his *The Age of Jackson*) who had left a Harvard professorship to join Kennedy as a special assistant and "court historian," could not resist the mythologizing mode. By 1965, he had completed *A Thousand Days,* his insider history of the Kennedy presidency. The book offered this appraisal of his former boss: "he quickened the heart and mind of the nation, inspired the young, met great crisis, led our society to new possibilities of justice and our world to new possibilities of peace and left behind so glowing and imperishable a memory."[214] The sober historian Schlesinger would never put it in exactly those terms, but his account of JFK reigning over a golden moment of idealism sounds a lot like Camelot.

Even as Schlesinger was beginning to write his history of JFK's presidency, Jackie and Robert Kennedy were inviting William Manchester to write the definitive history of the assassination, giving him unparalleled access to the Kennedy team in order to combat the disorder and misinformation already swirling around that fatal weekend in Dallas. Like Theodore H. White and Ted Sorenson before him, Manchester was to take control of the JFK narrative. The result, 1967's *The Death of a President,* chronicled not only the president's assassination but also the beginnings of his post-death mythologization.

But Manchester did not simply document JFK's transformation into a heroic legend—he contributed mightily to the process. An important element of Manchester's heroization of JFK was his corresponding vilification

---

214. Arthur M. Schlesinger Jr., *A Thousand Days: John F. Kennedy in the White House* (Boston: Houghton Mifflin, 1965), x.

of Dallas. Manchester's work would provide plenty of ammunition for those interested in casting the entire city as the president's killer.

•

The last words that John F. Kennedy heard in his lifetime were, "You sure can't say Dallas doesn't love you, Mr. President."[215] They were spoken by Nellie Connally, wife of Texas Governor John Connally. Riding in the forward seats of the presidential limousine, Mrs. Connally turned back to speak to Kennedy just as the motorcade began moving down Elm Street through Dealey Plaza. And she could point to plenty of evidence to support her assertion. Thousands of demonstrative JFK supporters had cheered his arrival at Love Field, and thousands more lined the streets all through downtown Dallas, greeting the motorcade with their pro-Kennedy signs and yelling out their well-wishes.

The Kennedy brain trust, and most of the rest of America, chose not to remember this obvious outpouring of support for the president. What they chose to remember instead were their pre-arrival suspicions that trouble awaited the president in Dallas, that he had been warned. After his UN Day speech had been so ingloriously interrupted, Adlai Stevenson suggested the president cancel his visit, and local luminary Stanley Marcus cautioned him against coming to Dallas. The anticipation of trouble had been so great that, in an announcement three days before Kennedy's arrival, Dallas Police Chief Jesse Curry authorized residents to take individual action against anyone who might perpetuate "an act that is harmful or degrading to the President of the United States." Despite what Nellie Connally witnessed on November 22, 1963, Dallas had not shown John F. Kennedy much love in 1960. Although Democrats dominated Texas politics and Kennedy's running mate was a senator from Texas, 63 percent of those who had cast their ballot in Dallas County voted against him. What America remembered most was that John F. Kennedy left Dallas in a coffin.

To eulogize the departed president in North Texas was tricky business.

---

215. Manchester, *The Death of a President*, 153.

While much of the nation held us responsible for JFK's murder, and we were often ostracized for being complicit in his demise, we were simultaneously expected to join in with the rest of the country in mourning. It was uncomfortable, to say the least. No wonder a major poll taken on the second anniversary of the assassination showed the percentage of people who mourned President Kennedy in Dallas "was dramatically below the national average."[216] We were damned if we did, and damned if we didn't.

Kennedy memorials were going up all over America. In Dallas, however, there was considerable foot-dragging as we struggled to meet our painful obligations. We were part of the story; Kennedy had died here, so it was clear some sort of memorial must go up. While it was inevitable, we understood it would draw more scrutiny—keep the wounds open. By the time we did finally complete our lone physical monument, the John F. Kennedy Memorial Plaza a block away from Dealey Plaza, seven painful years had passed. Even then, Philip Johnson's stark, modernist cenotaph was criticized for its vapid formality, its lack of any real content or feeling—the same faults evident in the state's early poetic responses to the assassination.

•

In Dallas, our local feelings of inadequacy were especially evident in our literature. Of all of our cultural endeavors, it was in our literary development that we felt most defensive. There was an unspoken understanding that our literary culture was second-rate, that we had never produced anything of enduring quality. There was nothing in our literature to compare with the glamour of Neiman Marcus's fashions or the Maria Callas days of the Dallas Opera. Writing two decades later, one of our own most widely praised authors, A. C. Greene, expressed his sense of our shortcomings: "Dallas has probably produced fewer important literary figures than any major American city."

In literature, at least, we were still a frontier town. We had not achieved the sophistication in the written word that we had elsewhere. "Dallas's artistic inferiority complex," Greene explained, "operates strongest in literary

216. Manchester, *The Death of a President*, 637.

areas."[217] We still labored in the shadow of J. Frank Dobie and Western-style regionalism, replete with longhorns and roadrunners, a style which had dominated the state's literary scene for decades. Even Lon Tinkle, the Sorbonne-educated head of SMU's French Department and our most urbane practitioner of the literary arts, was most well-known for his *Thirteen Days to Glory*, a historical account of the Battle of the Alamo.

Our city founder, John Neely Bryan, epitomized our frontier penchant for the practical over the literary. As a young man, he had read the law and been admitted to the Tennessee bar, but, as Dallas historian Darwin Payne noted, he "was not the kind of man who could be happy accumulating papers, keeping files, composing his thoughts, or sitting behind a desk. His dreams were visible only through direct action." The only written remains of Bryan's lifetime of frenetic activity are a couple of random letters.[218] In 1841, when he began the original encampment that would become the city of Dallas, it is hard to say what books, if any, graced the selves of his cabin.

In contrast, by 1841, many American cities already enjoyed long and distinguished traditions of writing and intellectual development. For example, Boston (John F. Kennedy's birthplace) was the birthplace of Transcendentalism. The same year John Neely Bryan built his cabin, Ralph Waldo Emerson gathered around him a group that included Margaret Fuller, a couple of years away from publishing *Woman in the Nineteenth Century*, and Henry David Thoreau, just on the verge of producing *Walden* and *Resistance to Civil Government*. Even more than a century later, how could we not be cursed with at least a little frontier defensiveness? According to *The WPA Dallas Guide and History*, the first documented literary work that comes close to being poetry produced in the city of Dallas was discovered on the flyleaf of a criminal docket from 1848–52. The county clerk had scribbled onto the flyleaf a parody on the song "O No, We Never Mention Him." It was "a lament on taking the temperance pledge."[219]

---

217. Greene, *Dallas USA*, 247–48.

218. Payne, *Dallas: An Illustrated History*, 19.

219. Maxine Holmes and Gerald Saxon, eds., *The WPA Dallas Guide and History* (Denton: University of North Texas Press, 1992), 211.

•

Dallas began life as a frontier city, but many of our early settlers were educated people. After taking care of the basic, necessary work of establishing a sustainable and secure settlement, education and literacy were always the next challenge. North Texas, like the rest of the developing West, was young and raw, but we were never illiterate. Even in the rural areas, literature was valued, and, by the turn of the century, poetry had become a popular form of entertainment among North Texas residents. As one Dallas poet recalled of her earlier days in 1910s Hillsboro, a small village fifty miles to the south of Dallas: "Everyone was writing poetry . . . They weren't writing very well, but everyone was writing it, and all the newspapers were publishing it . . . You went to someone's home, and someone read poetry or . . . played the piano, and that's what we did for entertainment back then."[220]

In the more sophisticated urban areas, the literary arts were already an important part of status display. By 1895, Dallas was already exhibiting its tendency toward a highfalutin style of living, as evidenced by the first volume about "high society" ever published in the state. The first Texas *Red Book,* along with its listing of "the best local society," demonstrated the important role literary pursuits played in maintaining one's elevated position. Of the nine local social clubs listed in the directory, fully five pronounced a study of serious literature as a primary function of their organization. From the Shakespeare Club to the Pierian Chatauqua Club, each emphasized working knowledge of the classics as an expected social grace. The Standard Club was typical; its members had "studied Goethe's *Faust,* Homer's *Iliad* and *Odyssey, Outlines of English History, Outlines of American History* and the works of Shakespeare. Each study covering one term of seven months."[221]

Anyone who has read Elizabeth Forsythe Hailey's 1978 epistolary novel *A Woman of Independent Means,* or seen Sally Field's performance in the 1995 NBC miniseries based upon it, might remember the importance the

---

220. Betty Holland Wiesepape, *Lone Star Chapters: The Story of Texas Literary Clubs* (College Station: Texas A&M University Press), 2004.

221. *1895–6 Red Book of Dallas Texas: A Facsimile Reproduction* (Dallas: A. H. Belo Corp., 1966).

Shakespeare Club played in the life of Bess Steed Garner. Garner was based on Hailey's Dallas grandmother and her struggles to create an autonomous life for herself within the strictures of early-twentieth-century Southern society. Hailey portrays Garner working to establish herself in Dallas society in 1913 by reading her first paper to the Shakespeare Club: "The most prominent women in the city comprise its membership, so I was extremely nervous when I stood to address them." A decade later, Garner is seeking to arrange work for her educated Black maid with the Shakespeare Club, educating the servants of her colleagues. "[S]he would be thrilled at the opportunity to make the glories of Shakespeare accessible to friends whose upbringing did not afford them the literary advantages she had," she writes.[222]

In Dallas, as in most American cities pushing to escape the embarrassing cultural backwardness of the frontier, the civilizing qualities of literature were obvious.

•

The opening of Dallas's first major institution of higher learning, Southern Methodist University, in 1915 (slightly less than three hundred years after the 1636 opening of Massachusetts's Harvard University), marked a significant breakthrough in the local literary arts. To deal with the overflow of students—reportedly the second-largest opening enrollment of any university at that point in the nation's history—SMU hired a young scholar who had not yet completed his doctoral work but showed great promise.[223] Jay Hubbell would help SMU become the nexus of Dallas's literary life.

It was Hubbell who called his best students together in 1922 to form the Makers. Assuming the modern English name for the Saxon *scop*, the equivalent of poet or minstrel in the Middle Ages, the Makers were the area's first serious writing group. "We wanted to be freaky and wear sandals and be far out," wrote one participant, "but [Hubbell] suggested that it would be better

222. Elizabeth Forsythe Hailey, *A Woman of Independent Means* (New York: Viking Press, 1978), 12, 155.

223. Payne, *Dallas: An Illustrated History*, 171.

to imitate the ancients . . . instead of imitating Greenwich Village."[224] Under Hubbell's tutelage, the Makers were active for roughly a decade and had a long-lasting and important influence on Dallas's evolving literary life. It wasn't the Boston Authors Club, which was founded in 1899 and would eventually be able to claim eighteen Pulitzer Prizes, but it was real progress.

The literary activity at SMU spread off campus. The first issue of the *Kaleidograph: A National Magazine of Poetry* appeared in 1929. Edited by Dallasites Whitney Maxwell Montgomery and Vaida Stewart Montgomery, the *Kaleidograph* published until 1959, and its circulation peaked at about two thousand, with subscribers in every state and several foreign countries. The Montgomerys' Kaleidograph Press also published over four hundred books by local and regional writers.[225] As members of the Makers and the writers involved with the *Kaleidograph* became intertwined with the Poetry Society of Texas, which had been organized in Dallas in 1921, Dallas emerged as the indisputable poetry capital of Texas. As one local bard put it in 1931: "It has gotten so that one cannot shake a bush without a poet or two falling out."[226]

While there was plenty of literary activity in our city during the first half of the twentieth century, we weren't quite yet ready to compete on the national stage. "Before World War II Texas poetry flourished," Texas literary critic Don Graham has written, "but without distinction."[227]

Despite this real progress, Dallas remained a literary frontier. The real action was still happening back east. After a decade of work at SMU, Jay Hubbell would leave for the greener pastures of Duke University, but he left an important legacy behind. Beyond inspiring local writing and writers, he was instrumental in connecting these local writers to the wider literary

224. Wiesepape, *Lone Star Chapters,* 40.

225. W. W. Bennett, "Kaleidograph," in *Handbook of Texas Online,* Texas State Historical Association, updated July 18, 2020, accessed April 7, 2012, https://www.tshaonline.org/handbook/entries/kaleidograph.

226. W. E. Bard, "An Aside to the Reader," in *Fountain Unsealed: A Collection of Verse by Texas Writers* (Dallas: Barrington Fiction Club/Clyde C. Cockrell, 1931).

227. Don B. Graham, "Literature," in *Handbook of Texas Online,* Texas State Historical Association, updated October 6, 2022, accessed July 21, 2020, http://www.tshaonline.org/handbook/online/articles/kzl01.

world. It was Hubbell, more than anyone, who brought the *Texas Review* from the University of Texas in Austin to Dallas in 1924, renaming it the *Southwest Review*. Following the lead of Harriett Monroe's influential *Poetry: A Magazine of Verse*, established in Chicago in 1915, the *Southwest Review* carried the name of SMU and Texas writers into major literary centers.

•

Hubbell also made an impact beyond the region by coediting *An Introduction to Poetry*, a bestselling college textbook. With this book, and through his affiliation with the American Literature Group of the Modern Language Association, which he would eventually chair, Hubbell championed the work of many of the leading American writers of his time. He published Carl Sandburg and Vachel Lindsay, affording them their first standing in the literary canon. Hubbell's influence granted him access to many of the leading contemporary American poets, and he was able to attract well-known writers to SMU for readings and speaking engagements. He scored his first big coup in the very first year of the Makers' existence: a visit by Robert Frost.[228]

Robert Frost would go on to become one of America's best-loved poets, and he would be profoundly influential in the development of North Texas's first critically significant poet. William Barney led Texas verse in its transition from provincialism to legitimacy. According to Texas poet and literary critic Paul Christiansen, "we may think of [Texas] poetry as being 'before Barney' and 'after Barney.' It grew up with this man's poetry." Barney, recognizing the same talent Hubbell had earlier, drew heavily upon Easterner Frost's work in achieving this local breakthrough. "Barney," Christiansen noted, "is the first writer of real size to drive the New England poem west, and make it register the life of the Southwest."[229]

Barney arrived in Texas in 1928 at age twelve, when his family moved to Fort Worth, and he came to love the area. He was a pastoralist, an appreciator

---

228. Wiesepape, *Lone Star Chapters*, 53.

229. Paul Christiansen, *West of the American* Dream (College Station: Texas A&M University Press, 2001), 184–89.

of the simpler rhythms of rural life. Barney worked for the US Postal Service for most of his life, but he also spent a good deal of his spare time as a naturalist. The rest he spent as a poet. Unsatisfied with the clichéd formalism that characterized the work of many of his contemporaries, Barney sought to raise the poetic standards of the region, "to sympathize with the land and its cruel history, and not to ignore it by throwing on an archaic and diversionary romanticism."[230] He was a longtime member of the Poetry Society of Texas, winning many of its contests, and its president in 1952 and 1953. He published nine books of poetry, many of them with Kaleidograph Press, and he was honored as the poet laureate of Texas in 1982.[231]

William Barney must have been thrilled with the participation of his distant mentor Robert Frost in John F. Kennedy's inauguration, but his biggest thrill would come later that year when the eighty-six-year-old Frost personally presented William Barney the Poetry Society of America's 1961 Robert Frost Award for his narrative poem "The Killdeer Crying." John Kennedy would in turn honor Robert Frost on October 26, 1963, just a month before his Dallas visit, delivering his stirring defense of the arts in America's public life at the groundbreaking of the new Robert Frost Library. The conservative Barney, however, was apparently not thrilled enough with John Kennedy to make the effort to greet the president on his Dallas visit.

On the morning of November 22, 1963, Barney, a distribution clerk in the inspection service at the Postal Service, reported to work at the Mercantile National Bank Building. This local landmark is located between Main and Commerce Streets in downtown Dallas and sits directly on the presidential motorcade route. The forty-seven-year-old Barney did not witness the passing of the president and his wife, but he did record his experience of that morning.

> I went out before noon, to do some Christmas shopping in the Dallas stores and let others in my office go later so they could see him. No

230. Christiansen, *West of the American Dream*, 86.

231. Kelli Tinervin, "William Barney," in *Handbook of Texas Online*, Texas State Historical Association, updated October 5, 2020, accessed April 7, 2012, www.tshaonline.org/handbook/online/articles/fbafm.

> one could walk through the streets without feeling an uneasiness in the air. I saw a traffic patrolman taking off his yellow raingear; the sun was breaking through the clouds. Later, back in my office, I heard the carillon in the Mercantile Bank playing: "Hail to the Chief." And shortly thereafter it turned suddenly to "What a Friend We Have in Jesus." "What in the world are they playing that for?" I asked a secretary. Abruptly, an engineer came to my door.
>
> "Can you stand a shock?" he asked. Sure. "The President has been shot!"[232]

This anecdote did not appear in print until 1993, thirty years after the fact. It was published in *Words from a Wide Land*, Barney's daybook, comprising 365 entries, running from January 1 to December 31. The November 22 entry, slipped in among snippets of observation and daily meditation, stands out as a striking deviation, an ugly accident. The topics Barney covers in *Words from a Wide Land*, and all his other work, are primarily natural and pastoral. Like Frost, he tends to stick to the small and the local; the world he writes of is primarily that of his Fort Worth home, the common rural folk he loved, and especially his trips to the natural areas around the state. The urban workplace of Fort Worth's sister city, Dallas, must have felt especially alien to Barney, its traffic and downtown canyons antithetical to his preferred subjects: cattle guards, mimosa, spiders, and wild roses. His "where-were-you-when" entry for November 22 is, however, representative of how a good portion of the local population experienced the assassination. It registers the shock of being suddenly pulled into a foreign world, of being a bystander to an event that you were not part of yet could not escape.

•

The first significant JFK assassination poem from a real Dallasite, an insider, was William Burford's "The Spell." Like Barney's *Words from a Wide Land*

232. Barney, *Words from a Wide Land*, 175.

anecdote, it would register that same sense that we were falling into something inescapably ominous. Burford's "The Spell," however, would also be prophetic of a larger gloom, a dark cloud that would fall across all of America.

The Dallas critic and poet Robert Trammell always referred to William Burford as "Dallas's first '*real*' poet." In a state dominated by poetic traditionalism, Burford was our original modernist. If Fort Worth's William Barney represented our rural poetic past, Burford's poetic style reflected the sophisticated urbanism upon which modern Dallas prided itself. Burford's continental influences paralleled the internationalism on display at Neiman Marcus's elaborate Fortnight Celebrations, which since 1957 had presented to Dallas the fashions and culture of the world, or at the Dallas Opera, which had recently earned the moniker "La Scala West."[233]

Even Burford's childhood home was reflective of the city's growing reputation for using its mercantile might to create high-profile cultural display. Today, the estate at the former 3417 Gillespie address (now Turtle Creek Boulevard) contains one of the country's premiere luxury hotels and five-star restaurants. The cream-colored Renaissance-style manor, with its distinctive arched and spired tower, is currently the Rosewood Mansion on Turtle Creek—"The Mansion," as it is most commonly called—and it is recognized nationally for its opulent hospitality.

This palatial estate, one of the first mansions to be built in Dallas's lush Turtle Creek neighborhood, was originally built by Sheppard King in the 1920s. The son of a Confederate War veteran, King migrated to the area in the late 1800s when cotton was still king. He amassed a fortune in the cotton trade and built a manor intended to display his impressive achievements. Filled with elaborate and very expensive replicas of European residential opulence, the estate became famous as the site of lavish parties and garish displays of wealth. However, the cotton industry fell upon hard times during the Great Depression, and Sheppard King sold the mansion in 1935.

By then, the oil boom was driving the local economy; in that year, the state's petroleum production doubled that of cotton. The estate fell into the

233. Ronald Davis, *John Rosenfield's Dallas: How the Southwest's Leading Critic Shaped a City's Culture, 1925–1966* (Dallas: Three Forks Press, 2002), 258.

hands of one of the industry's great family unions. In 1926, Freeman Burford, a pioneer oil producer and refiner who had established himself as a major player in the Texas oil business, married Carolyn Skelly, the scion of William G. Skelly, the founder of Skelly Oil. In the same year the couple moved into the Turtle Creek mansion, Freeman Burford sold his interest in his East Texas Oil Refining to Magnolia Oil, whose Dallas headquarters was the landmark Magnolia Hotel, the city's tallest building and the new home of its trademark neon Pegasus—the iconic symbol of mid-century Dallas.

William, the firstborn son, was eight years old when he took up residence at the estate on Turtle Creek, "a marvelous house, like a great F. Scott Fitzgerald fantasy," he would later recount. As a child, he was immediately thrust into the center of Dallas's cultural and political life. There was talk that his father might run for governor, and, when President Franklin Delano Roosevelt visited Dallas in 1936 to dedicate Lee Park and visit the Texas Centennial celebration, he stayed with the Burfords. In the early 1940s, the estate served as the first home of Margo Jones's groundbreaking Theater 45, and Tennessee Williams wrote his play *Summer and Smoke* while staying there. William's parents hoped that he might eventually serve in the diplomatic corps, so they sent him to Saint Mark's, Dallas's elite boys' prep school. Clearly, William Burford was destined to move in a large and connected world.[234]

Burford eventually matriculated at the Shattuck School, an Episcopal military academy in Minnesota, where he roomed with the young Marlon Brando. They performed together at Shattuck, and it was Burford who drove Brando to the train station when he left school to pursue a career in acting. After military service in WWII, Burford returned to Dallas, serving as assistant to the famous Fort Worth oilman and art collector Sid Richardson before heading off to Amherst College. It was at Amherst that Burford confirmed he would pursue a life of letters. He became close friends with James Merrill, and they produced the literary journal *The Medusa,* beginning a literary correspondence that would last decades. From there, it was on to Paris and the

234. Helen Sheehy, *Margo: The Life and Theater of Margo Jones* (University Park, TX: Southern Methodist University Press, 1989), 90.

Sorbonne in the early 1950s, then New York, where Burford befriended Anaïs Nin, the bohemian writer of erotica whose famous journals would occasionally mention their exchanges.

William Burford would have an impressive career as a teacher, poet, and translator. By the early 1960s, he had published two books of poetry and returned home to teach at SMU. Burford would become the first significant modernist writer from Dallas who chose to stay in the area throughout a good portion of his career, eventually becoming a member of the Texas Institute of Letters.

•

When John Kennedy was shot in Dallas in 1963, William Burford was a thirty-six-year-old professor of English at the University of Texas at Austin, a three-hour drive south down Interstate 35 from Dallas. What we know of Burford's reaction to the event lives on in his poem "The Spell," which finally appeared in 1966 in *A Beginning,* a collection of his work published by W. W. Norton.

"The Spell" is typical of Burford's poetic work in that it is short, contained, and austere. It features a mythic element, but, as in his other work, no allusions or literary references. Burford's imagery grows out of the local and specific, in that open, equivocal style of the French symbolists. (Burford studied French poetry at the Sorbonne and would later publish his translations of Arthur Rimbaud.) The archetypes that Burford utilizes in "The Spell" are drawn from the Zapruder film.

While the Zapruder film was not widely seen by the general public until 1975, it had quickly been disseminated in the form of still photographs. The November 29, 1963, issue of *Life* magazine contained a series of 31 of the 486 stills that compose the 26.6-second film. That sequence, documenting in gory detail the few seconds it took to kill the president of the United States, was instantly absorbed and internalized by the American public.

Burford, in his poetic reworking of the Zapruder film's imagery, attempted something that no other Texas poet had had the nerve to try to that point—explicitly depicting the assassination itself. Unlike previous poems by

Burford's local contemporaries, "The Spell" offers no avoidance or attempt at deflection. Instead, it transports the reader directly to Dealey Plaza at the very moment of the murder.

> You can almost see him, looking as if well,
> Shedding it, shaking it off,
> The least shadow on the shoulders
> Marking the hurt—as if absorbed almost;
> Then the face turning, alive—
>
> Only hesitating momentarily—
>
> Until you remember how the head
> Was horribly shattered
> And fell, with the lifted hair,
> As from an ax in back—Oswald
> Cutting a path for himself
> In the midst of America, a wedge;
>
> But was the thing as it sped,
> Coppered, leaden, not stopped
> Perhaps there in the invincible thick hair?
> Where the woman with her skill
> Could pick it away, in her lap,
> Breaking the spell? in the cloth of her dress—
>
> It was deeper than that;
> Neither burr nor dune thistle,
> Nor like the roses she held
> Black as blood in the light, so dark red—
> But a kind of blunt bud, splintered
> Into flower, that could not be touched,
> Having its own final force that spread throughout,
> The blind dark overwhelming him.

•

William Burford does not mention Camelot in “The Spell,” but that myth is present. Our two protagonists, the unnamed “him” and “the woman,” evoke the royal couple, and they are moving in that same field of tragic romance spawned by the Camelot narrative.

The central image in that romance, just as in Shuford’s “The Death in Our Family,” is the bloodied roses. Like Shuford, Burford brings into focus the profaning of those innocent flowers with spilled blood. But Burford comingles the image of the sodden roses with that of the bullet. The bullet becomes “the blunt bud, splintered / Into flower.” There is, of course, a double meaning here of “flower.” The bud becomes the bloodied flowers in the back seat of the presidential limousine, and the bullet / bud grows and transforms into something even more ominous—the spell.

In Burford’s poem, what flowers from that moment of the assassination, its enduring aftermath, is “the blind dark.” It overwhelms this one man, but this man is our leader. His kingdom is America, and the “blind dark” is the spell the assassination has cast upon all of us.

•

“Don’t let it be forgot,” Jackie reminded us in that December 6, 1963, *Life* magazine eulogy, “that once there was a spot, for one brief shining moment that was known as Camelot.” The real point, Jackie wished to emphasize, was that that era had passed—“it will never be that way again!”

The “wedge” that had created this great divide was, of course, the assassination: “Oswald / Cutting a path for himself / In the midst of America.” In Burford’s poem, as in the Kennedys’ Camelot, Oswald is the interloper who separates the prince and princess and initiates the tragic end of the mythic romance, terminating this great American fairy tale. Burford was unique among Texas poets in that he explicitly identified Oswald. Without exception, the early Texas assassination poets refused to utter the killer’s name, speaking of the assassination in the passive voice and treating it as a tragic result of some unnamed and inexorable malignant force. For example, Hoggard noted that "A man's become a legend in the twist / Of nonsense in an insane plan," but ultimately ended with the stoic diagnosis that it was all simply "the fatal involvement / Of man with man."

In retrospect, it was remarkable how smoothly the political transition transpired after the Kennedy assassination, a testament to the solidarity of the American state. Before Air Force One left Dallas that afternoon, the presidency had been transferred to JFK's successor, Lyndon Baines Johnson, and the wheels of power continued to churn efficiently. There was no great political transformation, no great governmental tumult. But obviously something had changed. Contemporary America had been separated from the Golden Age.

Today, looking back on the JFK assassination, Burford's invocation of a spell and a descent into darkness seems especially prescient. The assassination is almost universally recognized as a watershed moment in our history, and it is a common assertion that a dark, almost magical, transformation took place at that time.

The word "spell," an utterance or formula believed to have magic power, has a northern European etymology, linking it back to folktales like those of the Brothers Grimm. Those tales, of course, formed the bedrock of Walt Disney's mid-century animated films. Look at 1959's *Sleeping Beauty* and there it is: the hundred-year spell hovering over the stricken princess and her entire kingdom. In this narrative, the world waits for the arrival of the hero prince who will end the long, dread sleep with a simple kiss. In the Kingdom of Post-1963 America, the "blind dark" has spreads its thorns and brambles from the White House across the entire country, and, just as in *Sleeping Beauty*, there will be a very long wait for any relief from the deepening slumber.

Burford is no Walt Disney. "The Spell" offers no happy ending, just an endless suspension. The spell cannot be broken—"the woman with her skill / Could not pick it away." There are no words or magic incantations that can make things right again. The princess herself, Jacqueline Kennedy, had said it: "There will never be another Camelot again."

•

The myth of the spell fit the time and so, in a hundred variations, it spread. A decade and a half after the assassination, an acting American president would present a major address to the nation that would, in some important ways, codify the idea in our political history. In his July 15, 1979, address—which came to be commonly labeled the "Crisis of Confidence" speech—Jimmy Carter attempted, in a manner he intended to hearken back to the Periclean public duty summoned by Kennedy in his "Ask Not" inauguration speech, to call Americans to action. What Americans remember today about that speech was that Carter prefaced this challenge with an acknowledgment that we were suffering from a malaise. "We can see this crisis in the growing doubt about the meaning of our own lives and in the loss of a unity of purpose for our nation," he said. America was in an existential funk.

That malaise was already making itself evident in the work of some Texas literary artists as far back as 1968. While our Dallas writers generally acceded to muteness on the subject of the assassination, poet and editor Robert Bonazzi, running his Latitudes Press out of Houston, did not. His anthology *Towards Winter* carried the following subtitle: *a collection of poems (not necessarily encomia) for John F. Kennedy upon the occasion of the fifth november twenty-second.* The volume contained thirteen works from a diverse collection of national poets, including Robert Bly and Thomas Merton. Some of the work in the anthology directly addresses the assassination, but more prevalent was the theme of the disillusionment that followed it. Coeditor Harry Nash, in his poem "Here You Have It, Kennedy," notes that "four years have passed: gone down the nat'l drain," since November 1963, and Charlene Chesnut, in "Poem," bemoans that we "can't move disillusion back / to bright illusion." *Towards Winter* aimed not so much to honor John F. Kennedy as to document the debilitating aftermath of his murder. Closing the volume with a translation of the Vietnamese poet Nguyen Binh Khiem, W. S. Merwin left his readers with: "Why waste breath talking about the world?/It's better to be drunk and singing poems by the river."

Bonazzi's *Towards Winter* is emblematic of the darkening of the American mood in 1968, as the war in Vietnam escalated and the civil rights movement took a more violent turn. The optimism that marked Kennedy's 1960 inauguration was long gone. The great advocate of peaceful resistance, Martin Luther King Jr., was himself shot down in Memphis on April 4. Robert Kennedy, running for president to complete the unfinished work of his murdered brother, was shot down in Los Angeles on June 5. Throw in the assassinations of other prominent public figures like Medgar Evers in 1963 and Malcolm X in 1965, and by mid-1968, the killing of John F. Kennedy seemed like just the first spurt of a growing deluge of political violence—the Age of the Assassin.

We felt that particularly acutely in Dallas, where we were still hypersensitive to any mention of the topic of assassination. You could even see it in the pages of the *Southwest Review*. Margaret Hartley, the longtime editor, wrote this in the "Editor's Note" to the journal's Summer 1968 issue.

> Two months ago, on April 5, I began the Editor's Note of the Spring issue of *SWR* with the sentence, "This is being written on the day after the assassination of Dr. Martin Luther King." It is incredible that I should be sitting down again at the typewriter on June 8 of the same year to write, "This is being written on the day of the burial of Senator Robert F. Kennedy."

Hartley's reaction was typical of many Americans at the time, and she could not help but invoke her own variation of the spell, as the "blunt bud" of Oswald's bullet continued to splinter into flower. For Hartley, as for many other Americans, these killings were the signs of our "present place of division and peril"—that we were a "sick society."[235]

"Writing in the city where that other assassination occurred less than five years ago, and having watched the reactions that followed it," Hartley continues, it was especially clear that "something horrible had been unloosened." What had started here, it seemed, was becoming a national plague, and what Hartley asked in 1968—"What is happening to our country, that its fine and outspoken public figures are killed in rapid succession?"—would be echoed as a common narrative a decade later in Carter's "Crisis of Confidence"

235. Margaret Hartley, "The Editor's Notebook," *Southwest Review*, Spring/Summer 1968.

speech. "We were sure that ours was a nation of the ballot, not the bullet," Carter said, "until the murders of John Kennedy and Robert Kennedy and Martin Luther King Jr."

In the decade after 1968, there was, for many, a sense that the country was unraveling. In Dallas, many of us were uncomfortably aware that it had all started here.

•

It is a tricky business, attempting to heal the damaged psyche of a city. While our civic leaders were hard at work on their mission to rehabilitate the city's image, there was little else going on that might functionally mend our collective emotional scars. In the arts, the realm where one might most expect this sort of shadowy emotional work to take place, there was mostly silence. Dallas is a city of action, and the literary arts in particular have never been an important force in matters of public life. We had had an active poetry community, but we were like most American cities: our poets tended to be read mostly by each other, and even their best work left barely a ripple in the larger civic sphere.

Even our novelists, who could typically draw more public attention, were more or less alienated from the discussion. In 1972, when Bud Shrake published *Strange Peaches*, his caustic account of Dallas and the assassination, he had already exiled himself from Dallas and could be dismissed as an outsider. *Strange Peaches* sold well nationally and was often praised, but never achieved its deserved recognition here. Likewise, local journalist Bryan Woolley's 1981 novel *November 22* produced some initial positive discussion but would quickly fall off the local literary radar. Woolley could justifiably claim the city's taboo on discussion of the assassination was the cause.[236] Both of these books will be treated in much more detail in the next volume of this project, but suffice it to say here, they are inarguably among the finest literary works ever produced by Dallas authors. Neither, however, found the readership or recognition it deserved within the city limits.

---

236. Bryan Woolley, interview with Tim Cloward, July 22, 2012.

Gary Wills's critique of Dallas from a decade earlier was still relevant. "The printed word is severely controlled there," he wrote. "Both newspapers breathe symbiotically with the power structure." And the civic image was always that power structure's primary concern. As Wills pointed out, we had not demanded that our literary artists delve into uncomfortable subjects. After visiting Dallas in the mid-1960s, he wrote: "Dallas thinks of literary *responsibility* as the urge that fills shelves in the large alcove of the Cokesbury Bookstore devoted to celebration of Texas and things Texan."[237] It should come as no surprise, then, that locally produced literature about the assassination provoked such minuscule public reaction.

Touchy Dallasites, of course, could remind outsiders that we were not illiterate, and that, in fact, Cokesbury had been proclaimed by *Time* magazine in 1949 the single largest bookstore in the United States. The sparkling 1910 Main Street building, built by the United Methodist Publishing House, remained a showplace for our local literary accomplishment until it closed in the late 1970s. Kent Biffle, a *Dallas Morning News* columnist, called it "a city block of books reaching towards heaven." Lon Tinkle, the man of letters who founded the *Morning News*'s Books section, could even proclaim that "[b]ooks now seem as natural on the Texas prairies as oil derricks . . . or as they do in Boston or London."[238]

We sublimated the pain of the assassination with all manner of defensive boosterism, and, consequently, ended up with more slogans extolling our progress than poetry.

•

Given our local reticence, it should come as no surprise that some of the most insightful literary commentary on Dallas and its relationship to the assassination would come from exiles and outsiders. One of the most telling poetic

237. Gary Wills and Ovid Demaris, *Jack Ruby* (New York: Da Capo Press, 1994), 81.

238. Jane Lenz Elder, "Cokesbury Book Store: The Premiere Book Store in the Southwest," *Legacies: A History Journal for Dallas and North Central Texas* 24, no. 2, Fall 2012, 32–40.

comments on that legacy came from a Fort Worth poet. Sister cities, Dallas and Fort Worth have a long and storied rivalry, and Dave Oliphant's poem "Dallas" expresses both the love and loathing one associates with sibling attachment.

Dave Oliphant has was born in Fort Worth in 1939. A proud but philosophical Texan, he has spent a long career exploring what it is to be a poet and thinker in his home state. He works with an impressive array of technical expertise, allusion, and cultural history, yet his work is plainspoken and presented from the perspective of the common man. As the publisher of Prickly Pear Press, he has also done important work advancing the interchange between Anglo and Latin American literature. Prickly Pear's 1981 bilingual anthology *Washing the Cow Skull / Lavando la calavera de vaca,* for instance, includes a Spanish translation of William Burford's "The Spell." Oliphant is also one of the preeminent experts on Texas jazz music and stands today as one of the grand old men of Texas Letters.

Oliphant's most developed poetic exploration of Texas is his *Memories of Texas Towns & Cities.* This collection of thirty poems, each one focusing on a specific Texas locale, is comparable to William Carlos William's *Paterson.* Originally published in Oliphant's 1976 collection *Lines & Mounds,* "Dallas" is one of the earliest sections of this work to appear in print.

The poem begins with the depiction of a hard-edged, competitive business town. Downtown Dallas is a sort of coliseum with the business oligarchy safely overseeing "from box seats in tinted glass" the carnage that takes place at ground level.

encircled by freeway loops
has wished itself a Roman arena
styled more after Texas Stadium
where gladiators   this time
Christians from Abilene or SMU
take on Lions Bears Rams
while the lawyer-merchant class
spies down night and day
from box seats in tinted glass

spots the animals in goal-line stands
or last ditched along skid row

Developing his football/gladiator metaphor, Oliphant then directs our attention to the most notable blood spilled on the streets of Dallas: John F. Kennedy's in Dealey Plaza. This is what the tourists have come to see:

below
too are those looking for his-
tory staring at tobacco stains on
Federal Building walks visitors in from Boston
wondering
Is this where our hero bled?
buying his souvenirs windows Xed
in snapshots where Oswald took his aim
his bullet granting one more wish

As the great cosmopolitan center of North Texas, Dallas is a place that promises the fulfillment of desires; it is the urban paradise that might grant the wishes of the young Fort Worth native Oliphant. Mingled with these wishes, however, is a question that leaves the stanza hanging. Did Dallas wish Kennedy dead?

such carpet rides lift powerlines
overpasses skyscrapers high
rises hopes of masses recall
how they were raised for
days driving here as a family when fall
trips to the State Fair were long and hard
where at last in Sears would try
the cowboy boots had wanted so like Gene's
or Roy's but with narrow feet
dad said no they didn't fit
nothing in Dallas ever does

it's Texas but then it's not
it isn't the West it never was
would have it moved to an eastern spot

partly this comes out as
the talk of a Cowtown boy   Fort Worth-Dallas
called twin cities yet rivals from the start
the real Texas   with cattle and horses
rodeos at Will Rogers Coliseum   versus
the Airport

There is something else coupled with this critique—a desire to return to the simpler, more pastoral times of one's youth. This desire encompasses not only Oliphant's nostalgia for his own childhood but also more recent memories of taking trips to Dallas with his son, Dario. As Oliphant unravels the rivalry that exists between sister cities, he addresses a twin tension, one that exists between himself and his own rapidly coming-of-age son.

typical of towns grown near the closest father & son
are born to carry a rivalry on
Dario's red head sticks
out in any crowd
can be a pain yet will still claim him any time
like all of Texas or so would rhyme
Big D's a sore thumb too
though giving credit where credit's due
both share winning points
this city can boast of parks and lakes
are a blue-green sketch
for him to sit & draw match
with watercolor or tempera paints
outdo this description make a papa proud

carry him back to creeks shaded

by pecan & peach running clear and cold
over smooth & green-furred rocks   fresh
by willows   in summer a cool conversing   traded
for memos typed at the Apparel Mart to baskets sold
beside the bridge   their priceless wrinkled pits
brown-black nuts fallen at feet once bared to rip-
ples rainbow perch a movement Dario can better catch,

need for that his art need his love
needed Love Field too a where to land
& seek for him athletic fun a high-
er flight than had on fleetest jets   a swim
ming hole for deeper dives than
dips on tollway drives a where to buy
western boots for the skinny kid
right for walking streets can still recov-
er that magic word will trim shed blood
like a genii whisped
back inside an olym-
pic lamp overrubbed

Oliphant, in his allusions to the Kennedy assassination, does not evoke the by-then standard tropes of the Camelot myth. His is a more intimate approach, not concerned with the fate of the nation, but with his own relationship to his son. The final implied wish here is to go back, to "recov-/er that magic word" that will reclaim his own green youth through his son and return them to a more harmonious existence. But blood has been shed, and the genie that could grant Oliphant's wish is the same one that granted Dallas its wish to kill John F. Kennedy. And, try as he might, Oliphant can't wish (or whisper) the genie back into that "overrubbed" lamp.

An important parallel therefore connects Oliphant's "Dallas" and the Camelot myth—the idea of a lost and irrevocable Golden Age. For that sixties generation who came of age during the time of assassinations, there is the habitual pastoral desire for a return to innocence. Despite our most sincere yearning, we are trapped inescapably in our history. We all lose our innocence, and we must all come to understand there is no returning to the Garden.

•

One of the basic tenets of twentieth-century artistic modernism was that we all live in a condition of exile. If you were an artist with aspirations to create your own modern art in mid-century Dallas, that sense of alienation in your own home would have been easily achieved. Dallas was as conservative artistically as it was politically, and that was especially true of our local literature.

Poets such as Oliphant and Burford, developing their local variations of modernist poetics, were always swimming upstream in the literary waters of Texas. While Dallas liked to pride itself on being more sophisticated than the rest of the state, we had really not separated ourselves that much in our support of cutting-edged, adventurous literature. While our civic leaders had consistently strove to maintain the arts here as a symbol of our cultural ascendancy, what they supported was generally very conservative—efforts to maintain a symphony orchestra or to ensure the annual visit of the Metropolitan Opera, for instance. We were never really comfortable with international modernism, and our cultural traditionalism made Dallas poor soil for the germination of an avant-garde. If we were to take wild chances and embark upon ambitious risks, we would most commonly attempt it in commerce; in the arts, we generally played it safe.

We had exerted some significant influence on American culture, however. The Dallas Nine, a group of painters, printmakers, and sculptors led by Jerry Bywaters, had garnered national recognition for their unique brand of Southwestern regionalism in the 1930s and early 1940s. Margo Jones had put Dallas on the map of the theater world in the late 1940s and early 1950s by spearheading the regional theater movement. In both cases, these movements had garnered local support by developing distinctly American themes via a homegrown modernism that displayed few trappings of European avant-gardism. While our burgeoning skyline indicated we were comfortable with internationalist modernism in the more commerce-driven realm of architecture, it was generally understood that those artists who sought to produce radical work in other genres should best do it elsewhere.

By the mid-1950s, the political winds in the American heartlands were blowing ever harder against anything that might seem radical (and thus, perhaps, un-American). In Dallas, with our infernal drive toward conformity, we were even less tolerant of ideas that seemed to challenge standard convention. The city was fertile ground for the mid-century Red hunters. In the 1940s, our civic leaders had taken all the steps necessary to neutralize our local labor movement, and in the next decade our most fervent Red-baiters found that it was the arts that most needed purging of dangerous Communist infiltration. Echoing accusations that the modern art displayed by the Dallas Museum of Art was infected with "decadence, perversion, and revolutionary purpose," a bevy of local patriotic watchdog organizations attacked the institution. Insisting that it gave "a place of honor" to Communist art, along with "the work of others with notorious records of red front affiliations," these groups attacked the modernism of artists like Picasso, Diego Rivera, and Ben Shahn as inherently subversive. Jerry Bywaters, the populist modernist whose artistic talents and middle-of-the-road aesthetics had made him an obvious choice to head the museum, found himself in the awkward position of having to defend his display of modern art. These high-profile arts controversies spread to the Dallas Public Library as well, and, by 1956, Dallas had become the subject of national disapprobation, with coverage of the controversies in *Time*, the *New York Times*, and *Arts Magazine*.[239]

While high-profile battles were being fought over the visual arts, there was a lower-profile battle being waged in the local literary world. Again, the attention we would receive was not the result of any demonstration of local artistic excellence, but from the eruption of Cold War paranoia. In 1951, John Owen Beaty published *The Iron Curtain over America*, a book which would make him perhaps the most well-known and widely discussed Dallas author of the decade. Beaty was a distinguished SMU faculty member, having joined the English Department in 1919. He soon made a name for himself as an expert in Old

239. Francine Carraro, *Jerry Bywaters: A Life in Art* (Austin: University of Texas Press, 1994), 184.

English literature. He chaired the Modern Language Association's Old English group in the late 1930s, and, by all accounts, was an eminent scholar and civilized man. But *The Iron Curtain over America* was a highly controversial and widely criticized book. One journal called it the "most extensive piece of racist propaganda in the history of the anti-Semitic movement in America." Marshall Terry, then a student of Beaty's, summed up the work like this: "The thesis of the book was that all Jews were Communists, and all Communists were Jews."[240] Among Beaty's contentions were that Jews were largely responsible for the success of the Bolshevik Revolution in Russia and that those same Communist-friendly Jews currently dominated the Democratic Party in the United States. By 1953, the book, with its friendly depictions of Hitler and the Nazis, had sold forty-five thousand copies and was in its ninth printing. It was attracting national attention, especially among our nation's far-right-wing ideologues.[241]

At SMU, the acknowledged central locus of the city's literary life, there was real concern: How to muzzle Beaty and avoid civic embarrassment without trampling on his free speech rights? A group of SMU faculty joined with the Dallas Jewish community, led by Rabbi Levi Olin, to quarantine the book, asking the local press to limit its coverage of Beaty. SMU President Umphrey Lee sent a message to SMU trustees, urging them to disown Beaty's ideas. But, as some trustees were Beaty supporters, that exhortation went nowhere.

The controversy intensified when the *Houston Chronicle* raved about Beaty's book and quoted him as he accused the Dallas press of censorship. When Margaret Hartley of SMU Press published a review of Beaty's work in the *Southwest Review*, Beaty responded by issuing a pamphlet called *How to Capture a University*. In it, he claimed "a certain powerful non-Christian element was trying to take over SMU." Only then, as the controversy began to dominate Southern Methodist University and *Time* magazine sent a correspondent to cover the hullabaloo, did the university finally take definitive action. The faculty voted overwhelmingly to condemn Beaty's attacks as being "without any foundation in fact," and incoming President William Tate

240. Marshall Terry, *Loving U.: A Memoir by Marshall Terry* (University Park, TX: DeGolyer Library SMU, 2011), 30–31.

241. Hollace Ava Weiner, *Jewish Stars in Texas: Rabbis and Their Work* (College Station: Texas A&M University Press, 1999), 226.

confronted Beaty directly, convincing him to restrain the public advocacy of his more offensive views. Rather than make him a free speech martyr, SMU let Beaty quietly retire, finally bringing the matter to an end.[242]

The 1950s were not a sterling period for this city's literary life. Rather than championing the works of our best and brightest, many of our literary leaders had been drawn into a two-and-a-half-year struggle to divert attention from an obvious crackpot. The distinguished critic Lon Tinkle, in his special end-of-the-literary-year review in the *Dallas Morning News,* had to create a new special category for John Owen Beaty's work: books "that should not have been published."

•

Despite its pretentions as the center of the state's literary life, Dallas itself has not, until recently, created much cutting-edge literature. In fact, Dallas had established a long-standing tradition of driving its most talented writers into exile. The most adventurous of them have generally left town for the brighter lights of more culturally open cities. A list of authors who started, or attempted to start, their careers in Dallas and then left for greener pastures would make an impressive roster of literary talent. It would include eventual Pulitzer Prize–winner Katherine Anne Porter, noir master Horace McCoy, noted fiction writer William Humphrey, and New Journalism star Terry Southern. Almost all of them disowned the city once they left. After the assassination, the exodus would continue: novelist Bud Shrake, Texas New Journalist Gary Cartwright, and *Rolling Stone*'s Grover Lewis. Like the legendary Lost Generation of the 1920s, they chose exile, bemoaning the rampant materialism, religious intolerance, and knee-jerk patriotism that constricted the cultural life of their former home.

If you had literary ambitions and were disaffected by the provincialism of mid-1950s America, San Francisco—a city with a long history of literary innovation still bathed in the afterglow of the fabled San Francisco

---

242. Weiner, *Jewish Stars in Texas,* 225–27; "Education: The Friendly Professor," *Time,* April 12, 1954.

Renaissance—might have seemed like Mecca. As a teenager in 1950s Dallas, Stan Rice was probably already fantasizing about escape. After he met his future wife, Anne, in journalism class in suburban Richardson High School, they ended up attending classes at North Texas State University in nearby Denton. By 1962, just into their twenties and struggling with their aspirations to be writers, they married and moved to San Francisco.

That move placed Stan and Anne Rice in San Francisco just as it was becoming ground zero for the birth of America's 1960s counterculture. "In the middle of Haight-Ashbury in the 1960s," Anne later said, "I was typing away while everybody was dropping acid and smoking grass." Amid all this cultural turmoil, they both enrolled at San Francisco State University and began what would eventually become illustrious literary careers.[243]

Anne Rice, who had moved to Dallas from New Orleans at age sixteen, would go on to become one of America's most prominent literary celebrities. After the publication of her 1976 novel *Interview with the Vampire,* Rice's books would become perennial bestsellers, her Vampire Chronicles novels the basis for Hollywood blockbusters. Stan would go on to establish himself as an important poet and painter, running a gallery in New Orleans until his death in 2002.

Culturally, San Francisco would prove to be light-years away from the Dallas suburbs the Rices grew up in. Stan, in particular, felt liberated from the social claustrophobia of Dallas, and he was not alone. Other Texans traveled a similar road. Paul Foreman, a poet and important small-press editor from Granbury, a town an hour's drive southwest of Dallas, also ended up in California at that time, developing connections in the lively literary scene then brewing around Berkeley. To keep up with fellow travelers who had left their home state in search of greener literary fields, Foreman established TAWTE: Texas Artists, Writers, and Thinkers in Exile.[244] Like Rice, Foreman had discovered a larger world, but he remained inevitably attached to his Texas roots.

•

243. Stewart Kellerman, "Other Incarnations of the Vampire Author," *New York Times,* November 7, 1988.

244. Christiansen, *West of the American Dream,* 140–42.

When he heard that John F. Kennedy had been gunned down in his hometown in November of 1963, Stan Rice was twenty-one years old, studying literature, and living the bohemian life of a poor, aspiring poet. He was just beginning a journey that would quickly transform him into a poet of the first rank. Immersed in the thriving Bay Area literary scene and energized with the Black Mountain School and Beat poetics bouncing around the city, Rice developed a voice untethered from the innate conservatism and boosteristic optimism that characterized the city he had exiled himself from. "America the Beautiful" is typical of his early work and his personal immersion in the issues of his times:

> I pledge allegiance again,
> This time to the vivifications of our lost Body Politic,
> Nerves and follicles and arteries
> Ablaze in the suaveness of night.[245]

In his zeal to produce work that enacted this "vivification," Rice often produced poetry that was death-obsessed and filled with solipsistic brooding, savage in both style and content—verse that would have courted ostracism in Texas.

If Stan Rice ever wrote any poetry directly addressing the assassination of John Kennedy, it did not make it into any of his books, but he did create some significant work that illuminated his relationship with the city where the president was killed. In that work, he is hard on Dallas. There is none of the childhood nostalgia that can be found in Oliphant's "Dallas," but, like that poem, it is tinged with violence. The first poem from his 1983 collection, *Body of Work,* entitled "Texas Suite," is typical of many of the poems where Rice hearkens back to his earlier days in Texas. It begins: "The Murder Burger / is served right here."[246]

Elsewhere, Rice skewers Dallas, and his estranged younger self, for their bigotry and ignorance, most notably in his long poem "Whiteboy," published

245. Stan Rice, *Singing Yet: New and Selected Poems* (New York: Knopf, 1993), 7, 16, 17.

246. Stan Rice, *Body of Work* (Berkeley, CA: Mudra, 1983).

in 1976 by Mudra Press in Berkeley, California. What makes "Whiteboy" especially significant here is the fact that it deals with assassination—not John Kennedy's, but Martin Luther King Jr.'s. Yet Rice chooses to set his poem in Dallas. And this is not the Dallas you would see depicted in the local literature—it is a gloomier terrain. Borrowing both the imagery and the aesthetics of T. S. Eliot's epochal modernist poem "The Waste Land," Rice, the self-exiled Texan and budding modernist, has transformed the geography of his boyhood into a larger landscape of exile.

"The Waste Land" has long been considered the landmark poem of one of the masters of modernism, and Rice's work would naturally be colored by its long shadow. Eliot, as one of the great exemplars of the Lost Generation, would have served as one of Rice's spiritual mentors, with the topography of Rice's journey to San Francisco echoing Eliot's artistic flight to Europe. For a poet working in Rice's time and place, Eliot's image of the twentieth century as a wasteland was an easily adopted trope. It would not have been a huge leap for a reader then to recognize the congruencies between Eliot's wasteland and the prevailing funk of post–1960s assassination America. The wasteland was an effective objective correlative of our contemporary malaise.

For those few in Dallas who took notice of Stan Rice's work, there would have been reason to pause and reflect. By 1977, the year "Whiteboy" was published, Stan Rice had become a professor and the head of creative writing at San Francisco State. Most significantly, the collection in which "Whiteboy" appears (also titled *Whiteboy*) was honored by the Academy of American Poets with its Edgar Allan Poe Award, given to a poet forty-five or under in recognition of his continuing development. The Dallas expatriate had made himself a name in the larger literary world. But what might have drawn the most attention in Dallas was the fact that the image of the modern wasteland that Rice created in "Whiteboy," that stark and infertile landscape of dispossession, was so very specifically our own.

•

It is worthwhile to note the common origin of the wasteland mythology as developed by T. S. Eliot and the Camelot mythology that developed around the Kennedy White House. Both of these potent twentieth-century myths have their roots in the rich loam of the traditional tales of King Arthur and his Round Table. While the origins of the original Arthur are open to debate, lost in the murk of fifth-century historiography, we can assuredly trace the genesis of its twentieth-century offshoots to Sir Thomas Malory, who standardized for us the ever-expanding muddle of folk legends in his 1485 *Le Morte d'Arthur*. Before we had to contend with the deaths of Martin Luther King Jr. and John F. Kennedy, we reflected on the death of Arthur—one of the most enduring and immensely flexible myths in the Anglo-American heritage.

As William Manchester pointed out in *The Death of a President*, "Once a leader becomes a martyr, myth naturally follows." Even as he scrupulously labored to abide by the objective tenets of the historian, Manchester understood that the story of John F. Kennedy was already entering the realm of mythology. Citing *The Golden Bough*, Manchester noted this transformation of leader to martyr as an example of an archetypal pattern, a "custom that Sir James Frazer found in every early society: the ritualistic murder of the folk hero." It would be an agonizing experience for the society, Manchester wrote, "but it would also be a sign of contrition, and after the execution, their mighty friend would ascend into heaven, to temper the wrath of the Almighty and assure a green and abundant spring." It was a cycle that persisted in various manifestations across time and place. "[I]n Germany Siegfried, in France Roland," Manchester stated. "In Britain, he was Arthur."[247]

Manchester's implication was that John Kennedy was his generation's martyred hero, and the Camelot myth, as it was developing under Jacqueline Kennedy and Theodore H. White, happily embraced this idea. The public could not accept a death devoid of meaning. As with Arthur, there must be the promise, somehow, in some form, of redemptive return.

Sir Thomas Malory's Renaissance-era *Le Morte d'Arthur* noted that promise in the verse on Arthur's tomb: *Hic Iacet Arthurus, rex quondam rexque futurus.* "Here lies Arthur, the once and future king." By the mid-twentieth century, that promise of redemption receives even more emphasis. T. H. White ends his tale of Arthur, before the king has even died, with: *explicit liber*

247. Manchester, *The Death of a President*, 623.

regis quondam regisque futuri. "This is the story of the once and future king." This he follows with a final phrase: "The Beginning."

In his native Britain, King Arthur has been reborn in innumerable incarnations over the years. As Arthur crossed the Atlantic and T. H. White's novel was adapted for American consumption, his story began to take on an increasingly cheerier tone. In Lerner and Loewe's 1960 Broadway adaption, the court of King Arthur has been transformed into a place where, by royal decree, "The climate must be perfect all the year." An even cheerier and commodified, kid-friendly version of Arthur appeared in Disney's *The Sword in the Stone*, released in 1963. In these American pop culture versions of the Arthurian legends, the hero's martyrdom is increasingly sanitized of any tragedy. The Camelot that become the metaphor for the Kennedy White House was surprisingly jolly. Note Alan Jay Lerner's lyrics:

> In short, there's simply not a more congenial spot
> For happily-ever-aftering than here in Camelot

Stan Rice, in his depiction of that other great martyr of the late twentieth century, Martin Luther King Jr., makes use of an altogether darker facet of the Arthurian legend. His evocation of Eliot's "The Waste Land" also alludes to the antithesis of Camelot. Rather than Frazer's sacrificial king whose martyrdom revivifies the kingdom and assures the green and abundant spring, we are presented with the Fisher King. In the Arthurian tradition, the Fisher King sits by the river near the Castle Corbenic, fishing. A wound to the thigh makes him impotent and unable to father or support the next generation. His kingdom suffers as he does, his impotence affecting the fertility of the land and reducing it to a barren wilderness.

Eliot's promotion of this minor character in the King Arthur pantheon indicates the ultimate failure of Arthur's kingship. He and his Knights of the Round Table are unsuccessful in their final quest—they can neither claim the Holy Grail nor cure the suffering king. We are left with the image of the injured and disfigured Fisher King who neither dies nor is healed. As the king goes, so does the kingdom, condemned to a tragic stasis of inaction and futility. There is no place for successful martyrdom in the landscape of the wasteland. As created by T. S. Eliot and developed by Stan Rice in "Whiteboy," this landscape is barren of redemptive ritual—there is no chance for "happily-ever-aftering."

•

One testament to T. S. Eliot's profound influence on American literature was his 1958 visit to Dallas. In April of that year, in a presentation orchestrated by Lon Tinkle, Eliot drew over seven thousand people for a free talk and reading at SMU's Moody Coliseum. One scholar in attendance described the reading as "a performance of such unexpected power, splendor and eloquence that it became for me one of a handful of significant emotional events without equal." For many, it was proof positive that Dallas was *not* a cultural wasteland, and that we were not averse to challenging modernist literature.[248]

There is no evidence that future modernist Stan Rice, then a sixteen-year-old Richardson High School student, was at Moody Coliseum that night when Eliot read the "Fire Sermon," "Death by Water," and "What the Thunder Said" sections from "The Waste Land." We do know, however, that, years later, strands of imagery from Eliot's "The Waste Land" would be woven throughout "Whiteboy."

Just as April is "the cruellest month" in Eliot's masterwork, Martin Luther King Jr. was killed on April 4 in 1968. As "Whiteboy" unfolds, Rice weaves in more and more inescapable allusions to Eliot's work. The landscape itself, a variation of the standard North Texas suburban home and garden that Rice grew up in, takes on the aspects of an infertile and threatening wasteland. The garden is adorned with ivy, but it is a strange and mutated ivy with white tendrils: "their strength coils through the back yard like / a snake around a chicken egg / it swallows without breaking."

This is the ominous landscape in which the Whiteboy, more or less Rice himself, ponders MLK's assassination: "Im thinking of the meaning / this man's death has. / If it will last. / If any." In the process, Rice interrogates himself and his past; even the self-derogatory title is an admission of his provincial

248. Terry, *Loving U.*, 10–13.

ignorance. But the Whiteboy aims to educate and improve himself, and his introspection will take the form of a literary mediation. The poem's opening section is entitled "The Texan reads a book." It begins:

> Each night has new meaning
> in it. Tonight. Aeschylus, I hear your black and gold mask
> thunk in the yard . . .

The Whiteboy is reading the ancient Greeks, the tragedies of Aeschylus, and the poem's first allusion is to the Mycenaean warrior-king Agamemnon. It is his death mask that will "clink against the gravel" in the garden of the suburban wasteland, and his fate (he was assassinated by his own wife upon his return home from the Trojan War) that Rice will join with that of a more recently murdered hero.

> BANG! Aeschylus, you said:
> God marks the man with watchful eyes
> Who counts his killed by companies,
> And when his luck, his proud success,
> Forgets the law of righteousness,
> Then the dark Furies launch at length
> A counter-blow to crush his strength
> And cloud his brightness, till the dim
> Pit of oblivion swallows him.

But just as Aeschylus had his House of Atreus, and Agamemnon was just the first in a long line of tragically murdered protagonists, Rice had his 1960s equivalent—our own lineage of assassinated leaders. When you say "BANG!" here in Dallas, the hero you think of is always John Kennedy; you can still hear those echoes reverberating through Dealey Plaza. However, in his reworking of Aeschylus's archetypes, Rice is referencing a different victim of our contemporary curse.

> I am singing but I am sinking

into the little black hole
in Martin Luther King's black jaw.
Or, as one of his friends put it: "His face just exploded."
The language got too much.
His life stopped working.

As Rice reflects on "the meaning / this man's death has," he strives to be like Aeschylus—attentive to language.

So what is a dead Greek to this dead nigger?
At the Vice President's fund raising dinner where the news came
out the Chaplain said:
"The-king-is-dead-long-live-the-king-of-
peace-on-earth."
Meaning: each night has new meaning in it.
Meaning: we have heard the soft language before and it grew
white ivy.
Meaning: I am. My black roots are hair. Are
showing.

For Rice, who finds even himself implicated in the hero's death, the "soft language" common to eulogies is inadequate. He is distrustful of the traditional language of martyrdom and its usual bromides of redeeming sacrifice. He moves in the unsettled world of tragedy where there is no redemption for suffering—the world of the Eumenides. In "Whiteboy," as in Aeschylus's *The Oresteia,* the Eumenides—the Furies—hold sway. These ghastly subterranean deities dispense their primordial form of vengeance and retribution by relentlessly hounding their victims into insanity. This is not ancient mythology; this is our own time of the assassins.

•

The direct correlation of Dallas with Eliot's "The WasteLand" is most obvious in the third of "Whiteboy's four sections. Its title: "The Texan returns to the

Texas State Fair and sees Racism sitting in a glass cage over a tank of water," a reference to the epigraph with which Eliot prefaces "The Waste Land," itself a quotation from Petronius's *Satyricon*.

> For once I myself saw with my own eyes, the Sibyl of Cumae hanging in a cage, and when the children said to her, "Sibyl, what do you want?" she replied, "I want to die."

Petronius's Sibyl, the oracle / priestess of classical Roman legend, has been given eternal life by Apollo. However, she neglected to ask not to age, so she is growing smaller and smaller as her body wears away. In Stan Rice's poem, the Sibyl has become the embodied form of "Racism" and Cumae has been transformed into the State Fair of Texas.

The State Fair of Texas is the most quintessential of all Dallas landmarks. There is no more important event on the Dallas calendar, and even today children in North Texas are given a Fair Day: classes are dismissed, and they receive free tickets. As Dave Oliphant's "Dallas" demonstrates, the annual trip to the fairgrounds is an important ritual practiced by families across the region. Since the first Dallas fair in 1886, with its cattle sales, concerts, balloon ascents, and displays of farm machinery, the event has held a fun-house mirror up to our cultural life. Over the years, the State Fair of Texas has become the occasion when Dallas most shows itself off to the greater world. When presidents came to town—William Howard Taft in 1909, Woodrow Wilson in 1911 (then governor of New Jersey), and Franklin Roosevelt in 1936—they were whisked to the fairgrounds to address the populace.

The story of how R. L. Thornton and his fellow business leaders brought the 1936 Texas Centennial Exposition to those fairgrounds could be the foundation story of modern Dallas. Not only did the Texas-sized celebration draw six million visitors and transform Fair Park into an art deco landmark—it also gave birth to the Dallas Citizens Council. It would not be an exaggeration to say that Dallas history is inextricably linked to the history of the State Fair of Texas. And one truth inscribed in that shared history is the fact that the State Fair was created for white Dallas.

In the 1920s, when the Ku Klux Klan was at the height of its national popularity, Dallas was one of the movement's most important hubs. It's been estimated that thirteen thousand local citizens belonged to the Dallas chapter of the Ku Klux Klan, and the imperial wizard of the national Klan was Dallas dentist Hiram Wesley Evans. As always, we could count on the State Fair to put the "real" Dallas on display, and the annual KKK Day at the State Fair became one of the city's biggest spectacles. For example, the 1923 extravaganza featured fireworks and a marching band that could boast of being "the largest drum and bugle corps in the world." It drew seventy-five thousand citizens to watch Imperial Wizard Evans speak and witness the simultaneous swearing-in of two thousand new Klan members.[249]

Coming of age in 1950s Dallas, Stan Rice might not have been aware of this earlier history. It is also hard to say if he was aware, as he worked through grade school, of the series of home bombings then occurring around Fair Park as Blacks attempted to move into formerly all-white neighborhoods. He may have been too young then to be aware of the growing controversy surrounding "Negro Achievement Day," the single day when Blacks were allowed entrance to the State Fair. By 1953, the civic powers had bowed to Black pressure and agreed to allow them everyday access to the fair—with exception of the midway, the restaurants, and any ride where they might come into physical contact with whites. By the time Rice became a teenager, however, he must certainly have been aware that there was something in the air, and that Blacks in Dallas were making demands, pressing the city's white leadership. That pressure might have been most obvious to him in the events playing out around the State Fair. In 1955, just as Rice turned thirteen, Juanita Craft and her NAACP Youth Council volunteers began picketing the State Fair, calling for a boycott the State Fair's Negro Achievement Day and the integration of all fair attractions.

As the civil rights movement accelerated in Dallas, the larger-than-life symbolism of the State Fair of Texas made it a natural flashpoint. It is hard not to imagine that, as a youth growing up in the Dallas area, Rice's developing

249. Payne, *Dallas: An Illustrated* History, 106–108; "Flyer for Ku Klux Klan Day," *The Portal to Texas History*, accessed November 24, 2017, texashistory.unt.edu/ark:/67531/metapth31223/.

consciousness would be unimpressed by the State Fair. Surely he would have remembered the 1952 debut of Big Tex, the fifty-two-foot denim- and pearl-snap shirt–clad cowboy erected as our official mascot at the center of the grounds. Surely he was aware of the great State Fair ritual of the annual Texas-Oklahoma football game and its related pregame debauchery. Alongside all this blustering and braggadocious Texas culture, Rice surely would have also experienced the State Fair freak shows. As in all carnival settings, these tawdry exhibits were a fixture at the State Fair, displaying all manner of animal and human deformity. So the self-exiled Rice could look back at these memories a decade and a half later and add his own potent symbols to express the racial tension that underlay all this ostensible fun and patently Texan spectacle.

As Rice revisits the State Fair in "Whiteboy," he pulls those memories through the lens of Petronius's *Satyricon*. So the debauchery of ancient Rome becomes the debauchery of Dallas. The Satyrs, the goatlike companions of Dionysus, become the doubles of our own goatish behavior. (Bud Shrake modeled his outrageous 1973 parody of Dallas, *Peter Arbiter,* on *The Satyricon.*) Using the image of the caged Sibyl that Eliot incorporates into "The Waste Land," Rice collapses the public spectacle of the fairground dunking booth with the titillating allure of the freak show, giving us a personified "Racism sitting in a glass cage over a tank of water." The lines that follow indulge in all the obscene vernacular of white supremacy:

> And here is where the niggers wash.
> You can kill a nigger at last.
> You can throw a baseball at the target hooked to his body,
> You can pay him back for his sensual blackness,

In our greatest seasonal celebration, where Dallas displays itself to the world, Rice shows the city playing out the worst of its racial history. While it does not mention lynching, the poem's imagery evokes that horrific practice. Although lynching was a national problem in the early decades of the century, Dallas had a particularly brazen association with it, as evidenced by the murder of Allen Brooks. The fifty-nine-year-old Black laborer, accused of attempted rape, was pulled from the Old Red Courthouse by a vengeful white mob on March 3, 1910. He was hung from a telephone pole adjacent to the ornate ceremonial Elks Arch at the prominent downtown intersection of Akard and Main Street. His swinging corpse was witnessed by perhaps five thousand people before it was removed. Historians have gathered plenty of unsettling evidence suggesting that in Dallas, and elsewhere, lynchings during the Jim Crow era often functioned as significant social rituals for members of the white community. In "Whiteboy," you can detect the echoes of 1910, a time when the act of racial murder could be a form of mass entertainment.

> . . . You can make his seat snap open
> And down into the white filthy water he drops,
> His black hands and feet mixed in the foam,
> Staring at you through the glass tank
> Like an animal that you cant kill,
> You cant kill him,
> He keeps rising all oily and fresh, like a seal,
> Taunting you, virile, soiling you, soiled, your victim, your master.

In Rice's transformation of Eliot's parable, the compromised promise of eternal life for the Sibyl parallels the problematic promises of racial equality that America has proffered its Black population. The Black Man (as "Racism"), like the Sibyl, will not die. He is like the Arthurian Fisher King: left in a barren landscape where there is neither death nor healing. And we are there with him. "Racism" hangs before us, front and center in that great spectacle of the State Fair of Texas, as a grotesque carnival game that continues interminably and without resolution.

•

Martin Luther King Jr. also visited Dallas in 1963, some eleven months before JFK's fatal visit. On Friday, January 4, he stepped onto the stage of the venerable Fair Park Auditorium (today the Music Hall). The Spanish Baroque–style building was erected in 1925 and is still one of the fairgrounds, architectural highlights. It had long been a showplace for the city's high culture, most famously the 1957 premiere of the Dallas Civic Opera with the legendary soprano Maria Callas. Just two years before MLK's visit, the Fair Park Auditorium began allowing integrated seating at opera performances, and only after the touring Metropolitan Opera threatened it with a boycott.[250]

King had been invited to Dallas by Rev. H. Rhett James, NAACP organizer, chairman of the Dallas County United Poll Tax Committee, and head of the New Hope Baptist Church. He spoke for forty-five minutes to roughly 2,500 people, as a good number of local Black religious leaders (responding to pressure from congregants) joined local labor union representatives and a smattering of white Democratic Party leaders. Speaking eight months before making his memorable "I Have a Dream" speech during the March on Washington, King delivered a similar address in Dallas. He also took some time to praise President Kennedy, saying that the chief executive had "done some impressive things in civil rights, especially when compared to the previous [Eisenhower] administration." To support his claim, King cited Kennedy's fulfillment of his pledge to issue an executive order ending discrimination in federally funded public housing. King added, however, that this measure did not "do the full job." It was, he said, "a start," but Kennedy "must give the order teeth if it is to work."[251]

Those in attendance had to pass through some two hundred protesters outside as the police struggled to keep the teeming crowd the required twenty-five feet from the building. Their shouts could often be heard inside the auditorium, and the message that Dr. King was not welcome in Dallas—that he was a Communist agitator intent on destroying America—echoed across the fairgrounds.

Outside the Fair Park Auditorium that night you could have seen on display some of that same toxic brew of intolerance and righteous anger that would be broadcast across America ten months later, when a similar crowd accosted Adlai Stevens at the UN Day speech in the Memorial

250. Jim Schutze, *The Accommodation: The Politics of Race in an American City* (Dallas: Deep Vellum, 2021), 137.

251. Bill Minutaglio and Steven L. Davis, *Dallas 1963* (New York: Twelve, 2013), 189–92.

Auditorium (the event that would prompt *Time* magazine to label Dallas "A City Disgraced"). The protests surrounding King's Dallas visit, however, would garner no headlines. The *Dallas Morning News* and the other area media would decline to report on it at all. It was a "Black Thing," as former journalist Bud Shrake used to say: an event that occurred outside the white community and thus was unworthy of any mainstream news coverage. Likewise, the bomb threat that delayed King's speech and sent Dallas Police Department detectives scrambling to secure the Fair Park Auditorium would go completely unreported.

•

Martin Luther King was not killed in Dallas; he was assassinated in Memphis. Stan Rice was in San Francisco when he wrote the poem, but he drags the murdered civil rights leader's body back here—to the Dallas that was his childhood home.

In the closing section of "Whiteboy"—"The Texan re-reads a book"—Rice brings us back to myth-time. The book is again Aeschylus's *Oresteia,* with Martin Luther King and the murdered Agamemnon mirroring each other. Again, they share the landscape of the suburban-home-as-wasteland, and, as the poem closes, neither body has been given a proper burial.

> Im sure that Agamemnon's golden deathmask is a fake
> Martin Luther King's skin is awake in my garden.
> It talks.
> It says: your uncle's, your father's, your brother's, your own
> bones bones bones
> are pale and rotten and crushed and swallowed.
> The little black hole in his cheek
> sprouts water. Tonight.
> I see.
> I am.
> My own.
> Skin's father.

The unburied body here speaks for itself. In Stan Rice's Dallas, where we had failed to devise an adequate ritual to mollify our pain over the death of John F. Kennedy, he has delivered to us also the unburied body of Martin Luther King. What the Whiteboy has revealed to himself in his rereading of the Greeks, his epiphany, is his recognition of his own complicity in a murderous inheritance.

"Whiteboy" is not about mythologizing our dead heroes, finding meaning in their death and assuring ourselves that their spilled blood will ensure us green and verdant springs. It bears a starker message of self-implication. Examining the redneck culture of ignorance and racism from which he came, Rice's poem is both a reclamation and renunciation of his earlier self. Writing in that terrible time of recurrent assassinations, Rice challenges readers to gaze into the difficult mirror of American culture and recognize that we all bear some guilt for the murders.

When we see that "BANG!"at the beginning of "Whiteboy," the gunshot casts us back to where it all started—November 22, 1963. The lines that follow it, commemorating the life of the murdered leader, could have just as easily been written about John F. Kennedy as Martin Luther King or Agamemnon. For the audience of the Greek tragedy or the reader of the contemporary poem, the underlying question would be the same: what is it about ourselves and our society that could have unloosed these murderous passions?

The idea that we all held some collective guilt for that late-sixties period of notorious political assassinations had certainly made the rounds in our extended national discourse. But Rice's final cathartic lines—"I am. / My own. / Skin's father."—are a particularly brutal formulation of the idea. And it was an idea that was particularly unappetizing here in Dallas. In a city that had developed an unspoken consensus that the Kennedy assassination was a subject that should be discreetly avoided, discussion of complicity was especially vexing. If we heard the whispering or thought we saw the unburied body of the murdered, we knew to keep it to ourselves.

•

Here in the city of his birth, Stan Rice's "Whiteboy" sparked no great public discourse. It did not prompt introspection about the arts or their potential to transform our lives. But Stan Rice was asking difficult questions. He had left Dallas for literary San Francisco to find a place to ask these questions. For Rice, and many other ambitious writers who had left, Dallas was a wasteland in its intolerance and the sterility of its social and artistic life. In the modern wasteland myth that became such an influential trope in modernist thinking, the failure to ask difficult questions is exactly what traps us in that desolate landscape.

The roots of T. S. Eliot's version of the wasteland myth can be traced back to his reworking of material from Chrétien de Troyes's *Perceval,* an Arthurian romance composed in the twelfth century. At the heart of this is the quest for the Holy Grail. The grail is, of course, the great artifact of Christ's martyrdom—the vessel Jesus used at the Last Supper, and the cup which Joseph of Arimathea used to catch Christ's blood at the Crucifixion. In addition to its remarkable symbolic value, the grail was reputed to have miraculous powers. Finding the grail was the final great challenge taken up by King Arthur's Knights of the Round Table. It is in the pursuit of this grail that Perceval finds himself in the midst of the wasteland, specifically, in the Castle Corbenic, as the guest of the Fisher King. During a feast in honor of the visiting knight, Perceval is presented with a grand ceremonial procession. Paraded before him are the sumptuous treasures of the kingdom, concluding with a candelabra, a bleeding lance, and the grail itself (containing a single communion wafer which provided sustenance for the Fisher King). Perceval, having been warned against talking too much, watches the objects go by and fails to ask about their meaning. After the feast ends, he retires to his room. The next morning, he wakes to discover the castle abandoned and in ruins. Only later does Perceval come to realize that his failure to ask questions about the procession causes the Fisher King's wound, and thus his kingdom, to remain unhealed.

As the 1970s closed and the shroud of JFK's assassination hung still over the city, we lived in a sort of Castle Corbenic on the Trinity, heir to the same failures that were played out in the Perceval myth. Physically, the city flourished. We staged our processions, displaying for ourselves the impressive material wealth we had produced. Beneath that surface, however, there were wounds that would not heal. We could not find the grail with its magic power to release us and our kingdom from the oppressive shadow. We could not find that great ceremonial vessel that would hold the blood of the martyred hero.

A decade and a half after the assassination, our civic soul was stuck in a sort of psychic desert. While the rest of the country went about the business of fashioning their own variations on the myth of John F. Kennedy as our great national martyr, reassuring themselves that his spilled blood would be redeemed, we could not bring ourselves to join the program. Nor could we bring ourselves to ask those terrible questions that might set us free. Like Perceval, our deference and good manners consigned us to a consensus of public silence.

•

On October 26, 1963, less than a month before his death, President Kennedy traveled to Amherst College to speak at the dedication of the new Robert Frost Library. Honoring his favorite poet, the president spoke powerfully on the theme of the artist's role in society. "For he saw poetry as the means of saving power from itself," he said of Frost. "When power leads men towards arrogance, poetry reminds him of his limitations. When power narrows the areas of man's concern, poetry reminds him of the richness and diversity of his existence. When power corrupts, poetry cleanses." Kennedy reminded his audience that the poet is "the last champion of the individual mind and sensibility against an intrusive society and an officious state," and asserted that "The great artist is thus a solitary figure," engaged in, as Frost had said, "a lover's quarrel with the world."

From the time of the assassination through the early 1980s, those in Dallas interested in cutting-edge poetry were indeed solitary figures who receive very little support for their efforts. There were a few notable exceptions, but generally there was little institutional support for the type of deep reflexivity that modernist poetics propagated, and little audience for it. Despite the fact that T. S. Eliot's 1958 talk at SMU's Moody Coliseum had drawn seven thousand people, modernism had been slow to come to poetry in tradition-bound Texas. Those adventurous souls wishing to break the old molds had to extricate themselves from a system long dominated by the Poetry Society of Texas and a tendency toward bromides praising state, God, and the frontier tradition. Commonly, young Dallas writers with real poetic ambition hit the road.

Many of the exiles headed for the greener fields of the East or West Coasts. Paul Foreman, from nearby Granbury, migrated to Berkeley in the 1960s and founded the magazine *Texas Artists, Writers, and Thinkers in Exile.* The young Lewis MacAdams "bailed out" of Dallas to start his career as a Beat-inspired poet. In his 2001 book *Birth of the Cool: Beat, Bebop and the American Avant-Garde,* MacAdams recounts being a student in Dallas's elite Saint Mark's School in the late 1950s and coming to realize that the "cool" world was elsewhere. Like William Burroughs, who, as he wrote to Jack Kerouac and Allen Ginsberg from New Waverly in 1948, found "things very uncool in Texas," MacAdams realized that he would have to leave to satisfy his creative yearnings. He made his first start eastward, "following beat poet Gregory Corso around the Village and the Lower East Side of Manhattan," but eventually ended up in California. In the late 1970s, he teamed up with Rice to run the influential Poetry Center at San Francisco State University.[252]

Among the few serious poets who remained in Dallas through the 1960s and 1970s was a motley group of modernist strivers who had gathered at SMU. These young writers included Robert Trammell and David Searcy, both of whom would eventually become the vanguard of the city's literary resurgence. This group drew themselves together around the figure of Gerald Burns. Born in Detroit and Harvard-educated, Burns had been imported to the SMU faculty in 1975. A full-fledged modernist, he produced poetry in the vein of T. S. Eliot and Ezra Pound, dense and learnedly obscure, and he inspired a quirky devotion in his young charges. Marshall Terry, then head of the English Department, remembered that Burns would "wear tweed in summer and smell high," and that he "was the star of a group in Dallas that you knew were brilliant because you didn't know what in the world they were saying."[253]

While SMU remained the center of the city's literary life, as it had been since the early days of Jay Hubbell, it was an innately conservative institution. The only major university in a very conservative city, it was tucked away in the

252. Lewis MacAdams, *Birth of the Cool: Beat, Bebop and the American Avant-Garde* (New York: The Free Press, 2001), 13–14, 29, 137.

253. Terry, *Loving U.*, 171.

exclusive Park Cities section of Dallas, where today the median home value is over $2 million. SMU was where the Dallas's business elite would send their sons and daughters after prep school.

Gerald Burns did not last very long at SMU. Becoming sponsor for the campus Students for a Democratic Society probably did not endear him to the university authorities, nor did his eccentric individualism. After leaving SMU, he lived a sort of vagabond's life, often wandering off to work as a clown with small-scale touring circuses. (He even penned an instructional volume on the art of clowning.) Burns was one of the most accomplished poets to ever live and work in this city—his *Shorter Poems* was chosen by Robert Creeley as the 1992 National Poetry Series award winner—but he never really connected to the city. He became a belated exile when he left for good in 1995.

Burns's SMU crew would publish their work in literary journals around the country. However, with the exception of a very occasional publication in the *Southwest Review,* they experienced the harsh reality that Dallas was not an especially inviting place for the bohemian poet. Led by our business elite, we had created a social order predicated on perpetual economic progress and well-regulated order. Having developed this extraordinary, decades-long consensus, it was inevitable that the art that we produced would reflect these unspoken arrangements. In Dallas, you would find little support for art that challenged the status quo—this was especially evident in our poetry. If, in their own town, our poets were mostly invisible, they could at least take some solace in Robert Frost's admonition that the great artist is, indeed, "a solitary figure."

•

While Gerald Burns made himself a marginal figure at SMU, his boss, Marshall Terry, became an essential man in the English Department and within the administration. Having worked for the university for more than half a century, Terry would eventually earn the moniker "Mr. SMU."

Before hiring on as associate professor in 1969, Terry had worked as SMU's director of public relations for seven years. He would eventually become head of the English Department, but would have even greater influence as an administrator, writing the master plan which would revamp the university's curriculum and educational philosophy. But Terry was a writer first and foremost; he published his first novel, *Old Liberty*, in 1961, and five more over the course of his long career. He founded SMU's creative writing program in the late sixties, then the university's Literary Festival in 1975, and began to put SMU on the national literary map.

Widely appreciated for his work mentoring younger writers, Marshall Terry had considerable influence in the larger literary community. He was a longtime book critic for the *Dallas Morning News* and an influential fellow in the Texas Institute of Letters, serving some time as its president. Along with A. C. Greene, Terry was that rare area author who could bridge the gap between literature and the larger civic world.

In 1987, Terry published *Dallas Stories*, a collection of short stories spanning his twenty-year tenure here. As Terry wrote in the book's preface, *Dallas Stories* was an effort to "reflect the dynamism of a fascinating city with its own distinctive myth and metaphor." Like the tales in Joyce's *Dubliners*, they were "meant to be stories of the spirit as well as of the social scene." In his time, Terry had seen a considerable swath of the Dallas populace, often from very close to the centers of power. In *Dallas Stories*, those fictional folk mingle. From the volatile racial mixing at a Dallas Cowboys football game, to the homes of the privileged elite at its center, to the quirky abodes of its civic outliers, these stories intimately detail the life of the city as Terry experienced it.

In "Poet," Terry tells the story of Billy Blaubauch, a young man just out of a small Baptist college in West Texas who has come to Dallas to flee the restriction of a rural community that was "too tight."

> He knew he was a poet. He knew it at night, alone, as he smoked a little pot in his apartment, his cell off the expressway, sensitive to all the human sounds through the paper walls of the hive around him. He knew it but what true poet could afford to write a line? None, now. But God knew he was full of love, a poet who yearned to make art of the life around him.

Terry, as a man who had spent considerable time coaching young writers, understood the challenges of being a poet in Texas. In fact, he just barely avoided the fate himself. As he once related to a friend, Terry had aspired to be a poet while a sophomore at Kenyon College in Ohio. But one day his teacher, a poet himself, called Terry to his room and very politely offered him a glass of sherry. He then said: "'I wanted to tell you that your poems are the worst undergraduate poetry that I've ever read. Why don't you try prose?"[254]

It was good advice. If you look at the depiction of poetry and the poet in *Dallas Stories,* you'll see that Terry deemed the poet's role here as not just thankless but downright precarious.

Billy Blaubauch eventually proves himself to be an expert copywriter. He finds a decent job at a PR firm, but rather than the anticipation of accomplishment, each day begins with "the death-drive to work." A latent homosexual, Billy falls into a self-destructive spiral of drinking and drugs. Allowing himself the liberty of the poetic language his central character might produce, Terry leads the reader along in Billy's final hallucinogenic demise. The story ends with his death by drug overdose. The obvious message here is that Dallas is not a safe place for a sensitive soul.

•

Having worked so close to the center of the polis, Terry was also aware that there was still nothing so sensitive in Dallas as the topic of the Kennedy assassination. Despite the fact that the event had occurred more than two decades before, Terry chose to bookend *Dallas Stories* with two linked segments dealing explicitly with the Kennedy assassination. This new work made clear Terry's judgment that the memory of the events around November 22, 1963, still lurked at the core of our civic psyche.

Terry's depiction of the legacy of the Kennedy assassination in *Dallas Stories* echoes many of the trends already evident in works by other area authors. There would be no time spent memorializing the president and his

254. Joe Holley, "SMU legend Marshall Terry dies at 85," *Houston Chronicle,* December 30, 2016.

legacy; the concern would be for the effect his death had on our collective psyche. Just as our public figures did, Terry's fictional characters find it difficult to even say the president's name. Although we might deny it, Terry makes clear there was still here a great reservoir of pain, dangerously close to the surface, and we simply could not bring ourselves to talk about it.

Ben Ray Clark is "The Prince of Dallas," the opening work in *Dallas Stories*. The narrative opens with Clark in his corner office in the tower occupied by Texas Drilling Company, a powerful and influential Dallas oil company. From here, Clark can "see nearly as far as Fort Worth, and he could see the complex of industrial districts and the white cotton on the black earth between the two cities." Savvy in local culture as well as business, Clark can see spelled out in this landscape "the Myth of Dallas," the narrative in which powerful, civic-minded businessmen like himself had made this great city out of nothing—"the sustaining myth of the city that was now his."

It is clear that Clark is sophisticated and self-conscious; his office shelves are lined with books of poetry and history. On the wall is his favorite photograph: Robert Frost "hunched with his white hair blowing and scarf loose around his old neck reading—or saying —'The Gift Outright' at the Inauguration." The photo is mounted on the wall right next to his prized "Salesman Award." But Clark is particularly introspective on this day: "it was a big day for Big D, a hell of a big day for Dallas . . ." It is November 22, 1963.

Clark, the president of Texas Drilling Company, is about to meet Henry W. Fanch, the chairman. Fanch is a "hard little man with jowls and pinpoint eyes like hard blue onions," who has made his wealth as an oil wildcatter. A sort of archetype of the mid-century Dallas business leader, Fanch might very well be modeled on the plainspoken (and often profane) Mayor R. L. Thornton. As members of the business elite, the men are about to leave for the Trade Mart, where they will hear the president's speech.

We all know what happens next; Terry does not need to spell it out. Later, as a prominent spokesman for the city, Ben Ray Clark delivers a well-received post-assassination speech in the city's defense, but at the insistence of Henry Fanch he is forced to drop his reference to "our guilt and shame." Soon afterward, Clark mysteriously disappears.

The rest of "The Prince of Dallas" devolves into a quest to find what exactly has happened to Ben Ray Clark. The narration skips to Pete Elliot, a college friend who had come to Dallas with Clark and followed him into its business world. Because Clark is such a mover and a shaker, with important symbolic functions to play in the city's civic power structure, Elliot is tasked with the job of finding him and bringing him back.

Elliot, in a convoluted personal journey back to the idyllic youth he shared with Clark, finds himself back at Liberty College, where he and Clark had matriculated. This is where, "in another time and life [Clark] . . . presumed to desire to be a poet." It is at Liberty College in the old fraternity parlor where Elliot finally finds Ben Ray Clark—writing.

In their awkward confrontation, Clark explains to Elliot that he would like to stay there, maybe even endow himself with a chaired teaching position. Elliot assumes he will teach in his field—geology—but Clark hands Elliot the text he is working on:

> "No. Poetry. I'm going to do poetry. Here, want to see it—the first of it? My great work. Don't know what to call it—"'The King is Dead—Long Live—Our City!'"

Clark hands the poem to Elliot. It is his response to the Kennedy assassination, delivered from the very heart of Dallas's business community. "Burn it right now in this fire and forget it," Elliot tells him. "And come home. If you burn this now, then you can come back home."

> He said nothing, not a word.
>
> "My god," I said, "if anyone ever saw this crazy sophomoric poem, you'd be—"
>
> "An enemy of the people?"

Elliot cannot convince Clark to return to Dallas. The meeting ends badly, and Elliot storms out.

As the first story of Terry's *Dallas Stories* comes to an end, Ben Ray Clark does eventually return to Dallas, but his poem never sees the light of day.

Clark will never return to his former role at the center of the city's power structure. He discreetly removes himself from his civic responsibilities and arranges a long-term business tour that takes him away from Dallas. After his poetic epiphany, Ben Ray Clark walks away from it all.

•

Dallas Stories ends with "Elegy," the closing slice of Terry's assassination bookends. It is itself divided into three sections and is most notable for its break from the short story form; it suddenly shifts out of the fictional voice. In "November Noon," Terry speaks in the first person, and this is the real world. He begins at his home near SMU, having finished teaching his early classes and returning to eat lunch. It is November 22, 1963. Terry shares with us *that moment*, the story everybody shares, his own JFK "What-I-Was-Doing-When-I-Heard" story (most of which is included in one of our three opening epigraphs).

> My daughter, on the bed, paying closer attention to the TV, told [my wife]: "They've shot somebody."
>
> My wife called out again. "Something has happened," she said.
>
> I got up, stood stupidly. Then ran, stumbled into the bedroom.
>
> "Kennedy's been shot," said my little girl.

Terry then takes another abrupt leap. The second section is entitled simply "Poem," and without any preamble, seemingly out of nowhere, here is, apparently, the work that Ben Ray Clark had written in "Prince of Dallas"-- the great Dallas JFK assassination poem!

> He took a twelve-dollar gun
> Carcano (cheese?)
> And raised it into new-brilliant sun
> The rain had stopped we were bubbleless
> (Now it would take God's biggest plastic bubble)
> God it was a pretty day
> And yet if

Which goes to show
What poets can do
With their correlatives

The shots rang   shock and pain
We were numb   half-dead too
The shock   Why do we have these damn fanatics here?
The grief   anguish   shame
Numbed
But did the children cheer?

The sun warmed the snake and warmed it
Oh Big D little a double l asss
Me no questions I'll tell you no lies

What to do, boys? What we gonna do?
Why pray We all prayed, didn't we? Biggest
Baptist biggest Methodist   biggest Prebsy--
The Catholics too   And the Jews they know of this
Why pray, boys   then forget   roll up your sleeves
and
Build Dallas!

Blithe spirit to restore!   Dallas don't we love
You Back to normalcy
(The spirit of W.G. Harding or was it Coolidge
Clapped politely off the stage)

Yes Skyscrapers   some slums too   But he was
Left not right   Of course not right at all
Off his head a lone—Don't say guilt, boys

Okay   He's (don't say the name, say he) want us to
Go forward

Cheerleaders, three times the scared I mean sacred seven
Waving pom-poms of blood

Well, get the bastard a lawyer anyway   He don't
want a lawyer   Hi, Jack   you covering for
the Jewish press?   Ha ha   Why Jack you
Son of a bitch   like well   I'll be damned
They knew old Jack flawed ruby in our navel
No harm in him
He'd hung a round

Good words were said   we have a heavy heart
Yes (What is the matter, my Lord?)
Like a guest into our home   So welcome
Why we were empowered for
Citizens' arrest   By God I think I'll arrest old—
He'd better watch himself!

Well it could have happened anywhere
There's a Dallas Nevada and a Dallas this and a Dallas
Heaven and a Dallas Hell   Dallas is
everyone   So Big D little a big d little
Hester had her scarlet letter A

Pray and then forget   We don't want a monument
Let's call a moratorium
on it all   for our hearts are heavy and
The policeman's widow will have enough
Anyway it was Castro   The Mafia did it you know that
Grey pearl ruby hat is the mark—

Oh God!

Hester lived a good life after

Yet it did happen
Oh God
It happened here.

Here finally is our great civic confession—the poetic profession of all our feelings of guilt and shame! At the heart of this, however, is a troubling ambiguity—who exactly is speaking here? Should we ascribe the poem to the fictional Ben Ray Clark, or is it to be understood as the thinking of Terry himself?

Terry is clearly using the voice of Ben Ray Clark as the poetic avatar of the Dallas civic/business elite, and it is a voice that can speak from, and for, the very center of the city. Here Terry can harness the language that was denied Ben Ray Clark when, as president of Texas Drilling Company, he was appointed the task of speaking for the city. The difference here is that the author has given himself permission to freely address the collective "guilt and shame" that Clark, in his civic role, could not publicly articulate.

Terry was as aware as anybody that the topic of the assassination had been forbidden in Dallas's public discourse, but, for two decades, he had been witness to the whispered fables, fabrications, and folklore that seeped just under the surface. Here he has found a workable strategy to transfigure all of that into verse. "Poem" is the sound of something long pent-up suddenly loosened. The language is released in staccato gusts, strings of unpracticed and tentative thoughts, ideas long awaiting articulation but not fully formed. Using the vernacular of our early 1960s business elite, Terry parrots those tropes you might have heard in the back-slapping, fraternal boys' club of Dallas civic leadership.

Here is the booster's obsessive concern for public image and the cliquish desire to circle the wagons and protect our city against the accusations so unfairly hurled its way. Here is the shared desire for a return to "normalcy," the "Blithe spirit to restore!" Here is the frustration that all the direct avenues to action have been shut down. "What to do, boys? What we gonna do?" There is no way to practice "The Dallas Way"—how could we build our way out of this?

"Poem" works as an effective poetic reiteration of two decades of backroom, good-old-boy civic verbiage, but its author gives it at least one new twist. It's a literary allusion straight from sophomore-year American literature class—Nathaniel Hawthorne's scarlet letter. The transposition from colonial New England to twentieth-century Texas is strange but effective. Weren't we all trapped by that same burden of silence and victimized by the same puritanical collective judgment as Hester Prynne? Didn't we all experience the same sort of claustrophobic entrapment, and often at the hands of those contemporary heirs of the Puritans—the northern liberal elites?

Coursing beneath the surface of "Poem" is that brooding frustration that all Dallas citizens shared: the inescapable fact that if you were from Dallas, you could be smeared with the guilt of the murder of John F. Kennedy. It could happen anywhere and at any time. For instance, early Dallas Cowboys quarterback Eddie LeBaron recalled trips outside the state just after the assassination: "Someone would come up and ask, 'Where you from?' We'd say 'Dallas,' and they'd say, 'Oh . . . you're the ones that shot the President.' It was a tough deal for a long time."[255] Longtime residents of Dallas can share any number of variations on this tale, personal stories of traveling outside the state and being singled out as somehow complicit.

We would say Hester Prynne had it easy: she only had to wear an *A* for "adultery," not the bloody business of presidential assassination. With "Poem," Terry gives us a rendering of all the trauma we had to live with—the poem that we could not allow ourselves to write. There was no closure, however. Finishing *Dallas Stories,* Terry makes it clear that there was still much we needed to work out. In the final section (which we will devote more time to in our Epilogue), we find Terry standing before our John F. Kennedy Memorial at the twentieth anniversary of the assassination. Once again speaking in first person, unambiguously himself, Terry is still attempting to make his own peace with the legacy of the death of John F. Kennedy in Dallas.

•

255. Ray Buck, "1963 Dallas Cowboys were put in a bad light by the JFK game," *Fort Worth Star-Telegram,* November 28, 2008.

Marshall Terry's attempt at poetry aside, Dallas poets in the 1980s were not asking difficult questions about the city and the JFK assassination. They were, however, starting to ask harder questions about life in general and they were pushing the bounds of their craft accordingly. Thanks to a constant influx of outsiders and our own occasional efforts to rise above our provincialism, the city had gradually loosened up after the early 1960s. We had become more open and cosmopolitan, and our arts flourished accordingly. The most noticeable developmental leap was in our poetry. Dallas was now a different city than the one Stan Rice had grown up in—much less vulnerable to be tarred, as Rice does in "Whiteboy," as a wasteland of ignorance and racism. More and more often, poetic voices like Rice began to actually stay in town and find themselves some tolerable niche. Suddenly, you could find in Dallas a raft of poets capable of taking up President Kennedy's 1963 challenge to partake in that serious "lover's quarrel with the world."

By the early 1980s, Dallas was experiencing a burst of significant activity, if not quite a full-blown poetry renaissance. There were many more writers among us doing much more serious work. A number of local universities hired on poets of national stature and influence. At SMU, Jack Myers was well on his way to solidifying his place as a significant lyric poet, teacher, and editor. He also assisted Marshall Terry with the creation of the SMU Literary Festival, which, by the late 1970s , had become a significant event on the national literary calendar. At the University of Texas at Dallas, a newly opened satellite campus of the UT system in the bustling suburb of Richardson, Frederick Turner ensconced himself as the vocal leader of the New Formalist movement. The newly created community college system hired on writers as instructors; they, in turn, inspired more student writers. The recently established Dallas Institute of Humanities and Culture invited in and supported poets like Robert Trammell and William Burford. In the street-level arts revival occurring in Deep Ellum, poetry was being fused into a lively mix of theater, art, and music. Here, poets Tim Seibles, Roxy Gordon, and Sheryl St. Germain were giving voice to groups that had previously been treated as outsiders. While its influence waned, the Poetry Society of Texas still continued in its support of traditional verse and the sponsorship of verse contests.

Yet, with a few notable exceptions, the city of Dallas itself was not much present in the local poetry produced during this period. In the general effort to escape our past sins of parochialism and to connect ourselves to the larger, cosmopolitan world, there was little interest in local history. (If Dallas historians themselves neglected the topic, why should our poets be any different?) Mirroring the preexisting civic tendency to disregard the past for a more focused grasp on the future, the new generation of Dallas poets eschewed anything carrying even a whiff of the embarrassing clichés of Texas mythology. They scrupulously avoided cowboys, outlaws, and gunplay (you could find that in Fort Worth). Their aversion to stereotypes was so great that even football and J. R. Ewing were off-limits. Especially onerous—the topic loaded with the most incommodious freight—was the assassination of John F. Kennedy at Dealey Plaza. Many of these poets were too young to have the same visceral connection to the event as the preceding generation. Others had arrived in Dallas too recently to be aware of the real trauma longtime residents had experienced. To them, the assassination was simply a burden, the proverbial albatross around the neck. It was boring and redundant, something only the tourists were interested in. As they strove to create their brave new poetic world, it was the simplest thing in the world to ignore it.

•

There was one notable exception to this rule, and that was Robert Trammell's *Jack Ruby & the Origins of the Avant-Garde in Dallas.* Trammell was one of those smoky bohemian poets who had studied under Gerald Burns at SMU, and he had gone on to fashion himself into a unique, homegrown voice for this city. Trammell's *Jack Ruby* project first appeared in public in 1988, at the twenty-fifth anniversary of the assassination, and it has reappeared in a number of incarnations since. Trammell, who was fiercely independent, self-published most of his work, and *Jack Ruby* was his pet project. Archly modernist in its construction, it was staunchly vernacular and true to the local in its content. Packed with Xeroxed cut-ups and collages, each volume was a self-made work of art.

What is most exceptional about *Jack Ruby & the Origins of the Avant-Garde in Dallas* is that it unabashedly claims Jack Ruby as one of our own. By claiming Ruby, Trammell creates a work that is uniquely ours as well. It is arguably the most significant poem this city has produced. Because it is such a significant work, I will treat Trammell's *Jack Ruby & the Origins of the Avant-Garde in Dallas* at length in the next volume. Suffice it to say here, however, that *Jack Ruby* is not a book about John Kennedy. While the assassination provides the obvious backdrop and the inevitable, built-in momentum rushing toward the November 1963 climax, John Kennedy himself is almost completely absent from Trammell's text.

Elsewhere, the assassination appeared mostly in fragments that popped up at odd times and in unexpected places, often in poetic ephemera. William Barney's vignette on hearing about the assassination was not published until 1993. Poet Dave Oliphant came to realize that he had attended the same grade school as Oswald, Fort Worth's George C. Clark Elementary. "Future assassin and poet may have sat in the same classroom seat," he wrote, "even Oswald's last name and my own share the same initial letter."[256] This snippet appears in Oliphant's long, memoiristic poem "Austin," first published in 1985.

> down the road to learn Oswald too attended
> sat pen in hand in that Cowtown elementary
> in a same wooden seat with stained ink-well
> reading the same primers at George C. Clark
> on the very playground picked for kickball[257]

Dave Hickey, who would eventually become a fiction writer and celebrated renegade art critic, attended that same southwest Fort Worth elementary school with Oswald, and, according to Bryan Woolley, has been known to dish on exactly why Lee Oswald turned out the way he did. "His mother kept buying him Billy the Kid jeans." These specific jeans "had little horseshoes on

256. Dave Oliphant, *Harbingers of Books to Come* (San Antonio: Wings Press, 2009), 102.

257. Oliphant, *Memories of Texas Towns & Cities*, 283.

the back pocket," Woolly would recount. "They weren't cool; the other kids would tease him about his Billy the Kid jeans."[258] Hickey even began a recent *Paris Review* essay with this declaration: "I went to first grade in Fort Worth with Lee Harvey Oswald."[259]

Another childhood assassination remembrance popped up in a 2000 issue of the *Texas Review*, but here the strange thrill of being close to history retains some of the sting of the original event. Rebecca Spears's poem "Marina's Daughters, 1964" recounts what it is was like to grow up in the Dallas suburb of Richardson with Lee Harvey Oswald's widow for a neighbor. Marina Oswald had bought a house there not long after the assassination, and Spears (then ten years old) regularly saw her two daughters, Rachel and June, around the neighborhood. Marina attempted to shield her girls from any retribution linked to their father's fateful actions, but it would be a nearly impossible task—they were living just a few miles from where the president had been slain. Spears was drawn to her closest contemporary, the older, four-year-old Rachel: "I watched her / as I passed by / walking towards school." What she saw was ugly. Sometimes the girl's school bus would be followed by news teams, and someone shot up their mailbox.[260] "They taught us to hate her," Spears writes, "at school, hate her / and her kind, Russians, / all of them, / even her sister, / the baby."[261]

Rebecca Spears had been here when *it* happened, and it left a mark. Born in nearby Waco, she moved to Richardson before entering first grade, and was nine years old when President Kennedy visited Dallas. She left Dallas in 1980, moving to Houston with her husband, but the events of 1963 remained raw in her memory. "The assassination was the defining historical event of my childhood," she later explained, "and in fact, shaped my outlook on life for a long time."[262]

258. Bryan Woolley, interview with Tim Cloward, March 7, 2013.

259. Dave Hickey, "My Brief (Doomed) Surfing Days," *Paris Review*, July 27, 2017.

260. Keith Kathchik, "Growing up the daughter of an assassin: Shadow of Lee Harvey Oswald still hangs over daughter Rachel," *Texas Monthly*, March 1995.

261. Rebecca Spears, "Marina's Daughters, 1964," *Texas in Poetry 2*, Billy Bob Hill, ed. (Fort Worth: Texas Christian University Press, 2002), 366–67. (Originally published in *Texas Review*, 2000.)

262. Rebecca Spears, email message to Tim Cloward, November 3, 2020.

It took some time for that outlook to express itself poetically. Spears only began writing verse in the late nineties, after being encouraged by her primary mentor—Naomi Shihab Nye, a longtime resident of San Antonio—to complete her MFA at Bennington College.

Much of the mature work Spears has produced gravitates in some way to the JFK assassination and its aftermath. When she writes about these events, it is always in the voice of a Texan: Marina Oswald, Oswald's mother, Marguerite, Nellie Connally, Marie Tippit. Spears's most vivid work, however, delves into her personal experience. One notable example is the poem "My Father's Window." Spears's father was a freelance accountant for the fashion industry in Dallas, and he worked out of the venerable Kirby Building, the seventeen-story skyscraper built by beer magnate Adolphus Busch in 1913 to accompany his nearby Adolphus Hotel. The poem dwells on the chilling coincidence of her father witnessing the presidential motorcade from his office window while, just down the street, Oswald waits in his "snipers perch."

> That moment JFK passes the Kirby Building and looks up—
> does he sense in Daddy's wave, and the others,
> their relief: no rain and the limo's missing bubbletop
>
> surely gives our fathers the clearest view, good as
> one six blocks away, schoolbook depository,
> sixth floor, all windows cocked open.[263]

Tucked within the poem is another parallel, one that runs through most of the poems Spears has written about her relationship to the assassination: the difference between the president and his family and herself and her own family. In Spears's mind, there is a yawning gap between the glowing world of the Kennedys and the drab and mundane world of Dallas. As she notes in "My Father's Window," "JFK never imagines [her father] in the world," and "Caroline's dad can't see from our perch."

---

263. Rebecca Spears, "My Father's Window," *Dos Passos Review*, Fall 2005.

In her poem addressing the immediate aftermath of the assassination, "Last Things," Spears recalls how her family strained to cope with the incessant news coverage the day after the assassination: "We have watched enough (shamed, in silence)." For relief, they take a trip outside the city: "I will ask my mother to drive again into / the countryside to hunt pecans while I look for / the one unbruised pear." There will be no escape from the events in Dallas, however. Even in this pastoral setting, Spears is haunted by the assassination. "Last Things" closes with Spears pondering the event's aftermath: "Surely we haven't seen the last wild harvest."

In "Last Things," as in many of her Dallas poems, Spears's focus is on the Kennedy children:

> Hyannisport. The children and father
> roughhousing. Caroline under his desk.
> Caroline all blonde bob and tailored clothes:
> the image tags along with me all afternoon,
> a younger sister.[264]

Although the nine-year-old Spears feels empathy for the grieving Kennedy children, she cannot help but notice the distance that separates her from them. The separation originates from that same source that makes her father and the president such different men: privilege. (How far away is Hyannisport from the random East Texas roadside where she hunts for "the one unbruised pear"?) Moreover, in "Marina's Daughters, 1964," she notes that there were orphans here too. She contrasts the "sorrow we poured on / Jackie's children, / not on Marina's damned daughters: / Jackie's young drenched in it, / Marina's babies quiet,/burning."[265]

By the time Spears began to envision these poems, the Kennedy children were grown and had assumed their inherited role as a type of American royalty, basking in the redeeming glow of our reworked Camelot lore. A different reality existed in Dallas; the best Marina and her daughters could hope for

264. Rebecca Spears, "Last Things," *Nimrod*, Spring 2006.
265. Spears, "Marina's Daughters, 1964."

was anonymity. Just as for the rest of us, this was barren ground for the growth of any redemptive myth.

The bottom line here is summed up in another of Spears's Dallas poems. It is a recollection, via Nellie Connally as she talks to a CNN interviewer, of those moments in the presidential limo just after the gunshots. Amid the vertigo of that moment, with the horrid realization that both the president and governor have been shot, Nellie comforts her injured husband. The poem ends with these lines: "*Be still, be still,* I whispered into / John's ear. *We'll be blamed for this.*"

This was something we *all* realized in those very first moments after Kennedy was shot: *We'll be blamed for this.*

•

Rebecca Spears did not share her most personal assassination moment until two years after Dallas staged its fiftieth-anniversary ceremonies. She did so in a poem, "The Vanishing Point," that appeared in the 2015 *Texas Poetry Calendar.*

The morning of the assassination, Spears had been taken out of school by her mother for a dental appointment. Mother and daughter were driving back to school when Spears looked up and saw Air Force One taking off from Love Field for Washington, DC. Inside were the newly sworn-in president and the lifeless body of his predecessor.

> *—Look, Mama. The president's plane. In the sky.*
> *—Oh Lord.*

> The jet lifts so slowly it could be a memory
> made silver in the sun, that skims the surface
> of Bachman's Lake and takes time
> folding its reedy legs into itself, extending
> its white shawl of wings when it feels a wind
> to hold it aloft or

could be a dream: it passes like one before us,
moves beyond cambered cirrus
toward a vanishing point and wonder
why some god or chance left us to watch it
lumber so heavily, its great seal a plaster
on its side. We already

perceive what we've lost, don't we,
trapped inside this eye of improbability?
It turns to revolution, to a thing unimagined
and we are at the wellhead to raise
its sealing stone, but find nothing there,

when all we have to make sense with
are egrets rising from cattails and salt grass
while space around us fills with wind
invisible and whole, a thrust of air
bolsters us when we hold inside
much too much.[266]

This is Rebecca Spears's most personal brush with history. Like many of her JFK poems, it comes subtitled and time-stamped: "(Dallas Love Field, 22 November 1963, 2:45 PM)." In this exact moment, Spears had experienced a remarkable, coincidental event. Parallel to that historical image of Air Force One taking off from Love Field, she gives us this one personal image—an egret rising from the cattails and salt grass of Bachman Lake. It is something material and authentic that belongs to us and is part of our landscape.

Fifty years on, Spears is still working on her manuscript. For some of us who lived through it, the final word on the assassination is still a work in progress. We have not yet seen its "last wild harvest."

---

266. Rebecca Spears, "The Vanishing Point," in *Texas Poetry Calendar 2015* (Austin, TX: Dos Gatos Press, 2015).

•

By the time Spears began writing about her assassination experiences, she had survived almost three decades of the Camelot myth. It came prepackaged to us in our living rooms, via TV, magazines, and coffee-table books. Like the rest of us, Spears witnessed this idealization of the Kennedy family as our own American royalty.

When Air Force One vanished into the north Texas sky, Jack and Jackie did not leave any of that royal magic here. Their visit had left nothing but trauma. What Spears, and many fellow Dallasites, felt most when they witnessed this evolving myth of Camelot was the great distance between the shining world of the Kennedys and the comparative drabness here. Like everybody else, we were fascinated and intrigued by the glamour and the charm of this updated court of Camelot, but that admiration only seemed to widen the gulf we felt and stoke more resentment. For us, Camelot was always something that happened somewhere else.

Already, at the president's funeral in Washington, DC, we had seen our city's delegates treated as outcasts. In was clear already: the nation had judged us. The Kennedy family themselves continued, discreetly but very noticeably, to have nothing to do with Dallas.

John F. Kennedy and his family moved in a different world than we did. It was understood that we were not part of Camelot. When Gene Shuford wrote "The Death in Our Family," he had accepted Jack and Jackie as the prince and princess of our national family. But Shuford was writing from Denton, nearly fifty miles away from Dallas; it was easier for him to embrace this myth. By the time he received the Poetry Society of America's award for his assassination elegy, however, his poem was more reflective of the national perspective than the local.

You could say there's nothing surprising about Rebecca Spears's choice not to memorialize John Kennedy in her poetry. The predominant trends in recent lyric poetry tend more toward the autobiographical and a personal search for truth. The conventional hero narrative of the type that attached itself to John F. Kennedy after his assassination is unfashionable.

You might expect to find such homages in the work of our more traditional writers. Yet even the members of the Poetry Society of Texas produced almost nothing honoring John Kennedy. You could find tributes to the martyred Davy Crockett and Abraham Lincoln, but John F. Kennedy was not invited into the pantheon of fallen heroes. There were more tributes to Bonnie and Clyde than to Camelot. Even in that most significant of our assassination poems, Trammell's *Jack Ruby & the Origins of the Avant-Garde in Dallas,* we get an homage to the killer of Lee Harvey Oswald rather than the president.

•

When Jay Hogan, the scholarly old KRLD news pro, signed off late into that long night of the assassination with his impromptu elegy for John F. Kennedy, he ended a workday where he had been at the center of one of the century's great unfolding stories. To Hogan, it was a moment deserving of the pathos of poetry, and so he closed his broadcast with his "Good Night, Mr. President—good night." For fifty years, Jay Hogan's quickly composed poem would stand among our best efforts to find that mythic language that could express our relationship with the fallen president.

John F. Kennedy did find the "perpetual light" that Hogan wished him in his poem. Within days, he would be laid to rest beside his John F. Kennedy Eternal Flame in Arlington National Cemetery. In that less quotidian realm of myth, however, the question of the slain president's final resting place was still somewhat open. Hogan had offered up the possibilities of faraway Valhalla or the mystic Elysian fields, but the consensus among most Americans would mostly likely be that he was in Avalon.

When Jackie requested that her husband be honored with an eternal flame, she took at least part of her inspiration from T. H. White's *The Candle in the Wind,* the fourth book of *The Once and Future King*—the inspiration for Lerner and Loewe's *Camelot.*

It is important to remember that beneath the plotting of that feel-good Broadway musical flowed a millennium and a half of mythical British history. We built our Americanized version of Camelot upon the shifting sands of an already shaky foundation. Even today, the British continue their perpetual debate over the exact understanding of their great national myth.

There is even disagreement about the ultimate fate of the vanquished king. While everyone agrees that King Arthur, mortally wounded at the Battle of Camlann, was borne off to the mystical isle of Avalon, there is considerable disagreement about what happened next. In one version, the dead King is laid to rest and remains buried in Avalon.

In Dallas, where we had not been invited into Camelot, we were generally content to live with this latter version of events. As our updated American version of the Camelot myth unfolded around the country, however, the dead king would not stay at rest. John Kennedy, having become myth, proved to be as shape-shifting as any folkloric figure. He would not go away, and it seemed we were stuck with the ascendancy of the second version of that original Arthurian myth—the version where the wounded king returns, healed and rejuvenated, from the purgatory of Avalon. All around us, we could see evidence of the dead king's resurrection; the hero seemed still to move among us.

After the journalist Jay Hogan delivered his impromptu poem wishing the president good night, we spent most of the next half century content to let John Kennedy rest in peace. Even here, however, the lure of the story of the returning king proved irresistible. As we will chronicle in the third volume of this project, the resurrected hero would return. Dallas would find the opportunity to again address the departed president.

When we did finally, as a city, properly say goodnight to John F. Kennedy, it would be our civic leaders who found the poetry to do it. Through the commemorations of the Fiftieth, Mayor Mike Rawlings and those who worked with him would find the language and ritual that would finally close the circle and articulate our relationship to JFK. As a city, we would finally make our compromise with Camelot.

CHAPTER 4

Flashbulb Memories

"We do not know the true value of our moments until they have undergone the test of memory."

Georges Duhamel, *The Heart's Domain*[267]

EVERY SO OFTEN, there are certain, singular moments in our life when the freight train of history seems to collide head-on with the intimate world of our private existence. Psychologists have recently found it helpful to study these moments and the unique merging of individual sensation and public information that is embedded in our memories when this collision occurs. Observers have found that one of the most singular of these historical moments was the assassination of John F. Kennedy in Dallas on November 22, 1963.

This book opens with three examples of these memories: three passages excepted from literary sources to serve as our epigraphs. Each of these excerpts depicts that exact moment when its author found out the president of the United States had been killed. I chose them originally because they had been written by local authors, and because they serve as a very passable introduction to a work that deals with the city of Dallas and its reaction to the assassination of John F. Kennedy. They were concise, and they got right to the point. All three epigraphs also have something important to say about memory itself.

It turns out that each of these quotes, by Lawrence Wright, William Barney,

267. George Duhamel, *The Heart's Domain*, trans. Eleanor Stimson Brooks (New York: The Century Co., 1919), 132.

and Marshall Terry, could function as a near-perfect example of what has come to be known as "flashbulb memory." The term was coined to describe a type of shocking moment when we are introduced to a profound or momentous event. Because these moments have such an immense impact, they are imprinted into our memory in a remarkably vivid and long-lasting form. The effect of a flashbulb memory has been compared to a flare that instantaneously lights up a moment and burns it into one's mind forever. The researchers who first named it described it as "like a photograph that indiscriminately preserves the scene in which each of us found himself when the flashbulb was fired."[268] The idea of flashbulb memory, or FBM as the clinical shorthand goes, has had a great influence on recent cognitive psychology and has become one of the fundamental concepts used by researchers in the developing field of memory studies.

FBMs, of course, are analogous to those "where-were-you-when?" anecdotes that we throw around when we discuss a particularly stunning event that happened during our lifetime. We are all familiar with these, how they are a way we share events in common, but also make them distinctly our own. The when, where, and how we came to know of the event become a part of it; it's not just the event, but also the circumstances of our learning about it. It is worth noting that always at the center of these flashbulb memories is place. This link between memory and place, the *locus,* has deep and ancient roots in Western civilization.

The original science of memory was reputed to have been devised by the Greek lyric poet Simonides of Ceos. His system of mnemonics, commonly referred to as "the method of loci," became a staple of classical education. It was eventually taught as a core element in the practice of rhetoric by Greek and Roman orators, and you can see it later in the work of thinkers such as Thomas Aquinas and Giordano Bruno.

Simonides's method of loci was conceived through the experience of a devastating event. The Roman orator Cicero explained the origin of this idea in his 55 BC *de Oratore.* Simonides "was dining at the house of a wealthy nobleman named Scopas at Crannon in Thessaly, and chanted a lyric poem which he had composed in honor of his host." At one point in the proceedings,

268. Roger Brown and James Kulik, "Flashbulb Memories." *Cognition* 5, no. 1, 1977, 73–99.

Simonides was called outside and just then the roof of the building collapsed, crushing everyone within. All the guests were mangled beyond recognition. As Cicero relates the story, Simonides was able to recollect the place each of the victims had been reclining at the table in order to identify them for their proper burial. From this, Simonides surmised that it was the combination of place with images that created optimum memory, "as a wax writing tablet and the letters written on it."[269]

When the roof caved in on Dallas on November 22, 1963, the shock and trauma of that event were likewise imprinted in the memory of anybody who heard the news. The psychologists who developed the idea of flashbulb memory were especially aware of this phenomenon. "Almost everyone can remember with an almost perceptual clarity," they wrote of the JFK assassination, "where he was when he heard, what he was doing at the time, who told him, what was the immediate aftermath, how he felt about it, and also one or more totally idiosyncratic and often trivial concomitants."[270]

When our local authors recorded their recollections of their individual flashbulb moments, they might not have been as vivid and intense as those of Simonides at the moment of the disaster at Crannon. But each possesses its own power. In each telling, we see the particularities that have been seared into each writer's memory, each one's own "idiosyncratic and often trivial concomitants." And always, each account is situated in a place—where the teller was when they found out. One was pondering his way through math class at East Dallas's Woodrow Wilson High School; one was earning his keep working at the downtown Dallas post office; another was between freshman English classes, making himself lunch in his kitchen at home. Always in our JFK memories, there is the "where"—and almost always there is a sense of randomness to that location. It's as if randomness were the point. The event was so unexpected; it caught us by surprise as we were doing arbitrary things in unlikely places. Collectively, we were instantly joined together by the shock of it; we all became part of this bigger, inexplicable thing.

---

269. Marcus Tullius Cicero, *de Oratore*, trans. E. W. Sutton (Cambridge, MA: Loeb Classical Library, 1967).

270. Brown and Kulik, "Flashbulb Memories."

If you lived in Dallas, however, the place would not have seemed so incidental or insignificant. If you were here, you would understand the story in a different way. The flash would have seemed brighter, almost blinding.

•

The noted Harvard social psychologist Roger Brown and his assistant James Kulik first elaborated the concept of flashbulb memory in the journal *Cognition* in 1977. All scientific discovery is rooted in its time, and Brown and Kulik's work is rooted in that moment after the JFK assassination. As Brown and Kulik developed their theory of flashbulb memory, they came back, time and time again, to Dallas on November 22, 1963.

> "Hardly a man is now alive" who cannot recall the circumstances in which he first heard that John Kennedy had been shot in Dallas. Not just the fact that John Kennedy was shot and died; we remember that too, of course, but we really do not need to since it is recorded in countless places and in many forms. It is not the memory of the tragic news that invites inquiry, but the memory of one's own circumstances on first hearing the news.

It was not just that everybody of a certain age in America had a vivid memory of the assassination. It was that their lives seemed to be part of the memory. As Brown and Kulik developed the methodology for their memory work, they found nothing else could compare to the JFK assassination in its power to imprint potent recollection. "Is it only the news of John Kennedy's assassination that has ever set off the flashbulb registration of each person's circumstances on first hearing the news?" they asked themselves. "Anticipating our data, it seems to have precipitated the effect in greater strength, and for a larger number of persons than any other event in recent history."

Brown and Kulik tested responses to other recent political events, and even certain significant personal events of their participants, but they always found the same thing. The JFK assassination "precipitated the [FBM] effect in greater strength, and for a greater number of persons, than any other event in recent history." The event seemed to connect with their interviewees in an incredibly personal manner. "On the evidence, John Kennedy rated as a member of everyone's immediate family."

When the study was complete, Brown and Kulik summarized their findings. The abstract for that first article begins: "Flashbulb Memories are memories for the circumstances in which one first learned of a very surprising and consequential (or emotionally arousing) event. Hearing the news that President John Kennedy had been shot is the prototype case." In fact, the pull of this event was such that the authors themselves could not resist sharing their own JFK flashbulb memories. They put the standard, distanced objectivity of the scientific research paper into abeyance, and the researchers made themselves subjects.

On November 22, 1963, Roger Brown recalled, "I was on the telephone with Miss Johnson, the Dean's secretary, about some departmental business. Suddenly, she broke in 'Excuse me a moment; everyone is excited about something. What? Mr. Kennedy has been shot!' We hung up, I opened my door to hear further news as it came in, and then resumed my work on some forgotten business that 'had to be finished' that day."

Brown's younger colleague James Kulik remembered the event this way: "I was seated in a sixth-grade music class, and over the intercom I was told that the president had been shot. At first, everyone just looked at each other. Then the class started yelling, and the music teacher tried to calm everyone down. About ten minutes later I heard over the intercom that Kennedy had died and that everyone should return to their homeroom. I remember that when I got to my homeroom, my teacher was crying, and everyone was standing in a state of shock. They told us to go home."[271]

•

The concept of flashbulb memory did not appear out of the blue. Brown and Kulik were careful to credit Robert B. Livingston for laying the groundwork. Livingston was a man of varied interests. He was an influential neuroscientist

---

271. Brown and Kulik, "Flashbulb Memories."

who would become best known for his work on the computer mapping of the human brain, and he served as scientific director of the National Institute for Neurological Diseases under both Eisenhower and Kennedy. He was also a leader with the International Physicians for the Prevention of Nuclear War, an organization which won the Nobel Peace Prize in 1985, and afterward acted as the science advisor to the Dalai Lama.

The expansive scope of Robert Livingston's vision can be seen even in the 1967 textbook *The Neurosciences: A Study Program*. Here, Livingston was entrusted with the explication of "Brain Correlates of Functional Behavioral States." As was his wont, Livingston expounded upon the critical social importance of his scientific work. "We are engaged in activities that hold great promise for the future expansion of human consciousness and conscience," he writes. We are in "a moment of urgent, worldwide need for useful insights," a search driven by "man's capacity for intelligently directed self-development." To emphasize the urgency of our critical human endeavor, Livingston gives us some well-chosen quotes: "President Kennedy, with his flair for memorable contrast, declared in his campaign that 'ours will be known as the generation that turned this planet into a flaming pyre or that safeguarded succeeding generations from the scourge of war,' and, in his Inaugural Address, that ' . . . man holds in his mortal hands the power to abolish all forms of human poverty and all forms of human life.'"[272] Already in our scientific studies of memory, we find the hauntings of our recently assassinated president.

Included in this same chapter of *The Neurosciences* is Robert Livingston's presentation of his new theory of memory formation, what he calls "Now Print!" This is the work that drew the attention of Brown and Kulik and acted as the foundational idea behind their conception of flashbulb memory. The technical explication of Livingston's neurophysiological theory is filled with references to such activities as "limbic discharge into reticular formation" and "alterations of ionic barriers," but, in lay terms, it is pretty straightforward. What Livingston proposes is that the brain recognizes particularly "novel"

---

272. R. B. Livingston, "Brain Circuitry Relation to Complex Behavior," *The Neurosciences: A Study Program,* G. C. Quarton et al., eds. (New York: Rockefeller University Press, 1967), 499–515.

occurrences and instantly embeds them into its memory system. For practical evolutionary purposes, these novel events "will become incorporated into circuitry, presumably as a result of new molecular activations and local synaptic growth." Going further than Brown and Kulik ever would, Livingston suggests that these unique experiences actually create a permanent physical change in the neurological system.

Livingston does not go into great detail as to the nature of these "novel" experiences, but he gives us one illustration. "Let me give an example of an occasion which you probably all stamped with a 'Now Print!' order yourselves," he writes. "I suggest that almost all of you remember exactly where you were on November 22, 1963, when you heard the news that President Kennedy had been assassinated. You can probably tell us where you were, with whom, and very likely whether you were sitting, standing, or walking—almost which foot was forward when the awareness became manifest. Some people can even tell the details of the dial of a radio they happened to hear the news from, and so forth."[273]

Unlike Brown and Kulik, Livingston does not leave us with his own flashbulb memory, but he did have an equally vivid and long-lasting connection to the events of November 22, 1963. Having led two important government institutes dealing with mental health and neurological disease, Livingston took it upon himself to call and give his professional advice to James Humes, the pathologist at Bethesda Naval Hospital. Kennedy's body had just been returned to Washington, DC, and it would be Humes who would perform the critical autopsy. Subsequently, Livingston would question the results of that autopsy, and his expert testimony would provide important fodder for those who would question the Warren Commission's "lone gunman" interpretation of the assassination. Even as his groundbreaking work in the neurosciences and brain mapping is fading from our recollection, Livingston's contributions to the forensic sciences continue to live on in the eternal collective memory of internet JFK conspiracy lore.

•

273. Livingston, "Brain Circuitry Relation to Complex Behavior."

It is hard to overestimate the profound impact the JFK assassination had on America in 1963. Even veteran journalists, hardened by years of experience, struggled to display the calm objectivity that was the defining attribute of their profession. David Brinkley, who spent the day of November 22 fronting the marathon broadcast from NBC's news desk with cohost Chet Huntley, stated: "The events of those days don't fit, you can't place them anywhere, they don't go in the intellectual luggage of our time. It was too big, too sudden, too overwhelming, and it meant too much. It has to be separate and apart."[274]

Longtime CBS news anchor Dan Rather, who was on the streets of Dallas covering the motorcade, remembered: "I was just beyond the overpass, just beyond Dealey Plaza, and therefore I did not hear any shots. I didn't realize what had happened. I thought I saw the presidential motorcade whiz by, but when the rest of the motorcade didn't follow, I knew what was wrong and then I crossed over Dealey Plaza." Looking back at the immensity of the assassination, Rather explained: "I've never covered anything like it. Not before, not since, and I don't expect to in this lifetime, nor any lifetime beyond, to infinity and beyond."[275] In the half century since then, only the 9/11 attacks would generate an equivalent shock.

Our celebrities, of course, were no different from the rest of us. A decade after the assassination, amid all the media retrospectives, *Esquire* magazine presented an article entitled "Where Were You?" The celebrities interviewed all retained their flawless recollections of where they were and what they were doing when they found out. "Julia Child was in the kitchen eating *soupe de poisson.* Billy Graham was on the golf course, but he felt a presentiment of tragedy. Philip Berrigan was driving to a rally; Julian Bond was in a restaurant; Tony Randall was in the bathtub."[276]

It has commonly been noted that the assassination of John F. Kennedy in 1963 was a watershed moment in the history of electronic media, and so the idea that it would produce "flashbulb memories" seems doubly appropriate. The term retains the connotions of the traditional journalistic "news flash,"

274. Manchester, *The Death of A President*, 627.
275. Bugliosi, *Reclaiming History*, 1510.
276. Richard B. Stolley, "Where Were You?," *Esquire*, November 1973.

the urgent breaking news, something so exceptional as to cause a disruption in the flow of normal, everyday life. But "flashbulb memory" also captures something of a newer buzz that was in the air. The assassination occurred just a few months before the publication of Marshall McLuhan's *Understanding Media*, with its catchphrase "the medium is the message." In the new global village McLuhan describes, the sharing of information had a new instantaneousness and immediacy. We all shared the same flash.

In that remarkable weekend of unprecedented media coverage following the murder of JFK, the newspapers, the radio broadcasts, and the TV stations all focused on the same story. For three days, all three networks shut down their regular programming for endless coverage of this one remarkable event. NBC devoted seventy-two straight hours to the assassination and its aftermath. Everything else stopped; all else was trivial.

The recurring news flashes came so constantly they became one long, searing moment, a recurring loop that reset each time with the announcement, "Live from Dallas." Again and again, the return to the crime scene. In this charged new environment, the one thing that seemed ancient and unchanging was the sense of place. Simonides, when he devised his method of loci, understood: if something is to be remembered, it must be embedded and situated in a place. In our psyches, as well as the world, there has to be a landscape where things can "take place." Through hour after hour of this constant loop of broadcast information, we would all remember, at the center of it, Dallas.

As we experienced this media maelstrom from its very heart, we understood there would be no calm at its center. Like everybody else, we watched. Like everybody else, we could not take our eyes away. But we saw it differently. Numbed, but still cognizant of our place in the world, we attempted to make certain calculations. We struggled to gauge the effect of the images as they added up, the accumulating details of our culpability. In all of these hectoring announcements, we weighed the evidence, reckoned the judgments, endeavored to compute all of our sins. We watched, alone, and wondered: *What did we really look like to the rest of world?*

As we watched, there we were: accosting Adlai Stevenson, one of our society ladies banging him on the head with a protest sign as he left our

Memorial Auditorium just a month before. An unruly right-wing mob had disrupted his UN Day speech just moments before, and then came the subsequent write-up in *Time*—"A City Disgraced." There we were: our Mink Coat Mob gathered in the lobby of the elegant Adolphus Hotel jeering and spitting on Lady Bird Johnson and LBJ just before the last election. There we were earlier in the week, distributing "Wanted for Treason" flyers featuring the president's image throughout the city. There we were just that morning with our full-page *Dallas Morning News* "Welcome Mr. Kennedy" ad, accusing him of aiding and abetting Communism. Finally, there we were on Sunday, in the form of Jack Ruby, gunning down Lee Harvey Oswald on live, nationwide TV as our Dallas police stood idly by.

From that Friday afternoon onward, it never seemed to stop. "Flash" was exactly the right word; in that one blinding instant, we were connected both to the moment of the president's death and to the rest of the world. It was as if we were ensnared in a network of electrically charged filaments, caught in the electronic buzz of a world where the distance between private and public had collapsed, and there was just this one eternal moment endlessly recycling. It *was* a new kind of memory. Everyone remembered, and everyone remembered it happened in Dallas. As *Esquire* subtitled their "Where were you?" article a full decade later—"Nobody forgets."

•

It is not surprising that those of us in Dallas didn't talk much about the assassination. We accepted the tacit agreement that silence, given the circumstances, was best. Those unfortunate few who spoke publicly about the assassination and our part in it, who offered up anything that sounded like serious civic introspection, were shunned. It was best—if we could—to simply forget.

In the period just after the assassination, while the rest of the country pumped out writing about the Kennedy assassination at an astounding rate, there was virtually no serious writing on the subject in Dallas. The one notable exception was Warren Leslie. It would take a man of exceptional self-assurance to talk about the assassination in Dallas, and if Warren Leslie had anything, it was self-assurance. According to John Bainbridge, the author of *The Super Americans,* he affected "a long cigarette holder and an awesomely casual manner." But Leslie had good reason to be self-assured. In a few short years, he had made himself a prominent figure in Dallas. Born in Manhattan and educated at Yale, Leslie had come to Dallas as a journalist and was recruited away from the *Dallas Morning News* by Stanley Marcus himself, who made him the head of promotions for Neiman Marcus. This was a high-profile position: "The Alamo excepted," wrote Bainbridge, "Neiman Marcus has for years been the most celebrated institution in Texas"[277]

Having lived in Dallas for seventeen years, and having served almost a decade with Neiman Marcus, Leslie was as well connected as anybody in the city. This is abundantly clear in his book *Dallas Public and Private.* Published in April 1964, just four months after the assassination, it offers a definitive view of the city at the time of the assassination from a legitimate Dallas insider, a former journalist who moved freely within that tight-knit cabal of business and civic leaders who controlled the city.

Although our Dallas oligarchs lay low after the assassination, they were not resting. From his front-row seat in this well-concealed world, Leslie watched as Dallas's civic leaders struggled to find a way to reclaim the good name of their city. As he relates: "After the November events, several meetings were held throughout Dallas to consider what action, if any, the city should take." The city was under the scrutiny of the world; it was well understood that some action was required. But even these self-described men of action were paralyzed. In that pressurized atmosphere, any discussion of supporting a monument to the dead president could gain no traction.

Some of these meetings, however, attempted to go deeper than simply PR. "At a few of those meetings participants tried hard to get to the roots of the city's problems," Leslie writes, "and for one gathering, Dr. Robert E. Stolz, chairman of the department of psychology at SMU, prepared a professional report on aspects of Dallas." Over seven pages and eight sections, and in the blandly clinical language of the professional psychologist, Stolz offered up his analysis of the city's state of mind leading up to the assassination. It was not a pretty picture.

277. Bainbridge, *The Super Americans,* 131, 125.

Stolz's dispassionate description of "the current situation in Dallas" begins with this statement: "There are elements in the city that encourage irresponsibility in the conduct of civic, political, and personal affairs. The best organized and most vocal are the extreme right-wing groups." The second section starts: "Leadership of Dallas has given lip service to humane and moral values, but has shown that it values the physical and economic aspects of the community primarily . . . A strong emphasis on materialism is evident in this community." The third section explains that we had developed "a climate in which groups do not experience a mutual exchange of views and situations where rational and reasonable evaluation of facts and hypothesis is impossible . . . The newspapers in our community have contributed heavily to this condition." On the aftermath of the assassination, Stoltz pronounces: "Dallas today is frustrated. It would like to escape all blame and all its responsibilities . . . But it finds that this is difficult. It would like to believe that these events could have happened anywhere, but it is having trouble convincing even itself."[278]

What is most remarkable about Stolz's paper is not that it offered such serious and rigorous introspection among city insiders, but that it became public. While the report was originally delivered in full confidentiality, Dr. Stolz gave Leslie permission to publish it in its entirety in *Dallas Public and Private.* This was a remarkable break in the operational protocol, a trespass of the sacred agreement that the backroom discussions of the city's directing elite stay private.

In Leslie's book on Dallas, there is much that is unflattering. He chronicles our self-absorbed materialism, our lack of civic openness, and the oversize influence wielded by our far-right Absolutists. Worse, though, Leslie puts us on the couch, subjecting us to the gaze of Stolz's psychological examination as if we suffered from some collective mental disorder. Leslie prefaces his book with the famous quote from Socrates—"The unexamined life is not worth living"—but, in post-assassination Dallas, public self-examination was the last thing we longed for.

More than a few Dallasites might have nodded with approval if someone had reminded them that Socrates's city had responded to his unwelcome

278. Leslie, *Dallas: Public and Private,* 13–20.

exhortations by offering him the choice between exile and death. *Dallas Public and Private* was attacked prominently by the president of the Dallas Chamber of Commerce, and Leslie was taken to task in a *Dallas Morning News* editorial. From the moment the book was released, he became, in Dallas, a social pariah.

But it turns out that Warren Leslie would be one of the better writers Dallas ever produced. He had already written two novels by the time *Dallas Public and Private* was published. After he left here to work for the cosmetics giant Revlon, he turned that experience into the novel *Under the Skin.* He coauthored scripts for the soap opera *The Secret Storm,* and, in 1978, he recast his experiences at Neiman Marcus in the form of a wonderfully lurid pulp adventure entitled *The Starrs of Texas.* That book was well timed (the TV series *Dallas* debuted that same year), but Leslie's writing was the last thing we needed in 1964. After the assassination, we did not need more soap opera. The world stood in judgment of us, and, in our besieged bunker mentality, we feared that pondering our collective experience publicly might be seen as an admission of collective guilt.

While we were actively trying to forget, Warren Leslie broke all the rules. He had talked; not only that, he had shared our dirt. If we could not actually forget, we had resolved at least to maintain a collective silence. If you remembered, you remembered also to hold your tongue. Dallas has always been a future-oriented city. Warren Leslie had had the gall to talk about the past. Within the year he was gone, returned to Manhattan, where he had come from.

•

Warren Leslie would not be the first survivor of a traumatic event to be accused of profiteering from the experience. The wandering Greek Simonides was said to have been the first poet to push for proper pay for his work, and some have suggested that Simonides remembered the assembled guests at the collapsed banquet hall in Crannon because he had so assiduously checked them out as potential patrons. Likewise, many of the guests at the banquet hall in Dallas on November 22, 1963, would have been patrons of Leslie's employer. At the Trade Mart, the well-heeled guests assembled for the president's scheduled speech, especially the fashionable wives, were appareled in garb procured from

Neiman Marcus. Despite the political tension in the air, they wanted to look their best, perhaps even get that photo opportunity with the president and his wife: their own flashbulb moment with the glamorous Jack and Jackie. Those opportunities, of course, would never present themselves. After an uncomfortably long wait, Erik Jonsson took to the podium and made the announcement—and the roof fell in at the banquet hall.

As we have noted, it was out of that rubble of the collapsed banquet hall in Crannon that Simonides would develop his one great contribution to science, our first fully developed mnemonic system. Just as we in Dallas would have to deal with the proper arrangements for the bodies of the president, Police Officer Tippit, and Lee Harvey Oswald, in Crannon, they had their own dead to commemorate. Through his recollection of the architectural scheme of the banquet hall, Simonides was able to create a mental matrix that could then serve as an organizational scheme for recalling the individuals who had been dispersed within it. If you could maintain a stable image of a place, a "locus," you had an invaluable aid in recalling what was inside the place. From this idea, Simonides created his technique of mentally organizing large amounts of information, by translating that information into imaginal form, then placing those images in a predetermined mental location.

After November 22, 1963, Dallas itself became a sort of modern media memory palace for all Americans. The architecture of Dealey Plaza and the other locales associated with President Kennedy's death become a sort of standardized landscape that could be peopled with a thousand different images to produce a million different narratives about the assassination. As with the scale model of Dealey Plaza that the FBI had donated to the Sixth Floor Museum, you could move around the toy-sized cars in the motorcade and position the strings that represented the gunshot trajectories in whatever manner you wished. Each arrangement would result in a different scenario; each would create a new story; and each different story would have its own implications. Given the importance of the Kennedy assassination in our contemporary history, each story would also imply its own version of modern America.

In Dallas, we grew accustomed to watching these stories of the assassination broadcast back to us—a torrent of narratives about us, over which we had no control. We experienced the estrangement of seeing ourselves moved about like chess pieces in somebody else's memory palace; we experienced the doubleness of living in this city and seeing a different version of it represented in the media. We experienced the double bind of watching all this while we maintained our vows of silence. Warren Leslie's *Dallas Public and Private* was the first real story of our city and the Kennedy assassination that did not cast us, as the media had done, as ghosts of ourselves, haunting someone else's historical chessboard. Leslie's book was composed of the real flesh and blood of life in this city, and that caused its own discomfort. While the rest of us carefully stifled our own stories and suppressed our personal memories, here was one Dallas insider willing to share his story. Opening his book with a bold declaration—"What follows is not the story of an assassination. It is the story of a city."—Leslie became the first public figure in Dallas to stand above the rubble and show us where the bodies lay.[279]

While Leslie aimed to tell a bigger story, he would begin, like all of us, with that small, very specific moment: the instant he heard the news. Warren Leslie's version of the tale is set in the Club Imperial, the fashionable private club located in downtown Dallas's stately Baker Hotel. As Leslie presents it, the Imperial is a microcosm of the Dallas business world, one of a handful of places where the downtown business elite would gather for a few drinks and get things done. While many of his fellows were milling about at the Trade Mart, waiting for the president, Leslie was here working, "out of reach of extraneous minds and tongues."

On that late November day, Warren Leslie had just walked into the Club Imperial for lunch and a business discussion with Dr. Paul A. Goldschmidt of the United States-Austrian Chamber of Commerce. They had just seen the president pass by on Main Street and been impressed "by the great warmth and good will which emanated from the huge crowd." But the story continues:

> No more than minutes after our arrival at the club, the phone rang for me. It was brought to the table.
>
> My secretary said, "There's this awful rumor that the President's been

279. Leslie, *Dallas: Public and Private*, 12.

> shot. We can't get anybody—newspaper, radio stations—on the phone. Turn on the television."
>
> Goldschmidt, watching my face change, grabbed my arm. "My God, what is it?" he said.
>
> Before I could speak, a short, square man with a ruddy face burst into the club like a lunatic.
>
> "Turn on the television," he yelled. "The President's shot."
>
> A waiter turned it on. A face first, then its voice: "All we know," it said, "is that President Kennedy and Governor Connally *have* been shot . . . "
>
> In back of me, a man threw his head down on his arm against the table.
>
> "This God-damned Town," he said quietly.

Starting with this scene in the Club Imperial, Leslie presents an insightful and not entirely flattering picture of this city and its relationship to the death of John F. Kennedy. He writes, he says, feeling "that strange mixture of love and pain" that many people in Dallas felt at the time. "For this city, not nearly so black as the world press has painted it, was nevertheless not innocent in these matters. It was not innocent."[280]

•

In the aftermath of the president's murder, there was plenty of shame and embarrassment to go around. Dallas would take the worst of the beating, but the state of Texas would also take its share. Now all those Texas stereotypes that we had adopted as proud displays of our civic exceptionality were thrown back in our faces. According even to many outsiders who had played along in

---

280. Leslie, *Dallas: Public and Private*, 3–9.

the past, our hyperbolic Dallas self-confidence was revealed to be but a brittle veneer with which we stifled dissent. Our cowboy charisma was revealed to be simply a mask for our violent, macho gun culture. As Dallas was taken to task for creating the environment in which such tragic bloodshed could occur, so was the state of Texas tarred with the same charges—deemed guilty of the same sins.

In West Texas, where the frontier myths were especially embedded in everyday life, young James Pennebaker experienced the trauma of the assassination through the eyes of a teenager. Born in the oil field city of Midland, Pennebaker was thirteen years old in 1963. He would spend a good deal of his future career attempting to understand how our memories of the JFK assassination affected us here in Texas.

This is how James Pennebaker records his flashbulb memory of the events of November 22, 1963. He was sitting in a Midland dentist's chair when he heard the president had been shot. After his appointment, his mother drove him back to school. As soon as he arrived, the rest of the school learned what he had just learned.

> I was in physical education class in junior high when an announcement was made over the loudspeaker that John F. Kennedy had been assassinated . . . At the end of class, a group of us were silently standing by the door waiting for the bell to ring. Jan Taylor, a popular cheerleader, was quietly crying in the corner. To no one in particular, she angrily blurted out, "I hate Dallas. I'm ashamed to be a Texan."[281]

Like Warren Leslie, James Pennebaker would eventually find himself in a unique position to understand Dallas and its touchy relationship to the assassination. After high school, he left West Texas for college, eventually earning his Ph.D. in psychology at the University of Texas at Austin. In 1983, at age thirty-three, he moved to Dallas to continue his career as a professor of psychology at Southern Methodist University. Two decades after he heard the news of the assassination in Midland, Texas, James Pennebaker—a social

281. James Pennebaker, *Opening Up* (New York: Guilford Press, 1990),162

psychologist whose professional specialization was tending increasingly toward collective memory—found himself a new citizen of the city where John F. Kennedy had been killed.

In 1997, fourteen years later, the scholarly anthology *Collective Memory of Political Events: Social Psychological Perspectives* was published. It was edited and included articles by James Pennebaker. The book was a testament to the growing importance of the concept of flashbulb memory and how it had become a staple in the evolving field of memory studies.

•

In the twenty years since its introduction, Brown and Kulik's idea had become more than just a standard tool in the exploration of memory. Specialists outside the relatively narrow field of memory studies had begun using FBM to further their study of deeper psychological issues. For example, studies about the importance of the "self-defining function" of flashbulb memory were appearing. This research made clear that FBM is not simply "reproductive," or useful only for storing memory. FBM is "constructive," actually active in defining the individual. FBM serves "to structure autobiographical memory, which in turn defines the person's self/identity." It was becoming more and more clear, FBM was worth studying, and it was pliable. [282]

The primary focus of Pennebaker's anthology was not individual memory, however, but collective memory. The idea of collective memory had only fairly recently migrated from the social sciences and the works of such thinkers as Maurice Halbwachs into the harder sciences of cognitive psychology and cognitive biology. Flashbulb memory played a significant role in that transition. FBM allowed for fairly straightforward clinical study, and increasingly exposed to view the important link between individual and collective experience. These studies progressively indicated that memory was not simply the result of an instantaneous imprint of experience on the individual mind but that social factors shaped these imprints over time. There had been some inklings of this

282. James Pennebaker, *Collective Memory of Political Events: Social Psychological Perspectives* (Hillsdale, NJ: Lawrence Erlbaum Associates, 1997), 175–80.

from the beginning. In his "Now Print!" work, Robert Livingston had noted the importance of "rehearsal" in finalizing the imprinted memory. Brown and Kulik noted the effects of social mediation and how socially integrative "cues" affected how memories were elaborated to others. These were the first clues that the memory imprint was not quite finished until it had been articulated and presented to an audience. The more researchers built upon these earlier ideas, the more evidence accrued that memory had a social nature.

This was the weighty conclusion of Ulric Gustav Neisser, the "father of cognitive psychology." He had done important early work studying flashbulb memory. He attempted to replicate Brown and Kulik's original FBM work by looking at recollections of the 1986 Challenger space shuttle explosion. His results confirmed the vividness and long-lasting nature of FBM, but he proposed a profound shift away from the idea that memory is simply a mental snapshot of a moment. What Neisser found was that "memory, as it occurs in everyday life, was powerfully influenced by social factors." Memory did not happen instantaneously, but was a comingling of private and public impressions, an "active reconstruction of the past." Recognizing the critical role memory plays in the making of the self, Neisser asserted that "people gradually construct a story that matches the social demands of the interpersonal situation." This new science pronounced that memory, even FBM, is not simply individual and instantaneous, but is largely socially constructed over time.[283]

•

By the time that *Collective Memory of Political Events* was published, the field of social psychology had made remarkable advances. Both Pennebaker and the city of Dallas had played an important role in this process. When James Pennebaker first moved to Dallas in 1983, Brown and Kulik's cutting-edge work on flashbulb memories was just beginning to make the rounds, and it was obvious that those initial memories of the JFK assassination in Dallas formed the core of their FBM work. As FBM became the primary device by

283. Pennebaker, *Collective Memory of Political Events*, 191.

which we would study memory itself over the next few years, Pennebaker would be constantly reminded of his close proximity to the origin point of the idea. As Pennebaker pushed the concept of FBM further into his developing ideas of collective memory, there was always the question of *this* city and that benchmark memory event—the murder of John F. Kennedy.

Thirty years after Pennebaker first moved to Dallas, he had the opportunity to share his recollections of his first trip to Dealey Plaza, the "locus" of all of this compacted memory. In a newspaper article marking the fiftieth anniversary of the assassination, a reporter for the *Austin American-Statesman* related the story of how Pennebaker, just after he and his family had moved to Dallas in 1983, made his first pilgrimage to the great Mecca of memory studies.

> Curious, he drove down to the former Book Depository, which had become a county administration building, to get a look at the sniper's nest. He had his infant daughter, Teal, with him. Wife Ruth was at work.
>
> "We went to the elevator and I pushed the sixth-floor button. It didn't go up," he says. He went into an office and asked how to get to the sixth floor. You can't, he was told.
>
> "I went outside, and all these people were wandering around outside trying to figure out where the assassination was," Pennebaker recalls. "It was like there was a big sign on the building: "Nothing happened here. Go to Southfork."

Pennebaker was discovering just how challenging researching memory in Dallas might be. Although the Kennedy assassination would provide him with a profoundly unique case study, dealing with his local witnesses would not be an easy task. "They wanted to bury it and avoid any reminders of it," he said.[284]

•

284. Helen Anders, "JFK anniversary: Austinites remember when an assassination shattered an ordinary day," *Austin American Statesmen*, November 16, 2013.

James Pennebaker did eventually gain access to the sixth floor of the former Texas School Book Depository. A few years later, when the exploratory process of creating the Sixth Floor Museum began, he volunteered his expertise and became an active participant in the work that would lead to the institution's creation. For a social psychologist specializing in memory, Dallas was not just an interesting workshop; it was the mother lode.

Pennebaker's first job was to document the full extent of the local memory vacuum. It was a fairly straightforward task to record our lack of public commemoration. While the rest of the country was ambitiously building things for and naming things after JFK, there was no school, street, or building named after Kennedy here in Dallas. This was convincing material evidence of our neglect, but Pennebaker was most interested in the internal workings of our denial.

Pennebaker took surveys of museum visitors, gauging their thoughts and memories regarding the assassination. What he found was remarkable. While the rest of the nation tended to forget Dallas's part in the assassination, we tended to remember. A nationwide survey a week after the assassination reported that 15 percent of the respondents blamed the city of Dallas itself. In his 1988 survey, Pennebaker found comparable results—that less than 20 percent of out-of-town respondents still blamed Dallas. By contrast, a full 80 percent of Dallas natives above thirty years of age felt that the rest of the country still blamed Dallas. Of the recent Dallas transplants or those too young to remember, 60 percent perceived the rest of the country stilled blamed us. After twenty-five years, the shame was still with us. Our perception of external judgment still echoed in our memories, out of all proportion to actual fact.[285]

According to Pennebaker, "Dallas was uniquely affected. It was an anxiety-provoking, shameful experience for the community." Having documented the lingering presence of that shame, he aimed further: to understand its consequences. Pennebaker's interest in the correlation of psychological factors with physical well-being led him to take a deeper look at public health data. Joining with fellow SMU faculty member Rhonda Polakoff, he conducted a study of the city in the five years following the assassination.

285. Pennebaker, *Opening Up*, 165.

They discovered that Dallas deaths due to heart disease increased 4 percent over the four years after the assassination, while there was a 3 percent decrease in the nation as a whole during this period. Our murder and suicide rates increased significantly. In the year after the assassination, murder rates in Dallas jumped 25 percent compared with 1 percent nationwide. In 1964, the suicide rate in Dallas increased by 20 percent compared with 1 percent across the country, this rise occurring while underlying economic indicators in the city were improving.

There were those who disputed Pennebaker's statistical methodology, but he adamantly stood by his basic conclusion: the failure to properly acknowledge the death of John F. Kennedy in Dallas had done real damage to the city's population. In his words: "the failure to admit to the psychological effects of the assassination was ultimately unhealthy."[286]

As Pennebaker continued his research on collective memory, he also began exploring therapeutic methods for dealing with traumatic memory. Dallas, of course, continued to play a leading role in his work. In a 1997 publication, Pennebaker included a chapter entitled "Inhibited Cities." In it, he leapt around the world, examining how different communities had processed various traumatic events. The closing, and most critical, section was labeled "Community Shame: The Case of Dallas and the Assassination of Kennedy." Once again, Dallas and JFK were held up as the exemplar—the prototypical model—as modern psychology worked out its clinical understanding of memory. And it wasn't just a matter of abstract or historical interest. According to Pennebaker at least, there were consequences: "People who are at the most risk for illness are those who have experienced a trauma, who continue to think about it, and who do not talk about it—in short, a thumbnail sketch of our Dallas natives."[287]

•

In 1997, James Pennebaker also published *Opening Up: The Healing Power*

286. Pennebaker, *Collective Memory of Political Events*, 9–10.
287. Pennebaker, *Opening Up*, 165.

of Expressing Emotions. This book was a culmination of his developing work on trauma disclosure. By then, he had built an impressive and wide-ranging career, having dug down even to the level of the dynamics of language analysis (*The Secret Life of Pronouns*). At the heart of all his work is the idea that the mental state affects the physical state. His focus in *Opening Up* is on inhibition, and how inhibition is physical work that affects short-term biological changes, even causing long-term health issues. Keeping secrets influences a person's thinking abilities and impacts their health, Pennebaker asserts. The cure, according to Pennebaker, is to speak and write. Expression, he argues, is the avenue to mental and physical health.

An unspoken trauma, the Kennedy assassination has always been there beneath the surface for many Dallasites. Pennebaker had his own story, and he knew we had them too. Each time he visited the Sixth Floor Museum, Pennebaker was reminded how vividly those memories still burned. Each time he passed through the entry lobby, he saw what they call today "The Memory Book." Here, visitors were invited to add their responses as they experienced Dealey Plaza and the museum. It became a grand repository of striking impressions and flashbulb memories.

Pennebaker could not help but note that many of these entries were emotionally charged. Many were cathartic or conveyed a sense of therapeutic cleansing. The guests who entered their stories came from all over, but Pennebaker took special notice of those who lived in the Dallas area. Here was evidence, not only of inarticulate pain but also a vivid spark that remained locked in our memories. Here was a hint of the writing on the JFK assassination that had otherwise never quite made it to the page.

Pennebaker would not have been the first to note the remarkable lack of correspondence between the effects that the Kennedy assassination had on the city of Dallas and the amount of art and writing the city has produced in response. It is a striking imbalance. The palpable absence of response from Dallas is even more remarkable when considering those uncounted thousands of offerings (flowers, letters, keepsakes) that descended upon Dealey Plaza immediately after the assassination, each an individual expression of mourning. That river of passion seemed, somehow, to trickle away quickly. With the absence of any form of notable official civic eulogy for the murdered president, the immediate pushback against those who did speak out about the killings, and the general shock at the country's insistence on blaming Dallas, the walls went up. We cemented ourselves into a self-censoring silence that became second nature.

Pennebaker was not a historian or a chronicler of the arts, but he understood that something was missing. While libraries elsewhere filled up with JFK literature, there was very little produced here. There were some notable exceptions (often conspiracy related), but, in general, if you wrote about the assassination, there was no place to publish and no place to speak. If you painted, there were no gallery walls available to hang your work. Because there was so little to begin with, there were no anthologies or retrospectives.

It was primarily our journalists, duty-bound by profession, who kept the memory public. In the first two decades, on the significant anniversaries of the assassination, the *Dallas Morning News* and *Dallas Times Herald*, still competing against each other for journalist preeminence, produced fairly impressive retrospectives. On non-anniversary years, we got much less. After a few years, the output dwindled to one or two unrelated newspaper articles or a few fast TV news segments. Routinely, these concentrated on individual stories: the experience of a police officer in the motorcade; a doctor working at Parkland.

At home, as we read the newspapers or watched the TV, we would perform our own obligatory retrospectives. Prompted by these journalistic reminders, the sparks of our recollections would flame up again, and perhaps some of us might rehearse all our memories again. We might enhance them, deepen them, burnish them up a bit, but if we did, we did it sequestered off by ourselves. And, in general, we kept those memories to ourselves; we did not share. The annual reporting, in its distanced, just-the-facts journalistic style, made us remember, but it did not give us the space to disclose anything more of ourselves.

Every year, we all remembered November 22, but we had no Simonides. There was no great patron here in Dallas willing to hire on that poet who could present for all of us that great final epitaph. There was no local bard who would step up and perform the necessary final oration. That stage remained empty.

•

After the Kennedy assassination, the city of Dallas engaged in a massive project of civic sublimation. In place of mourning or outward displays of grief, we built things. If this was a collective defense mechanism, it was a very efficient one. If it was a protective reaction, it had impressive results. (We should note that this was a type of conscious suppression, not repression, which is unconscious.) Ultimately, it was a recognition that, even though we were unable to express ourselves in the traditional language of grief and mourning, we could still choose to express ourselves in the language with which we were most comfortable—new construction. It made us more like we already were.

Carl Jung once wrote: "Sublimation is part of the royal art where the true gold is made."[288] Freud before him credited certain aspects of repressed behavior as an important and positive aspect of civilized life, and the physical evidence of the city's successful sublimation was everywhere on display. The results of Mayor Erik Jonsson's "Goals for Dallas" building initiative were visible in our public buildings, parks, transportation, and educational institutions. By almost any economic accounting, the city had reacted with resolve and vigor. Already by 1970, *Look* magazine had declared Dallas an "All-American City." As the city continued to expand, its downtown development was especially impressive. Even James Pennebaker could see it. He noted that "our logical strategy was highly successful in boosting the economic and social prospects of the city." But, he observed, "it also produced some unexpected cost." [289]

There is the physical city and there is the psychic city, and the reconciling of these two geographies is the challenge of any city dweller. If there is an imbalance between our physical world and that more ephemeral world of our collective memory, how are the maps made right? Pennebaker, and a few others, warned us of the cost of the denial of our own memory. "As a city, Dallas responded by pretending nothing had happened," Pennebaker reminded us. "It became the city of the future, and, at the same time, the city without a past."[290]

---

288. Carl Jung, *Letters of C. G. Jung*, Gerhard Adler and Aniela Jaffé, eds., vol. 1, 1906–1950 (Princeton, NJ: Princeton University Press, 1974), 171.

289. Pennebaker, *Opening Up*, 167.

290. Pennebaker, *Collective Memory of Political Events*, 10.

Pennebaker was only half right here. The assassination did not initiate an entirely new state of pastlessness. Dallas had, from the beginning, been the city of the future. Our post-assassination sublimations only made it more so—made us now even more heedless of our own history. We have always been undeniably forward-looking, and one of our defining features has been our unbounded optimism. With an ethos rooted in mercantile boosterism, we've always been a sales pitch for something more. We've always been an unfinished project.

When Pennebaker further noted that "Dallas historians report that the assassination forced the city to become extremely image conscious," he was, again, only half right. A relative newcomer to Dallas, Pennebaker did not realize that here it was always understood it was better to be a master at public relations than history. We were long practiced at claiming the easy myth rather than the difficult truth. Because of our impressive civic success—our astounding growth and relative prosperity—we could justify making outrageous claims and subsequently attempting to achieve them.

Our recent history offered plenty of evidence of this. Whenever the city was faced with a particularly daunting problem, our inevitable first move was to mount a PR campaign. In the early 1960s, we had Sam Bloom, advertising man par excellence, and he was happy to serve. First, Dallas called on Bloom to handle the task of spearheading the rollout of our court-mandated school desegregation program. Then Dallas made him the man behind the arrangements for the 1963 Kennedy visit. After that exploded in our face, Dallas assigned Bloom the crucial task of civic press liaison to Judge Joe Brown in the trial of Jack Ruby. This unprecedented reliance on public relations as public policy became standard procedure for our city leaders. It was all about public perception, and Sam Bloom was the man.

Dallas is a business city, and we have always known the value of a little blue-sky sales, the fizz of those ephemeral enticements that don't always quite fit into the standard accounting. But some, exemplified by Pennebaker, suggested that a type of accounting was necessary. History has its own bottom line, and we had not, Pennebaker asserted, made any investment in the "symbolic acknowledgment that a trauma occurred." That account had to be reconciled. In Pennebaker's view, "An overconcern with images and appearances comes at the expense of self-reflection."[291]

It is no exceptional thing for a city as young as Dallas to lack a very developed sense of its own history. That type of self-reflection must be nurtured deliberately. It was common for such cities to be guilty of mistaking civic boosterism, familial ancestry research, and folklore for full-blown, legitimate history. In our neglect of a full and objective assessment of our civic past, we were not alone among American cities, but were certainly among the most well-practiced in the disregard of our history.

At the time of the assassination, however, we had made at least one very readable stab at a civic history. *The Lusty Texans of Dallas: Their First Hundred and Twenty-Five Years* was first published in 1951, then updated and reissued in 1965 by Cokesbury Bookstore, our local literary Mecca. If not of exacting historical standards, the book is at least lively and well informed. It was written by John Williams Rogers, a noted local newspaper man, columnist, and critic who had very often been a part of the history he wrote about. Rich with telling anecdotes, Rogers's history lays out the endearing qualities of these rough-and-ready people, leaping from the train robber Sam Bass to fashion merchant Stanley Marcus and back with the same gusto so characteristic of its subjects. In fact, Rogers casts Dallasites as a bunch of ambitious self-fashioners, constantly jumping, as the situation demanded, between folksy Texanism and worldly cosmopolitanism. "Certainly, if you scratch the marble and chromium that adorn Dallas," Rogers writes, "its origins as a frontier community close to the soil are not far beneath."[292]

After the assassination, however, the blustery, self-assured tone of Roger's mythic narrative could no longer be sustained. When *The Lusty Texans of Dallas* was reprinted in 1965, it still detailed how we "had grown to be by far the largest American city completely landlocked and remote from navigable water" to nonetheless become a "'port' in our own right."[293] It still celebrated our remarkable growth, our nationally recognized grand opera,

291. Pennebaker, *Opening Up*, 168.

292. John William Rogers, *The Lusty Texans of Dallas: Their First Hundred and Twenty-Five Years* (Dallas: Cokesbury Book Store, 1965), 396.

293. Rogers, *The Lusty Texans of Dallas*, 387.

and the new Graduate Research Center of the Southwest. But it also contained an amended final chapter entitled "World Confusion about Dallas." This new section is a wistful attempt to convince readers that the world was wrong about us; we had not killed the president. Sadly, it is more effective in demonstrating our sense of being trapped under the glaringly bright lights of national scrutiny. The lustiness is gone; the new tone is humbled and self-defensive. "World Confusion about Dallas" is like a Band-Aid that only manages to draw more attention to the wound.

After the assassination, it would be a while before anyone in Dallas attempted another civic history. We did not know how to tell the story anymore, and no one really wanted to talk about anything like collective memory. This was all part of the cost. The type of self-reflection that required a backward glance was no longer an option. If Dallas had always tended to ignore its past, that tendency became more profoundly entrenched than ever before.

•

Ironically, as Dallas dug into its communal memory blackout, the nation as a whole was experiencing a "memory boom." As one expert explained, this memory boom was a drastic expansion of popular and scholarly work dealing with how we form and process our recollections of the past. According to the editors of Oxford Press's *The Collective Memory Reader*, all this "began sometime in the late 1970s and has only begun to wind down since the turn of the millennium."[294] In the rapidly expanding field of memory studies, the editors explain, there was a growing recognition of the importance of memory formation in the creation of personal identity and an increasing appreciation of how memory is influenced by social and technological factors.[295] At the core of these developments was the notion that memory was pliable—that it could be adjusted and realigned. One of the emerging goals of this new memory work was the healing of the individual with traumatic

294. Jeffery Olick et al., eds., *The Collective Memory Reader* (Oxford: Oxford University Press, 2011), 4.

295. Olick et al., *The Collective Memory Reader*, 37.

memories. This developing science had an amazingly quick and significant effect on the larger culture.

Not that many people in Dallas would have been familiar with Livingston's "Now Print!" or Brown and Kulik's flashbulb memory work, much less keeping up with advancements in memory studies. Nor would many have registered that the JFK assassination was the "benchmark" for some of the most critical memory studies. What everyone in Dallas knew, however, was that we had been scrutinized and judged from the very beginning. As soon as those first news flashes went out, we were placed under the microscope. It seemed a natural reaction to shut down, to root ourselves into a collective reticence. It was not amnesia; we could not forget. We were not negligent or indifferent; it was more complex than that. While we maintained our outward composure, there was a roiling discomfort under the surface.

It cannot be refuted; there was some undeniable hatred of Kennedy here. That much had been well documented. There were many in Dallas who wished not to honor the president, even in death. He was not from here and could be honored elsewhere. Obviously, however, there were also those cheering thousands who lined the streets for the motorcade. They had seen fit to publicly honor Kennedy then—where were they now? Even they had shrunk back after the initial shock of the judgment cast upon the city. For many, that judgment had left them resentful, wary to take any public action. Inaction became a type of voiceless pushback. There existed a type of communal paralysis, a hopelessness that there was anything we *could* do. It was the classic double bind; it was well understood that anything we offered up would itself be judged and proclaimed insincere and feigned. For a thousand reasons, nothing ever happened. We knew what it looked like: a sore spot, a black eye, a black hole. The weight of the assassination was always there, but we didn't know quite how to put it into words, even if we wanted to.

There was a term, however, that was just then beginning to come into use that we might have used to articulate our experience. It was an idea that had been brewing in, of all places, European post-structuralist philosophy. It was called, simply, "the gaze." In its developing philosophical usage, "the gaze" evoked the anxious state of mind that comes with the self-awareness that one can be seen and looked at, turned into an object for judgment. While you are trapped in the gaze, you are subjected to a loss of autonomy.

In 1963, the same year as the Kennedy assassination, French theorist Michel Foucault published his *Naissance de la clinique,* translated into English as *The Birth of the Clinic.* Although very few of us were privy to how Foucault had extended Jean-Paul Sartre's ideas of epistemology, we would all experience the psychological effects of the gaze he described. We would have felt instinctually the loss of control. While *The Birth of the Clinic* would not be made available and widely read in the United States until 1973, those of us in Dallas had already felt "the gaze"—and the mortification and humiliation that came with it.

A critical aspect of Foucault's work was his treatment of power dynamics. *The Birth of the Clinic* may focus on science and the relationship between patients and medical experts, but we would have recognized the disproportionate distribution of power Foucault describes in our own situation. Just as the patient is put at the mercy of the medical expert who observes and scrutinizes him, so we were powerless before of critics. And everyone, it seemed, had given themselves the authority to pass their judgment upon us.

The biggest culprits—our most unavoidable tormentors—were the media and political power centers of Washington, DC, and New York. In Texas, we had always harbored that love/hate tension that comes from courting the approval of the official arbiters of truth and beauty. Now their gaze was insufferable. We became keenly aware of the biases of the East Coast elites and their Yankee disdain for the South, their self-satisfied urban superiority. As Foucault noted, the gaze doesn't simply rob an individual of their freedom as a subject; it also allows the arbiter an opportunity to display their superiority. With each condescending pronouncement from the East Coast came another reminder of their smug preeminence.

That was the worst of it, but this sense of being judged came from all sides, and it was paralyzing. We had the feeling of being reduced to a specimen, labeled, tagged, and pinned up for exhibit. We might not have called it "the gaze," but we could feel something at work that kept us awkward and self-conscious, reduced to a sense of collective inertia.

Of course, it was not just the constant examination that paralyzed us; there was our dissatisfaction with the diagnosis as well. From the beginning, we resented the collective psychoanalysis, that we should be put all together on the therapist's couch and pronounced a "sick city." If we were not convinced of the idea of collective guilt, we did eventually learn to feel at least some justification for harboring a collective resentment. What was particularly galling, of course, was when that psychiatric scrutiny came from within our own ranks. (But when Warren Leslie published Dr. Stolz's self-impaling psychological profile of the city in 1964, Leslie understood he had relinquished the right to be "one of us.")

By the time the concept of "the gaze" pulled itself into mainstream usage, we had much less inclination to think of it in terms of our own situation. Three decades after Kennedy's death, we were well practiced in the arts of deflection. By the time James Pennebaker's work was published, asserting that Dallas was the model of the "inhibited city," the practical work of sublimation had worked itself into our civic DNA. When Pennebaker warned us that the traumatic experience we had not translated into language and purged was "likely to surface in the forms of ruminations, dreams and associated thought disturbances," we didn't run for therapy. We had already learned how to deal with the ruminations. Our reactions fit comfortably into the developing backlash against the excesses of therapeutic memory work. Even the editors of *The Collective Memory Reader* expressed some concern about the limits of the talking cure. The demands for public expiation now went beyond mere cities: "The memory boom thus unleashed a culture of trauma and regret, and states are allegedly now judged on how well they atone for their past misdeeds rather than how well they meet their fiscal obligations and inspire future projects."[296]

A good portion of the nation went a little crazy with their "memory boom," developing their identity politics and writing self-help memoirs. Meanwhile, we tended to spend less time parsing the difference between sublimation and repression. In Dallas, we continued to scrupulously meet our financial obligations and emphasize more active pursuits. Memory had never been our strong suit; we specialized in the future!

But, without thinking about it much, we had made a profound contribution to the science of memory. Like Simonides's city of Crannon, Dallas

296. Olick et al., *The Collective Memory Reader*. Oxford Press, 3–4.

has a peculiar double legacy. We have hosted a horrific and tragic event, and that event, in turn, provided the raw experience that has impelled critical new developments in our understanding of memory.

I do not know if, there on the broad plains of Thessaly within sight of Mount Olympus, there is some memorial for those dead in the party of Scopas. I do not know if the citizens of Crannon have made any attempt to remember where the banquet hall was where the roof came down and their fellows were crushed by fate. The wandering poet Simonides would go on to his deserved fame, and the history of the tragic incident at Crannon would be spun and respun out of his telling. The people of Crannon would come to understand that, in these tales, their city would be made out as a backwater (say, as 1963 Dallas might have looked to New York or Washington, DC). They would see the proud clan of Scopas depicted as crass, ignorant, and concerned only with their own self-glorification (as, maybe, our own aristocrats awaiting the presidential banquet at the Trade Mart were). In Crannon, they too might have resented the gaze of those superior outsiders. But they must, at least, be heartened to this day that their city still has some place in our history.

By the time Cicero recounted the disaster some four centuries later, his aim was not the lofty goal of memorializing the tragic dead. Cicero referenced Crannon, and we remember Crannon today, because of its contributions to Simonides's development of his method of loci. We remember Crannon for its contributions to remembrance itself.

Has Crannon, two and a half millennia later, marked, in some public manner, its profound contributions to the science of memory? Here in Dallas, it's an interesting question to ponder. Likewise, should we ourselves consider establishing some civic observance of our status as a landmark in the science of memory? I fear that many here might respond to this question in the same manner as Simonides's good friend Themistocles. When he was offered the chance to master Simonides's new science of mnemonics, Themistocles replied, "I would rather a technique of forgetting, for I remember what I would rather not remember and cannot forget what I would rather forget."[297]

297. Cicero, *de Oratore*.

•

Jorge Luis Borges is reported to have said: "Creativity is suspended between memory and forgetting." Indeed, the method of loci is an active, not a passive, system, and it requires a constant stream of decisions, many of them aesthetic. Undoubtably the most extravagant development in the art of memory as conceived by Simonides, the very pinnacle of its elaboration, is Giulio Camillo's "Memory Theater." Camillo was a Renaissance philosopher born in northern Italy around 1480. In his lifetime he was recognized as one of the great minds of the age. Camillo's great claim to fame was his ambition to move memory beyond the individual mind and construct a literal, physical palace for its storage. Camillo's ambition was to create a memory machine so comprehensive that it could contain everything.

Camillo's Memory Theater would take the form of the amphitheater, and it would draw its organizing principles from Vitruvian architecture. Seven sections in rising tiers would radiate from the stage, and each of the seven rows would be spanned with an arch, tagged with one of the seven planets and seven classical Greek mythological motifs. Across this matrix would be spread the vital information from all the fields of study, all encoded within an elaborate symbolic system. A plethora of supplementary information would be organized within this structure, tucked into various drawers and cubbyholes, instantly at hand. All of this would be perfectly aligned to enable its users to instantly recall every imaginable relationship, from the micro- to the macrocosmic.

Perhaps the most remarkable thing about Camillo's Memory Theater, its most radical twist, is its reversal of the theater's normal division between the audience and stage. In the Memory Theater, the audience would consist of a single person, at once both spectator and actor. This one participant was to stand onstage and look out into the amphitheater. In this strange transposition, all the action, all the images and symbols, would be located where the audience would normally be seated. The goal of this theater was for the single participant to experience the epiphany of the "magic memory moment," an encounter with the divine mind and everything contained within it.[298]

298. Frances Yates, *The Art of Memory* (London: The Bodley Head, 1966), 173–74.

Camillo's Memory Theater was the last, final burst of occult development of the memory practices that originated with Simonides. Already, when Giulio Camillo died in 1544, Johannes Gutenberg's Bible had been circulating for almost a century, as had the new techniques of printing and movable type. The mass-produced book was profoundly transforming the idea of memory storage. Increasingly this artificial, outside-the-body memory was becoming the order of the day. Increasingly, we would have not just more accessible units of artificial memory, but more elaborate systems for their accumulation and distribution.

The library, of course, was an already ancient idea. Ashurbanipal had amassed a collection of more than thirty thousand cuneiform tablets in seventh-century-BCE Nineveh, and the great project of collecting all the world's knowledge was well under way at the library of Alexandria before it was burned in 48 BCE. After Gutenberg, the accumulation and accessibility of all this artificial memory accelerated exponentially. In the Western world, the seventeenth and eighteenth centuries became the Golden Age of libraries. Britain established the first national library in 1753, and then the first public library system in 1850. As Western democracies developed, so did ideas of increasing access to information, creating a commons of recorded memory.

Parallel to our basic human propensity to create faster, better communication, there is an equal urge to devise ways to record and remember those communications. The technological revolution gave us, in an accelerating sprint, these electronic communication systems: in 1837, Samuel Morse developed his code for the telegraph; in 1876, Alexander Graham Bell patented the telephone; in 1901, Guglielmo Marconi perfected his radio. Each invention proved more instantaneous and immediate than the last, and each presented new challenges in producing systems to archive and access all this newly produced information, all this new memory. This was a communications revolution, but it was equally a revolution for the acquisition of memory.

What was changing was not simply the speed of communication but also its sensory immediacy. By the 1960s, we were coming to understand that electronic media were not just a part of our lives but had become part of our way of being. Critics like Marshall McLuhan made us more reflective in gauging its influence, and, by 1960, we were already publicly assessing the impact of media on the presidential campaign. There was coverage of the relative effects of radio versus TV during the Nixon/JFK debates, and we understood John F. Kennedy as our "first TV president."

It would not be outrageous to say that the unprecedented public impact of the Kennedy assassination had at least something to do with the unique media landscape of the period. When all three television networks shut down regular programming to focus exclusively on the events in Dallas, this became the core of a mammoth information feedback loop. There was a new type of connectedness that produced an almost instantaneous common experience of remarkable immediacy, a communal example of what has come to be known as "prosthetic memory." The term is a recognition that the echo chamber of the modern media environment had moved inside our heads. Our memories become "prosthetic" as they are altered by what Alison Landsberg calls "engaged and experientially-oriented encounters with mass media." Our field of experience has exploded due to the inescapability of electronic communications. Landsberg further explains that prosthetic memory is a new type of memory, one which allow individuals "to have a personal connection to an event they did not live through."[299]

It was no coincidence that Brown and Kulik, performing their research a decade after the assassination, found the "flash" in their flashbulb memory in the news flash of the Kennedy assassination. By then it had become commonplace to note the parallel between the electric buzz of our own neural network with that of the media network. In their original definition of FBM, Brown and Kulik clearly stated that one could stem from a private trauma just as well as a public event. From the beginning, however, their clinical research was pulled toward public events that were shared via the electronic media. Of course, public events were easier to compare and study, but there was also a growing recognition that the realm of memory had expanded. In the late twentieth century, we moved in a new, more connected, more media-saturated memory environment. As our social scientists further developed

299. Alison Landsberg, "Prosthetic Memory: the ethics and politics of memory in an age of mass culture," in *Memory and Popular Film*, Paul Granger, ed. (Manchester: Manchester University Press, 2003).

the idea of FBMs, there was a growing interest in the interchange between the microcosm and the macrocosm—the negotiation that takes place between individual and societal memory. Always, deep beneath the surface of these developments, was that original model memory: the experience of the Kennedy assassination in Dallas.

One could argue that the JFK assassination was the first case of a great communal prosthetic memory. Here was that first moment in history when a profoundly significant event was almost instantaneously shared with the world through a modern media system dominated by television. Never before had there been such immediacy in our experience of the larger world. Furthermore, the news media presented both the original experience, the flash, and the remediated follow-up, the instant replay, a type of second memory. It was something new, and it would take our social scientists a few years to find the exact terms for it. One thing was becoming clear, however: we didn't simply move within this new media environment; it was also inside our heads.

If all of the reportage didn't seem instantaneous enough—if there still seemed a lag in the system—even that could be remedied. If you were tuned in to NBC at 12:21 on November 24, you saw Jack Ruby step up to the handcuffed Lee Harvey Oswald in the basement of the Dallas police headquarters and shoot him dead. You watched it live as it happened; you were part of it! Was there ever a starker reminder of how synced-up we had become?

•

On that long weekend in November 1963, we sensed that a revolutionary change had occurred, and we had our first inkling that this mammoth media machine had become an active partner in the making of our individual memories. But hadn't Giulio Camillo proposed something very similar five hundred years before? With his Memory Theater, didn't he attempt to construct an analogous machine that would produce a swirling field of visual images and language, a vast and systematic inventory of instantly accessible information that would dwarf regular experience? This too was a machine that would link the individual microcosm to the macrocosm of the larger world. How different is our contemporary epiphany of connectedness from Camillo's magic memory moment?

Since the 1960s, we've experienced nothing but constant acceleration in the development of our external memory systems. In this ever more connected world, our libraries, computerized and digitized, have branched themselves into larger libraries, this huge collective entity encompassing all the functions of the state, academia, business, and entertainment. The information collective we now know as the internet—so vast and amorphous, it would have boggled the mind of the most visionary thinkers of the 1960s—is light-years beyond anything that could have been devised by any individual, even a singular genius like Giulio Camillo. Camillo did, however, seek the same end as our contemporary information engineers—infinite connectivity. How different from, say, Steve Jobs with his iPhone, was Camillo's goal of creating a memory machine for his audience of one? Whether it was the Renaissance conception of access to the divine *mens* (mind) or today's concept of a networked world brain, the dream was the same: instant access to all possible information, the chance to have it all instantly at the tip of our finger (or our tongue).

It is worth remembering that even in this grand digital information boom, all these systems still have their human constraints. They cannot exist without us; all this memory is useless without a human being to activate it. Just as with Camillo's Memory Theater, the central node in all of these memory networks is the individual consciousness. In our virtual age, we can almost forget our consciousness is actually nested within our physical bodies—and that these bodies are always, inevitably, situated in a specific place. As Simonides reminds us, our memory is always contained in a "locus." If you are from, say, Dallas, Texas, this will have its effect.

In these geographies of our recollection, there are some places that come filled with such concentrated memory that they demand our specific attention—some places where we might even say "the past is present." There are some historical sites so burdened that we make them into monuments, official receptacles of past experience: memorials. Dealey Plaza is one of those places, one of our great national sites of common memory.

If you are from Dallas or have lived here a long time, you have some understanding of how Dealey Plaza is the modern-day equivalent to Giulio

Camillo's Memory Theater—a literal, physical memory machine, the memory "locus" supreme. It is a place where you walk onto the stage, and all this cargo of the past suddenly unloads itself. If you are a Dallasite, however, this is most likely neither the machine you are looking for nor the information you want. Most of us might feel like Simonides's Athenian friend Themistocles, who desired rather a machine for forgetting.

If Dealey Plaza is a memory machine, it is one with no on/off switch. Simply entering the physical space activates it. The locus itself is the memory.

•

We've discussed how we've developed our systems to augment memory, but we have not yet addressed the question why. What is the purpose of harnessing all this information? Historically, in the classical mnemonics systems that began with Simonides, the ultimate goal of all this harnessed knowledge was to augment the practice of rhetoric—public speaking.

Our best source on this is Cicero's 55 BCE dialogue *de Oratore.* Cicero himself was the widely respected master and model of rhetoric, and here he describes the ideal orator. Cicero was working in an already well-developed tradition, one which held that memory (along with arrangement, style, delivery, and invention) was one of the central elements in the canon of rhetoric. The accomplished orator was obliged to combine all these techniques with a wide knowledge of the world. Memory, of course, was the immediate repository of that knowledge. Combining this with the proper ethical principles, the rhetorician would utilize his skills for the benefit of his society. He would, through his public pronouncements, act as the state's moral guide.

This was exactly the type of man for whom Giulio Camillo had designed his Memory Theater. In fact, Camillo used Cicero as a constant inspiration, and worked Ciceronian text into his design wherever he could. Camillo's intention was that participants in the Memory Theater, having immediate access to this immaculately organized receptacle of knowledge, would instantly find themselves able to perceive as well as express all-encompassing truths. The idea was that this great mnemonic machine would allow speakers to become Ciceros themselves.

Like Camillo's memory machine, Dealey Plaza provokes a great inrush of remembrance. Packed within its compact physical bounds is an immense amount of tightly wound information—historical, scientific, cultural, conspiratorial—crammed in from books, newspapers, films, TV, the internet, and a million different individual stories, ready to explode into the consciousness of whoever steps inside. Never, though, has Dealey Plaza inspired a great and fitting work of oratory, a public speech worthy of the loftiest goals of rhetoric. There have been speeches made in the plaza, but never anything that was officially sanctioned and widely recognized. Between 1963 and 2013, the city of Dallas hosted not a single official speech or ceremony in Dealey Plaza addressing the assassination of John F. Kennedy.

The irony here is that trauma recovery was a hot topic in post-sixties America. It was a given that the way to deal with trauma was to go public; to "talk it out." It bordered on societal cliché. In our burgeoning self-help movements, our growing networks for social therapy, and in the mounting evidence from clinical studies, there was a constant chorus that open expression was the cure for disruptive memories. Emblematic of this trend was the recognition of PTSD, post-traumatic stress disorder, as an official mental disorder in 1980.[300] Our own James Pennebaker, of course, was in the vanguard of this movement. His *Opening Up: The Healing Power of Expressing Emotions,* published in 1997, laid out this new science for the lay reader (and specifically pointed out Dallas as the model of an "inhibited city.") It was becoming apparent that our contemporary art of memory was no longer about augmenting our recollections but assuaging the pain caused by the persistence of our traumatic memories. We were no longer burdened with the needs of memory storage; technology had taken care of that. Our goal now was to manage the consequences of *too much* memory.

In Dallas, of course, we never got that classic oratory of closure—almost no one talked about JFK or the assassination. But, to keep things in perspective, Giulio Camillo's Memory Theater never did produce the great oratory it promised, either. In fact, Camillo's project, despite all the attention it garnered

---

300. *Diagnostic and Statistical Manual of Mental Disorders: DSM III* (Washington, DC: American Psychiatric Association, 1980).

at the time, ultimately proved a failure. When Camillo passed away in 1544, he had just completed a manuscript of his scheme. It would eventually be transcribed and posthumously published as *L'Idea del Theatro.* He never did, however, complete the construction of the actual Memory Theater. It perhaps existed in prototype form in France, and in a nearly complete form in Venice. And there exists one account of a visitor there: Viglius Zuichemus wrote a 1532 letter to Erasmus describing the tour Camillo gave him of the Venice theater.[301] After his death, all physical evidence of Camillo's idea seemed to instantly disappear. One of the most storied men of learning during the Renaissance, Giulio Camillo himself fell almost entirely out of history.

Giulio Camillo's Memory Theater survives today as a fascinating but obscure historical novelty. When Camillo is mentioned today, he might be cited by the rare historically minded cybernaut as the forefather of the concept of pan-mnemism, "the dream of a universal, encyclopedic machine," or proclaimed the "Bill Gates of his age." His Memory Theater might be credited as the original attempt at a universal storage and retrieval system. Yet mentions of Camillo's Memory Theater show up slightly more often in the arts. (Even at the height of his fame, Camillo was criticized by Renaissance rationalists such as Erasmus for his use of less-than-scientific mysticism such as the Kabbalah and Hermeticism.) Recognizing Camillo's intentions to produce a machine that would stimulate the imagination as much as the memory, a few modern and contemporary artists have produced significant works that explore his ideas. A series of paintings by Jean Dubuffet, a project by video artist Bill Viola, and an orchestral work by British composer John Buller are all inspired interpretations of Camillo's Memory Theater.[302]

•

All of these Memory Theater–inspired works create what we might call aesthetic "magic memory moments" for their audiences, but none of them

---

301. Yates, *The Art of Memory,* 135.

302. Peter Matussek, "The Renaissance of the Theater of Memory," *Janus* 8, 2001, 66–70.

attempt that grander gesture, the transcendent, all-encompassing scope, toward which Camillo's creation aspired. Likewise, those memory moments created here, as our visitors step into Dealey Plaza and experience that inevitable whirl of history for themselves, are inevitably singular and individualized. Unlike Camillo's theoretical Memory Theater, Dealey Plaza offers no organized support structure by which to orient all that swirl of incoming information. There is nothing there to focus the visitor's impressions—everything feels centrifugal, discouraging a unified experience. All the societal ambiguity about what actually happened at Dealey Plaza, the myriad interpretations of its history, mingle with the general openness of the park. Dealey Plaza, so long lacking any sort of historical markers, and even today missing any significant memorial structure, is unique among our major historical sites for its lack of direction—for how little it coaches visitors or helps them shape their experience. The pressure of that charged moment, confronting the history there in all the vividness of its physical reality, inevitably produces a significant experience, but those experiences tend to be incredibly diverse, extraordinarily individualized, and sometimes downright idiosyncratic.

Dealey Plaza's pilgrims, or at least a good portion of the people you'll find milling around there, have come preprogrammed. They have planned their trips; they have some intentionality about the experience they want to have. To take a pilgrimage requires some near-theological practice, a developed mindset, and an understanding of the path that must be followed. When you get to the altar, you know what to do. You know how to feel.

About the rest of the visitors, it is hard to tell. The majority of them are out-of-towners. I have seen the full gamut. There are those who are here on a lark, who caper around and shout and joke —an acknowledgment of the great amount of junk content that has accumulated in Dealey Plaza. But there are more of those who are clearly moved, whose reaction is a silenced reverence. All of these people mingle here, and the pressure of the moment produces reactions both funereal and carnivalesque. There is always a vague sheen of confusion simmering in the air.

Those of us who live in Dallas are less likely to visit Dealey Plaza. The people of San Antonio, similarly, do not constantly visit the Alamo—tourist attractions are for tourists. But here there is something different going on; our history is not so glorious and celebrated. If we do visit Dealey Plaza, often when we visit, it is to accommodate out-of-town guests, to accompany them patiently as they have their JFK experience. For newcomers here, Dealey Plaza is a distraction, a relic from the past that constantly distracts visitors from what we are really all about today. It is something constantly imposed on us, and we are bored with it. We are a big, thriving city; who has time for all this? And if you have been here a while, are one of those old-timers who experienced it all firsthand and know what the assassination has long meant to the city, you would agree that there are better things to think about. Dealey Plaza sits at the heart of the city, physically and psychically, but we have never worked up any commonly accepted script by which to present it. When the visitors came, the general strategy, even after the Sixth Floor Museum opened, was to stand mutely aside and let them have their time.

If Dealey Plaza has been bereft of any locally unifying oratory, it has been equally devoid of artistic expression. For fifty years, it contained no significant monument related to the assassination or images of the president. Before the Fiftieth, it had hosted no official assassination-related public rituals or concerts. After the bouquets and votive offerings that filled the plaza immediately after the assassination faded away, virtually nothing by way of aesthetic gestures took their place, no symbols appeared that might order and give meaning to the lingering memories of the president and his fate.

With one exception: the dramatic reenactments. They continued one after the other. Cinema, the dream of our great collective unconscious, was the one artistic form that could not be denied. The nation demanded a certain level of realism from these reenactments, and they needed Dealey Plaza. Again and again, the film crews moved in, the action started, and our recurring feedback loop of traumatic memories replayed themselves. What a therapist might label triggers, dissociative experiences, flashbacks—all of that became available via standard thirty-five-millimeter film. We would suffer through it, and the next time the location scouts showed up in town, the proper city official would approve the proper forms, and soon the moviemakers were at it again. We could not deny Hollywood, but these constant cinematic revisitations always reminded us of something we already knew: Dealey Plaza is not just a stage. It is a perilous place, a sort of low-level Pandora's box. It's best to keep a lid on it.

We kept our guard up, but very, very occasionally, there were provocations. There were cases in which wayward local artists, drawn to the plaza precisely because of our delicate sensitivities, made unofficial forays into that space. The most notorious of these was the intrusion of March 17, 2010, when the immensely popular neo-soul singer—and native Dallasite—Erykah Badu sashayed into Dealey Plaza, discarding her clothing piece by piece. Documented by a coconspirator with his handheld camera, Badu's was clearly an act of incitement, an intentional prodding of the open wound. As Badu mimed her own shooting as if it were the president's, she didn't just succeed in bringing all those painful memories back into play. She made all of it intensely personal. Find the footage on YouTube: when, after Badu falls, the camera rises and scans the entire plaza, recording in one slow spin all of downtown Dallas, it is as if you yourself have just stepped onto the stage of Camillo's Memory Theater and been instantaneously presented with this huge panorama of recollected history, all of it spiraling back to this singular point in the middle of this plaza, where you stand at the very center of Dallas, at the X marking the spot where President Kennedy was assassinated.

As the video ends, Badu rises from the ground. A voice-over accompanies her symbolica rebirth.

> They play it safe, are quick to assassinate what they do not understand. They move in packs ingesting more and more fear with every act of hate on one another. They feel most comfortable in groups, less guilt to swallow. They are us. This is what we have become. Afraid to respect the individual. A single person within a circumstance can move one to change. To love herself. To evolve.

It isn't Cicero, exactly, but Badu's words constitute an audacious rhetorical act. They take a stab at expressing, if not our great common experience of the assassination, at least the fact that the assassination could be used as a platform for individual expression. America took notice of Badu's guerrilla-art invasion of Dealey Plaza; the general consensus was that this was intriguing work by a fearless artist. But in Dallas, there were very few here ready to take up Badu's challenge to be reborn through an unprotected, naked engagement with our traumatic past.

Badu's action demonstrated in a very public way how haunted Dealey Plaza still was. It remained our local Memory Theater. (You could even speak of the memory of the memories, as Badu was born seven years after the assassination.) Even for this next generation of Dallasites, memories of November 1963 hung over Dealey Plaza like fumes; they could be set off with a spark. Even after forty-seven years, when Badu stepped onto that stage, it was our own nakedness she wore. And when she mimed being shot, we could all imagine the flash.

•

If you are from Dallas or lived in Dallas at the time of the assassination, you'd feel the burden of a formidable, obdurate memory. The landscape of your life would have a strange doubleness. This was the place where you went about the routine business of your quotidian life, but it would also be the stage set of a mammoth historical drama that never quite seemed to fade away. Simply by living here, you were "caught in the action."

There *were* a few who, like Badu, understood that this glaring spotlight of memory presented a stage where you could play with the tension between these worlds. There was here another option, an opportunity, or maybe an obligation, to consciously respond—to make some art of it.

Memory, according to the Greeks, is the mother of the nine Muses. The Greeks recognized that kings and poets received their authoritative powers of speech through the inspiration of Mnemosyne herself. It is from those traditional guardians of the arts, the nine Muses, Calliope to Urania, that we receive the scroll, the lyre, and the mask. Calliope, for instance, is the protector of rhetoric as well as heroic poetry, and she gives us the writing tablet and the stylus in addition to the lyre. All of this artistic activity is born from memory. In Dallas, we would do well to remember that even the underworld Hades had its two parallel rivers: the river of forgetfulness, Lethe, and the river of remembrance, Mnemosyne.

William Wordsworth wrote of poetry as "the spontaneous overflow of powerful feelings" taking "its origin from emotion recollected in tranquility."[303] What our nine Greek Muses, those sentinels of our Western artistic traditions, give us are the tools by which we can manage these powerful feelings and the receptacles in which they can be contained. Properly encoded in the forms the Muses have provided, these memories can be purged of their toxins. Via this magical aesthetic transformation, even the most traumatic memories can be translated from poison into nourishment.

Today, when we talk about the "spontaneous overflow of powerful feelings," we are just as likely to invoke the cognitive sciences and psychology as aesthetics. We could just as easily find ourselves discussing how these feelings are contained in flashbulb memories and focus on the receptors in our neural circuitry as how we might pour these feelings into the aesthetic receptacles of the scroll, the lyre, or the mask. We would still, however, be talking about the same thing as Wordsworth. What are the means (aesthetic and otherwise) by which we might take our most intense memories, store them, and then shape them in ways that might be useful to ourselves as we move through this precarious world?

•

We need to return now to where we began, to the smallest particle of the vast communal experience of the assassination of John F. Kennedy—our flashbulb memories. All of us, a whole generation, are still working through our memories of this same moment, figuring out what to do with these microbursts of remembrance and the Wordsworthian emotions that come with them. "Almost everyone can remember with an almost perceptual clarity," wrote Brown and Kulik of the JFK assassination, "where he was when he heard, what he was doing at the time, who told him, what was the immediate aftermath, how he felt about it, and also one or more totally idiosyncratic and

303. William Wordsworth, "Preface," in *Lyrical Ballads* (Oxford: Oxford University Press, 2013).

often trivial concomitants."[304] We are still working on explicating and amending this memory—on bringing some final meaning to it.

In Dallas, we knew the instant JFK was shot that *we* were linked to history. We already understood; it had happened *here*. Whoever pulled the trigger, we were implicated. It was that feeling you'd have as you were lined up for a mug shot: hustled in, set in that perfunctory frame, and *flash!* There you were, caught suddenly unawares and unprepared, stuck in that one pose, set to be judged forever. We were trapped, it seemed, in that eternally arrested moment, caught standing naked onstage in the Memory Theater.

When the president was murdered here in Dallas, we were closer to the event than the rest of America. We were caught in the flash.

304. Brown and Kulik, "Flashbulb Memories," 73–99.

EPILOGUE

Guardians of the Ghost

> "Ghost stories are never just reflections. They are social critiques camouflaged with cobwebs; the past clamoring for redress."
>
> —Parul Sehgal, *New York Times,* October 22, 2018[305]

AFTER A CAMERA FLASH, we are often left with an afterimage, a lingering visual remnant left floating in our eye. This is often referred to as a ghost. A specialist in human optics might explain these persisting images in terms of photochemical activity in the retina. They might also note that we might see such an afterimage after staring at a single image for an extended period of time. Our expert might even go further and explain a rare visual malady called palinopsia. Derived from the Greek word "palin" for "again" and "opsia" for "seeing," the disease causes pathological distortion in visual processing. In its especially chronic form, hallucinatory palinopsia can produce continuously replayed, intense, and long-lasting afterimages. Literally, the ghost will not go away.

Photography presents us with a parallel to this ghostly phenomenon. Technically termed "lens flare" or" ghosting flare," these intrusions occur when a particularly strong light source is reflected off of lens elements, leaving unseen images, often called "artifacts," in the picture frame. A common

305. Parul Sehgal, "The Ghost Story Persists in American Literature. Why?", *New York Times,* October 22, 2018.

technical problem, these "ghosts" can also be manipulated to create remarkable visual effects.

Both memory and optical anomalies are at work in the creation of what we have come to call "ghost photography." The "spirit photographers" responsible for these images were enterprising artists who enjoyed a heyday that lasted from the years immediately following the American Civil War until the 1920s. They gained great notoriety by mastering the technique of surreptitiously inserting images of dead souls into their photographs. Their customers were generally spouses or relatives who had recently lost loved ones and hoped to maintain some flicker of a connection to the past.

The most famous of these ghost photographs, and our link to presidential assassinations, is the photo of Mary Todd Lincoln taken by William H. Mumler in the 1870s. In it, the spectral image of the deceased Abraham Lincoln drapes his hands over the shoulders of his seated widow. Mumler pioneered ghost photography, calling himself a "spirit photographic medium." Setting up studios in New York and Boston, Mumler reigned preeminent in his field for some time, but he was eventually revealed to be a fraud in a trial that included testimony against him by none other than P. T. Barnum.

•

In Dallas, of course, we do not believe in ghosts. We tend to be materialists without much sympathy for such insubstantial claims on reality. When it comes to our iconic JFK assassination photos, however, we have to admit there might be something strange going on.

Take, for instance, that famous Love Field photograph. Picture it: there is our handsome and well-coiffed president and his smiling wife, Jacqueline, in her pink Chanel suit with its matching hat. She has just been welcomed with a bouquet of red roses. With Air Force One silhouetted behind them, they walk to mingle with the crowd of well-wishers. You know this photo—you can vividly recall it to your memory through this simple description—and you know the story behind it.

It might be that, as you stare at this photo, a vague afterimage begins to leak into the frame. Subtly juxtaposed upon the original image is the translucent, misty black-and-white image of a limousine abandoned just outside Parkland Hospital. The vehicle's back door remains slung open, exposing to view the bouquet of roses strewn across the back seat and floorboard.

If you looked into this phenomenon more closely, you would realize you were simply collapsing two famous photographs from the November 29, 1963, issue of *Life* magazine. These two images formed the introduction spread for the magazine's initial assassination coverage: on the left, the full-page image of the president and Jackie at Love Field; on the right, the smaller black-and-white image of the limousine at Parkland, wedged between the headline and the text.

Life magazine, of course, is the source of so many of these iconic images of the assassination. Looking back, it was in the pages of *Life* that we saw all the promise of mid-century American photojournalism realized. There was a general consensus that the magazine showed us the reality of ourselves. It seemed this was what photography had promised us from the very beginning, the kind of clinical, scientific truth that only a witness as impartial as a camera's lens could record. But the photography in *Life* gave us even more.

It was only recently that I went back to that November 29, 1963, issue of *Life* and read the fine print. I discovered that the limo abandoned outside of Parkland in the *Life* spread was not the president's but the vice president's. When I look now, this much is clear. The limo in the photo is obviously white; the president's limo was black. Moreover, the roses on the floorboard appear to be yellow. In my mind, those flowers had always belonged to Jackie; this was the same bouquet from the Love Field photo, and they would have been splattered in the president's blood. I suspect I was not the only one who remembered it that way.

Of course, Jackie's blood-soaked roses became a common trope in assassination lore. As we've seen, Gene Shuford repeats the image of bloodied roses throughout "The Death in Our Family." Addressing the president, he write: "you bled, as red as roses that the princess dropped / from trembling fingers on the day you died." And, in William Burford's "The Spell," we find "the roses she held / Black as blood in the light, so dark red—."

Of course, Jackie did have red roses with her in the back seat of the presidential limo; you can spot them on the seat in some of the pre-assassination motorcade photos. However, it is the afterimage of the November 26 *Life* photo that leaks back into the Love Field photo. This should come as no surprise. If it is *Life* imagery that fills our memory, it will be *Life* imagery that also fills our imagination.

Poured into this imagery were yet deeper elaborations. There were all those traditional associations of the red rose, from the medieval connections between the spilling of holy blood and the martyrdom of saints. Jackie's memory-soaked roses, in turn, would become a foundational trope within the larger narrative of another updated tradition from the Middle Ages: the Camelot myth. By the next issue of *Life,* with its elaborate spread on Kennedy's Washington, DC, funeral, Jacqueline Kennedy and Theodore White had created the outlines of the Camelot myth and sent it off to assume a life of its own.

There is no outright fraud here, of course, but think about how much has been added to these JFK assassination photos. How much have the editors, photographers, and writers at *Life,* collectively working as our mid-twentieth-century "spirit photographic mediums," filled in the emptiness around these images? It is also worth remembering our own part in this process.

In the high-tech media landscape we live in today, with its relentless emphasis on the visual, we always speak of our desire for better resolution. We push for sharper definition, more fine-grained detail, megapixels. We go to astounding lengths to ensure that we can see more clearly. However, it could be that what we really want is something more fundamental. We want things to be resolved!

Cognitive specialists would tell you that our brains constantly augment our visual input, and that this process is a critical part of how we survive in our complex and dangerous world. We are hardwired to fill in the gaps. How, then, would we know when we have gone too far? Could we gauge when, exactly, we are approaching that state of palinopsia in which we pathologically superimpose these images from our memory onto our current reality? We are our own doctors here, and it is our burden to diagnose whether we are finding deeper truths or simply courting dysfunction.

It would be easy to ridicule the bereaved Mary Todd Lincoln for posing with William Mumler and furthering his obviously fraudulent manipulations.

However, it might be worthwhile to ask ourselves: When we look at our JFK assassination photos, what ghosts are *we* haunting *them* with?

•

"'Can you stand a shock?' he asked. Sure. 'The President has been shot!'"

Suddenly, you are back with William Barney in the Mercantile Building post office on November 22, 1963. The memory appears out of nowhere, and it takes you on a three-decade leap backward.

When this passage appears in Barney's *Words from a Wide Land,* it feels like a tear in the fabric of time—and Barney's poetic daybook (finally published in 1993) is all about time. Comprising 365 entries, running from January 1 to December 31, it tracks the annual cycle of nature as experienced through Barney's daily interaction with his rural North Texas environment. Within *Words from a Wide Land,* the November 22 entry stands as something profoundly *unnatural.* Here is Barney's flashbulb memory, blasted into the daybook totally undigested. It stands completely alone and separate, totally at odds with everything around it: an abomination in the garden.

With this November 22 entry, you are pulled instantly out of the rhythms of the natural world and into the capricious, artificial cycle of human history. Here, Barney reminds us that, for many, November 22 is a date that still haunts the calendar. For Dallasites, the date is not simply a harbinger of unpleasant and painful memories. Every time it appears on our calendars, it introduces again those questions of our personal relationship and obligations to that brutal historical event. Unlike the natural cycles Barney tracks throughout the rest of *Words from a Wide Land,* November 22 is an aberration, an annual disturbance imposed by our collective trauma.

We know that in literature, just as in photography, there is a developed repertoire of artistic techniques that can be used to depict these eruptions of untamed memory. The less civilized inverse of Proust's madeleines, these are those moments when things are abruptly out of place; there is a disruption of the normal flow of time; the elements of ordinary reality are somehow disconnected. These unnatural and mysterious disruptions, like Barney's outburst, have been represented in about all forms of art. All of these troubling disturbances, coincidentally, could also be explained as the result of malfunction, deception, or madness.

In the quotidian world, all of this might justifiably call for a quick diagnosis of the psychological disturbance, with the idea that some remedial treatment be initiated. These memory eruptions are, if you remember, remarkably similar to the "ruminations, dreams and associated thought disturbances" that James Pennebaker warned us about. They are the result of traumatic experiences that must be translated into some restorative expression before they can be banished via the talking cure.

It is, however, a little embarrassing to admit to being plagued by such undigested experience. When these artifacts show up in our photographs, our poetry, or our psyches, their appearance can be very difficult to explain. Admittedly, it *is* hard to find exactly the right words for this phenomenon. However, when some unprocessed remnant from the past inexplicably intrudes upon our rendering of the present, couldn't we all just agree to call it a ghost? What is a ghost, after all, but the unnatural manifestation of an unresolved issue? There are a million variations, but essentially ghosts are relationships from the past demanding to be worked out.

Ghost stories are universal, and there are many cultures where ghosts are always present. In Dallas, we take great pains to protect the line between present and past, but in many locales this line is considerably more permeable. In cultures that practice ancestor worship, the management of ghosts is a central preoccupation. In ceremonies such as the Chinese Ghost Festival or Mexico's Day of the Dead, you can see well-practiced strategies for maintaining proper relationships with the dearly departed. In Dallas, these are foreign cultures indeed. We often prefer to preach the efficiency of forgetting. However, if you look beyond the city limits, you can see the same lesson delivered over and over again. In all cultures everywhere, the dead demand their due.

Ghosts are elemental. They hide in the nexus of all of our ideas about time, and they lie concealed in our most important ideas about place. For all their vagueness, the one most definite thing about ghosts is that they are invariably grounded in a specific place. They bring human meaning to mere geography.

•

There are some cities you could say are "ghost" cities, places that have harbored a type of unique spiritualism and whose residents celebrate it to the extent that it becomes part of their history and identity. New Orleans is a ghost city, as are San Francisco, New York, Boston, and Savannah, Georgia. When you visit these cities, you might schedule a ghost tour to get to know them.

Dallas has never been a very welcoming place for ghosts. We do have a number of reputed spirit presences, but none that can make any real claims on our identity. Ghosts do call two of our most venerable hotels home: a jilted bride roams the nineteenth floor of the Adolphus, and the murdered hotel manager's mistress wanders the upper floors of the Stoneleigh. I've heard reports of a ghost in the old wood-framed Sons of Hermann Hall, a 1911 clubhouse for a German fraternal organization in Deep Ellum. There was a reputed ghost in the bathroom of my favorite hamburger joint, Snuffers on Lower Greenville, but it apparently disappeared after the building was renovated. Our most widely documented and disseminated local ghost lore over the last half century has involved our so-called "lady of the lake." There have been repeated reports of a young woman, soaking wet in a beautiful white dress, standing by the roadside near White Rock Lake. She solicits a ride to her nearby home, only then to disappear into a puddle of water in the back seat. While the various reiterations of these sightings almost always feature local particularities—in some, the lady is definitely wearing a dress from Neiman Marcus—our lady of the lake seems to be a hometown variation of the "Lady in White" story that is common throughout much of the world. For a city our size, these tales don't amount to much.

Dallas is a future-oriented place; we don't like unfinished business. Ghosts require us to look the wrong direction. We are also a city dominated by Protestantism. When specters appear, they take the form of either demons or angels. When you die here, you go to heaven or hell; there is no room for those who would brood about in limbo. And ghosts require a sort of suspension of disbelief that we are generally not willing to grant. Some have even suggested that Dallas doesn't have many ghosts because of a housing shortage; we are famous for tearing down our old historic buildings.

Instead of a ghost tour, Dallas has an assassination tour. Visitors here can load up on their buses, trams, or limousines at Dealey Plaza and make the rounds of the city. There are a number of well-established tours that will shuffle you to Oswald's old rooming house or the emergency room entrance at Parkland Hospital. After a couple of hours, you can come to know Dallas intimately by reviewing the events of late November 1963. But the most surprising, even astounding, thing you might discover on your assassination tour is that, in Dallas, the sighting of the ghost of John Kennedy is virtually unheard of.

Although we remain haunted by the assassination of John Kennedy, we do not seem to be plagued by the personal presence of the actual murder victim. Meanwhile, it is said you can find his ghost in a rocking chair in the rooms and halls of the third floor of the Ahwahnee Hotel in Yosemite National Park. (Kennedy stayed there once in 1962.) There have been reports of John Kennedy's ghost waving from the back seat of the Lincoln limousine housed in the Henry Ford Museum in Dearborn, Michigan, on the anniversary of his assassination. There are rumors that JFK is occasionally seen strolling around in the White House. But in Dallas? Nothing.

•

According to at least one reliable source—Lawrence Wright—the ghost of JFK departed Dallas in 1984. The story goes like this: Wright had come to Dallas to cover the Republican National Convention. As a visitor attending the convention, he was offered a choice of junkets to tour the city. Wright decided on the JFK assassination tour.

With his fellow conventioneers, Wright retraced the JFK parade route from Love Field to downtown, saw the Municipal Building, where Oswald was shot, and was driven to the former location of Jack Ruby's nightclub. The trip ended at Dealey Plaza and culminated with a climb up to the sixth floor. It was there, near Oswald's legendary sniper's nest, where Wright had his epiphany.

Wright recounts this experience in his memoir *In the New World: Growing Up with America from the Sixties to the Eighties*, published in 1987. As the book nears its conclusion, Wright returns to Dallas. After a decade and a half, he has reconciled himself with his past—with his family, his country's politics, and, most importantly, with Dallas. It was Dallas and JFK that had held this tightly packed narrative together, and so it must be Dallas and JFK that serve as the emblem of Wright's reconciliation. Wright stands on the sixth floor of the former Texas Book Depository, meditating on all of this, and gives this final benediction to his former home. "I saw the city now, bursting with 'vigor,' as Kennedy would have said," he writes. "I saw the new world fulfilled in the place of his death."[306]

Wright's *In the New World* is an accomplished exercise in the taming of traumatic memory. As a work of psychological reconciliation, it is all that a social psychologist like James Pennebaker could ask for. Wright, using all the pertinent tools the Muses have to offer, has produced a work that heals the individual psyche while also attending to the entire civic body. It is a wonderful example of successful writing therapy, and a model for the ritual banishing of ghosts. Indeed, the final line of Wright's memoir is: "I suddenly saw the ghosts rise and depart."

Wright left Dallas disgruntled and returned to Texas reconciled with his hometown and his father's world. Dallas gladly welcomed him back, proud to call him one of our own. Wright is arguably the most accomplished writer ever to have come from this city. A Pulitzer Prize winner, he has made a name for himself as an open-minded and wide-ranging journalist. He has taken on tough subjects, but his work inevitably leaves you feeling more edified than outraged. Through his work, his readers have experienced empathy for al-Qaeda operatives, confessed Satan-worshippers and celebrity Scientologists. He was prescient enough to release his well-researched novel concerning a fictional international pandemic at exactly the time the actual international pandemic hit the news cycle.

By the time Lawrence Wright banished the ghosts of JFK from Dallas in 1984, he had been absent from Dallas for roughly a decade and a half. He stepped into the former Texas School Book Depository as a visiting journalist, admitting that, after so long an absence, he felt like something of a tourist. He

306. Wright, *In the New World*, 307.

had returned to Texas a few years earlier, moving to Austin to work with the thriving *Texas Monthly*. He became one more in a long list of excellent Dallas writers who had left to seek the more generous literary climes of our capital city, and he was returning to reclaim his links not to Dallas but to Texas.

Wright did speak for many Dallasites when he pronounced the ghosts gone. For many, it was well past time that we set aside all this JFK assassination guilt. We had already paid our dues, whatever they were, and it was time to move on. Others, however, were not quite so sure. They might not have said it aloud, but many had the sense that something was still haunting us here in Dallas.

Nevertheless, Lawrence Wright was correct in his assessment that John Kennedy himself no longer haunted us. Kennedy, the man, had had a certifiably proper burial. In the stately and majestic ceremony which occurred on November 25, 1963, in Washington, DC, Kennedy was laid to rest before 220 foreign dignitaries from 92 foreign nations, including 19 heads of state. The ceremony was an international event that received unprecedented media coverage. It might be that more eulogies were delivered for John F. Kennedy than any other human being. Kennedy received his deserved remembrances; his was not a spirit who needed to return to seek his due.

The departing of Kennedy's ghost may close Wright's *In the New World*, but it did not close the book on the assassination in Dallas. There was still an active presence here that demanded to be dealt with. It was ghostly because we failed to reduce it to a workable form; it was amorphous and indistinct, and we could not get our hands around it. While the figure of John Kennedy lived its afterlife of amorphic shape-shifting, it did so in the realms of celebrity, history, or myth, not that metaphysical realm of ghosts. If ghosts still haunted Dallas, they were the ghosts of our past selves, grappling with our relationship to this protean figure of John F. Kennedy.

Today, John Kennedy still casts a giant shadow over Dallas, but this is a much different phenomenon than some traditional ghost wafting about seeking personal vengeance. As with the shades in classical Greece, it would require taking a long journey elsewhere to contact him. If you were seeking a séance with the dead president, it would be best to look elsewhere.

•

"It is Sunday morning. Twenty years after." Marshall Terry is standing a block southeast of Dealey Plaza, at the corner of Main and Market at the John Fitzgerald Kennedy Monument. Slightly less than a year before Lawrence Wright experiences his assassination epiphany at the former Texas Book Depository, Terry is about to stage his own JFK assassination ceremony.

Unlike Lawrence Wright, who left the city just as he became an adult, Terry came here as a young man in 1951 and stayed. In *Dallas Stories,* assuming his role of literary guardian for his adopted city, Terry also confronts this central issue of Dallas life—the legacy of the Kennedy assassination. In the book's final section, following his recounting of his own "where-were-you-when-you-heard" story and his introduction of the long-lost assassination poem from "The Prince of Dallas," Terry closes with "Elegos." Here again, Terry forgoes the voice of the fiction writer, and recounts directly his attempt at the ritual of resolution. He is waiting for the proper time to begin. "Now it is noon, as it was that day so many years ago"—

The memorial site is nearly abandoned on this quiet Sunday morning. While people flock to Dealey Plaza a block away, they rarely come here. In Philip Johnson's stark cenotaph, everything is stripped down to its bare essentials, and the architecture itself creates a sense of emptiness. Terry observes a single spray of roses left on the central platform. A few people pass through, quickly and quietly, some apparently uncertain as to exactly what all this is about. After a few minutes, a lone woman enters and places down her own roses. When she is done, Terry will say his prayer.

> I stop and say a brief prayer of wonder, for his life and yours and mine, for all the joy and insanity of it, the grief and love, the purpose that eludes us. I ask forgiveness for my part in it, all the sins of omission and commission."[307]

This is a solitary act, but Terry makes his best attempt at crafting a common prayer. It is brief, but implied here are all of those difficult questions we all face. Just what are our obligations to the deceased? To ourselves and each

307. Terry, *Dallas Stories,* 152.

other? To history? Terry has no answers, however, and his prayers feels fragmentary and incomplete.

Less than a year later, Lawrence Wright would banish Kennedy's ghost. But Terry can barely find the president. In Terry's prayer, Kennedy's life is jumbled up with "yours and mine." Elegies are traditionally a lament for the dead, but, in Dallas, our communications with the dead president have tended to be about ourselves. Terry's elegy is no different.

If Terry cannot quite find a common language for all of us here, he can at least share his common experience, and one thing many Dallasites would recognize is exactly how solitary all this is, how disconnected. Terry cannot muster much of a common prayer, because we had not had enough of a mutual conversation to figure out what we shared. Like many of us, Terry was stuck with a personal reckoning—this tiny, solitary prayer—but when he closes his prayer, asking forgiveness for his own "sins of omission and commission," he speaks for all of us who have likewise failed to find the proper language for this communal tragedy.

Dallas is a large and vibrant city, and it does have its great common rituals that tie us all together. Terry has already reminded us that on this Sunday morning, most of Dallas was in church, and he ends *Dallas Stories* with these lines:

> Then I drive back up Main Street. Most of Dallas will be home soon, waiting for the Cowboy game to come on television.

We have our rituals, among them church and football, but at the twentieth anniversary of the assassination, we had not really devised anything for November 22.

•

Twenty years after the assassination, things in Dallas were still unsettled. The figure of John F. Kennedy was still a powerful presence, and we were the guardians of the physical location of his monumentally famous death. It was clear a great calamity had occurred here, something profoundly sad and senseless.

That long weekend of November 1963 had all the pathos of classical Greek tragedy. Just as in those ancient theater rituals, there were the dead strewn about the stage: the president, Police Officer J. D. Tippit, Lee Harvey Oswald, and Jack Ruby (who died of cancer in early 1967 while still in jail). They would all have their burials, but just as in traditional tragedy, not everything had been put to rest.

We had all of the elements of classic tragedy, but we lacked the form. In Dallas, this theater of contemporary history played out haphazardly. The assassination was restaged in a thousand different versions. The very bloody business of the JFK assassination became a constant media circus, a soap-opera version of tragedy, always with a new episode scheduled to air tomorrow. It was a play that went on and on and never ended.

Because we could never find the vessel that could hold all of this painful commotion, things remained unsettled. In classical tragedy, of course, the plot would lead to some process of purification and purgation—that final climactic catharsis. Here, however, we had no Sophocles; the citizenry never marched to that stage beneath the acropolis to participate in the Dionysian rites. We just watched TV and read the paper and stood silent witness as the muddled spectacle passed by.

As tragedy developed as a theatrical tradition, playwrights developed an important tool to deal with exactly this type of accumulating, unresolved tension—adding a ghost to the plot. In Rome, Seneca reworked Sophocles, Aeschylus, and Euripides to give us our first respectable tragic ghosts. (Shakespeare's reworkings of Senecan tragedy would give us the tragic ghosts we most remember: *Macbeth*'s Banquo, and the ghost of Hamlet's father.) From Seneca, we get those first specters that grew out of the pricking conscience, the products of the tormented psyche that calls us out. Here was the ghost of the internal conscience (and isn't it exactly our internal conscience that makes ghosts?) As Seneca wrote: "Every guilty person is his own hangman."

It was Seneca, incidentally, who also gave us our first example of the playwright himself caught up in the assassination conspiracy. In 65 CE, Seneca was forced to take his own life for his alleged complicity in the Pisonian conspiracy to assassinate Nero. Sadly, he was likely innocent.

"The brain makes its own ghosts." That's how Julie Beck puts it—at least, that's the title of her 2014 article on the then-latest research concerning FOPs. FOP is the acronym for "feeling of presence," that ghostly sensation you get when you think there is an unseen human nearby. Recent clinical tests have successfully induced these sensations in people with the hopes of understanding how they are produced in the brain. Beck further writes that researchers have noted the occurrence of FOPs not only in neurological and psychiatric patients but also in healthy individuals.[308]

Even Lawrence Wright, mentally healthy by any standard, could find himself susceptible to these ghostlike "feelings of presence." On March 30, 1981, Wright was driving around Austin. He was crossing the Congress Avenue Bridge when he heard the news on the radio: John Hinkley had just shot Ronald Reagan. "By the time I crossed the river," Wright wrote, "I was sobbing and pounding the steering wheel."

Suddenly, here was an eruption of untamed memory, a flashback to seventeen and a half years before. For Wright, it was "something dreadfully familiar"—it was "like Kennedy, he was shot . . . It was all happening again." While the clinical tests Beck describes had used a robot to induce FOPs, here it was a radio news report that produced a ghostly "feeling of presence." The ghost of Dallas 1963 had returned in the living form of John Hinkley.[309]

Here was another presidential assassin from Dallas, and Wright, the boy from Dallas, felt it in the same way many of us here did—personally. Here again was this ghost we all lived with—the killer of presidents. "That is the mark of the native son; I had come to expect the worst. I believed that somehow the finger would point at me." Wright was experiencing a visitation of the classic Shakespearean ghost of internal conscience, and, if you were from Dallas, you felt it pointing too.

If others wanted to point, they had ample justification. John Hinkley was very much a product of Dallas. He had graduated from affluent Highland Park

---

308. Julie Beck, "The Brain Makes Its Own Ghosts," *The Atlantic,* November 8, 2014.

309. Wright, *In the New World,* 295–99.

High School. His father had been a successful oilman, and his family socially prominent. He had been eight years old when John Kennedy was shot, and the assassination had a huge influence upon him. Like Oswald, by the time he reached his mid-twenties, he was an alienated and delusionary political outcast with a gun.

Reagan survived the shooting. We would not be responsible for the assassination of another president. Three years later, the Republicans would even bring their 1984 national convention to Dallas to launch Reagan into his second term. Lawrence Wright would come back to town to cover that convention, reconciled with Dallas. He would pronounce his forgiveness of the city and see "the ghosts rise and depart." If it was not quite a moment of catharsis, he had at least achieved some critical distance.

The brain makes its own ghosts, and so the brain can make them disappear.

•

Today we do not need a William Mumler and his trick photography to see that our iconic JFK assassination photographs are haunted. Look at those half-century-old photos of LBJ being sworn in on Air Force One, or Jack and Jackie waving from the limo to the enthusiastic crowd in downtown Dallas. For my generation, there are ghosts present in those frames. In our contemporary, highly mediated, visually overladen world, we are light-years beyond the age in which photography was born. With our data-crammed memory; it is a simple mental procedure, almost automatic, to fill in the gaps ourselves. Look at the stills of the Zapruder film. We know that each of these 486 frames has been endlessly parsed and plotted. We have divided those 26.6 seconds, 18.3 frames per second, into a chronology of our times. Today, each individual frame operates as a sort of tarot card that, lined up properly, might explicate the great mystery. This is not just the necromancy practiced by the conspiracy buffs. We are all involved in assigning these images their occult meaning. In each are the clues, the signs, the symbols we need to decipher the whole story. They are, as DeLillo has said, worlds inside the world.

We ask of an ordinary photo that it show us its meaning; these JFK assassination photographs interrogate us. They challenge us to answer that one big question: What does it really mean that these things happened in Dallas in late November of 1963?

It is generally agreed that the JFK assassination was a watershed moment in our history, but no one, it seems, can agree on exactly why. Yet most still believe that something changed in America then. DeLillo called it "the seven seconds that broke the back of the American century," but what, exactly, does that mean?

When I tell people that I am writing a cultural history of Dallas after the assassination, they inevitably ask one question (and it is *always* the same question): Who do *you* think killed the president? Always, my response is to sigh and repeat that Oswald alone killed President Kennedy and Jack Ruby alone killed Oswald. There was no great conspiracy; the Warren Commission essentially got it right. This is, of course, generally unsatisfying to my listener. They will generally have a much more interesting take on events than I have, and this is where the conversation will go as they fill me in on the details.

I have heard a hundred versions of the story, with every manner of embellishment. Everybody adds their own ghosts. When the stories are over, however, there is still that one question we all must address: What do the ghosts demand of us?

•

It would be impossible to describe all the motivations driving the visitors who have made their pilgrimages to Dealey Plaza. There have been those appreciators of history, admirers of John Kennedy—both as a president and a celebrity. We have made accommodations for annual conspiracy conferences, and we have welcomed those who simply come here to pray. There are doubtless hundreds who might not be able to express even to themselves why they've come (or came) here. Dealey Plaza has served, seemingly simultaneously, as a crime scene, a circus, and the site of a funeral service.

We are the custodians of this hallowed site, and there are certain obligations you assume as a guardian of a place such as this. Over the years, we have strained to understand exactly what those obligations are. Lawrence Wright has described one of our most essential responsibilities—"a function nearly every Dallasite has served"—that of "subsidiary guide." We accompany our out-of-town guests to Dealey Plaza and stand with them while they tell us about their connection to the assassination and where they were when it happened. As Wright explains, "you listen, and receive it, because that's your special privilege as a Dallasite, to be the bearer of their stories."[310]

Over the years, a lot of people have said a lot of things about the JFK assassination; we have borne all these stories and attempted to make sense of them. Our obligations are to be the caretakers of a very amorphous inheritance, and it might be that we have become the guardians of something *we* don't really understand.

•

In Dallas, we don't believe in ghosts, and yet all these people continue to come, beckoned here by some phantom of the past. We struggle to explain it. While we don't really believe in ghosts, we could maybe understand all this as a ghost *story.* We believe in ghost stories. They show up in commodities like books and movies, making them real at least in the mercantile sense. We could even understand all this bustle in Dealey Plaza as a ghost story movie.

Film might be just the genre to reveal to us the truth of all this. Just a few years back, the *New York Times* proclaimed the ghost story a legitimate and ongoing part of our American literary canon, and we certainly don't need to justify the legitimacy of movies. Especially helpful here is the fact that ghost stories have certain rules, trusted formulas that are flexible enough to accommodate all sorts of variables. There are a lot of visitors here, with all sorts of motivations, and all this has to fit into the plot.

Because we don't believe in ghosts, we would play the role of the doorman, or maybe the groundskeeper, in this movie. The haunted place that needs to be looked after is an essential trope in these films; it could be a

310. Wright, *In the New World,* 306.

haunted mansion, a hotel, a theater, or a cemetery. Here, it is Dealey Plaza. Our job, of course, is to open the door, greet the visitors, and beckon them in. It is not an exciting or glamorous role, but it recognizes that function of "subsidiary guide" that Wright reminds us is our role to play.

The rules of the genre require that we, as doorman or groundskeeper, go about our business as if nothing unusual is going on. After all, this haunted place is simply where we work and live. Our job is to help along the main players as they pursue their goals. There are so many of them, but they each have some expectation. Remember what the experts say: "how hardy the ghost story proves as a vessel for collective terror and guilt, for the unspeakable. It alters to fit our fears."[311] There is a plot for everybody, and the movie could play out in a million intriguing ways.

The players might come to Dealey Plaza to perform their seances or to conduct their investigations. They might come to perform a ceremony to honor the dead or even to ridicule the memories contained in Dealey Plaza. All of them have come here to confront something, and it is understood that there will be a reckoning.

All this time, we are secondary characters, always in the background. The major characters will barely notice us, except maybe to comment on our local eccentricities. Sadly, we will seem very small, stock characters devoid of inner life. But we will always be present (because this is where we live and work), and there will always be the understanding that we are somehow implicated in this thing that is going on.

It is understood, to play the role of the doorman/groundskeeper, that we must cultivate a practiced aloofness. We must feign disinterest in everything going on around us. We are to remain aloof from all of the visitors' shenanigans—with one exception. In this movie, we are an audience. It is our job to listen to the visitors' stories.

As a sort of a coping device, we might, because we don't believe in ghosts, occasionally caution our guests when their stories get a little out of hand. We might hint that those mysterious flashes might be only optical tricks, or gently suggest the possibility that their memories have become distorted. It could be

311. Sehgal, "The Ghost Story Persists in American Literature. Why?"

that we are here to remind our visitors that these might not be ghosts at all but merely some form of misapprehension.

You can see now that this doorman/groundskeeper role is a fairly thankless job, and how this movie might eventually start to irritate. The visitors continue to arrive, and it seems to just go on and on, always others talking about this thing, and you listening and listening and listening. Before long, it is just too much. It all becomes gibberish, a sort of constant glossolalia that begins to crowd your consciousness. You begin to wonder: What is this thing that is clamoring for redress?

Now we are trapped in this movie, living in this constant, ongoing tension. We continue to play our role: we feign indifference, that we are only half paying attention while these outsiders wander about asking their big questions about the ghosts of America. We listen to their stories, but we are out of sorts.

Then something will happen! We remember that these movies follow their own logic, and something always happens. Our expert scriptwriter reminds us there are demands the ghost story makes of us: "It understands us—how strenuously we run from the past, but always expect it to catch up with us. We wait for the reckoning, with dread and longing."[312]

This is when we realize the movie is actually about us!

312. Sehgal, "The Ghost Story Persists in American Literature. Why?"

Acknowledgments

My gratitude to these, my biggest inspirations: Lisa Huffaker, whose proofreading, moral support, and patience made this all possible; Steven Davis, whose early work on Texas literary history became a model for this work and who contributed some early encouragement and editorial feedback; Ben Fountain, whose constant support for local writing includes some critical support for this project.

Special thanks must go to Will Evans for both his larger vision of Dallas as a significant literary center and his specific belief in and support for this project. Thanks also to the crew at Deep Vellum Publishing—Sara Balabanlilar, Serena Reiser, and Walker Rutter-Bowman—for all their inspired efforts. A special thanks goes to Joe Milazzo, whose painstaking editing and thoughtful feedback have been invaluable.

I cannot thank enough those many individuals who guided me to the richest veins of our hidden local culture, especially those writers who assisted in my research: Rebecca Spears for generously sharing her current work, Dave Oliphant for his knowing perspective on our longer regional history, and Antoinette Barksdale Terry, who helped me amplify the critical place of her husband, Marshall, in our common literary life. Particularly helpful were those significant culture workers, people like John Slate and Bryan Woolley, who offered their time for interviews or provided me critical materials. Last, but not least, I must express my gratitude to those vital institutions that support research into our local cultural history, in particular SMU's DeGolyer Library, the Sixth Floor Museum, and the UNT Archives.

Bibliography

Bard, W. E. "An Aside to the Reader." In *Fountain Unsealed: A Collection of Verse by Texas Writers*. Dallas: Barrington Fiction Club/Clyde C. Cockrell, 1931.

Barney, William. *Words from a Wide Land*. Denton: University of North Texas Press, 1993.

Broderick, James F. *Web of Conspiracy: A Guide to Conspiracy Theory Sites on the Internet*. Medford, NJ: CyberAge Books, 2008.

Bugliosi, Vincent. *Reclaiming History: The Assassination of President John F. Kennedy*. New York: W. W. Norton and Co., 2007.

Carraro, Francine. *Jerry Bywaters: A Life in Art*. Austin: University of Texas Press, 1994.

Cartwright, Gary. *Turn Out the Lights: Chronicles of Texas During the 80s and 90s*. Austin: University of Texas Press, 2000.

Christiansen, Paul. *West of the American* Dream. College Station: Texas A&M University Press, 2001.

Cicero, Marcus Tullius. *de Oratore*. Translated by E. W. Sutton. Cambridge, MA: Loeb Classical Library, 1967.

Condon, Richard. *Winter Kills*. New York: Dell, 1974.

Curran, Barbara. *25 Years of Dallas: The Complete Story of the World's Favorite Prime-Time Soap*. College Station, TX: VBW Publishing, 2004.

Davis, Ronald. *John Rosenfield's Dallas: How the Southwest's Leading Critic Shaped a City's Culture, 1925–1966*. Dallas: Three Forks Press, 2002.

Dealey, Jerry. *D in the Heart of Texas*. Garland, TX: JEDI Management Group, 2002.

DeLillo, Don. *Libra*. New York: Viking, 1988.

Diagnostic and Statistical Manual of Mental Disorders: DSM III. Washington, DC: American Psychiatric Association, 1980.

1895–6 Red Book of Dallas Texas: A Facsimile Reproduction. Dallas: A. H. Belo Corp., 1966.

Foreman, Paul. *Feather River*. Berkeley, CA: Thorp Springs, 2003.

Graham, Don. *Cowboys and Cadillacs: How Hollywood Looks at Texas*. Austin: Texas Monthly Press, 1983.

Hailey, Elizabeth Forsythe. *A Woman of Independent Means*. New York: Viking Press, 1978.

Hartley, Margaret. "The Editor's Notebook." *Southwest Review* (Spring/Summer 1968).

Hellman, John. *The Kennedy Obsession: The American Myth of JFK*. New York: Columbia University Press, 1997.

Hinckle, Warren. *If You Have a Lemon, Make Lemonade*. New York: G. P. Putnam's Sons, 1974.

Holmes, Maxine, and Gerald Saxon, eds. *The WPA Dallas Guide and History*. Denton: University of North Texas Press, 1992.

Huffaker, Bob, Bill Mercer, George Phenix, and Wes Wise. *When the News Went Live: Dallas 1963*. Lanham, MD: Taylor Trade Publishing, 2004.

Hunt, Conover. *Dealey Plaza National Historic Landmark*. Dallas: Sixth Floor Museum, 1995.

Hunt, Conover. *JFK for a New Generation*. University Park, TX: Southern Methodist University Press, 1996.

Jones, Penn. "The Philosophy from a Weekly Editor." *Southwest Review* 49, no.1 (Winter 1964): 36–43.

Jung, Carl. *Letters of C. G. Jung*. Vol. 1, *1906–1950*, edited by Gerhard Adler and Aniela Jaffé. Princeton, NJ: Princeton University Press, 1974.

Kay, Jonathan. *Among the Truthers: A Journey through America's Growing Conspiracist Underground*. New York: HarperCollins, 2011.

Kelin, John. *Praise from a Future Generation: The Assassination of John F. Kennedy and the First Generation Critics of the Warren Report*. San Antonio: Wings Press, 2007.

Knight, Peter. *Conspiracy Nation: The Politics of Paranoia in Postwar America*. New York: New York University Press, 2002.

Knight, Peter, ed. *Conspiracy Theories in American History: An Encyclopedia*. Santa Barbara: ABC-CLIO Inc., 2003.

Knight, Peter. *The Kennedy Assassination*. Edinburgh: Edinburgh University Press, 2007.

Kopkind, Andrew. "Slacking Toward Bethlehem." *Grand Street*, no. 44 (1993): 176–78.

Kuhn, William. *Reading Jackie: Her Autobiography in Books*. New York: Doubleday, 2010.

Lansdale, Joe R., and Don Coscarelli. *Bubba Ho-Tep*. San Francisco: Night Shade Books, 2005.

Leslie, Warren. *Dallas: Public and Private*. University Park, TX: Southern Methodist University Press, 1998.

Livingston, R. B. "Brain Circuitry Relation to Complex Behavior." In *The Neurosciences: A Study Program*, edited by G. C. Quarton, T. Melnechuk, and F. O. Schmitt, 499–515. New York: Rockefeller University Press, 1967.

Lubin, David. *Shooting Kennedy: JFK and the Culture of Images*. Berkeley: University of California Press, 2005.

MacAdams, Lewis. *Birth of the Cool: Beat, Bebop and the American Avant-Garde*. New York: The Free Press, 2001.

Mailer, Norman. *Oswald's Tale: An American Mystery*. New York: Random House, 1995.

Matussek, Peter. "The Renaissance of the Theater of Memory." *Janus* 8 (2001): 66–70.

McAdams's Kennedy Assassination Home Page Index. Accessed May 17, 2011. http://mcadams.posc.mu. edu/organ4.htm.

McGirr, Lisa. *Suburban Warriors: The Origin of the New American Right*. Princeton, NJ: Princeton University Press, 2001.

Manchester, William. *The Death of a President*. New York: Harper & Row, 1967.

Manchester, William. *One Brief Shining Moment*. Boston: Little Brown, 1983.

Marrs, Jim. *Crossfire: The Plot That Killed Kennedy*. New York: Carroll & Graf, 1989.

Marrs, Jim. *The Terror Conspiracy: Deception, 9/11 and the Loss of Liberty*. New York: Disinformation, 2006.

Mayhew, Andrew. *The World's Tribute to John F. Kennedy in Medallic Art*. New York: William Morrow and Co., 1996.

Minutaglio, Bill, and Steven L. Davis. *Dallas 1963*. New York: Twelve, 2013.

Newton, Violette. "Texas Poetry." In *Texas in Poetry 2*, edited by Billy Bob Hill. Fort Worth: Texas Christian University Press, 1971.

Olick, Jeffery, Vered Vinitzky-Seroussi, and Daniel Levy, eds. *The Collective Memory Reader*. Oxford: Oxford University Press, 2011.

Oliphant, Dave. *Harbingers of Books to Come*. San Antonio: Wings Press, 2009.

Oliphant, Dave. *Memories of Texas Towns &* Cities. Austin: Host Publications, 2000.

Payne, Darwin. *Dallas: An Illustrated History*. Woodland Hills, CA: Windsor Publications, 1982.

Payne, Darwin. *Dallas Citizens Council: An Obligation of Leadership*. Dallas: Dallas Citizens Council, 2008.

Payne, Darwin. *Indomitable Sarah: The Life of Judge Sarah T. Hughes*. University Park, TX: Southern Methodist University Press, 2004.

Pennebaker, James. *Collective Memory of Political Events: Social Psychological Perspectives*. Hillsdale, NJ: Lawrence Erlbaum Associates, 1997.

Pennebaker, James. *Opening Up*. New York: Guilford Press, 1990.

Phillips, Michael. *White Metropolis: Race, Ethnicity, and Religion in Dallas, 1941–2001*. Austin: University of Texas Press, 2006.

Pierson, James. *Camelot and the Cultural Revolution*. New York: Encounter Books, 2007.

Rice, Stan. *Body of Work*. Berkeley, CA: Mudra, 1983.

Rice, Stan. *Singing Yet: New and Selected Poems*. New York: Knopf, 1993.

Rogers, John William. *The Lusty Texans of Dallas: Their First Hundred and Twenty-Five Years*. Dallas: Cokesbury Book Store, 1965.

Schlesinger, Arthur M., Jr. *A Thousand Days: John F. Kennedy in the White House*. Boston: Houghton Mifflin, 1965.

Schutze, Jim. *The Accommodation: The Politics of Race in an American City*. New York: Citadel Press, 1986.

Shrake, Edwin. *Strange Peaches*. Austin: Texas Monthly Press, 1987.

Slate, John. *Historic Dallas Parks*. Charleston, SC: Arcadia Publishing, 2010.

Spears, Rebecca. "Last Things." *Nimrod* (Spring 2006).

Spears, Rebecca. "Marina's Daughters, 1964." In *Texas in Poetry 2*, edited by Billy Bob Hill. Fort Worth: Texas Christian University Press, 2002.

Spears, Rebecca. "My Father's Window." *Dos Passos Review* (Fall 2005).

Spears, Rebecca. "The Vanishing Point," In *Texas Poetry Calendar 2015*, edited by David Meischen and Scott Wiggerman. Austin, TX: Dos Gatos Press, 2015.

Stone, Oliver, and Zachary Sklar. *JFK: The Book of the Film*. New York: Applause Books, 1992.

Strong, Julia Hurd. "Day of Crisis." In *A Book of the Year 1965*. Poetry Society of Texas.

Terry, Marshall. *Dallas Stories*. University Park, TX: Southern Methodist University Press, 1987.

Terry, Marshall. *Loving U.: A Memoir by Marshall Terry*. University Park, TX: DeGolyer Library SMU, 2011.

Texas State Historical Association, *Handbook of Texas Online*. https://www.tshaonline.org/handbook.

Weiner, Hollace Ava. *Jewish Stars in Texas: Rabbis and Their Work*. College Station: Texas A&M University Press, 1999.

White, Theodore H. *In Search of History*. New York: Warner Books, 1978.

Wiesepape, Betty Holland. *Lone Star Chapters: The Story of Texas Literary Clubs*. College Station: Texas A&M University Press, 2004.

Wills, Gary, and Ovid Demaris. *Jack Ruby*. New York: Da Capo Press, 1994.

Womack, John Davenport. "Epitaph." In *A Book of the Year 1965*. Poetry Society of Texas.

Wright, Lawrence. *In the New World: Growing Up with America from the Sixties to the Eighties*. New York: Vintage, 1989.

Yates, Frances. *The Art of Memory*. London: The Bodley Head, 1966.

Index

La Reunion

La Reunion Publishing is an imprint of Deep Vellum established in 2019 to share the stories of the people and places of Texas. La Reunion is named after the utopian socialist colony founded by Frenchman Victor Considerant on the west bank of the Trinity River across from the then-fledgling town of Dallas in 1855. Considerant considered Texas as the promised land: a land of unbridled and unparalleled opportunity, with its story yet to be written, and the La Reunion settlers added an international mindset and pioneering spirit that is still reflected in Dallas, and across Texas, today. La Reunion publishes books that explore the story of Texas from all sides, critically engaging with the myths, histories, and the untold stories that make Texas the land of literature come to life.